W9-AGO-017

Millions of
Years Ago

TRIASSIC **JURASSIC** **CRETACEOUS**

245 208 145 65

335
First
Reptile

230
First
Pterosaur

225
First
Dinosaur

145
First
Bird

65
End of
Dinosaurs

1.5
First
Man

The Dinosaur Society's
DINOSAUR ENCYCLOPEDIA

DON LESSEM & DONALD F. GLUT

Illustrations by
Tracy Ford, Brian Franczak, Gregory Paul, John Sibbick
and Ken Carpenter

Scientific Advisors
Drs. Peter Dodson, Catherine Forster and Anthony Fiorillo

DEDICATION

Cheryl Frost, Steve Gittelman, Ray Ann Havasy, Liz Isherwood, Doug Jones, Dan LoRusso, Tammi Palmeri, Greg Wenzel and the many others whose support has helped build The Dinosaur Society.

THE DINOSAUR SOCIETY

The Dinosaur Society is an international nonprofit organization devoted to furthering paleontological education and research.

Dinosaurs are a key to science education and a vibrant field of scientific inquiry. Yet less than $1,000,000 per annum is presently spent worldwide on field research on dinosaurs.

By creating exhibits, publishing popular and technical works, sponsoring research, programs, and trips, and advising upon and creating educational products, The Dinosaur Society aims to further dinosaur science worldwide.

Directed by paleontologists and featuring the world's leading artists, educators, authors, and researchers on dinosaurs, it welcomes individual members. It publishes a quarterly newsletter for adults, a catalog of dinosaur products, a listing of scientifically recommended dinosaur books, and a monthly newspaper for children, *Dino Times*.

For information on Society programs, including individual adult and children's memberships, write:

The Dinosaur Society
200 Carleton Avenue
East Islip, NY 11730

CONTENTS

INTRODUCTION

You might imagine that dinosaurs need little introduction. They have become a cultural phenomenon during the century and a half since they were first scientifically recognized. Their horned and crested images pop out at us from television shows, horror movies, coloring books, animated cartoons, and popular science magazines. There are dinosaur toys, trading cards, toilet paper, cookies, and spaghetti. Dinosaur skeletons—whether real fossils or casts—are the star attractions at major natural history museums around the world. Children have no trouble remembering dinosaurs' tongue-twisting names, and they delight in confounding adults with their superior knowledge. As a result of this commercialization, a great deal of dinosaur misinformation has seeped into the public consciousness.

This is the first popular book to collect and illustrate, where possible, the significant dinosaur species and all the genera in a single volume. It should dispel many persistent myths. But we still don't know the real-life dinosaurs well. We wrote this book to reveal the fascinating, real-life side of dinosaurs, to show that dinosaurs were far more diverse and complex than the cutesy little critters found in children's storybooks and television sitcoms. Millions of years ago, dinosaurs lived, reproduced, and died right where humans and other animals live today. Some of these dinosaurs were the largest, most fearsome creatures ever to have walked the earth; many others were dainty and delicate little animals that might have made great house pets. Altogether, they were among the most varied, successful animals in earth's history.

Everything we know about dinosaurs comes from the earth. But only recently have we learned how to decipher some of the evidence of their former existence. This knowledge does not come easily; it requires years of difficult, patient, expert work—work that will continue for as long as clues emerge out of the ground and new techniques develop for re-examining the material we already have. We find fossilized dinosaur bones weathering out of the sedimentary rocks on every continent, even Antarctica. Sometimes the bones are still joined together—articulated—as they were in life. Much more often, the bones are isolated and broken, barely identifiable as dinosaurian. Sometimes we find dinosaur bone beds where the bodies of dozens of dinosaurs were jumbled together after an ancient herd perished in a terrible catastrophe. We also find remnants of dinosaur nests, including not only the eggs, still arranged as if waiting to hatch, but even the very embryos within. Traces of tooth marks on fossil bones give us clues to dinosaur feeding behavior. Major recent discoveries of baby dinosaurs have informed us about dinosaur mating habits, parental care, and growth patterns. Dinosaur trackways—fossilized footprints laid down in serial order more than a hundred million years ago, tell us how dinosaurs walked, ran, and herded. Fossilized dinosaur droppings disclose what they ate. Deformed, fractured, and healed bones inform us about dinosaur diseases. Rare skin impressions in fine-grained rock show the patterns of dinosaur scales. The even rarer dinosaur mummies have preserved fragments of their soft tissue, allowing us to reconstruct with considerable confidence what dinosaurs looked like when they were alive. And high-tech CAT scans have begun to reveal the innermost anatomy of dinosaur skulls too precious to break apart.

With a new generation of better-equipped and better-trained paleontologists hard at work, our inventory of new dinosaur species is growing at the rate of about one new species described every seven weeks—a pace unequaled since the late nineteenth century's tremendous "dinosaur rush."

Despite a rapidly accumulating wealth of information, most people still have only a vague idea about what dinosaurs were. The very term "dinosaur" has come to mean something oversized, inefficient, archaic, unsuccessful, and doomed to extinction. We have assumed that dinosaurs must have been slow and sluggish, because for many years dinosaurs were classified as large reptiles, and that is how we picture the large reptiles of today. We think of tortoises, crocodiles, pythons, and Komodo dragons, for example, as lethargic and inactive, though they are all capable of rapid, deadly movement. Still, our image of dinosaurs as torpid giants, roaring and bellowing as they wallowed in swamps, is persistent, and even older than the motion picture industry that fostered that myth.

Dinosaur skeletons and trackways tell a different story. Dinosaurs walked erect, with their legs positioned vertically beneath them and their tails held well off the ground. They were similar to today's birds and large mammals, but quite unlike today's creeping, crawling, sprawling reptiles. Some dinosaurs pursued prey and may have escaped from predators at speeds approaching those of race horses. Some plant-eating dinosaurs lived in huge, structured herds, providing them with protection from fierce meat-eating dinosaurs. Such herds may have migrated thousands of miles, foraging for food and searching for breeding grounds as the seasons changed.

In fact, dinosaurs (and other fossil animals) have forced paleontologists to rethink the very meaning of the term "reptile." Some dinosaurs were so advanced and birdlike that it has become clear that birds are either dinosaur descendants or very closely related to the dinosaurian evolutionary lineages. On the vertebrate family tree, crocodiles are more closely related to birds than they are to lizards and snakes, and dinosaurs are the transitional group that emphasizes this intimate relationship.

Contrary to popular belief, not every giant or bizarre-looking prehistoric animal was a dinosaur. Mammoths and woolly rhinos were mammals, not dinosaurs. They had fur and nursed their young, like other mammals, and unlike dinosaurs, and they lived millions of years after the last dinosaurs vanished from the earth. Finbacked pelycosaurs, such as *Dimetrodon*, which is often included with dinosaurs in plastic model sets, were not dinosaurs either; they were the precursors of mammals that lived well before the dinosaurs. (This is not to say that there were no finbacked dinosaurs. There were. And there was even a dinosaur, *Amargasaurus,* that had two fins side-by-side along its back.) Giant marine reptiles, such as plesiosaurs, ichthyosaurs, and mosasaurs, prevailed in the seas at the same time that dinosaurs occupied the land. Although they were only very distantly related to dinosaurs, they must have been equally terrifying. Also, the leathery-winged pterosaurs, the first vertebrates to develop the ability to fly (rather than simply glide), were not dinosaurs, although they were closely related to them.

Enough of what dinosaurs were not. What *were* they? They were either one, two, or three groups of animals, distinguished by having skeletons adapted for a particular kind of fully erect stance.

The idea of a "group" of living things is very precise among scientists. Organisms make up a group when they share a common evolutionary ancestor. This is why mammoths, pelycosaurs, plesiosaurs, ichthyosaurs, mosasaurs, and pterosaurs were not dinosaurs. Although all of them were four-limbed vertebrates (tetrapods) and possessed very distant ancestors in common with dinosaurs, those ancestors were neither dinosaurs, mammoths, pelycosaurs, plesiosaurs, ichthyosaurs, mosasaurs, nor pterosaurs. Common ancestry is usually signaled by resemblance, not the superficial "sort of" resemblance of fish to dolphins, but the deeper, more detailed anatomical and biological similarities shared, for example, by all birds, or by all bats, or by all carnivorous mammals. These special similarities were first developed in the group's common ancestor. This idea, termed "shared derived characters," is a cornerstone of the modern theory of evolution.

Scientists do not yet know enough about dinosaur origins to say from which ancestors they arose and when. However, they do think dinosaurs are a natural group of their own, because they have found a number of shared derived characters common to all dinosaurs, hinting that they all shared a common ancestor. That ancestor, or an animal sufficiently closely related to it, has so far eluded fossil hunters. The earliest known dinosaurs are already different enough from one another that we can confidently place them in one of the recognized dinosaurian lineages. We will have more to say about this when we discuss the dinosaur family tree and the classification of dinosaurs later in this Introduction.

The oldest known dinosaur fossils are found in rocks about 230 million years old, and dinosaurlike footprints occur in rocks even older than that. The youngest

known dinosaurs come from rocks about 65 million years old, and not a single reliably dated dinosaur bone or footprint is more recent than this. The span of time from 215 to 65 million years ago is often called the "Age of Dinosaurs," because, except for a few crocodiles and rare large lizards, all known land-living animals from that age that measure more than about three feet long are dinosaurs. During the period of time immediately before that, from 230 to 215 million years ago, dinosaurs shared the earth with other large reptiles, including their more primitive relatives. The Age of Dinosaurs makes up the major portion of what geologists and paleontologists call the Mesozoic Era. The Mesozoic, which extended from 248 to 65 million years ago, is popularly known as the "Age of Reptiles."

During this time, dinosaurs lived all across the earth, and are represented on every continent from equatorial lands to within the Arctic and Antarctic Circles. They did indeed live in swamps, but they also lived in forests, and in near-desert environments. They were truly world-dominant. If we don't find their remains everywhere, it is only because we don't have rock of dinosaur age exposed everywhere. Nor is every period of dinosaur time represented by the dinosaur-age rocks that can be surveyed. But we know enough to say that the dinosaurs were a great and long-lived success.

Sixty-five million years ago, dinosaurs became extinct everywhere in the world, all at once and seemingly overnight. When the huge reptiles vanished, the world was rapidly recolonized by mammals that had survived during the Mesozoic Era by remaining small (and probably, in many cases, nocturnal) in order to stay out of reach of dinosaurian meat-eaters. Dozens of explanations have been put forward for why the dinosaurs vanished after more than 150 million years of unmitigated dominance, but none—not even the asteroid impact whose traces are found worldwide, and which marked the end of the Mesozoic Era—seems to tell the whole story. The abrupt disappearance of the dinosaurs remains the most famous unsolved mystery of paleontology.

Although the last dinosaurs died out 65 million years ago, that is not a long time compared to the eons since the origin of the earth or the entire universe. To put it into perspective, imagine the time span since the origin of the universe— the Big Bang—as a skyscraper 1,500 feet tall. Not all scientists agree on how long ago the universe burst into existence, but we may adopt 15 billion years (give or take 5 billion) as a rough estimate. On this scale, every 100 feet of skyscraper represents a billion years, so every foot represents 10 million years, and every inch a little more than 800,000 years—833,333 years and 4 months, to be exact. Six thousand years of recorded human history is, on this scale, less than 1/100 of an inch, about the thickness of a manila file folder. Compare that to the height of the entire skyscraper to gain some perspective on the significance of humanity to the universe as a whole.

Of the skyscraper's 1,500-foot height, only the uppermost 465 feet (less than ⅓) represents the age of the earth, which was "born" 4.65 billion years ago. The oldest known life forms, the "blue-green algae" that created mound-shaped colonies called stromatolites, appeared about 3.5 billion years ago. They would appear a mere 350 feet from the top of the skyscraper, were we to take an elevator ride to the top. From that level, the elevator would have to rise another 280 feet before we reached a floor where individual life forms would be visible without a microscope. The "Cambrian explosion" that filled the earth's oceans with vast numbers of easily fossilized, hard-shelled aquatic animals occurred somewhat later, about 580 million years ago. Although it seems unimaginably distant from the present, it actually corresponds to a level only 58 feet—about five floors—below the 1,500-foot skyscraper's top. And the dinosaurs? Their age occupies most of the top two floors of the skyscraper, from 23 feet to a mere 6.5 feet from the top.

The point of this exercise is to show that although dinosaurs may appear to have been primitive animals that lived millions of years ago, they were, in the grand scheme of things, quite close to us in time. (Compare 6.5 feet of skyscraper to 465 feet or 1,500 feet.) The world in which dinosaurs lived was quite modern in its aspect, not really very different from the world we live in today. They were also highly successful animals. Their heyday occupies 17.5 feet of our skyscraper, quite a lot more space than the top three inches (2.5 million years) during which recognizable human beings have existed on earth.

So we are not reaching back very far, comparatively, into earth's history in trying to reconstruct the evolution of dinosaurs. But paleontologists do not yet know exactly when or in what order the major dinosaur groups originated. No fossil animal discovered so far can be considered a truly ancestral dinosaur. We do not have a dinosaur fossil record from earlier than about 228 million years ago.

When dinosaurs first appeared in the fossil record, they were already easily separable into two distinct lineages: the herbivorous sauropods and carnivorous theropods in the "lizard-hipped" line of saurischian dinosaurs, and the herbivorous ornithischian line of "bird-hipped" dinosaurs. As their names suggest, these lines were distinguished by the orientation of their hip bones, and in particular the pubic bone. In the saurischian dinosaurs this bone pointed forward and down. In the ornithischian dinosaurs, the pubic bone was backward parallel to another pelvic bone. How these lineages might be related to each other is still anybody's guess.

As far as we know, the ornithischians (bird-hipped dinosaurs) originated sometime during the Triassic Period, but we do not know the details of their early evolution. The group's origin lies in as-yet-undiscovered fossils at the base of the dinosaur family tree. Until only a few years ago, almost all dinosaur experts agreed that the ornithischians were quite different anatomically from the

sauropods and theropods. Ornithischians and saurischians were considered only distantly related. More recent studies, however, have pointed out certain characters common to ornithischians and each of the other two dinosaur groups in the saurischian order. However, these characters are not specific enough to determine which of the two groups Ornithischia might be closer to.

The fact that ornithischians and sauropods were plant-eating dinosaurs with somewhat similar tooth and limb anatomy does hint that the Ornithischia branched off along with sauropods.

Early ornithischians gave rise to several distinct orders of dinosaurs. Perhaps the most primitive of these was the Ankylosauria, which includes the well known armored, quadrupedal plant-eaters, ankylosaurs and nodosaurs. The order Stegosauria, or plated dinosaurs, probably branched away from the Ankylosauria soon after the latter order developed. Members of the Pachycephalosauria seem to have been less primitive; they evolved into the very specialized dome-headed dinosaurs. The order Ceratopsia, the horned dinosaurs, branched away from the Pachycephalosauria well before the end of the Jurassic Period, and long before the pachycephalosaurs had evolved their domed skulls. The Ornithopoda, the most advanced ornithischian order, included various-sized bipedal plant-eaters, and eventually culminated in the hadrosaurs, the "duckbilled" dinosaurs.

The lizard-hipped sauropods were plant-eating dinosaurs that walked on all fours, had small heads at the end of long necks, and possessed long, thick tails that were sometimes armed with a whiplash or a tail club. Among the sauropods were the longest and heaviest animals ever to have walked the earth. There were two distinct branches of the sauropod family tree: the earlier, smaller, more lightly built, primitive prosauropods; and the later, enormous, advanced ones known as sauropods. They almost certainly shared a common ancestor that lived at least some 235 million years ago, about halfway through the Triassic Period. From this progenitor, prosauropods and sauropods evolved independently.

The other lizard-hipped branch (aside from the sauropods) are the theropods, the most diverse dinosaurian order (or suborder, depending on classification scheme). Like sauropods and ornithischians, the earliest theropods appear suddenly in the fossil record. There is little hint of their origins except for their obvious but general anatomical resemblances to the earlier archosaurs, reptiles with teeth set in sockets, and a special bone that supported their brain.

The theropods *Eoraptor*, *Herrerasaurus*, and *Staurikosaurus*, the earliest known dinosaurs, were medium-sized, bipedal meat-eaters, obviously related to the later small-to-giant-sized dinosaurian predators (such as *Tyrannosaurus rex*) so well known to the public.

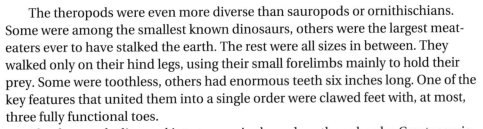

The theropods were even more diverse than sauropods or ornithischians. Some were among the smallest known dinosaurs, others were the largest meat-eaters ever to have stalked the earth. The rest were all sizes in between. They walked only on their hind legs, using their small forelimbs mainly to hold their prey. Some were toothless, others had enormous teeth six inches long. One of the key features that united them into a single order were clawed feet with, at most, three fully functional toes.

The theropods diverged into two major branches: the suborder Ceratosauria, in which the tail was flexible throughout most of its length, and the branch recently named Tetanurae ("stiff tails"), in which the vertebrae in the back half of the tail were to some extent interlocked, and not as free to move as were the vertebrae in the front half. All the earliest known theropods were ceratosaurians, whose fossil record extends from the Late Triassic Period through at least the Late Jurassic Period, with a Southern Hemisphere branch that carried on through the end of the Mesozoic. Tetanurans appeared in the Middle Jurassic, diversified in the Late Jurassic, and remained the dominant Northern Hemisphere predators to the end of the Late Cretaceous Period.

Theropod dinosaurs, or at least their descendants, birds, live on. Those dinosaurs profiled here are at least 65 million years dead. But they remain wonderful and, despite a fast-advancing science, largely mysterious.

HOW TO USE THIS BOOK

This book is an alphabetical, illustrated catalogue of all the dinosaur genera and many of the species that have ever been formally named. These totals are now calculated at 446 genera, 113 of which are of doubtful validity, and 665 species, 213 of which are of doubtful validity. These totals do not include synonyms, many of which are also listed here. So many popular dinosaur books call dinosaurs only by their first, or generic, names that we forget that several, quite different, species may sometimes be included in any one genus. Imagine a book about living animals that referred to them only by genus. Which big cat would we exhibit for the genus *Panthera*, the tiger (*Panthera tigris*), the lion (*Panthera leo*), or the leopard (*Panthera pardus*)? Likewise, by focusing on the individual species rather than just the genera, we obtain a more realistic picture of dinosaurian diversity.

Unfortunately, this approach also presents some problems. Many dinosaurs are identified by mere fragments. More than half of all dinosaurs are known from just a single fossil. And many more paleontological debates center on the species than on the genera. Consequently, some species are passed around from genus to genus for what must seem like unfathomable reasons, and every time a species changes genus, it acquires a new first name. This happens often enough, and in obscure-enough publications, that even professional paleontologists may be unaware of all the ways a particular species has previously been renamed, as in the now-celebrated case of "Brontosaurus," identified nearly a century ago as the previously named *Apatosaurus*.

In fact, we cannot guarantee that we have unearthed all the different renamings. We are reasonably certain, however, that we have found all the different genera—excluding renamings—through about 1990, and most of the ones thereafter, through this book's publication date in 1993. We have sifted through all the available bibliographies and systematic indices in our "name chase." Nevertheless, in a few original papers read while we were researching the entries, we encountered further renamings not listed in any of those bibliographies. Since no one, including us, has read every single scientific dinosaur paper ever written, we cannot guarantee that we have picked up every last renaming. So if you chance upon a dinosaur species name elsewhere that is different from any you find in this book, it might just be one that fell through the cracks—unless it's one coined after this book was printed, or one whose name is so badly misspelled as to be unrecognizable. (This happens more frequently than you might imagine.) Or it could be a species that is no longer considered dinosaurian. However, to our knowledge this book represents the most complete description of dinosaurs available for a popular audience.

In the section "Not a Dinosaur," we list genera and species of fossil animals (and at least one plant) that some paleontologists thought at one time or another were dinosaurs, but now do not. We have not striven for completeness in this respect, but we have included the ones we have come across in our research.

The names of dinosaur families, genera, and species (but not higher-level groups) are governed, along with the names of all other animals, living and extinct, by the International Code of Zoological Nomenclature, a system of rules that makes a name "official," or scientific. In order for the name of any animal to have formal standing in science, it must be created according to the rules in the Code.

First of all, if you are a paleontologist, you have to have a specimen—the actual physical remains of the dinosaur. Then you must describe it in a research paper, and then have that paper published and distributed. In the description, the specimen must be compared with specimens of closely related dinosaurs, to show how it is different from the others. Then you must also list a set of anatomical characters that could be unique to this species. These characters would allow other scientists to identify specimens of their own as belonging to your species. The all-important specimen in your description becomes the "type specimen" of your new species. (Among fossil animals, every new species must have a type specimen to be valid.) Finally, you must make a good attempt at classifying the species, that is, explaining where on the Tree of Life your newly created little branch might fit.

The name of your new species must be a two-word Latin or Greek noun phrase. The first word of the name is the name of the genus to which your species belongs. The second word is a Latin or Greek adjective or noun that modifies the generic name. Both names together form the name of your species. The specific name must be unique; no other animal in the animal kingdom is allowed to have the same specific name.

Sometimes your species is different enough from other species so that it will not fit into any established genus. Then you have to create a new genus for it, and it then becomes the type species of the new genus. For your generic name, you are free to use almost any pronounceable combination of letters, but most generic names are capsule descriptions of the specimens that have been translated into Greek or Latin, and then "Latinized" into a unique noun. As with species, the generic name must be unique. To prevent confusion, no other animal is allowed to have the same generic name. And just as a species must have a type specimen to be valid, so a genus named after 1931 must have a type species to be valid.

Finally, your new genus may not fit into any established family. Therefore you create a whole new family for your genus, and your genus becomes the type genus of the new family. The name of the new family must be derived from that of the type genus. This is done by altering slightly the ending of the generic name, according to the rules of Latin grammar, and adding the suffix "-idae."

Tangles involving dinosaur names occur when a species is established on a type specimen that is not complete enough to fully characterize the species. For example, dinosaur species based only on teeth, no matter how distinctive the teeth may be, often turn out to be of doubtful validity.

When any information about any aspect of a dinosaur is doubtful, a question mark is placed in front of that entry. Question marks are reminders of the uncertainty of an attributed date, name, size, or classification.

There are two kinds of entries for this book, for genera and for species. They are listed in alphabetical order, so the listing for the genus and its type species is followed by all the significant species known to us.

All listings follow the same pattern:

Genus

The name for a particular group of dinosaurs, and the level of classification at which most dinosaurs are commonly known. The genus name is represented phonetically, with commonly accented syllables in uppercase. Since pronunciations of dinosaur names vary considerably, these are not the only acceptable ways of saying their names.

Status

Here the validity of a name is assessed. Some species and genera (the plural of *genus*) have been listed as *Invalid* either because they were previously otherwise named, or because they refer to mistakenly classified fossils. If they are now known by another scientific name, that name is given. When their classification is uncertain—usually because of insufficient fossil data—they are listed as *Doubtful*. Those few dinosaurs that have been unofficially described, or mentioned in publications without a scientific description, are noted as *Unofficial*. Their names appear in question marks, not italics.

Type Species

The species for which this group, or genus, of dinosaurs was named. The species, like the genus, was named for a distinctive set of fossil remains, the type specimen.

Classification

Each genus entry contains the classification of the genus to the level of order. That is, the names of the order, suborder, and family (as appropriate) in which the genus and all its included species are placed. Similar genera of dinosaurs belong to the same *Family*, like families to *Suborders*, like suborders to *Orders.* Uncertain aspects of a dinosaur's classification are marked by question marks. These levels correspond to particular branches of the dinosaur family tree, so they tell us what the anatomy of the dinosaurs in the genus was like, and also how other dinosaur genera were related to it.

Name

This entry describes how the name was created from Greek or Latin roots to form a Latin word. Nowadays, an original describer almost always supplies an etymology, but during the nineteenth century, scientists were expected to know enough Greek and Latin to make etymologies unnecessary.

Size

The average length of a representative adult of this particular dinosaur. A range of sizes may be given, especially when a genus encompasses species of widely varying sizes. Often, a genus is named from such fragmentary fossil evidence that its size cannot be estimated beyond an approximate description ("similar in size to a…") or perhaps it can't be estimated at all. (Most dinosaurs, by the way, were smaller than cars, though they—and humans for that matter—are among the largest of animals.)

Gauging the weight of a dinosaur from even the most complete skeleton is a dicey matter, and so weight estimates, which appear widely and with varying totals, are not reliable. When nearly complete specimens have allowed for some reasonable scientific estimate, we have noted the weight in the text.

Place

This entry provides a general idea of where this animal lived, and is based on where its fossil remains have been found. The animal might well have had a far wider range.

Period

This is the period in which this genus of dinosaur lived. This date is based on many variables. It may include a range of dates for the sediments in which various species of the same genus have been found. The time range given for this genus should not be interpreted as the entire length of time it lived. It is only the best available approximation for a period within which this dinosaur may have lived.

Diet

This entry describes the dinosaur as a meat- or plant-eater, with some variations if the primary diet has not been determined, or if more specific dietary preferences are indicated by jaw and tooth structure or fossilized stomach contents.

Entry

A text section that describes what is known or speculated about this animal, based largely upon its type species. If other species are known for this genus, they are listed, alphabetically, following the type species.

ILLUSTRATIONS

We have supplied three kinds of illustrations with the entries. If a species is known from good enough fossil material to merit a reasonably accurate life restoration, then we have tried to supply one. Many species, however, are known from incomplete type skeletons or only a few isolated bones. For such species we supply either skeleton silhouettes that show where the bones of the type specimen would fit together in a hypothetical, complete skeleton, or bone illustrations if the type specimen is too meager for us to attempt a skeleton silhouette.

ILLUSTRATION CREDITS

Tracy Ford

2, 3, 8, 12, 23, 33, 36, 40, 43, 46, 53 (top), 57, 63, 65, 69, 70, 71, 78, 79, 89, 98, 103 (bottom), 108, 109, 120, 126, 128, 132, 139, 145, 154, 157, 165, 170, 176, 179, 190, 193, 201, 202, 204, 206, 207, 209, 220, 224, 229, 230, 231, 232, 236, 238, 253, 261, 265, 272-273, 275, 279, 281, 289, 293, 297, 298, 300, 308, 318, 319, 321, 323, 324, 325, 333, 343, 351, 356, 358, 369, 374, 378, 380-381, 384, 386, 388, 393, 401, 404, 405, 415, 446, 448-449, 452, 455, 460, 462, 464, 465, 467, 473, 482, 483, 489, 499, 504, 510, 512, 513, 519, 520, 524, 527

Brian Franczak

5, 14 (bottom), 15, 17, 24-25, 30 (bottom), 39, 47, 53 (bottom), 58, 59, 60-61, 74, 76, 83, 92 (top), 125, 141, 146-147, 153, 171, 172, 184-185, 187, 188, 203, 205, 216, 219, 222, 249, 258-259, 268-269, 270, 278, 290, 292, 295, 315, 317, 329, 335, 346, 347, 357, 383, 395, 402, 407, 408, 410, 418, 421, 423, 424-425, 427, 428, 430, 440, 443, 453, 457, 469, 475, 487, 491, 493, 495, 525

Gregory Paul

4, 13, 14 (top), 19, 20, 30 (top), 51, 64, 73, 74, 84, 86, 87, 91, 92 (bottom), 97, 103 (top), 118, 123, 127, 136, 137, 142-143, 148, 149, 150, 152, 161, 162-163, 173, 174, 175, 189, 195, 225, 227, 228, 250, 254, 271, 274, 287, 339, 342, 348, 349, 350, 359, 360, 361, 366, 367, 375, 390, 433, 434, 442, 447, 451, 484, 486, 488, 490, 496, 497, 498, 508, 509, 522, 523

John Sibbick

197, 212-213, 218, 266, 372, 429

Ken Carpenter

32, 56

DINOSAUR CLASSIFICATION

Scientists group dinosaurs according to their significant shared characteristics. The broad outlines of dinosaur classification have been agreed upon for a century, but many of the details and the methods of analysis have changed in recent years. As a result, dinosaur classification is presently in flux. In the classification entries for each dinosaur described in this book we have noted how some paleontologists presently classify these animals at the species, genus, family, suborder and order levels. This is by no means the only, or most complete, attempt at classification, and is meant only as a guide.

Dinosaurs, like other organisms, are organized at more levels within their orders. Here we define more fully the various levels of classification of dinosaurs. Groupings are presented within an evolutionary hierarchy. Levels of classification descend from the superorder Dinosauria to the two orders (Ornithischia and Saurischia) to the many suborders, infraorders and families within each order. Genus and species listings are to be found within the body of the book.

Dinosauria
Superorder

Small-sized to gigantic terrestrial archosaurs, "ruling reptiles," characterized by a suite of technical features including the pelvis, thigh bone, shin bone, ankle and foot. The net result of these features is to permit an erect gait. All of the following levels of classification of dinosaurs belong to the Dinosauria.

Saurischia
Order of Superorder Dinosauria

Small- to gigantic-sized, bipedal, semi-bipedal and quadrupedal dinosaurs, including both carnivorous and herbivorous types.

Theropoda
Suborder of Order Saurischia

Tiny to very large, two-legged or bipedal, carnivorous dinosaurs, with small to very large heads. Theropods had either sharp teeth or were toothless. They had relatively short forelimbs and birdlike feet, the first digit of which was reduced and spurlike; toothless forms possibly herbivorous or omnivorous. Theropoda include:

Ceratosauria

Infraorder of Suborder Theropoda, Order Saurischia

Small- to large-sized carnivorous dinosaurs, some bearing cranial horns or crests, some possibly having dorsal "fins."

Ceratosauridae

Family of Infraorder Ceratosauria, Suborder Theropoda, Order Saurischia

Large- to very large-sized, massively built carnivores, with large heads bearing a prominent nasal horn; short neck; and short forelimbs with a four-fingered hand. Ceratosauria include several families:

Herrerasauridae

Family of Infraorder Ceratosauria, Suborder Theropoda, Order Saurischia

The most primitive of the theropods.

Megalosauridae

Family of Infraorder Ceratosauria, Suborder Theropoda, Order Saurischia

A "junk-basket" of little-known carnivores, including the most generalized forms; all large-sized, with large heads with long jaws and teeth with double edges; very short forelimbs with three-fingered hands; powerful hindlimbs; and toes with large talons.

Segisauridae

Family of Infraorder Ceratosauria, Suborder Theropoda, Order Saurischia

Small, lightly built carnivores, proportionally similar to the Coeluridae, with relatively long necks.

Staurikosauridae

Family of Infraorder Ceratosauria, Suborder Theropoda, Order Saurischia

Primitive, bipedal, slender carnivores, with moderately long necks; relatively small forelimbs with probably five-fingered hands; long hindlimbs with five-toed feet; and slender tails. Relationships are uncertain. These dinosaurs may be more primitive than either the Saurischia or the Ornithischia.

Velocisauridae

Family of Infraorder Ceratosauria, Suborder Theropoda, Order Saurischia

Small carnivores, with the upper part of the foot relatively long; probably agile runners.

Podokesauridae

Family of Infraorder Ceratosauria, Suborder Theropoda, Order Saurischia

Small- to moderate-sized carnivores, lightly built, with somewhat elongated heads. Some more specialized forms bore cranial crests; had moderately long necks; short and slender forelimbs with four-fingered hands; and birdlike feet with three functional toes.

Abelisauridae

Family of Infraorder Ceratosauria, Suborder Theropoda, Order Saurischia

Large carnivores, having high, broad heads, with short snouts and large eyes.

Tetanurae

Infraorder of Suborder Theropoda, Order Saurischia

Small- to giant-sized carnivores of great diversity, including all theropods that are more closely allied with birds than they are to the Ceratosauria. Tetanurae include:

Carnosauria

Microorder of Suborder Tetanurae, Suborder Theropoda, Order Saurischia

Very large-sized meat-eaters, including the largest terrestrial carnivores of all time. Large heads, with most or all forms bearing cranial ornamentation, and large teeth; short necks, barrel-like trunks; reduced forelimbs; and claws on all toes. Carnosauria include these families:

Spinosauridae

Family of Microorder Carnosauria, Infraorder Tetanurae, Suborder Theropoda, Order Saurischia

Large carnivores with three-fingered hands; "sail" backs supported by long spines. Possibly quadrupedal.

Eustreptospondylidae

Family of Microorder Carnosauria, Infraorder Tetanurae, Suborder Theropoda, Order Saurischia

Carnivores with long heads and shallow snouts.

Allosauridae

Family of Microorder Carnosauria, Infraorder Tetanurae, Suborder Theropoda, Order Saurischia

Large- to giant-sized carnivores, with large heads; short necks; and short fore-limbs bearing three fingers with formidable claws.

Tyrannosauridae

Family of Microorder Carnosauria, Infraorder Tetanurae, Suborder Theropoda, Order Saurischia

Large-sized, of the general plan as allosaurids, but more massive and power-ful. Extremely small forelimbs with a functionally two-fingered hand, the third digit a splintlike vestige. Tyrannosaurs include these subfamilies:

Aublysodontinae

Subfamily of Family Tyrannosauridae, Microorder Carnosauria, Infraorder Tetanurae, Suborder Theropoda, Order Saurischia

Medium- to large-size, more slender carnivores; head lower and with relative-ly more teeth than in the Tyrannosaurinae (see below), with a long, low muz-zle, relatively large teeth, smooth-edged premaxillary teeth; and more gracile limbs.

Tyrannosaurinae

Subfamily of Family Tyrannosauridae, Microorder Carnosauria, Infraorder Tetanurae, Suborder Theropoda, Order Saurischia

Large-sized, more massive forms of tyrannosaurids, with all teeth serrated.

Coelurosauria

Microorder of Infraorder Tetanurae (the present division of coelurosaurs and carnosaurs within the Tetanurae is now in question)

Primitive carnivores capable of moderately fast locomotion. Relatively large hands, and (probably) three-toed feet. Coelurosauria include:

Ornithomimosauria

Superfamily of Infraorder Tetanurae, Suborder Theropoda, Order Saurischia

Large-sized forms, lightly built, superficially resembling modern ground birds. Long snouts, beaklike and usually toothless jaws (small teeth present in

primitive forms), which were probably covered by a horny beak; large eyes and long necks. Their long forelimbs (about half the length of the hind limbs) ended in hands with three long fingers. They had slender hind limbs, thighs shorter than shins. With three to four toes, they were probably fast runners, and possible omnivorous or herbivorous. The Ornithomimosauria includes:

Harpymimidae

Family of Superfamily Ornithomimosauria, Infraorder Tetanurae, Suborder Theropoda, Order Saurischia

Very primitive "bird-mimic" dinosaurs, the only known forms of these dinosaurs to have teeth. Their hands were relatively large, their feet probably three-toed, and they were capable of moderately fast locomotion.

Garudimimidae

Family of Superfamily Ornithomimosauria, Infraorder Tetanurae, Suborder Theropoda, Order Saurischia

These were very primitive dinosaurs, with a four-toed foot that retained a short first toe. They were capable of moderately fast locomotion.

Ornithomimidae

Family of Superfamily Ornithomimosauria, Infraorder Tetanurae, Suborder Theropoda, Order Saurischia

These were medium-sized bird-mimic dinosaurs, with no first toe and the third toe longer than the second and fourth. These were capable of the fastest locomotion among ornithomimosaurians, and perhaps all dinosaurs.

Maniraptora

Microorder of Microorder Coelurosauria, Infraorder Tetanurae, Suborder Theropoda, Order Saurischia

These dinosaurs were even more birdlike than above-described forms. All had long hands with predatory claws.

Elmisauridae

Family of Microorder Maniraptora, Microorder Coelurosauria, Infraorder Tetanurae, Suborder Theropoda, Order Saurischia

Small, lightly built forms, with slim hands and large feet.

Oviraptorosauria

Superfamily of Microorder Maniraptora, Microorder Coelurosauria, Infraorder Tetanurae, Suborder Theropoda, Order Saurischia

Small-sized dinosaurs, with toothless beaks. Their necks were moderately long, their hands had three fingers, and they were possible herbivorous.

Oviraptoridae

Family of Superfamily Oviraptorosauria, Microorder Coelurosauria, Infraorder Tetanurae, Suborder Theropoda, Order Saurischia

These were small forms, whose heads had short jaws with parrotlike beaks. They had relatively large braincases. Their front limbs were quite long and similar to those in ornithomimids, differing from the latter in that the claws were more sharply curved and the first finger was somewhat longer than the other two. Oviraptorids include these subfamilies:

Ingeniinae

Subfamily of Family Oviraptoridae, Superfamily Oviraptorosauria, Microorder Coelurosauria, Infraorder Tetanurae, Suborder Theropoda, Order Saurischia

More robust than oviraptorines, these small theropods had an apparently crestless head, and relatively smaller claws on second and third fingers.

Oviraptorinae

Subfamily of Family Oviraptoridae, Superfamily Oviraptorosauria, Microorder Coelurosauria, Infraorder Tetanurae, Suborder Theropoda, Order Saurischia

More lightly built than the subfamily Ingeniinae (see above). Some of these had crested heads.

Troodontidae

Family of Microorder Maniraptora, Infraorder Tetanurae, Suborder Theropoda, Order Saurischia

These were small-sized carnivores with long, narrow heads and the largest brain size of all dinosaurs. They had long, slender, delicate jaws with small, closely spaced teeth; and very long, slender hind limbs, with enlarged second toes that bore large claws.

Dromaeosauridae

Family of Microorder Maniraptora, Infraorder Tetanurae,
Suborder Theropoda, Order Saurischia

Small, lightly built meat-eaters with large heads, narrow snouts, moderately deep, straight lower jaws, and backwardly curved teeth. They had unusually long forelimbs, a hand with a mobile wrist, three long fingers, and large curved claws. Their feet had second toes which developed into a uniquely raptorial "sickle claw." They all had long, stiff tails.

Alvarezsauria

Microorder of Microorder Coelurosauria, Infraorder Tetanurae,
Suborder Theropoda, Order Saurischia

Small forms, possibly similar in some ways to ornithomimids.

Alvarezsauridae

Family of Microorder Alvarezsauria, Microorder Coelurosauria, Infraorder Tetanurae, Suborder Theropoda, Order Saurischia

Sauropodomorpha

Suborder of Order Saurischia

Herbivorous, bipedal, semi-bipedal, and quadrupedal forms, small- to gigantic-sized, with small heads, long necks, heavy bones, stocky hind limbs, five-fingered forefeet, and five-toed hind feet.

Prosauropoda

Infraorder of Suborder Sauropodomorpha, Order Saurischia

Small- to large-sized, bipedal, facultatively bipedal or quadrupedal. Small heads, leaf-shaped teeth, elongate necks, first finger powerfully developed, fourth and fifth fingers reduced and clawless, fifth toes very small. Prosauropoda families include:

Thecocontosauridae

Family of Infraorder Prosauropoda, Suborder Sauropodomorpha,
Order Saurischia

Small, erect-postured forms, the only fully bipedal prosauropods.

Anchisauridae

Family of Infraorder Prosauropoda, Suborder Sauropodomorpha, Order Saurischia

Primitive, small, slender-limbed forms.

Massospondylidae

Family of Infraorder Prosauropoda, Suborder Sauropodomorpha, Order Saurischia

Medium-sized forms, with small head and jaws.

Yunnanosauridae

Family of Infraorder Prosauropoda, Suborder Sauropodomorpha, Order Saurischia

Large forms whose heads were tall and narrow, with short snouts, and teeth similar to those in sauropods.

Plateosauridae

Family of Infraorder Prosauropoda, Suborder Sauropodomorpha, Order Saurischia

Medium to large-sized forms, with stout limbs. Some of these animals were heavily built.

Melanorosauridae

Family of Infraorder Prosauropoda, Suborder Sauropodomorpha, Order Saurischia

More advanced forms, large-sized, with a tendency toward quadrupedal locomotion, some fully four-legged.

Blikanasauridae

Family of Infraorder Prosauropoda, Suborder Sauropodomorpha, Order Saurischia

Medium-sized, stockily built, with proportions similar to those in sauropods. Hind feet had a backwardly directed "spur."

Sauropoda

Infraorder of Suborder Sauropodomorpha, Order Saurischia

Very large to gigantic, including the largest land animals of all time. These plant-eaters were quadrupedal, had small heads and the smallest brain-to-body sizes of all dinosaurs. They had long necks; strong, upright limbs; and broad feet with the first toes of the forefeet sporting a claw. They had tails ranging from very short to very long. Some forms had skin armor. The families include:

Vulcanodontidae

Family of Infraorder Sauropoda, Suborder Sauropodomorpha, Order Saurischia

Large-sized, primitive forms, with forelimbs almost as long as the hind limbs, but also having several prosauropod features, including an enlarged thumb claw on the first toe.

Cetiosauridae

Family of Infraorder Sauropoda, Suborder Sauropodomorpha, Order Saurischia

Primitive, unspecialized forms, moderate- to large-sized, with front and hind legs of equal or subequal length.

Cetiosaurinae

Subfamily of Family Cetiosauridae, Infraorder Sauropoda, Suborder Sauropodomorpha, Order Saurischia

These are more generalized forms of cetiosaurid sauropods.

Shunosaurinae

Subfamily of Family Cetiosauridae, Infraorder Sauropoda, Suborder Sauropodomorpha, Order Saurischia

Forms which apparently bore a bony club at the end of the tail.

Brachiosauridae

Family of Infraorder Sauropoda, Suborder Sauropodomorpha, Order Saurischia

Gigantic animals, the heaviest ever on land, with short, shallow snouts; very long necks; front legs almost as long as or longer than hind legs; and relatively short tails.

Camarasauridae

Family of Infraorder Sauropoda, Suborder Sauropodomorpha,
Order Saurischia

Conservative sauropods of medium to very large size, with short heads with a short snout; nostrils in front of the eyes; heavy spatula-shaped teeth that extend along the jaw margins; front and hind limbs of nearly equal length; and a back held horizontally.

Camarasaurinae

Subfamily of Family Camarasauridae, Infraorder Sauropoda,
Suborder Sauropodomorpha, Order Saurischia

Same description as for Camarasauridae.

Opisthocoelicaudinae

Subfamily of Family Camarasauridae, Infraorder Sauropoda,
Suborder Sauropodomorpha, Order Saurischia

Similar to camarasaurines, but with relatively short tails.

Diplodocidae

Family of Infraorder Sauropoda, Suborder Sauropodomorpha,
Order Saurischia

Whip-tailed plant-eaters, very large or gigantic; both massive and slender forms, some extremely long; a long head with the nostrils located at the top; delicate teeth at the front of the mouth; and with a long, tapering tail. They include these three subfamilies:

Diplodocinae

Subfamily of Family Diplodocidae, Infraorder Sauropoda,
Suborder Sauropodomorpha, Order Saurischia

Very large-sized, some with tails ending in a whiplash.

Dicraeosaurinae

Subfamily of Family Diplodocidae, Infraorder Sauropoda,
Suborder Sauropodomorpha, Order Saurischia

Similar to diplodocids, especially in the form of the head and teeth; with short necks and high backs.

Mamenchisaurinae

Subfamily of Family Diplodocidae, Infraorder Sauropoda,
Suborder Sauropodomorpha, Order Saurischia

Asian sauropods with extremely long necks, some more than 30 feet in length.

Titanosauridae

Family of Infraorder Sauropoda, Suborder Sauropodomorpha,
Order Saurischia

Slender to heavy, small-sized, rather primitive forms, with wide, sloping heads; peglike teeth; front limbs about three-fourths as long as the hindlimbs; long whiplash tails. Some or all possessed armor in the form of body plates or ossicles imbedded in the skin.

Segnosauria

Suborder of Order Saurischia

These distinctive, if rare, animals have been assigned their own suborder. Medium-sized, somewhat resembling prosauropods, but with a beak, probably covered with a horny sheath in life, followed by a toothless area, which was, in turn, followed by a series of cheek teeth. These peculiar, barrel-chested dinosaurs, best known from Mongolia, had theropod-like hands, stout hind limbs and broad feet with claws.

Segnosauridae

Family of Suborder Segnosauria, Order Saurischia

Same description as for the Segnosauria.

Ornithischia

Order of Superorder Dinosauria

"Bird-hipped" dinosaurs with pubic bone parallel to another hip bone, the ischium. Stegosaurs, armored, dome-headed, and duckbilled dinosaurs are all among the Ornithischia, which features the following groups:

Thyreophora
Suborder of Order Ornithischia

Small- to large-sized, mostly quadrupedal but including primitive bipedal forms, all possessing body armor.

Scelidosauridae
Family of Suborder Thyreophora, Order Ornithischia

Same description as for Thyreophora.

Stegosauria
Infraorder of Order Ornithischia

Medium to large quadrupeds, with proportionally small heads. They had short, massive forelimbs. Columnar hind legs were longer than front legs, which ended in five hooflike toes. These animals had two rows of backward-directed dermal plates that graded into backward-directed spines. Some had shoulder spines.

Huayangosauridae
Family of Infraorder Stegosauria, Order Ornithischia

Medium-sized, with retained premaxillary teeth; apparently two rows of small, paired dorsal plates; and spines on their tails.

Stegosauridae
Family of Infraorder Stegosauria, Order Ornithischia

Medium-to large-sized herbivores, whose feet had three toes. They had armor plates that were small to very large, arranged in two paired or alternating rows.

Ankylosauria
Infraorder of Suborder Thyreophora, Order Ornithischia

Stocky, quadrupedal herbivores, with forelimbs about two-thirds to three-fourths as long as the hind limbs. They had short, broad feet; wide heads, which they carried low and which were covered by a mosaic of armor plates; and leaf-shaped teeth. Their body armor was usually made up of small rounded plates forming a continuous bony shield on the back. Their tails comprised about half of their body length.

Nodosauridae

Family of Infraorder Ankylosauria, Suborder Thyreophora,
Order Ornithischia

In these armored dinosaurs the body was held more upright than in the club-tailed Ankylosauridae. The nodosaurids had pear-shaped, hornless heads with small teeth. Their heads were fortified with bony plates. Their body armor coverings sometimes bore large lateral spikes; however, they had no tail clubs.

Ankylosauridae

Family of Infraorder Ankylosauria, Suborder Thyreophora,
Order Ornithischia

These armored dinosaurs had triangular heads with horns, armor "shells" with small lateral spikes (if present at all); and tails terminating in a club.

Ornithopoda

Suborder of Order Ornithischia

Includes the most diverse of dinosaur herbivorous groups, from small to very large-sized forms, the former bipedal and the latter sometimes semi-bipedal to quadrupedal.

Heterodontosauridae

Family of Suborder Ornithopoda, Order Ornithischia

Among the smallest and earliest ornithischians, these animals had a horny beak, followed by a large tusklike tooth (except apparently in juveniles), then a row of closely packed cheek teeth which show extensive wear.

Hypsilophodontidae

Family of Suborder Ornithopoda, Order Ornithischia

Small- to medium-sized slender plant-eaters with cheek teeth; probably a horny beak; short forelimbs with five-fingered hands; and long hind limbs with four-toed feet.

Iguanodontia

Infraorder of Suborder Ornithopoda, Order Ornithischia

Small- to very large-sized bird-hipped plant-eaters, including dryosaurids, iguanodontids, and duck-billed dinosaurs.

Dryosauridae

Family of Infraorder Iguanodontia, Suborder Ornithopoda,
Order Ornithischia

Medium to large-sized, unspecialized bipedal herbivores, with sharp ridged
cheek teeth, five-fingered hands, and long, stiffened tails.

Camptosauridae

Family of Infraorder Iguanodontia, Suborder Ornithopoda,
Order Ornithischia

Medium-sized plant-eaters, bipedal to semi-quadrupedal, with elongate
snouts; tails without tall spines; hands with large wrists and short, spurlike
first fingers; and broad, stocky feet.

Iguanodontidae

Family of Infraorder Iguanodontia, Suborder Ornithopoda,
Order Ornithischia

Medium- to large-sized plant-eaters; bipedal, semi-bipedal and quadrupedal;
having a skull with a long snout, a broad (more so than in camptosaurids)
horny beak and numerous grinding teeth. The iguanodontids had large shoulders and forelimbs. Their second and third fingers were blunt and hooflike.
Their thumbs had developed into "spikes," and their hind limbs and feet were
broad.

Hadrosauridae

Family of Infraorder Iguanodontia, Suborder Ornithopoda,
Order Ornithischia

Large-sized, with a body plan quite similar to that in the Iguanodontidae (but
without the "spiked thumb"). They had heads with duckbills formed by the
broad, toothless areas at the front of the jaws. Beaks at the front of the head
were followed by a toothless area and then a battery of teeth. Some bore cranial crests. Some or all had a back "frill." They had relatively long forelimbs
with long forearms; fingers covered in a fleshy "mitten;" and hooved fingers
and toes.

Hadrosaurinae

Subfamily of Family Hadrosauridae, Infraorder Iguanodontia,
Suborder Ornithopoda, Order Ornithischia

These were more lightly built duckbills, with a longer head, either flat-headed
or with a solid cranial crest.

Lambeosaurinae

Subfamily of Family Hadrosauridae, Infraorder Iguanodontia, Suborder Ornithopoda, Order Ornithischia

More robust duckbills whose heads had a hollow crest. Their heads were taller toward the back than hadrosaurines, and their forelimbs were shorter and stouter.

Marginocephalia

Suborder of Order Ornithischia

Small- to large-sized, bipedal and quadrupedal, mostly Late Cretaceous forms, including dome-headed and also parrot-beaked, frilled and horned ornithischians. All had some development of a frill or shelf at the back of the head.

Pachycephalosauria

Infraorder of Suborder Marginocephalia, Order Ornithischia

Small- to medium-sized, bipedal bone-headed dinosaurs, whose heads had a relatively short facial region, a thickened skull roof, small leaflike teeth, and bony ornamentation of varying degrees in the snout and back regions.

Homalocephalidae

Family of Infraorder Pachycephalosauria, Suborder Marginocephalia, Order Ornithischia

Small- to medium-sized, flat-headed bone-heads.

Pachycephalosauridae

Family of Infraorder Pachycephalosauria, Suborder Marginocephalia, Order Ornithischia

Small- to medium-sized bone-heads, whose heads had domes of various sizes.

Ceratopsia

Infraorder of Suborder Marginocephalia, Order Ornithischia

Small- to giant-sized, bipedal but mostly quadrupedal horned dinosaurs. Their heads usually had large frills and horns, their snouts were probably horn-covered beaks in life, and their front feet had five toes.

Psittacosauridae

Family of Infraorder Ceratopsia, Suborder Marginocephalia, Order Ornithischia

Small-sized, primitive, bipedal forms, with tall parrot-like beaks comparatively shorter than in any other ornithischians without horns or frill; rather long forelimbs with four fingers; and feet with four functional toes. These dinosaurs superficially resembled primitive ornithopods in general body proportions.

Neoceratopsia

Microorder of Infraorder Ceratopsia, Suborder Marginocephalia, Order Ornithischia

Small- to large-sized, mostly quadrupedal horned dinosaurs. Their heads were quite large in relation to the size of their bodies. Their prominent beaks were probably covered with a horny material in life. They had frills of varying shapes and sizes, some of these bearing bony processes. The larger forms had horns.

Protoceratopsidae

Family of Microorder Neoceratopsia, Infraorder Ceratopsia, Suborder Marginocephalia, Order Ornithischia

Small-sized, relatively primitive, mostly quadrupedal, basically hornless "horned" dinosaurs (although in adults the region above the snout and eyes can be raised and roughened, with a rudimentary nose horn sometimes present). These animals had variably developed neck frills. Some forms may have been capable of rapid, bipedal locomotion.

Asiaceratopsinae

Subfamily of Family Protoceratopsidae, Microorder Neoceratopsia, Infraorder Ceratopsia, Suborder Marginocephalia, Order Ornithischia

More primitive Asian protoceratopsids, lacking premaxillary teeth, differing mainly in having a relatively shorter heads, longer facial regions, and teeth that were enameled on both sides.

Protoceratopsinae

Subfamily of Family Protoceratopsidae, Microorder Neoceratopsia, Infraorder Ceratopsia, Suborder Marginocephalia, Order Ornithischia

More derived protoceratopsids, with a shorter facial region than that of Asiaceratopsinae.

Ceratopsidae

Family of Microorder Neoceratopsia, Infraorder Ceratopsia, Suborder Marginocephalia, Order Ornithischia

Medium- to large-sized horned dinosaurs. They were quadrupedal, and had prominent frills sometimes developed to very large size; horns of varying sizes, and the largest brains compared to body size of all quadrupedal dinosaurs. Their forelimbs were slightly shorter than their hind limbs, their hind feet were short, and the toes on front and hind feet were hooflike.

Centrosaurinae

Subfamily of Family Ceratopsidae, Microorder Neoceratopsia, Infraorder Ceratopsia, Suborder Marginocephalia, Order Ornithischia

Relatively small- to medium-sized horned dinosaurs, with short, high faces, usually with longer nasal horns, and shorter to nonexistent brow horns. Their frills were usually (possibly always) laced with openings. The frill was usually shorter than length of the basal part of the head, with a scalloped border, that had a more elaborate degree of border ornamentation than in chasmosaurines.

Chasmosaurinae

Subfamily of Family Ceratopsidae, Microorder Neoceratopsia, Infraorder Ceratopsia, Suborder Marginocephalia, Order Ornithischia

Large-sized forms (larger and more highly derived than centrosaurines), with long, low facial regions; pronounced beaks; shorter nasal horn (when present), and longer paired brow horns. They had long usually "windowed" frills.

NOT A DINOSAUR

The following list comprises genera that have appeared in the paleontological literature, and which had been, either in their original or some subsequent publication, classified as dinosaurs or footprint types attributed to dinosaurs. Currently, however, they are excluded from accepted classifications.

Name	Identification
Aachenosaurus	Petrified wood
Aggiosaurus	Crocodile
Albisaurus	Non-dinosaurian
Ankistrodon	=*Epicampodon*, Theocodontian (earliest "ruling reptile")
Anthodon	Cotylosaur
Archaeopteryx	=*Archaeornis, Griposaurus*, Bird
Artiodactylus	*See Kouphichnium*
Avalonia	*See Avalonianus*
Avalonianus	=Theocodontian
Avisaurus	Bird
Basutodon	Theocodontian
Bathygnathus	Pelycosaur
Brachychirotherium	*See Chirotherium*
Brasileosaurus	Crocodile
Chienkosaurus	=*Hsisosuchus*, Crocodile
Chirotherium	=Brachychirotherium, Theocodontian tracks
Cladeidon	Theocodontian
Clarencea	Theocodontian
Clepsysaurus	=*Palaeoctonus, Suchoprion, Phytosaur*
Colonosaurus	=*Ichthyornis dispar*, Bird
Cosesaurus	?Megalosaurid
Cybele	Trilobite
Dahutherium	?Crocodilian tracks
Dakosaurus	Crocodile
Dasygnathoides	*See Ornithosuchus*
Dasygnathus	*See Ornithosuchus*
Deinisuchus	=*Phobosuchus*, Crocodile
Deuterosauropodopus	=*Brachychirotherium, See Chirotherium*
Deuterotetrapous	Therapsid tracks
Doratodon	=*Crocodilus charcharidens*, Crocodile Rhadinosaurus

Name	Identification
Elopteryx	Bird
Epicampodon	*See Ankistrodon*
Eupodosaurus	Nothosaur
Galesaurus	Procynosuchian
Gobipteryx	Bird
Gracilisuchus	Theocodontian
Gwyneddosaurus	Lepidosaur
Hallopus	Crocodile
Herbstosaurus	Pterosaur
Hypornithes	*See Kouphichnium*
Hypselorhachis	Theocodontian
Ignotornis	Bird tracks
Jurapteryx	Bird
Kouphichnium	Invertebrate tracks
Krokodilopus	?Crocodilian tracks
Kuangyuanpus	=*Batrachopus*, Crocodilian tracks
Lagerpeton	Theocodontian
Lagosuchus	Theocodontian
Lewisuchus	Theocodontian
Longisquama	Theocodontian
Macelognathus	Crocodile
Macrodontophion	Non-dinosaurian, ?crocodile or ?plesiosaur
Macrocelosaurus	*See* in Meyer 1847; *See Tanystropheus*
Megalancosaurus	?Theocodontian
Micrichnus	*See Kouphichnium*
Nuthetes	Non-dinosaurian, ?lizard
Ogliosaurus	Crocodile
Ornithichnites	Obsolete term formerly used to label any three-toed footprint fossil
Ornithoides	Carboniferous or Permian fossil footprint
Ornithosuchus	=*Dasygnathoides, Dasygnathus*, Theocodontian
Otouphepus	Invalid term for tracks
Otozoum	Theocodontian or crocodilian tracks
Palaeoctonus	*See Clepsysaurus*
Palaeonornis	=*Rutiodon carolinense*, Phytosaur
Palaeopteryx	Bird
Palamopus	Lacertilian tracks

Name	Identification
Pentasauropus	Dicynodont tracks
Plectropus	Non-dinosaurian tracks
Pneumatoarthrus	=*Archelon?* Turtle
Poposaurus	Theocodontian
Procerosaurus	*See Tanystropheus*
Protoavis	Bird
Pseudolagosuchus	Theocodontian
Pseudotetrasauropus	=*Brachychirotherium; See Chirotherium*
Ptorornis	*See Kouphichnium*
Rachitrema	Ichthyosaur, possibly synonymous with *Merriamia*
Rhadinosaurus	*See Doratodon*
Rhopalodon	Titanosuchian
Rigalites	Theocodontian tracks
Riojasuchus	Theocodontian
Saltoposuchus	Theocodontian
Saurischichnus	Theocodontian tracks
Sauropodopus	=*Brachychirotherium; See Chirotherium*
Sclermochlus	Theocodontian
Smilodon	*See Tanystropheus*
Spinosuchus	Theocodontian
Stereosaurus	Plesiosaur
Succinodon	Filled burrowings of bivalve mollusk Kuphus
Suchoprion	*See Clepsysaurus*
Tanystropheus	Eosuchiomorph
Tapinosaurus	Plesiosaur?
Tarsodactylus	Crocodilian tracks
Tarsoplectrus	Non-dinosaurian tracks
Teratosaurus	Theocodontian
Tetrasauropus	=*Brachychirotherium; See Chirotherium*
Trialestes	Theocodontian
Triassolestes	*See Trialestes*
Trichristolophus	Theocodontian tracks
Unicerosaurus	Fish
Venatiosuchus	Theocodontian
Xishuangbanania	Lizard tracks
Yezosaurus	Plesiosaur
Zanclodon	*See Tanystropheus*

GLOSSARY

Wherever possible we have used everyday language to describe dinosaurs and their environments. Still, there are a few scientific or uncommon terms that appear regularly, and which may require definition.

Advanced Used to describe features that have evolved within a group as more specialized, or derived, than those of other members of its group. For instance, a two-fingered hand is an *advanced* condition in meat-eating dinosaurs. It is a feature that evolved from the more primitive condition of three or more fingers.

Bird-hipped *See* Ornithischian

Bone-headed A descriptive term for the thick, rounded or flattened skull rooves of some dinosaurs, particularly the pachycephalosaurids.

Crest A descriptive term used here for the ridge or other projection found on the skulls of many dinosaurs, particularly the lambeosaurine hadrosaurs.

Cretaceous The third and last period of the Mesozoic Era and of dinosaur life, from 145 million to 65 million years ago.

Family A grouping of similar genera.

Finback A descriptive term for what may have been a fin or sail-like projection on a dinosaur, as indicated by the elongated projections on the vertebrae of the animal's back. (*See* "sailbacked.")

Formation A geological term for the strata of rock deposited at a particular time and region.

Frill A descriptive term for the bony border or fringe of the dinosaur's skull, particularly the sometimes enormous, decorative fringe of bone on the horned, or ceratopsian, dinosaurs.

Genus (plural, *genera*) A grouping of species with common characteristics, but distinct from other members of the same family.

Jurassic The second period of the Mesozoic Era and of dinosaur life, from 208 million to 145 million years ago.

Lizard-hipped *See* Saurischian

Mesozoic One of the major eras of earth's history, from 245 million to 65 million years ago. It was the time when dinosaurs, flying reptiles, and many other life-forms lived, and when mammals and birds first evolved.

Order A classification of organisms with common characteristics between the smaller suborder and larger family levels of classification.

Ornithischian One of the two orders of dinosaurs, based by traditional analysis on hip anatomy. These are bird-hipped dinosaurs which, like birds, have a pubic bone that lies parallel to another hip bone, the ischium. Stegosaurs and armored, dome-headed, and duckbilled dinosaurs are ornithischians.

Plate A smooth, flat, bony piece that formed part of an armored covering on many dinosaurs, including all ankylosaurs and some titanosaurid sauropods.

Primitive This term is used to describe dinosaur features that are simple, or conservative, within the evolution of a group. For instance, among dinosaurs, a five-toed foot is a primitive condition. While such features appear in the earliest members of a group, later animals of that group may still retain certain primitive features.

Saurischian The second order of dinosaurs based on hip anatomy. These lizard-hipped dinosaurs had a long pubis pointing forward and down from the hip socket. The meat-eating theropods and the giant herbivore sauropods are saurischians.

Sailback A descriptive term for the sail-shaped arch that may have appeared along the backs of many dinosaurs, as indicated by prominent series of bony projections along the animals' back vertebrae. (*See* "finback.")

Sauropod Large plant-eating saurischian dinosaurs. This group included the largest dinosaurs known, some of which were more than one hundred feet long.

Species A group of organisms that are similar in appearance and might interbreed.

Spine A bony, pointed projection, often used here interchangeably with "spike," which refers to the large, tapering bone outgrowths on many armored and plate-backed dinosaurs.

Suborder A group of organisms with similar characteristics. This group lies between the smaller family and larger order in the classification hierarchy.

Synonym An alternative name, used here to refer to the many dinosaurs which have been named, mistakenly, more than once. The "junior synonym" is the more recent name, and not valid in scientific usage.

Tail club A large knob of bone at the tip of the tail vertebrae that was present on ankylosaurid armored dinosaurs and some sauropod dinosaurs.

Theropod Largely bipedal, predatory saurischian dinosaurs from smaller-than-duck-size hunters to forty-foot _Tyrannosaurus rex._

Triassic The first of the three periods of the Mesozoic Era, and of dinosaurs, from 245 million to 208 million years ago.

Whiplash A descriptive term for the long, flexible, whip-like tails of many dinosaurs, such as _Diplodocus._

ABELISAURUS

(ay-BEE-li-SAW-rus)

Type Species: *comahuensis* (KOH-muh-hoo-EN-sis)

Classification:

Order:	Saurischia
Suborder:	Theropoda
Family:	Abelisauridae
Name:	*Abeli* = Latinized name for Roberto Abel, director of the Museo Provinciale de Cipolleti + Greek *sauros* = lizard
Size:	About 8 meters (25 feet) long
Period:	Late Cretaceous, 70 million years ago
Place:	Argentina
Diet:	Meat

   Abelisaurus comahuensis, was a large carnivore about the same size as *Allosaurus fragilis*. *Abelisaurus* is known only from an incomplete skull, which shows that it had a long head, with a deep face, and had no horns or ornamentations over its eyes. Although we do not know what its body looked like, it may have been similar to *Carnotaurus sastrei*, another large carnivore known from Argentina with long, slender hind limbs, and, possibly, short forelimbs.

ABRICTOSAURUS

(ih-BRICK-tuh-SAW-russ)

Type Species: *consors* (KON-surz)
Classification:
   Order: Ornithischia
   Suborder: Ornithopoda
   Family: Heterodontosauridae
Name: Greek *abricto* = awake + Greek *sauros* = lizard
Size: About 1 meter (3 feet) long
Period: Early Jurassic, 208 million to 200 million
              years ago
Place: Southern Africa
Diet: Plants

   Abrictosaurus was an early bird-hipped plant-eater from the heterodontosaurid family. Like all heterodontosaurids, *Abrictosaurus* had cheek teeth and was a bipedal herbivore. What set *Abrictosaurus* apart from all other heterodontosaurids is that it had no pointed canine teeth at the front of its lower jaw. *Abrictosaurus* had a turkey-size body and a long tail. Its head was about 10 centimeters (4 inches) long. Its forelimbs were small and delicate, with hands that were probably used for plucking choice tidbits from the local plant life. Its hind limbs were much larger and were adapted for rapid running.

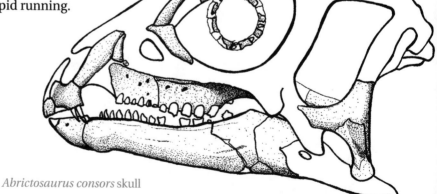

Abrictosaurus consors skull

ACANTHOPHOLIS

(uh-KAN-thuh-FOH-lis)

Type Species: *horridus* (HOR-i-dus)

Status: Doubtful

Classification:

  Order: Ornithischia

  Suborder: Ankylosauria

  Family: Nodosauridae

Name: Greek *akantha* = prickle, thorn; backbone or spine of animal + Latin *folium* = composed of many layers

Size: About 3 to 4 meters (10 to 13 feet) long

Period: Late Early Cretaceous, 115 million to 91 million years ago

Place: England

Diet: Plants

   Acanthopholis was a small member of the nodosaur family, armored dinosaurs without tail clubs. Although illustrations and descriptions of this dinosaur have often appeared in popular books, we know little about its appearance. What we do know suggests that most of the illustrations are incorrect. Its hefty spines, about 24 centimeters (9 inches) long, are often omitted from representations.

   What we now know about *Acanthopholis* suggests that this dinosaur did not differ greatly in size from its earlier British relatives, *Hylaeosaurus* and *Polacanthus*, nor in appearance from its larger North American relative *Sauropelta*. It may have had a long tail like that of *Sauropelta*. Most likely, it belonged to the same branch of the nodosaurid family tree. The major problem with *Acanthopholis horridus* is that no complete specimen has ever been found, and almost all of its known remains are isolated bones scattered among several museums. These do not give us a true description of *Acanthopholis*.

Acanthopholis horridus
dermal spine

ACROCANTHOSAURUS

(ACK-roh-KAN-thuh-SAW-rus)

Type Species: *atokensis* (AY-toh-KEN-sis)
Classification:
    Order: Saurischia
    Suborder: Theropoda
    Family: Allosauridae
Name: Greek *acro* = high + Greek *akantha* = prickle,
thorn, or backbone or spine of animal +
Greek *sauros* = lizard
Size: About 9 meters (30 feet) long
Period: Early Cretaceous, 115 million to 105 million
years ago
Place: Oklahoma, Texas
Diet: Meat

This huge carnivorous dinosaur, a theropod, is famous for the tall spines on its neck, back, and tail. These spines were as much as 60 centimeters (2 feet) high in large individuals, and gave this dinosaur a powerful-looking profile. The tall vertebral spines served as attachment points for powerful neck, back, and tail muscles, and may have been useful in grabbing, holding, or dismembering prey.

ACROCANTHOSAURUS *continued*

Tall spines evolved in various dinosaur groups, plant-eaters and meat-eaters alike. In some instances, the spines supported a thin sail that may have helped keep the dinosaur cool. In other instances, such as the *Acrocanthosaurus*, the spines were embedded in a thick ridge of flesh.

Acrocanthosaurus may have been a close relative and possibly a descendant of the Late Jurassic theropod *Allosaurus*. Unlike *Allosaurus*, *Acrocanthosaurus* did not possess tall horns above its eyes.

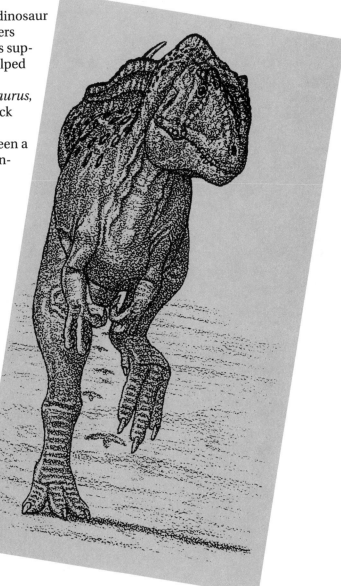

ADASAURUS

(AD-uh-SAW-rus)

Type Species: *mongoliensis* (mon-GOH-li-EN-sis)
Classification:
   Order: Saurischia
   Suborder: Theropoda
   Family: Dromaeosauridae
Name: Mongolian *ada* (an evil spirit from Mongolian
             mythology) + Greek *sauros* = lizard
Size: About 2 meters (6 feet) long
Period: Late Cretaceous, 80 million to 73 million
             years ago
Place: Southwestern Mongolia
Diet: Meat

    This small carnivore, similar to the North American *Dromaeosaurus*, is known only from parts of a skull and some skull fragments. The chief difference between *Adasaurus* and other dromaeosaurids is that the "killer claw" on its second toe was less imposing than the fearsome, sickle-shaped, disemboweling claws possessed by its larger relatives. The pelvis of *Adasaurus* was unusual among theropods, having more backwardly-directed pubic bones than those of *Deinonychus* and *Velociraptor*. We do not know what effect these anatomical distinctions had on *Adasaurus's* hunting style.

AEGYPTOSAURUS

(ee-JIP-tuh-SAW-rus)

Type Species: *baharijensis* (buh-HAR-ee-EN-sis)
Classification:
   Order: Saurischia
   Suborder: Sauropoda
   Family: Titanosauridae
Name: Latin *Aegypto* = Egypt + Greek *sauros* = lizard
Size: About 15 meters (50 feet) long; 3 meters
               (10 feet) tall at the hip
Period: Mid-Cretaceous, 100 million to 95 million years ago
Place: Egypt
Diet: Plants

    This large dinosaur is seldom heard about today. The only skeleton ever found, excavated from an oasis in the middle of the Egyptian Sahara Desert, was pulverized during a World War II bombing raid. Unfortunately, even this type skeleton was incomplete, consisting mainly of leg bones and three fragmentary vertebrae. There was, however, enough to classify the animal and to provide some idea of its general size and appearance, and so we know that *Aegyptosaurus* was a titanosaurid, a moderate-sized, primitive, four-legged sauropod, perhaps with armor.

AEOLOSAURUS

(ee-OH-luh-SAW-rus; ay-OH-luh-SAW-rus)

Type Species: *rionegrinus* (REE-oh-NEG-ri-nus)
Classification:
   Order: Saurischia
   Suborder: Sauropoda
   Family: Titanosauridae
Name: Greek *Aeolo* = Aeolus, god of the winds, from both
               Greek and Roman mythology + Greek *sauros* =
               lizard
Size: About 15 meters (50 feet) long;
               3 meters (10 feet) tall at the hip
Period: Late Cretaceous, 75 million
               to 70 million years ago
Place: Argentina
Diet: Plants

This bulky four-legged herbivore belonged to the titanosaur family of medium-sized, often armored sauropods. It was similar enough to the Indian dinosaur *Titanosaurus* to place them both in the same subfamily, but *Aeolosaurus* had peculiar tail vertebrae with long, forward-pointing prongs on them.

Aeolosaurus was probably about the same size as *Aegyptosaurus*, that is, average for a titanosaurid. It was among the last of the titanosaurids, which ranged far across the earth in the Cretaceous Period, especially in the southern hemisphere.

AEPISAURUS

(EE-pi-SAW-rus; EP-i-SAW-rus)

Type Species: *elephantinus* (EL-uh-fan-TYE-nus)
Status: Doubtful
Classification:
  Order: Saurischia
  Suborder: Sauropoda
  Family: ?
Name: Greek *aepys* = steep or tall + Greek *sauros* = lizard
Size: About 17 meters (55 feet) long
Period: Late Early Cretaceous, 113 million years ago
Place: France
Diet: Plants

    Although this was one of the first sauropod dinosaurs to be described, we still know next to nothing about it. The only specimen that we are sure belongs to this species is a single upper arm bone about 1 meter (3 feet) long. Although *Aepisaurus* is sometimes listed as a titanosaurid, it could belong to any sauropod family. The bone is evidence that a fairly large sauropod lived in what is now France.

    Aepisaurus has the distinction of being one of the most often misspelled dinosaur names, having appeared as *Aepysaurus, Aepyosaurus, Aeposaurus,* and *Oepysaurus* in various publications.

AETONYX
(ee-TON-icks)

Status: Invalid name — *See Massospondylus*

AGATHAUMAS
(ag-uh-THAW-mus)

Status: Invalid name — *See Triceratops*

AGILISAURUS

(AJ-i-li-SAW-rus)

Type Species: *louderbacki* (LOU-dur-BACK-eye;
                LAW-dur-BACK-eye)

Classification:

Order: Ornithischia

Suborder: Ornithopoda

Family: Hypsilophodontidae

Name: Latin *agilis* = light, easily moved, and nimble +
            Greek *sauros* = lizard

Size: 1.2 to 1.7 meters (3.5 to 4 feet) long

Period: Middle Jurassic, 170 million years ago

Place: China

Diet: Plants

Agilisaurus was a hypsilophodontid, one of a worldwide family of small plant-eating, bird-hipped dinosaurs. Like some other hypsilophodontids, *Agilisaurus* had several sharp front teeth, probably for nipping leaves and cones off plants. It chewed with serrated, leaf-shaped teeth that lined the sides of its mouth.

Agilisaurus's hind legs were large and strong, and clearly belonged to a swift runner. Its skeleton was one of many well-preserved dinosaurs to emerge from the Dashanpu quarry in Sichuan, China.

Agilisaurus multidens (MUL-ti-denz): This was a larger species of hypsilophodontid than the type species of *Agilisaurus*, about 2 meters (7 feet) long. It was previously known as *Yandusaurus multidens*.

AGROSAURUS

(AG-roh-SAW-rus)

Type Species: *macgillivrayi* (muh-GIL-i-VRAY-eye)
Status: Doubtful
Classification:
   Order: Saurischia
   Suborder: Prosauropoda
   Family: ?
Name: Greek *agros* = field + Greek *sauros* = lizard
Size: 2 to 3 meters (6 to 10 feet) long
Period: Late Triassic, 225 million to 213 million years ago
Place: Northern Australia
Diet: Plants

    Agrosaurus was the first and oldest dinosaur found in Australia. It was a small prosauropod, or primitive four-legged plant-eater. Its few remains—a forelimb, a hand, and a leg bone—closely resemble the bones of the British prosauropod, *Thecodontosaurus*. Some scientists therefore postulate that *Agrosaurus* was a similar small, primitive, prosauropod that ran on its hind legs, walked on all four, and used its relatively large hand claws for defense.

    The astonishing thing about *Agrosaurus* is that we know anything about it at all. The British survey ship HMS *FLY* landed along the coast of northern Queensland in 1844. An explorer came ashore, did a bit of digging around, and made off with not only the first dinosaur fossils ever found in Australia, but also the only known Triassic Australian dinosaur. Dinosaurs of any sort, in any condition, are rare finds in Australia, and no more *Agrosaurus* fossils have ever been found.

    The discovery of *Agrosaurus* helps to prove that prosauropods lived all over the world during the Late Triassic Period.

ALAMOSAURUS

(AL-uh-moh-SAW-rus)

Type Species: *sanjuanensis* (SAN-wahn-EN-sis)
Classification:
    Order: Saurischia
    Suborder: Sauropoda
    Family: Titanosauridae
Name: Spanish *Alamo* = The Alamo, the Texas trading
                 post near which the type specimen was discovered
                 + Greek *sauros* = lizard
Size: 21 meters (69 feet) long
Period: Late Cretaceous, 73 million to 65 million
                 years ago
Place: New Mexico, Texas, Utah
Diet: Plants

    A large, four-legged browser, *Alamosaurus* is the only sauropod known from the Late Cretaceous Period of North America. Giant sauropods dominated the American West at the end of the Jurassic Period, 145 million years ago. Then, for at least 25 million years, they seem to have been absent from North America.

    Alamosaurus was a titanosaurid, one of a family of primitive sauropods, some of which had armor. It may have come to North America from South America, where sauropods—titanosaurs in particular—remained abundant throughout the Cretaceous Period. *Alamosaurus's* body was as large as that of *Apatosaurus*; its tail, however, seems to have been a few yards shorter than the famous *Apatosaurus* whip-like tail.

ALBERTOSAURUS

(al-BUR-tuh-SAW-rus)

Type Species: sarcophagus (sahr-KOF-uh-gus)
Classification:
  Order: Saurischia
  Suborder: Theropoda
  Family: Tyrannosauridae
Name: Latinized Alberto (for Alberta, Canada) + Greek
           sauros = lizard
Size: 8 to 10 meters (25 to 30 feet) long
Period: Late Cretaceous, 76 million to 68 million
           years ago
Place: Western North America
Diet: Meat

This large carnivore stalked western North America some eight million years before *Tyrannosaurus rex*, and eleven million years before the end of dinosaur time. Both *Tyrannosaurus* and *Albertosaurus* belonged to the tyrannosaurids, the last and largest group of dinosaur carnivores discovered in both North America and Asia.

Like *Tyrannosaurus*, *Albertosaurus* had a huge skull with sharp, serrated teeth for sawing meat.

Albertosaurus libratus
adult and juvenile

ALBERTOSAURUS *continued*

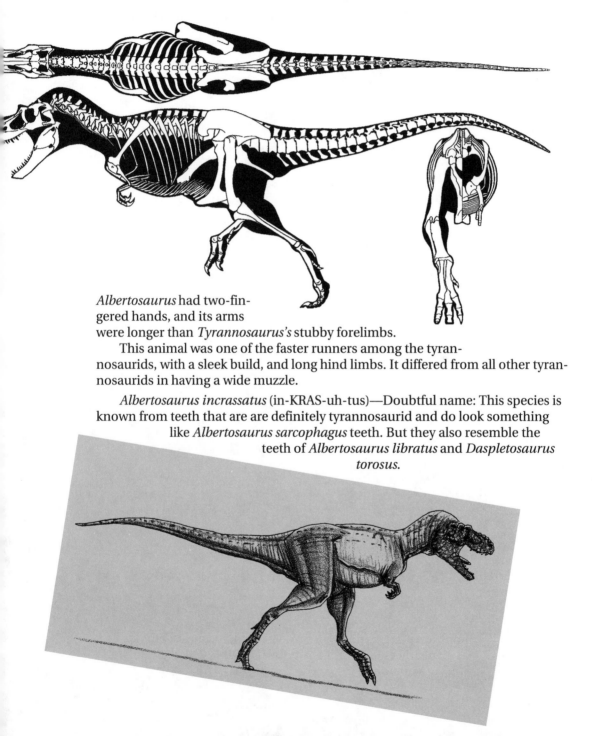

Albertosaurus had two-fingered hands, and its arms
were longer than *Tyrannosaurus's* stubby forelimbs.

   This animal was one of the faster runners among the tyrannosaurids, with a sleek build, and long hind limbs. It differed from all other tyrannosaurids in having a wide muzzle.

   Albertosaurus incrassatus (in-KRAS-uh-tus)—Doubtful name: This species is
known from teeth that are are definitely tyrannosaurid and do look something
like *Albertosaurus sarcophagus* teeth. But they also resemble the
teeth of *Albertosaurus libratus* and *Daspletosaurus
torosus.*

ALECTROSAURUS

(uh-LECK-truh-SAW-rus)

Type Species: *olseni* (OHL-si-nye)
Classification:
   Order: Saurischia
   Suborder: Theropoda
   Family: Tyrannosauridae
Name: Greek *a* = without + Greek *lektron* = bed + Greek *sauros* = lizard
Size: 8 to 9 meters (25 to 30 feet) long
Period: Late Cretaceous, ?98 to ?88 milllion years ago
Place: Mongolia, China
Diet: Meat

This large carnivore was, for many years, a puzzle to paleontologists. All scientists had to go on were arm bones and leg bones found about 100 feet apart in the Gobi Desert in the 1920s. Although the leg bones resembled those of tyrannosaurids such as *Albertosaurus* and *Torvosaurus*, the arm bones—particularly the claw—were much larger than those of other tyrannosaurids.

In the early 1970s, more *Alectrosaurus* specimens were found in Mongolia. These included leg bones similar to those described by paleontologist Charles Whitney Gilmore more than forty years before, as well as skull and arm bones. The original leg bones were later determined to belong to *Alectrosaurus*. The arm bones belonged to an as-yet-unidentified member of a peculiar, family of theropods with large front limbs, the segnosaurs.

Alectrosaurus had a long, toothy skull. Its snout was smooth on top, rather than rough and bumpy as in later tyrannosaurids. The forelimbs were larger than those in later tyrannosaurids, but not nearly as large and powerful as those found near the first skeleton.

ALGOASAURUS

(al-GOH-uh-SAW-rus)

Type Species: *bauri* (BOU-uh-rye)
Status: Doubtful
Classification:
  Order: Saurischia
  Suborder: Sauropoda
  Family: ?
Name: Portuguese Algoa (Algoa Bay, South Africa) + Greek *sauros* = lizard
Size: About 9 meters (30 feet) long (or longer)
Period: Late Jurassic to Early Cretaceous, 145 million to 135 million years ago
Place: South Africa
Diet: Plants

This four-legged plant-eater is not well known, since its description is founded on one vertebra, a single leg bone, and a hoof. Before quarrymen realized that they had found a dinosaur skeleton, most of the bones of this dinosaur were pulverized to make bricks. This was doubly unfortunate, because only a few dinosaur fossils have ever been collected in this part of South Africa. Nevertheless, it appears *Algoasaurus* was a small sauropod less than half the size of an adult *Diplodocus.* From the shape of its back vertebra, some paleontologists have included *Algoasaurus* in the diplodocid family, but others have classified it as a titanosaurid sauropod, or even as an ornithischian.

The small size of the fossil suggests that it may be a half-grown juvenile.

ALIORAMUS

(AH-lee-uh-RAM-us)

Type Species: *remotus* (ri-MOH-tus)
Classification:

Order:	Theropoda
Suborder:	Carnosauria
Family:	Tyrannosauridae
Name:	Latin *alio* = different + Latin *ramus* = branch
Size:	5 to 6 meters (16 to 20 feet) long
Period:	Late Cretaceous, 73 million to 65 million years ago
Place:	Mongolia
Diet:	Meat

Alioramus was one of the tyrannosaurids, the last and most advanced large carnivores in dinosaur evolution. Its most striking features were six small horns on top of its snout: two side by side, and four more in a single row ahead of them. These little horns were too small to have been useful in defense, but they probably helped distinguish males from females, or mature individuals from immature ones.

Only one fragmentary and incomplete *Alioramus* skeleton has been found. *Alioramus* had a longer head than other tyrannosaurids, and smaller and more numerous teeth than its relatives. It was small and slender for a tyrannosaurid.

ALIWALIA

(AL-ee-WAW-lee-uh)

Type Species: *rex* (RECKS)
Classification:
   Order: ?
   Suborder: ?
   Family: ?
Name: *Aliwa* (named for South Africa)
Size: 8 meters (25 feet) long
Period: Late Triassic, 225 million years ago
Place: South Africa
Diet: ?

    Aliwalia rex was a large predator, fragments of which were found in a shipment of fossils of the primitive prosauropod *Euskelosaurus*, sent in 1873 to an Austrian museum. For a long time these were assumed to be parts of the prosauropod, leading scientists to think prosauropods were carnivores.

ALLOSAURUS

(AL-uh-SAW-rus)

Type Species: *fragilis* (fruh-JIL-is)

Classification:

Order:	Saurischia
Suborder:	Theropoda
Family:	Allosauridae
Name:	Greek *allos* = different + Greek *sauros* = lizard
Size:	9 to 12 meters (30 to 40 feet) long
Period:	Late Jurassic, 156 to 145 million years ago
Place:	Colorado, Utah, Wyoming, Montana
Diet:	Meat

Allosaurus is the best known large carnivore of the Late Jurassic Period of western North America. A powerful flesh-eater, it had a one-meter-long (3 feet) head armed with more than seventy 7.5-centimeter-long (3 inches) teeth. Like many other large theropods, *Allosaurus* had lower jaws which were hinged in front and so could expand slightly sideways when it opened its mouth. A movable joint in the skull enabled the snout to move up and down relative to the back of the head. This made it possible for *Allosaurus* to wolf down huge chunks of meat.

Allosaurus's hind legs were large and powerfully muscled, and may have been able to carry it along at speeds of perhaps twenty miles per hour or more. Its forelimbs were much smaller, but each was armed with three sharp claws as much as 25 centimeters (10 inches) long that it may have used to hold prey. Short, well-developed horns, the function of which is unknown, were located above and in front of each eye.

ALLOSAURUS *continued*

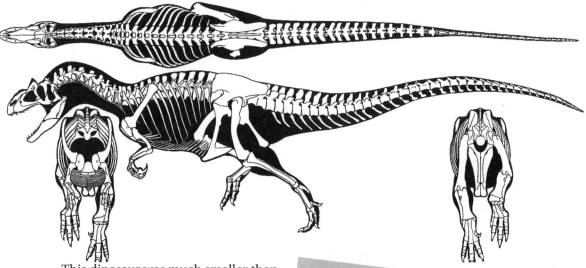

This dinosaur was much smaller than the enormous browsers, the diplodocid sauropods, with which it coexisted. It was probably not large enough to single-handedly bring down a healthy adult sauropod, although calves would have been fair game. Some paleontologists speculate that *Allosaurus* hunted in packs. Like most meat-eaters, it may have been a scavenger.

There are two large carnivores going under the name *Allosaurus*, as indicated by the distinctly different skulls in various museums. There are not enough complete specimens of the two forms to determine whether the differences are individual, or represent different species or genera.

Allosaurus was possibly the most common carnivore of the Late Jurassic period. Thousands of individual bone specimens have been collected, indicating individuals ranging in size from juveniles 3 meters (10 feet) long to huge adults almost 12 meters (40 feet) long.

ALOCODON

(uh-LOH-kuh-don)

Type Species: *kuehnei* (KYOO-ee-eye)
Status: Doubtful
Classification:
   Order: Ornithischia
   Suborder: ?
   Family: ?
Name: Greek *aloco* = furrow + Greek *odontos* = tooth
Size: 1 meter (3 feet) long
Period: Late Jurassic, 164 million years ago
Place: Portugal
Diet: Plants

    This species is named for the crowns of its teeth, which show that *Alocodon* was a small plant-eater. One school of thought contends that *Alcodon* is an intermediate species between *Lesothosaurus* and *Hypsilophodon*; another suggests it evolved independently from a small ornithischian (bird-hipped) ancestor. Most dinosaur experts agree, however, that there is too little material available to speculate meaningfully on *Alocodon's* ancestry.

ALTISPINAX

(AL-ti-SPYE-nacks)

Type Species:	*dunkeri* (DOONG-kuh-rye)
Status:	Doubtful
Classification:	
Order:	Saurischia
Suborder:	Theropoda
Family:	?
Name:	Latin *altus* = high + Latin *spin* = spine + Latin *ax* = suffix to create noun
Size:	9 meters (30 feet) long
Period:	Early Cretaceous, 125 million to 119 million years ago
Place:	Germany, Belgium, England
Diet:	Meat

    Altispinax was a large carnivore described from a peculiar broken tooth crown found near Hanover, Germany. Instead of serrations (like the teeth of other carnivorous dinosaurs), this tooth had a thickened, bladelike edge. However, there is no reliable way to tell whether the serrations were present in life, or were in fact worn away after death.

    The isolated teeth from which this genus is known were later linked to several vertebrae found at an English site, and belonging to the dinosaur *Altispinax*.

ALVAREZSAURUS

(AL-vuh-rez-SAW-rus)

Type Species: *calvoi* (KAL-voh-eye)
Classification:
   Order: Saurischia
   Suborder: Theropoda
   Family: Alvarezsauridae
Name: Spanish *Alvarez* = (for historian Don Gregorio Alvarez) + Greek *sauros* = lizard
Size: 2 meters (6 feet) long
Period: Late Cretaceous, 80 million years ago
Place: Argentina
Diet: Meat

    The partial skeleton of this small, meat-eating dinosaur was found on a riverbank near the Argentine National University's Museum of Natural Science. Like most of the other Late Cretaceous dinosaurs of South America, *Alvarezsaurus* was quite different from its northern-hemisphere relatives—in this case, it was so different that a whole new family of theropods, Alvarezsauridae, was created just to accommodate it.

    Alvarezsaurus was lightly built, with the slender legs and long feet of a fast runner. Whether this animal's speed evolved to help it escape from larger and slower predators, or to chase down small, quick prey, we cannot tell.

    No forelimb bones have yet been found for *Alvarezsaurus*, but a shoulder blade suggests that its arms and hands were not used for walking, but for catching and holding prey. The tail was very long, slender, and flattened from side to side. It probably made up more than half of this dinosaur's total length.

    Perhaps *Alvarezsaurus's* oddest feature was the extremely short spines on its vertebrae, making this dinosaur's back very smooth, without the ridge that other theropods had. What purpose this served, and how it might be related to the dinosaur's other adaptations for speed, cannot be guessed without knowing more of the animal's skeleton.

AMARGASAURUS

(uh-MAHR-guh-SAW-rus)

Type Species: *cazaui* (KAZ-ou-eye)
Classification:
   Order: Saurischia
   Suborder: Sauropoda
   Family: Diplodocidae
Name: *La Amarga* (a canyon in Argentina) + Greek
              sauros = lizard
Size: 10 meters (33 feet) long
Period: Early Cretaceous, 131 million to 125 million
              years ago
Place: Argentina
Diet: Plants

Recently discovered, *Amargasaurus* may be the one of most bizarre-looking of all dinosaurs. The large, four-legged browser was distinguished from all other sauropods by the elongated spines on its neck, back, and tail vertebrae. These spines were paired, so the living animal had not one, but two, rows of spines up its back.

Unfortunately, we cannot tell whether the spines in the living dinosaur supported two thin parallel sails running down the neck and back, or one thick sail. In either case, *Amargasaurus cazaui* must have presented a striking appearance.

AMARGASAURUS *continued*

The purpose of this bony "mane" is uncertain. The scientists who described *Amargasaurus* speculated that the elongated spines served a defensive function, presenting an obstacle to a large predator that tried to bite through the *Amargasaurus's* neck. In addition, the spines may have proved useful in intimidating rivals during the mating season. Finally, all these spines—particularly if they formed two parallel sails—would have significantly increased the animal's body surface, thus helping to keep it cool. Tall neural spines evolved in a variety of dinosaur groups that lived near the equator, especially during the Early Cretaceous Period. Perhaps all of them used their sails for cooling in a hot environment.

The skeleton of *Amargasaurus* is complete from the back of the skull to the base of the back. Elephant-sized, it was small for a sauropod, and very similar to the Late Jurassic Period African dinosaur *Dicraeosaurus*.

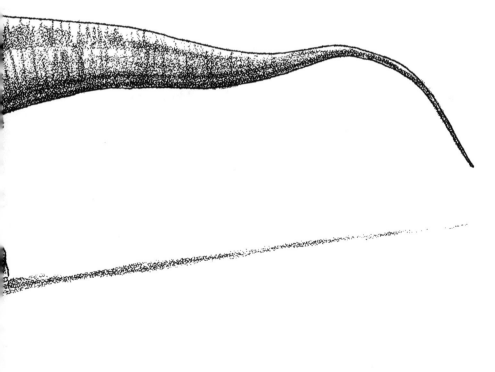

AMMOSAURUS

(AM-uh-SAW-rus)

Type Species: *major* (MAY-jur; MAH-yor)
Classification:

Order:	Saurischia
Suborder:	Prosauropoda
Family:	Plateosauridae

Name: Greek *ammos* = sandy ground + Greek *sauros* = lizard

Size: 4 meters (14 feet) long

Period: Early Jurassic, 198 million to 187 million years ago

Place: Connecticut, ?Nova Scotia, ?Arizona

Diet: Plants

Ammosaurus was a medium-sized member of the prosauropod family—primitive, large plant-eaters with small heads, long necks, and large bodies. This animal was discovered by quarrymen and described more than a century ago. The great Yale University dinosaur scientist, Othniel Charles Marsh, managed to salvage only the back half of the specimen, because the sandstone block containing it had already been broken apart and built into a bridge near South Manchester, Connecticut. In 1969, a nearby sandstone bridge was demolished, and more parts of *Ammosaurus's* skeleton were found. But all we have now of this animal are the incomplete remains—three vertebrae, some hip bones, and both hind limbs—of a few specimens of varying sizes.

AMPHICOELIAS

(AM-fi-SEEL-yus)

Type Species: *altus* (AWL-tus)
Status: Doubtful
Classification:
  Order: Saurischia
  Suborder: Sauropoda
  Family: Diplodocidae
Name: Greek *amphi* = both + Greek *koilos* = hollow + *-ias*, a suffix that creates a noun
Size: 21 meters (70 feet) long; at least 4 meters (13 feet) high at the hip
Period: Late Jurassic, 150 million to 145 million years ago
Place: Colorado
Diet: Plants

    This large four-legged plant-eater belonged to the diplodocid family, which was distinguished by its members' long whip-like tails. *Amphicoelias* may be the same animal as one of the better known diplodocids, *Diplodocus* or *Barosaurus,* from the American West.

    Amphicoelias has the honor of being the first sauropod to have a published life restoration. In 1897, famed dinosaur artist Charles R. Knight showed an underwater group of *Amphicoelias* feeding on plants and sticking their heads above the surface, snorkel-fashion, to breathe. This image was responsible for the now-outmoded idea that sauropods were aquatic animals.

AMTOSAURUS

(AM-toh-SAW-rus)

Type Species: *magnus* (MAG-nus)
Status: Doubtful
Classification:
   Order: Ornithischia
   Suborder: Ankylosauria
   Family: Ankylosauridae
Name: Mongolian Amtgay (location in eastern Mongolia)
           + Greek sauros = lizard
Size: 6 to 7.5 meters (20 to 25 feet) long
Period: Late Cretaceous, 95 million to 85 million
           years ago
Place: Mongolia
Diet: Plants

This dinosaur was first described as a large ankylosaur, or club-tailed, armored dinosaur, related to *Talarurus*. Unfortunately, the only known specimen is an incomplete braincase. Recent reexamination of the fossil raised the possibility that the braincase comes from a duckbilled dinosaur, a hadrosaur.

AMYGDALODON

(uh-mig-DAW-luh-don)

Type Species: *patagonicus* (PAT-uh-GON-i-kus)
Classification:
  Order: Saurischia
  Suborder: Sauropoda
  Family: Cetiosauridae
Name: Latin *amygdalo* (combined form of the word
               amygdala) = almond + Greek *odontos* = tooth
Size: 12 to 15 meters (40 to 50 feet) long
Period: Middle Jurassic, 180 million to 175 million
               years ago
Place: Argentina
Diet: Plants

    This medium-sized, four-legged herbivore, a sauropod known from an incomplete skeleton, is the most primitive sauropod known from South America. Its almond-shaped teeth resemble those of the British sauropod *Cardiodon*, which is thought to be a synonym of *Cetiosaurus*. *Amygdalodon* was closely related to the later South American cetiosaurid, *Patagosaurus*.

    Assuming it was a cetiosaurid, it would not have been a large one. *Amygdalodon's* discovery indicates that cetiosaurids enjoyed a worldwide distribution during the Middle Jurassic Period.

ANATOSAURUS

(uh-NAT-uh-SAW-rus)

Status: Invalid — *See Edmontosaurus*

ANATOTITAN

(uh-NAT-uh-TYE-tan)

Type Species: *copei* (KOH-pye)
Classification:
  Order: Ornithischia
  Suborder: Ornithopoda
  Family: Hadrosauridae
Name: Latin *anas* = duck + Greek *titan* = giant
Size: 9 to 12 meters (30 to 40 feet) long; about 2 to 2.5 meters (7 to 8 feet) high at the hip
Period: Late Cretaceous, 70 million to 65 million years ago
Place: Montana, South Dakota
Diet: Plants

This large duckbilled plant-eater was one of the last of the dinosaurs, living close to the end of the Mesozoic Era. Its muzzle was flattened into the longest, broadest duckbill among the hadrosaurids. *Anatotitan's* key feature is that the entire front half of its snout lacked teeth, a longer toothless section than in any other duckbill.

Anatotitan also had longer and more slender limbs than its relative *Edmontosaurus*, and although *Anatotitan* was almost as long as *Edmontosaurus regalis*, it was more lightly built. *Anatotitan* was also comparatively scarce: dozens of specimens of *Edmontosaurus annectens* have been collected in the American West, but only five or six of *Anatotitan copei*.

Anatotitan longiceps (LONG-i-seps): This species grew to 12 to 14 meters (40 to 45 feet) long and 3,000 to 4,000 kilograms (3 to 4 tons) in weight, judging from a jaw bone. There is some speculation that this animal is an intermediate between *Edmontosaurus annectens* and *Anatotitan copei*.

ANCHICERATOPS

(ANG-ki-SER-uh-tops)

Type Species: *ornatus* (or-NAY-tus)

Classification:

Order:	Ornithischia
Suborder:	Ceratopsia
Family:	Ceratopsidae
Name:	Greek *anchi* = near to + Greek *keras* = horn + Greek *ops* = eye or face (or Greek *keratops* = horn face)
Size:	4.5 to 6 meters (15 to 20 feet) long
Period:	Late Cretaceous, 73 million to 70 million years ago
Place:	Alberta
Diet:	Plants

Anchiceratops was a medium-sized, horned dinosaur with a large head and long frill. Like other dinosaurs of the ceratopsid family, its distinguishing features were the shapes and arrangement of its horns and frill. *Anchiceratops's* outwardly diverging brow horns were larger than its nose horn. Its long, rectangular frill was decorated with large bones that gave it a distinctive, strongly scalloped edge. Some individuals had additional knobs sticking up from the back of the frill. Since we know only the skull, we cannot be certain about the rest of *Anchiceratops.*

ANCHISAURUS

(ANG-ki-SAW-rus)

Type Species: *polyzelus* (POL-i-ZEL-us)
Classification:

Order:	Saurischia
Suborder:	Prosauropoda
Family:	Anchisauridae

Name: Greek *anchi* = near to + Greek *sauros* = lizard
Size: 2 to 3 meters (6 to 8 feet) long
Period: Early Jurassic, 200 million to 188 million years ago
Place: Massachusetts, Connecticut, and Nova Scotia
Diet: Plants

Anchisaurus was one of the most primitive lizard-hipped, saurischian prosauropods, or plant-eating dinosaurs. We know it was a plant-eater because it had finely serrated, leaf-shaped teeth, quite unlike the sickle-shaped teeth of meat-eating dinosaurs. Equipped with large eyes, *Anchisaurus's* narrow, lightly-built skull tapered to a blunt point in front. Its neck was long and slender, and its body had a long trunk. Its forelimbs ended in large, five-digit hands. The first digit was strong and affixed with a thick claw. For most of the 100+ years after its discovery, *Anchisaurus* was thought to be a Triassic Period dinosaur. This notion was overturned in the late 1970s, when the rocks in which it was found were determined to be from the Early Jurassic Period. This made *Anchisaurus* one of the later prosauropods.

Anchisaurus sinensis (sy-NEN-sis): Anchisaurids were not confined solely to North America during the Early Jurassic Period. This species existed in China during that time. A small, long-necked plant-eater like *Anchisaurus polyzelus*, it shared the landscape with its much larger relative, *Lufengosaurus huenei*.

ANDESAURUS

(AN-di-SAW-rus)

Type Species: *delgadoi* (del-GAH-doh-eye)
Classification:
  Order:

                Saurischia
  Suborder: Sauropoda
  Family: Titanosauridae
Name: Spanish Andes (Andes Mountains) + Greek *sauros* = lizard
Size: 18 meters (60 feet) long
Period: Late Early to early Late Cretaceous, 113 million to 91 million years ago
Place: Argentina
Diet: Plants

    Andesaurus was a large four-legged herbivore, about the same size as the Late Jurassic sauropod *Camarasaurus* from the western United States. Titanosaurids, *Andesaurus* included, were abundant in South America during the last dinosaur period, the Cretaceous, even though sauropods had almost entirely disappeared from North America by then.

    The tail anatomy of the *Andesaurus* was unusual among titanosaurs. In this species, the tail vertebrae were joined together by ball-and-socket joints. Both the front and back ends of the vertebrae were flattened. *Andesaurus's* rear back vertebrae had tall spines, which helps to set it apart from other sauropods. The vertebrae are well over 0.6 meters (2 feet) high, and are similar to those of the even larger titanosaurid *Argyrosaurus*.

ANKYLOSAURUS

(ang-KYE-luh-SAW-rus; ANG-ki-luh-SAW-rus)

Type Species: *magniventris* (MAG-ni-VEN-tris)

Classification:

    Order: Saurischia

    Suborder: Ankylosauria

    Family: Ankylosauridae

Name: Latin *ankylo*, combined form of *ankylos*, a Greek word meaning curved, crooked, or bent + Greek *sauros* = lizard

Size: 7.5 meters (25 feet) long; some possibly longer

Period: Late Cretaceous, 70 million to 65 million years ago

Place: Montana, Wyoming; Alberta

Diet: Plants

   Ankylosaurus is among the best known of all the armored, club-tailed dinosaurs for whom its family—the ankylosaurids—is named. This animal has been widely (and wrongly) illustrated with drawings based on a mistaken description by American Museum of Natural History prospector Barnum Brown. Brown thought *Ankylosaurus* was a stegosaur, and reconstructed its skeleton with a high arch. He also thought *Ankylosaurus's* mostly-circular armor plates were arranged like cobblestones.

   Later studies have shown that *Ankylosaurus* was built lower to the ground, and its body was not completely plated. Armor did extend to the animal's bony eyelids, which worked like window shades to protect the eyes from attackers. The armor pattern of *Ankylosaurus* was similar to that of its earlier relative, *Euoplocephalus,* though on a larger scale.

   Ankylosaurus's tail club was a formidable weapon. The vertebrae of the back one-third of the tail were immobilized by overlapping connections that turned it into a solid handle. The club itself was made out of several armor plates fused into a single unit, with the two largest plates on either side of the club.

   Ankylosaurus was not just the last of the ankylosaurids; it was also the largest one. A skull about 76 centimeters (30 inches) long would have belonged to an animal perhaps 9 meters (30 feet) long.

ANKYLOSAURUS *continued*

Ankylosaurus's bones are not common. Only three good specimens and a handful of fragmentary remains are known. This may be because *Ankylosaurus* did not live in the river deltas where most dinosaur fossils were buried. It may have lived on higher ground, and the bits and pieces we have may be from animals that died along a riverbank and were washed downstream.

ANOPLOSAURUS

(an-OP-luh-SAW-rus)

Type Species: *curtonotus* (KUR-tun-O-tus)
Status: Doubtful
Classification:
    Order: Ornithischia
    Suborder: Ornithopoda
    Family: Iguanodontidae
Name: Greek *an-* = without + Greek *hoplon* = weapon + Greek *sauros* = lizard
Size: ?
Period: Late Early Cretaceous, 98 million years ago
Place: England
Diet: Plants

    Anoplosaurus was an iguanodontid, a large, bird-hipped dinosaur with big, spike-like thumbs. It was named, and long misidentified, from fragmentary remains originally thought to belong to a small, possibly juvenile, armored dinosaur. The lower jaw measured only 6 centimeters (2.4 inches) long, and the upper arm would have been only 24 centimeters (9 inches) long. The absence of armor plates on what he thought were the skeletal remains of an armored dinosaur caused Harry Govier Seeley, the British scientist who named this find in 1879, to call it *Anoplosaurus*—unprotected lizard. Because of the fragmentary nature of the fossils, we do not know what kind of dinosaur *Anoplosaurus* represents.

ANSERIMIMUS

(an-SER-i-MYE-mus; an-SER-i-MEE-mus)

Type Species: *planinychus* (PLAN-i-NYE-kus)
Classification:
    Order: Saurischia
    Suborder: Theropoda
    Family: Ornithomimidae
Name: Latin *anser* = goose + Greek *mimos* = mimic
Size: 3 meters (10 feet) long
Period: Late Cretaceous, 75 million to 70 million years ago
Place: Mongolia
Diet: Meat

    Anserimimus was an "ostrich-mimic" dinosaur, one of the long-legged, nearly-toothless carnivores of the ornithomimid family. It is known from a single partial skeleton from which the skull is missing.

    Anserimimus had more powerful forelimbs than other ornithomimids. Like other ornithomimids, its arms, hands, and spade-like claws all seem designed for rooting through loosely-packed soil or plant matter, and perhaps were used for digging up insects or nests of dinosaur eggs.

    The discoveries of *Anserimimus* and several other Asian ornithomimids indicate that these animals may have been more diverse in Asia than in North America.

ANTARCTOSAURUS

(ant-ARK-tuh-SAW-rus)

Type Species: *wichmannianus* (VIKH-man-YAN-us)
Classification:

Order:	Saurischia
Suborder:	Sauropoda
Family:	Titanosauridae
Name:	Antarctic (from the Latin) + Greek *sauros* = lizard
Size:	19 to 30 meters (60 to 100 feet) long
Period:	Late Cretaceous, 83 million to 65 million years ago
Place:	Argentina, Uruguay, Chile
Diet:	Plants

Antarctosaurus was the largest dinosaur known in the Southern Hemisphere, and one of the biggest animals ever to walk the earth. Weighing as much as 50 tons, this enormous four-legged browser was a member of the titanosaurid family of short-tailed, and primarily medium-sized sauropods, some of which were armored.

This species is one of the few titanosaurids for which some of the skull bones have been described. The skull would have been only about 60 centimeters (2 feet) long and quite high, with large eye holes and weak jaw muscles. The teeth were located only at the very front of the mouth.

As in some other titanosaurids, *Antarctosaurus's* hind limbs were substantially longer than its forelimbs. This would have given its back a majestic arch, like those in *Diplodocus* and *Apatosaurus*. The neck may have been short and upwardly inclined.

Antarctosaurus was named from a number of bones, probably belonging to a single individual, found in Argentina in 1916. Other finds in Uruguay and Chile seem to indicate that this species was widespread in South America during the closing stages of the Mesozoic Era.

ANTRODEMUS
(AN-truh-DEE-mus)

Status: Invalid — *See Allosaurus*

APATODON
(uh-PAT-uh-don)

Status: Doubtful — *See Allosaurus*

APATOSAURUS

(uh-PAT-uh-SAW-rus)

Type Species: *ajax* (AY-jacks; AY-acks)
Classification:
  Order: Saurischia
  Suborder: Sauropoda
  Family: Diplodocidae
Name: Greek *apato* = fraud + Greek *sauros* = lizard
Size: 21 to 27 meters (70 to 90 feet) long
Period: Late Jurassic, 156 million to 145 million years ago
Place: Colorado and Utah
Diet: Plants

    This giant dinosaur is among the best known and most commonly represented of all dinosaurs, usually referred to by the name "Brontosaurus."

    Apatosaurus, though not quite as colossal as *Antarctosaurus*, *Seismosaurus*, *Supersaurus*, and *Ultrasaurus*, was an enormous, four-legged, browsing dinosaur. It was a member of the diplodocid family of long-necked sauropods with whip-like tails. *Apatosaurus's* thick neck and prominent lower back ribs distinguished it from other diplodocids. Its backbones had forked spines at the base of

APATOSAURUS *continued*

the neck and in front of the tail, which in life would have given the animal twin ridges along part of the neck and back. These spines supported the large ligaments or tendons that held up the neck and tail.

A short back and forelimbs suggest that this dinosaur may have been able to rear up on its hind legs, using its tail as a "third leg" for support. Standing on all four legs, an *Apatosaurus* would have been able to raise only the front third of its neck to fully vertical. By rising up on its hind legs, it would have increased its feeding range to as much as 15 meters (50 feet) into the treetops.

Apatosaurus may have been a solitary forest forager. Remains are relatively rare, and are among the least likely to be found with other skeletons. *Apatosaurus* skeletons are found distant from large bodies of water, and from the fossils of aquatic animals such as fish and crocodilians. This indicates that *Apatosaurus*, like most sauropods, spent much of its time on land, contrary to its once-popular image as a swamp-dweller.

The confusion over *Apatosaurus's* name is longstanding and unrelated to the widely publicized, incorrect mounting of another dinosaur's skull on its body in museum exhibits.

All we have of *Apatosaurus ajax's* skull are a few badly-preserved bones. The first permanently mounted sauropod skeleton in the world was the *Apatosaurus* at the American Museum of Natural History in New York City. It was based on a half-complete skeleton without a skull, and a *Camarasaurus*-like skull was created for it.

APATOSAURUS *continued*

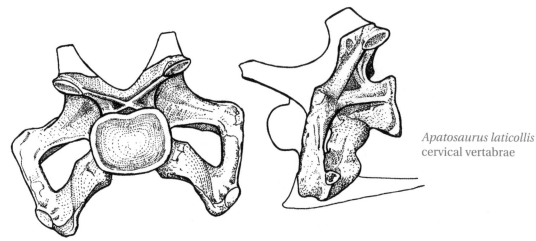

Apatosaurus laticollis
cervical vertabrae

The confusion over the names *Apatosaurus* and "Brontosaurus" occurred when the same animal was mistakenly given two different names. Othniel Charles Marsh described these as two separate animals, not realizing they were separate species of the same genus. Since *Apatosaurus* had precedence over "Brontosaurus" as the first animal described, *Apatosaurus* became the correct scientific name. (*See Apatosaurus excelsus.*)

Apatosaurus excelsus (ek-SEL-sus): This animal became the type specimen of the genus "Brontosaurus" shortly after it was unearthed in 1879. It was first pointed out in 1903 that this animal was more likely a different species of *Apatosaurus* than a new genus. It differed only in that its features were those of an adult, whereas the type specimen of *Apatosaurus ajax* was not fully grown. This species is based on one of the best preserved and most complete large sauropod skeletons ever found, though it was found without a skull. "Brontosaurus" was renamed, but the name was already so well-known and beloved that it remains in use.

Apatosaurus louisae (loo-EE-zay, loo-EE-zye): *Apatosaurus louisae* differed from *Apatosaurus excelsus* in minor, but significant, anatomical details, such as the shape of its neck, ribs and vertebrae. This species is based on an almost-complete sauropod skeleton excavated in 1909 at the site now known as Dinosaur National Monument near Jensen, Utah. Another, smaller, skeleton was found lying directly beneath the larger one, and later excavations unearthed four different skeletons. These finds included a complete, long, slender skull, with nostrils on top, and peglike teeth. For many years, scientists thought this skull belonged to *Diplodocus*.

*Apatosaurus
minimus* pelvis

ARAGOSAURUS

(AR-uh-goh-SAW-rus)

Type Species: *ischiaticus* (is-kee-AT-i-kus)
Classification:

Order:	Saurischia
Suborder:	Sauropoda
Family:	Camarasauridae
Name:	Spanish Aragón + Greek sauros = lizard
Size:	18 meters (60 feet) long
Period:	Early Cretaceous, 130 million to 120 million years ago
Place:	Spain
Diet:	Plants

This large, four-legged plant-eater is known, like many other European dinosaurs, from fragmentary finds. For *Aragosaurus* we have some tail vertebrae, a forelimb, and parts of the pelvis, suggesting this animal had a powerful, muscular tail and a heavy body. The overall anatomy and proportions of the bones resemble those of the earlier North American sauropod *Camarasaurus*.

ARALOSAURUS

(uh-RAL-uh-SAW-rus)

Type Species: *tuberiferus* (TOO-buh-RIF-uh-rus)
Classification:

Order:	Ornithischia
Suborder:	Ornithopoda
Family:	Hadrosauridae

Name: Aral (Sea) + Greek *sauros* = lizard
Size: 9 meters (30 feet) long
Period: Late Cretaceous, 90 million to 85 million
                years ago
Place: Kazakhstan
Diet: Plants

   The only known skull specimen of this large duckbill is the back half of a skull, which includes part of a nasal bone. This bone had a "Roman nose"-like swelling on top similar to that of the crestless Canadian hadrosaur, *Gryposaurus*.
   This skull belonged to a subadult animal. Various limb bones and vertebrae of several other *Aralosaurus* individuals were unearthed from the same deposits.

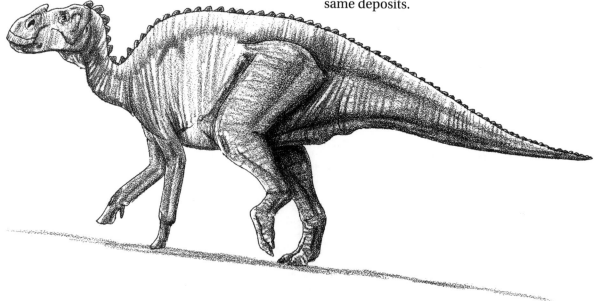

ARCHAEORNITHOIDES

(AHR-kee-OR-ni-THOY-deez)

Type Species: *deinosauriscus* (DIE-no-sore-ISS-cuss)
Classification:
   Order: Saurischia
   Suborder: Theropoda
   Family: Archaeornithoididae
Name: Greek *archaeornith* (generic "first bird") =
            Archaeornis (junior synonym of *Archaeopteryx*)
            + Greek *oides* = known as
Size: 90 centimeters (3 feet) long
Period: Late Cretaceous, 84 million to 80 million
            years ago
Place: Mongolia
Diet: Small vertebrates and insects

    Archaeornithoides, named in 1992, is one of the smallest of all dinosaurs, perhaps weighing less than 1.5 kilograms (3 pounds). It is known from slender bones from the bottom of its snout. Many of this fossil's features are reminiscent of bird bones, hence its name. These remains also appear to link *Archaeornithoides* with the troodontids—small, advanced carnivores. And, surprisingly, some features of this dinosaur, such as its cone-shaped, unserrated teeth, link it with the spinosaurid dinosaurs. The spinosaurids include what were perhaps the largest of all carnivorous dinosaurs, *Spinosaurus*, from North Africa.

Archaeornithoides deinosauriscus skull

ARCHAEORNITHOMIMUS

(AHR-kee-OR-ni-thoh-MIM-us)

Type Species: *asiaticus* (AY-zee-AT-i-kus)
Status: Doubtful
Classification:
  Order: Saurischia
  Suborder: Theropoda
  Family: Ornithomimidae
Name: Greek *archaio* = ancient + Greek *ornithos* = bird + Greek *mimos* = mimic
Size: Small
Period: Late Cretaceous, ?97.5 to 91 million years ago or ?73 to 65 million years ago
Place: China
Diet: Meat

Archaeornithomimus was the oldest ornithomimid, or "ostrich-mimic," dinosaur. Unlike later ornithomimids, which had three short fingers, *Archaeornithomimus* had a small, short, third finger. This is among the few fragments of this dinosaur found, and there is some question as to whether *Archaeornithomimus* is a true ornithomimid, or another, as-yet-unidentified, carnivorous dinosaur.

ARCTOSAURUS

(AHRCK-toh-SAW-rus)

Type Species: *osborni* (OZ-bor-nye)
Status: Doubtful
Classification:
   Order: Saurischia
   Suborder: Theropoda
   Family: ?
Name: From the Latin *arcticus* = north + Greek *sauros* = lizard
Size: Almost 3 to more than 3.5 meters (10 to 12 feet) long
Period: Late Triassic, 231 million to 208 million years ago
Place: Arctic North America
Diet: ?

   Arctosaurus was the first dinosaur discovered in the Arctic region, but was named from just a single crushed, partial neck vertebra. It has been variously classified as a prosauropod plant-eating dinosaur, a theropod meat-eating dinosaur, or even a turtle. Because of the poor quality of the specimen, scientists cannot even determine whether or not it is a dinosaur.

ARGYROSAURUS

(AHR-gye-ruh-SAW-rus)

Type Species: superbus (soo-PUR-bus)
Classification:
    Order: Saurischia
    Suborder: Sauropoda
    Family: ?Titanosauridae
Name: Greek argyros = silver + Greek sauros = lizard
Size: ?21 meters (70 feet) long
Period: Late Cretaceous, 73 million to 65 million
           years ago
Place: Argentina, Uruguay
Diet: Plants

This was a massive, four-legged plant-eater, apparently even larger than *Apatosaurus*. It was the first sauropod described from South America. The specimen consists of a very large forelimb with foot bones. Other isolated material has been assigned to it, but without good reason. *Argyrosaurus* may or may not be a titanosaurid, one of a family of sauropods, some of which were armored. Titanosaurs were particularly abundant in South America.

Argyrosaurus
superbus
front leg

ARISTOSAURUS

(uh-RIS-tuh-SAW-rus)

Status: Invalid name — *See Massospondylus*

ARISTOSUCHUS

(us-RIS-tuh-SOOK-us)

Status: Invalid name — *See Calamospondylus*

ARRHINOCERATOPS

(ay-RYE-noh-SER-uh-tops)

Type Species: *brachyops* (BRACK-ee-ops)
Classification:

Order:	Ornithischia
Suborder:	Ceratopsia
Family:	Ceratopsidae
Name:	Greek *a* = without + Greek *rhinos* = nose + Greek *keratos* = horned + Greek *ops* = face
Size:	About 6 meters (20 feet) long
Period:	Late Cretaceous, 72 million to 68 million years ago
Place:	Alberta
Diet:	Plants

This large horned dinosaur is known from just two specimens, one of which is a nearly complete skull, 1.5 meters (5 feet) long, found in western Canada in 1923. The skull of *Arrhinoceratops* had a short, thick nose horn and moderate-sized brow horns which pointed forward and to the sides, possibly the result of deformation. Its rectangular, bony frill had four small oval-shaped holes within it.

Compared to other ceratopsids, *Arrhinoceratops* had a very short nose and face. Only skull bones have been found, so far, for this dinosaur.

ARSTANOSAURUS

(ahr-STAN-uh-SAW-rus)

Type Species: *akkurganensis* (uh-KUR-guh-NEN-sis)
Status: Doubtful
Classification:
   Order: Ornithischia
   Suborder: Ornithopoda
   Family: Hadrosauridae
Name: Arstan (locale in Kazakhstan) + Greek *sauros* = lizard
Period: Late Cretaceous, 87.5 million to 73 million years ago
Place: Kazakhstan
Diet: Plants

    Arstanosaurus was named from an upper jaw bone, and is considered a duck-bill, though one of its teeth is characteristic of horned dinosaurs' teeth. Although this fragment does appear to be from a hadrosaur, it has no special features that set it apart from all other hadrosaurs.

ASIACERATOPS

(AY-zhuh-SER-uh-tops)

Type Species: *salsopaludalis* (SAL-soh-puh-LOO-duh-lis)

Classification:

Order:	Ornithischia
Suborder:	Ceratopsia
Family:	Protoceratopsidae

Name: Asia + Greek *keratos* = horned + Greek *ops* = face

Period: Late Cretaceous, 97.5 million to ?90 million years ago

Size: 2 meters (6 to 7 feet) long

Place: Central Asia

Diet: Plants

Asiaceratops belongs to the protoceratopsids, a family of primitive and relatively small horned dinosaurs which includes the well known *Protoceratops*. It appears to be closely related to at least one species of *Montanoceratops*, a North American horned dinosaur. The resemblance between these two dinosaurs, like that of many North American and Asian dinosaurs from the end of dinosaur time, indicates that many kinds of dinosaurs moved between the continents when land masses were joined in the Late Cretaceous Period.

Asiaceratops is known only from a few teeth, a jaw, and some leg and foot fragments. It was a very small animal.

ASIATOSAURUS

(A-zee-AT-uh-SAW-rus)

Type Species: *mongoliensis* (mong-GOH-lee-EN-sis)
Status: Doubtful
Classification:
   Order: Saurischia
   Suborder: Sauropoda
   Family: ?
Name: Asia + Greek *sauros* = lizard
Size: Very large
Period: Early Cretaceous
Place: Mongolia, China
Diet: Plants

   Asiatosaurus was a large four-legged browser of unknown family affiliation. It was named from fragmentary fossils, including two teeth which bear similarities to those of *Camarasaurus*. Its back vertebrae appear to be nearly identical to those of *Euhelopus*, a Chinese sauropod, and these animals may be one and the same.

   Asiatosaurus kwangshiensis (KWANG-shee-EN-sis): Doubtful name. This species is based only on teeth.

ASTRODON

(AS-truh-don)

Type Species: *johnstoni* (JON-ston-eye)
Status: Doubtful — *See Pleurocoelus*
Classification:
   Order: Saurischia
   Suborder: Sauropoda
   Family: Brachiosauridae
Name: Greek *astro* = star + Greek *odontos* = tooth
Size: ?10 meters (33 feet) long
Period: Early Cretaceous, 130 to 120 million years ago
Place: Maryland; ?Niger, West Africa
Diet: Plants

Astrodon was a relatively small sauropod, named from its spoon-shaped tooth, discovered in Maryland. Because of striking similarities between its tooth and that of the better-known *Pleurocoelus*, and because they were found in the same place, these two dinosaur names may represent the same animal.

Astrodon johnstoni

ATLANTOSAURUS
(at-LAN-tuh-SAW-rus)

Status: Doubtful — *See Apatosaurus*

ATLASCOPCOSAURUS

(AT-lus-KOP-kuh-SAW-rus)

Type Species: *loadsi* (LOHD-zye)
Classification:

    Order: Ornithischia

    Suborder: Ornithopoda

    Family: Hypsilophodontidae

Name: Atlas Copco Corporation (providers of drilling equipment) + Greek *sauros* = lizard

Size: 2 to 3 meters (6.75 to over 10 feet) long

Period: Early Cretaceous, 114 million to 110 million years ago

Place: Southeastern Australia

Diet: Plants

    Atlascopcosaurus was a plant-eater found in Australia, an area well within the Antarctic Circle during this dinosaur's time. *Atlascopcosaurus* is known from fragments of jaws and teeth. The teeth resemble those of another hypsilophodontid, *Zephyrosaurus*, from North America.

    Both *Atlascopcosaurus* and *Leaellynasaura*, another hypsilophodontid from the same site in Australia, were small dinosaurs. No large dinosaurs have yet been recorded from southeastern Australia.

AUBLYSODON

(oh-BLIS-uh-don)

Type Species: *mirandus* (mi-RAN-dus)
Classification:

    Order: Saurischia
    Suborder: Theropoda
    Family: ?

Name: Latinized Greek *au* = backward, +
              Greek *odontos* = tooth

Size: 4.5 meters (15 feet) long

Period: Late Cretaceous, 76 million to 65 million
              years ago

Place: Western North America

Diet: Meat

   Aublysodon may have been a tyrannosaurid, a large and advanced carnivore from the end of dinosaur time. Unlike all other tyrannosaurids, *Aublysodon* had front teeth without serrations. Since it was named nearly a century ago from fragmentary remains of teeth and skull pieces, many fossils of hard-to-define carnivorous dinosaurs have been assigned to *Aublysodon*.

AUSTROSAURUS

(AW-struh-SAW-rus)

Type Species: *mckillopi* (muh-KIL-uh-pye)
Classification:
    Order: Saurischia
    Suborder: Sauropoda
    Family: ?
Name: Latin *auster* = south + Greek *sauros* = lizard
Size: About 15 meters (50 feet) long
Period: Early Cretaceous (Albian), 113 million to 98 million
                 years ago
Place: Queensland, Australia
Diet: Plants

    Austrosaurus is only the second sauropod dinosaur, or large four-legged browser, found in Australia. The first was *Rhoetosaurus*.

    Like most Australian dinosaurs, *Austrosaurus* was named from incomplete fossils (some vertebrae and limb fragments). Its family is unknown. It had long limbs and features which resembled both the giraffe-like brachiosaurid sauropods and the smaller, boxy-headed sauropods, the camarasaurids. However, its closest relations may be among the cetiosaurid sauropods, which were primitive, long-tailed browsers.

AVACERATOPS

(AY-vuh-SER-uh-tops)

Type Species: *lammersi* (LAM-ur-sye)
Classification:
  Order: Ornithischia
  Suborder: Ceratopsia
  Family: Ceratopsidae
Name: Ava (Cole) + Greek *keratos* = horned +
             Greek *ops* = face
Size: About 2 meters (about 7 feet) long
Period: Late Cretaceous, 77 million to 73 million years ago
Place: Montana
Diet: Plants

Avaceratops was one of the smallest true horned dinosaurs. It represents the most complete dinosaur specimen ever collected from Montana's Judith River Formation, a major source of dinosaur remains.

Avaceratops had a solid neck frill. Although certain features of the bones suggest that the type skeleton represents a small adult individual with a fused braincase, some paleontologists think that *Avaceratops* is a juvenile of an already-known horned dinosaur species, such as *Centrosaurus.*

AVIMIMUS

(AH-vee-MIM-mus)

Type Species: *portentosus* (POR-ten-TOH-sus)

Classification:

Order:	Saurischia
Suborder:	Theropoda
Family:	Avimimidae

Name: Latin *avis* = bird + Greek *mimos* = mimic

Period: Late Cretaceous, ?85 million to 75 million years ago

Size: About 1.5 meters (5 feet) long

Place: Mongolia

Diet: Meat

Avimimus was a birdlike dinosaur, with a slender body, a long and birdlike neck, slim legs, and birdlike feet. As in modern birds, the front of its jaws were toothless. *Avimimus* may belong to the tetanurian group of stiff-tailed meat-eaters, but it was considered distinct enough to warrant its own family, the Avimimidae. However, where it fits into the family tree of meat-eating dinosaurs is uncertain.

Avimimus seems to have been among the longest-legged and swiftest of the dinosaurs. It probably caught insects and small reptiles for food.

Because of its avian characteristics, some researchers have suggested that *Avimimus* had feathers, though no feather impressions were found with it, or any other dinosaur remains. Russian scientists suggested that *Avimimus's* forearm bone showed marks indicating the possible attachment of feathers. This interpretation has been questioned by other scientists. If feathers were present on *Avimimus*, they may have been used for body insulation, not flight. If, as some paleontologists speculate, fast-running small dinosaurs like *Avimimus* were hot-blooded, then feathers could have helped to limit their loss of body heat.

AZENDOHSAURUS

(ay-SEN-doh-SAW-rus)

Type Species: *laaroussii* (lah-ROO-see-eye)
Status: Doubtful
Classification:
  Order: ?Saurischia
  Suborder: ?Prosauropoda
  Family: ?
Name: Azendoh (village) + Greek *sauros* = lizard
Size: ?1.8 meters (6 feet) long
Period: Late Triassic, 228 million years ago
Place: Morocco
Diet: Plants

   This is a poorly known plant-eater, the description of which is based on portions of a jaw with teeth. First believed to be a bird-hipped plant-eater, an ornithischian related to *Lesothosaurus*, *Azendohsaurus* was later identified as a prosauropod.

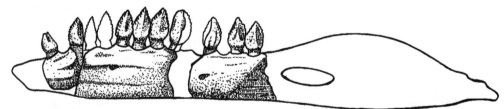

Azendohsaurus laaroussii
jaw fragment

BACTROSAURUS

(BACK-truh-SAW-rus)

Type Species: *johnsoni* (JON-suh-nye)
Classification:
  Order: Ornithischia
  Suborder: Ornithopoda
  Family: Hadrosauridae
Name: Bactria (province of Asia) + Greek *sauros* = lizard
Size: 6 meters (20 feet long)
Period: Late Cretaceous, 97 million to 85 million years ago
Place: Mongolia, China
Diet: Plants

Bactrosaurus is the oldest known member of the true lambeosaurines, the hollow-crested and more solidly built (than the crestless hadrosaurines) subfamily of duckbills. This browser was more massive and more powerful than its contemporary from the hadrosaurine subfamily of duckbills, *Gilmoreosaurus*. *Bactrosaurus* bears a superficial resemblance to the iguanodontids, earlier plant-eaters, and is among the most primitive of the duckbills.

Bactrosaurus was discovered in Inner Mongolia (now part of the People's Republic of China) in 1923 by scientists who were part of the American Museum of Natural History's expedition to the Gobi Desert.

The age of the Gobi sediments in which *Bactrosaurus* was found is not yet established, but *Bactrosaurus* has long been ascribed to the early part of the Late Cretaceous Period.

Since *Bactrosaurus* was more primitive than the duckbills already known from western North America, its discovery supports the expedition leaders' theory that Asian dinosaurs crossed into North America via now-submerged land connections during the Late Cretaceous Period. While dinosaurs did move between these continents, it is not clear whether Asian dinosaurs were the ancestors of those found in North America.

BAGACERATOPS

(BAG-a-SER-uh-TOPS)

Type Species: rozhdestvenskyi (ROZ-des-SVEN-skee-eye)

Classification:

Order: Ornithischia

Suborder: Ceratopsia

Family: Protoceratopsidae

Name: Mongolian *baga* = small + Greek *keratos* = horned + Greek *ops* = face

Size: 1 meter (3 feet) long

Period: Late Cretaceous, 70 million years ago

Place: Mongolia

Diet: Plants

Bagaceratops was a small and primitive horned dinosaur with a short frill over its neck, which may have been laced with openings. Its snout was short, and had a small nose horn. *Bagaceratops* most closely resembles *Leptoceratops gracilis* (though its nose horn and frill are larger) and *Microceratops gobiensis*.

Skulls of this dinosaur were discovered in the Gobi Desert of Mongolia in an expedition led by Polish women scientists.

BAHARIASAURUS

(buh-HAYR-ee-uh-SAW-rus)

Type Species: *ingens* (IN-jenz)
Classification:
   Order: Saurischia
   Suborder: Theropoda
                Family: ?
Name: Baharija (Oasis in Egypt) + Greek *sauros* = lizard
Period: Early to Late Cretaceous, 105 to 95 million
                 years ago
Size: ?4.5 to 6 meters (15 to 20 feet) long
Place: Egypt, perhaps North Africa
Diet: Meat

   This poorly known large carnivore may have been smaller than *Albertosaurus*, but some of its backbones were twice as long. It was apparently a powerfully built animal. *Bahariasaurus's* relationship to other carnivorous dinosaurs is unclear.

   Bahariasaurus, like the giant sail-backed carnivore *Spinosaurus*, was brought to Stuttgart by its German collectors. Unfortunately, until more specimens are found, we cannot understand much about *Bahariasaurus* or *Spinosaurus*, as their namesake specimens were destroyed in 1944 by bombs.

BARAPASAURUS

(buh-RAP-us-SAW-rus)

Type Species: *tagorei* (tuh-GOR-ee-eye)
Classification:
    Order: Saurischia
    Suborder: Sauropoda
    Family: Vulcanodontidae
Name: Hindi *bara* = big + Hindi *p* = leg + Greek *sauros* = lizard
Size: 20 meters (60 feet) long
Period: Early Jurassic, 208 to 188 million years ago
Place: India
Diet: Plants

    Barapasaurus was a large browser with spoon-shaped teeth and relatively slender limbs. It may be one of the earliest sauropods, the giant four-legged herbivores, though some scientists consider it a prosauropod.

    Parts of more than 300 of these mysterious animals have been found in the Godavari Valley of southern India, but how *Barapasaurus* looked and what it was remains uncertain. No skulls or feet have been found, and the proportions of the limbs are uncertain.

Barapasaurus appeared at the time when the supercontinent Pangea broke up, and India began drifting north from the southern supercontinent of Gondwana.

BAROSAURUS

(BAYR-uh-SAW-rus)

Type Species: *lentus* (LEN-tus)
Classification:
   Order: Saurischia
   Suborder: Sauropoda
   Family: Diplodocidae
Name: Greek *baros* = heavy + Greek *sauros* = lizard
Size: 20 meters (60 feet) or longer
Period: Late Jurassic, 156 million to 145 million years ago
Place: Western North America, East Africa
Diet: Plants

   Barosaurus is a relatively rare sauropod, a longer-necked close relative of the whip-tailed giant, *Diplodocus. Barosaurus's* tail was shorter than that of *Diplodocus,* and its hind limbs stockier.

   The cast of a *Barosaurus* rearing up on its hind legs to defend its young from an *Allosaurus* stands in the rotunda of the America Museum of Natural History in New York City. It is, at more than fifty feet high, the tallest dinosaur display in the world. In life, it is questionable whether *Barosaurus* could adopt such a dramatic pose.

   Barosaurus was the first dinosaur found in the Black Hills of South Dakota. It was named in 1890 by the most prolific namer of dinosaurs, Yale scientist Othniel Charles Marsh. It has also been discovered in Wyoming and western Colorado.

   Barosaurus gracilis (GRAS-i-lus): From limited evidence, this species appears to have been a large sauropod much like *Barosaurus lentus.* It was named from isolated limb bones found in Tanzania in 1908. The discovery of *Barosaurus* in now widely dispersed habitats reflects the close contact between the modern African and North American continents in Late Jurassic times.

BARSBOLDIA

(bahrz-BOHL-dee-uh)

Type Species:	*sicinskii* (si-CHIN-skee-eye)
Status:	Doubtful
Classification:	
Order:	Ornithischia
Suborder:	Ornithopoda
Family:	Hadrosauridae
Name:	Named for (Rinchen) *Barsbold*, Mongolian paleontologist
Size:	?10 meters (30 feet) long
Period:	Late Cretaceous, 73 million to 70 million years ago
Place:	Mongolia
Diet:	Plants

This big duckbilled dinosaur was found in Mongolia in the late 1960s. It is one of the hollow-crested duckbills, and it is among the largest of the lambeosaurines. The high spines on its backbone and other characteristics of *Barsboldia's* skeleton more closely resemble *Hypacrosaurus* of North America than they do other Asian duckbills. Perhaps *Barsboldia* had a humped back or a slight fin. As yet, it is very poorly known, and questionable as a valid name, since it was named from a single incomplete specimen.

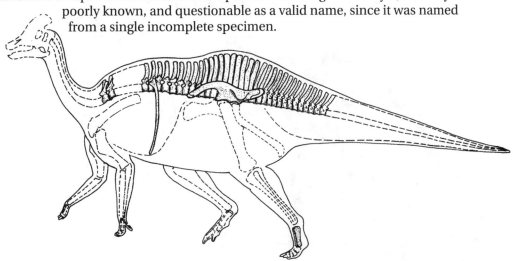

BARYONYX

(BAYR-ee-ON-icks)

Type Species: *walkeri* (WAW-kuh-rye)

Classification:

    Order: Saurischia

    Suborder: Theropoda

    Family: ?

Name: Greek *baros* = heavy

               + Greek *onux* = claw

Size: 10 meters (30 feet) long

Period: Early Cretaceous, 125 million years ago

Place: England

Diet: Meat (fish?)

    Nicknamed "claws," *Baryonyx* was an unusual, large meat-eater. Perhaps its most distinctive characteristics were its long crocodile-like snout with many teeth, and its enormous talons, nearly one foot long. The first fossil of *Baryonyx*, one of its claws, was discovered in a British claypit in January, 1983, by an amateur collector. British Natural History Museum scientists excavated a nearly complete skeleton at the site, the first carnivorous dinosaur ever found in England from any time, and the first from the Lower Cretaceous Period anywhere in the world.

Baryonyx's long snout and abundant teeth suggest it was a fish-eater, perhaps crouching on river banks to snap up its prey. Its enormous claw is shaped much like that of *Allosaurus*, though it is considerably larger. It is not certain whether the claw belongs to the hand or foot of *Baryonyx*. If it was a hand claw, it would have been held clear of the ground, and may have been used to spear fish as a grizzly bear swipes at salmon with its paw.

BECKLESPINAX

(BECK-ul-SPYE-nacks)

Type Species: *altispinax* (AWL-ti-SPYE-nacks)
Classification:

Order:	Saurischia
Suborder:	Theropoda
Family:	?Eustreptospondylidae

Name: (Samuel H.) *Beckles* + Latin *spina* = spine
Size: ?5 meters (15 feet) long
Period: Early Cretaceous, 125 million years ago
Place: England
Diet: Meat

All we know of *Becklespinax* are three massive, linked, and unusually tall vertebrae with very high spines that were discovered in Battle-near-Hastings, in East Sussex, England, during the early 1850s by Samuel H. Beckles. *Becklespinax's* spines most closely match those in the South American carnivore, *Piatnitzkysaurus.* These spines may have given this theropod a humpbacked or finbacked appearance.

Becklespinax was originally described by Sir Richard Owen, the scientist who coined the name "dinosaur" in 1842. Owen considered *Becklespinax* to be an example of another predator, the first dinosaur named, *Megalosaurus bucklandi.*

Becklespinax altispinax
dorsal vertabrae

BELLUSAURUS

(BEL-uh-SAW-rus)

Type Species: sui (SOO-eye)
Classification:

Order: Saurischia
Suborder: Sauropoda
Family: ?Cetiosauridae

Name: Latin *bellus* = beautiful + Greek *sauros* = lizard
Size: 5 meters (16 feet) long
Period: Middle Jurassic, 188 million to 163 million
            years ago
Place: China
Diet: Plants

Bellusaurus was a small four-legged browser with spoon-shaped teeth. Its short forelimbs suggest it may belong to the cetiosaur sauropods. Skull fossils are very rare for any sauropods, animals with small and light heads. But Chinese scientists in Xinjiang, in far northwestern China, discovered the lightly built skull of *Bellusaurus*, which features nostrils set on the side of the head. The animal's neck was short for a sauropod, yet longer than its trunk.

BETASUCHUS

(BAY-tuh-SOO-kus)

Type Species:	*bredai* (BREE-dye)
Status:	Doubtful
Classification:	
Order:	Saurischia
Suborder:	Theropoda
Family:	?
Name:	Greek *beta* = b, second letter of Greek alphabet + Greek *souchos* = crocodile
Size:	?
Period:	Late Cretaceous, 70 million to 65 million years ago
Place:	The Netherlands
Diet:	Meat

    Betasuchus is an old historical name for a poorly known carnivorous dinosaur. The animal was originally described by British scientist Harry Govier Seeley as a species of *Megalosaurus*. Its description was based on a single incomplete leg bone found in the famous Maastricht fossil beds of the Netherlands, the site of the first scientifically identified fossils.

    German dinosaur paleontologist Friedrich von Huene identified the specimen as a coelurosaur, a small predator he originally named *Ornithomimidorum genus b.* He later gave it a new generic name, *Betasuchus.*

    The one known bone of *Betasuchus*, its femur, closely resembles that in both *Elaphrosaurus* and *Sarcosaurus*. It may, as von Huene thought, have been an ornithomimid, or ostrich-mimic dinosaur, the only one known from Europe. The bone is in too poor condition for any kind of positive classification, so *Betasuchus's* status as a valid dinosaur name is in doubt.

"BIHARIOSAURUS"

(bi-HAR-ee-uh-SAW-rus)

Type Species: *bauxiticus* (bawk-SYE-ti-kus)
Status: Unofficial name
Classification:
   Order: Ornithischia
   Suborder: Ornithopoda
   Family: Iguanodontidae
Name: Bihor (region) + Greek *sauros* = lizard
Size: ?
Period: Late Jurassic to Early Cretaceous, 150 milliion to 138 million years ago
Place: Eastern Europe
Diet: Plants

    A primitive member of the Iguanodontid family, *Bihariosaurus* may have evolved from *Camptosaurus,* a bulky plant-eater known from both western North America and western Europe. *Bihariosaurus* is known only from some teeth and bones found in a bauxite mine in Romania in 1978. It has not yet been scientifically described.

BLIKANASAURUS

(bli-KAN-uh-SAW-rus)

Type Species: *cromptoni* (KROMP-tuh-nye)
Classification:
  Order: Saurischia
  Suborder: Prosauropoda
  Family: Blikanasauridae
Size: ?
Name: Blikana (Trading Store) + Greek
                sauros = lizard
Period: Late Triassic, 225 million to 215
                million years ago
Place: South Africa
Diet: Plants

Blikanasaurus was a stoutly built prosauropod, one of the early dinosaurian plant-eaters. Most prosauropods were capable of walking either on four legs or just their hind limbs, but the heavy-legged *Blikanasaurus* may have walked only on all fours. Some paleontologists have suggested that *Blikanasaurus* may be more closely related to the sauropods, the giant four-legged plant-eaters of later dinosaur times, than other prosauropods.

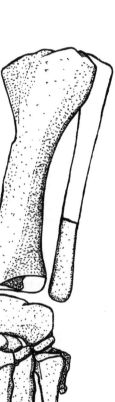

Blikanasaurus cromptoni
lower leg

BOROGOVIA

(BOR-uh-GOH-vee-uh)

Type Species: *gracilicrus* (gruh-SIL-i-krus)

Classification:

Order:	Saurischia
Suborder:	Theropoda
Family:	Troodontidae

Name: *Borogove* (a fantastic creature in Lewis Carroll's *Alice in Wonderland*)

Size: ?2 meters (6.5 feet) long

Period: Late Cretaceous, 80 million to 70 million years ago

Place: Mongolia

Diet: Meat, ?insects

Borogovia was a medium-sized member of the troodontid family of small, nimble, and unusually larged-brained dinosaurs. It appears to have been long-legged, as it has the longest shin bone known for those dinosaurs, at least 280 millimeters (approximately 11 inches) long. In other known troodontids, the second digit is strongly curved, with a toe equipped with a sharp claw and carried off the ground. This toe was used as a weapon. Although the second toe of *Borogovia* touched the ground, the sharpness of its bone indicates that it, too, may have functioned as a weapon.

Borogovia gracilicrus
lower leg

BOTHRIOSPONDYLUS

(BAH-three-uh-SPON-di-lus)

Type Species: *suffosus* (suh-FOH-sus)

Classification:

    Order: Saurischia

    Suborder: Sauropoda

    Family: Brachiosauridae

Name: Greek *bothrion* = trench + Latin *spondylus* = vertebra

Size: ?15 meters to 20 meters (49 to 66 feet) long

Period: Late Jurassic, 170 million to 156 million years ago

Place: England, Madagascar

Diet: Plants

In 1875, Sir Richard Owen, the scientist who coined the term "dinosaurs", described this long-legged, long-toothed, bulky sauropod from the backbones in its hip region. At the time, *Bothriospondylus* was the only dinosaur known to have large openings in its backbones, hence its name. That feature is now known to be common to many sauropod dinosaurs.

The hind legs of *Bothriospondylus* were nearly equal in length to those in the front, and its overall appearance resembled the sauropod *Camarasaurus*, well-known from North American Late Jurassic sediments.

This dinosaur was once known by the dubious name of *Marmarospondylus*.

BRACHIOSAURUS

(BRACK-ee-uh-SAW-rus)

Type Species: *altithorax* (AWL-ti-THOR-acks)
Classification:
   Order: Saurischia
   Suborder: Sauropoda
   Family: Brachiosauridae
Name: Latin *bracchium* = arm + Greek *sauros* = lizard
Size: 25 meters (82 feet) long
Period: Late Jurassic, 156 to 145 million years ago
Place: Colorado, Tanzania
Diet: Plants

The giraffe-like *Brachiosaurus*, standing up to 16 meters (52 feet) high, is one of the best known of all the giant sauropod browsers. The biggest land animal known from nearly complete remains, it is the rarest of all the large sauropods found in the Morrison Formation of the American West.

Brachiosaurus was first collected in 1900 in Fruita, Colorado, by Elmer G. Riggs, and was displayed for half a century at the Field Museum in Chicago. Riggs recognized that this immense, big-chested animal was not only a new genus of dinosaur, but also a member of a previously-unknown family of sauropods, the brachiosauridae.

More information on *Brachiosaurus* came with the discovery of spectacularly complete material in the early twentieth century in Tanzania. These remains are the basis for a second-named species, *Brachiosaurus brancai*.

The African remains showed that *Brachiosaurus's* skull was similar to that of its relative, *Camarasaurus*: stout, with strong jaws and large chisel-shaped teeth. Its most unusual skull feature was a flat snout with enormous nasal openings at the front of the skull. These were viewed as snorkels by those who thought sauropods were swimmers. However, recent studies indicate that a large sauropod could not have lived long partially submerged in water.

Scientists now see *Brachiosaurus* as a landlubber and a treetop browser. The high-placed nostrils may have been covered by a fleshy chamber that amplified

BRACHIOSAURUS *continued*

sound. The placement and structure of the nostrils may also have served to increase the sense of smell, or perhaps they functioned as a cooling surface for the blood.

Though at home on land, *Brachiosaurus* was probably not a nimble runner, for it had small, narrow feet for its size, and short hind legs. The first digit of the front foot had a claw, and the hind foot had large claws on the first three digits. The function of the claws is unknown; they may have been used for raking plants, or in defense.

Brachiosaurus was adept at getting food from the forest canopy. Fossils indicate that *Brachiosaurus* could hold its long neck high and maneuver it well. Muscle scars on the neck ribs indicate that these bones accommodated large muscles. The cervical vertebrae have a ball-and-socket design, which gave the neck strength and flexibility. *Brachiosaurus* is also distinguished by its lightly built and undivided back vertebrae, unusually long chest ribs, and slender upper arm (humerus), which measures 2.04 meters (80 inches) long.

What may be the biggest of all known dinosaurs, the giant "Ultrasaurus" discovered by "Dinosaur Jim" Jensen, may well be a *Brachiosaurus*. This giant sauropod reached an approximate length of 30 meters (98 feet) and weighed as much as 130 metric tons (70 tons).

This dinosaur was named from a huge, crushed back vertebra found in 1979 in Colorado. After it was named in 1985, it was discovered that the name "Ultrasaurus" had already been claimed for a Korean fragmentary dinosaur. It has been provisionally renamed *Ultrasauros*, but further finds are required before it can be determined if it merits a distinct genus.

BRACHIOSAURUS *continued*

Brachiosaurus brancai (BRANG-kye): This species is based upon the remains of a number of individuals discovered in Tendaguru, Tanzania. A composite skeleton (the largest mounted dinosaur skeleton in the world) of *B. brancai* is on display in the Humboldt Museum fur Naturkunde in Berlin. This skeleton measures some 22.5 meters (74 feet) long and 12 meters (39 feet) tall, although there are bones in the museum collection belonging to an even larger individual.

Brachiosaurus brancai may represent a different genus. The structure of the vertebrae of its back, and perhaps its shoulder, differ somewhat from *Brachiosaurus altithorax*.

BRACHYCERATOPS

(BRACK-i-SER-uh-tops)

Type Species: *montanensis* (MON-tan-EN-sis)
Classification:
   Order: Ornithischia
   Suborder: Ceratopsia
   Family: Ceratopsidae
Name: Greek *brachy* = short + Greek *keratos* = horned +
             Greek *ops* = face
Size: 1.8 meters (6 feet) long
Period: Late Cretaceous, 80 million to 70 million
             years ago
Place: Montana
Diet: Plants

   Brachyceratops was a small horned dinosaur, with diminutive brow horns and a slight upward curve on its nose horn. Its frill had a scalloped border and a relatively sharp crest in the middle, an area perhaps pierced with small openings.

   This dinosaur was first collected in 1913 in Glacier County, Montana by Charles Whitney Gilmore of the Smithsonian Institution. Five small *Brachyceratops* were found near an adult dinosaur nearly twice their size, suggesting this may have been a family of young horned dinosaurs cared for by a parent.

BRACHYLOPHOSAURUS

(BRACK-i-LOH-fuh-SAW-rus)

Type Species: canadensis (KAN-uh-DEN-sis)

Classification:

   Order: Ornithischia

   Suborder: Ornithopoda

   Family: Hadrosauridae

Name: Greek brachy = short + Greek lophos = crest +
              Greek sauros = lizard

Size: 7 meters (23 feet) long

Period: Late Cretaceous, 75 million years ago

Place: Alberta, and Montana

Diet: Plants

   This primitive, late, duckbill had a low, solid crest with a short spike that pointed backward between its eyes. This prominent nasal spike may have been used in head-pushing during contests between brachylophosaurs. *Brachylophosaurus* had long forelimbs for a duckbill.

   Brachylophosaurus was first believed to be a new species of *Gryposaurus*, but further study showed it was a new genus of duckbill, distinguished by its relatively high skull and paddle-shaped crest.

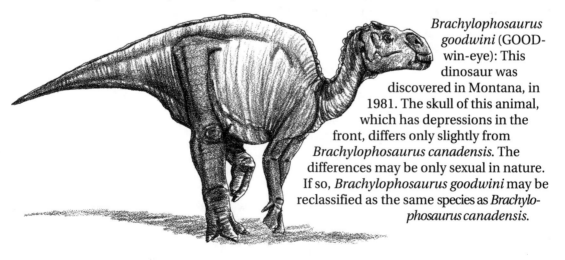

Brachylophosaurus goodwini (GOOD-win-eye): This dinosaur was discovered in Montana, in 1981. The skull of this animal, which has depressions in the front, differs only slightly from *Brachylophosaurus canadensis*. The differences may be only sexual in nature. If so, *Brachylophosaurus goodwini* may be reclassified as the same species as *Brachylophosaurus canadensis*.

BRACHYPODOSAURUS

(BRACK-i-POH-duh-SAW-rus)

Type Species: *gravis* (GRAH-vis)
Status: Doubtful
Classification:
  Order: Ornithischia
  Suborder: Ankylosauria
  Family: ?
Name: Greek *brachy* = short + Greek *podos* = foot +
               Greek *sauros* = lizard
Period: Late Cretaceous, 88 million to 73 million
               years ago
Place: India
Diet: Plants

   Brachypodosaurus was a short, stoutly-built dinosaur that may have been an ankylosaur, or, perhaps, related to the stegosaurids. The type specimen, which consists only of a lower leg bone, does not permit a sure identification of this animal.

BRACHYROPHUS

(BRACK-ee-ROH-fuss)

Status: Doubtful — *See Camptosaurus*

BRADYCNEME

(BRAY-dee-kuh-NEE-mee)

Type Species: *draculae* (DRACK-yuh-lye)
Classification:
    Order: Saurischia
    Suborder: Theropoda
    Family: ?Troodontidae
Name: Greek *bradus* = slow + Greek *kneme* = leg
Period: Late Cretaceous, ?73 million to 65
               million years ago
Place: Romania
Diet: Meat

    This little known small carnivore represents one of the most stupendous misnamings in paleontology. Two British scientists thought that the tip of a shin bone collected in Transylvania in 1923 by Lady Smith-Woodward belonged to a new family of giant owls. Its species name honors Count Dracula of Transylvania.

Bradycneme draculae shin bone

BRONTOSAURUS

(BRON-tuh-SAW-rus)

Status: Invalid name — See
             Apatosaurus

CAENAGNATHUS

(SEE-nig-NAY-thus)

Type Species: *collinsi* (KOL-in-zye)
Classification:

Order:	Saurischia
Suborder:	Theropoda
Family:	Caenagnathidae

Name: Greek *kainos* = recent + Greek *gnathos* = jaw
Size: 2 meters (7 feet) long
Period: Late Cretaceous, 75 million years ago
Place: Western North America
Diet: Meat

   Caenagnathus was a slightly built carnivore. Some paleontologists thought it was identical to another small meat-eater from the same time in Alberta, *Chirostenotes*. However, current scientific thinking is that *Caenagnathus* is a more primitive dinosaur, belonging to its own family. Since it is known only from its lower jaws, deducing its identity is particularly difficult.

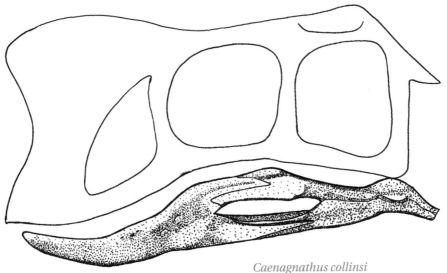

Caenagnathus collinsi
lower jaw

CALAMOSAURUS

(KAL-uh-muh-SAW-rus)

Type Species: *foxi* (FOCK-sye)
Status: Doubtful
Classification:
  Order: Saurischia
  Suborder: Theropoda
  Family: ?
Name: Latin *calamus* = reed + Greek *sauros* = lizard
Size: Small
Period: Early Cretaceous, ?125 million to 119 million years ago
Place: England
Diet: Meat

    Calamosaurus was a small, early meat-eater, too poorly known for any definite assignment to a particular family. It was named on the basis of two neck vertebrae and a lower leg bone found more than a century ago on the Isle of Wight, where many British dinosaurs have been found. *Calamosaurus* may be the same animal as *Calamospondylus.*

CALAMOSPONDYLUS

(KAL-uh-moh-SPON-dil-us)

Type Species: *oweni* (OH-en-eye)
Status: Doubtful
Classification:
   Order: Saurischia
   Suborder: Theropoda
   Family: ?
Name: Latin *calamus* = reed + Greek *spondylus* = vertebra
Size: Small
Period: Early Cretaceous, 125 million years ago
Place: England
Diet: Meat

    Another small meat-eater of uncertain identity, *Calamospondylus* is known from incomplete fossil remains found on the Isle of Wight. Among the few facts known about this dinosaur is that its toes were small. The claws of its hands, however, were relatively large. An unusual feature of this dinosaur is its pubic bone. The so-called "foot" of this bone seems to be much longer than that of most other meat-eaters, suggesting that *Calamospondylus* had a bigger stomach region.

CALLOVOSAURUS

(kaw-LOH-voh-SAW-rus)

Type Species: *leedsi* (LEED-zye)
Status: Doubtful
Classification:
  Order: Ornithischia
  Suborder: Iguanodontia
  Family: ?
Name: Callovian for Jurassic time stage + Greek *sauros* = lizard
Size: ?3.5 meters (11 feet 6 inches) long
Period: Middle Jurassic, 166 million years ago
Place: England
Diet: Plants

Although known from only one upper leg bone, *Callovosaurus* is an important dinosaur, because it marks the earliest known occurrence of the Iguanodontia, a group of large two-legged plant-eaters to which all iguanodonts and duck-billed dinosaurs belong.

When remains of this dinosaur were discovered, they were first thought to belong to a new species of *Camptosaurus* (*leedsi*), then to another dinosaur, *Dryosaurus*. Not until 1980 was *Callovosaurus* recognized as a new kind of dinosaur.

CAMARASAURUS

(KAM-uh-ruh-SAW-rus)

Type Species: *supremus* (soo-PREE-mus)
Classification:
   Order: Saurischia
   Suborder: Sauropoda
   Family: Camarasauridae
Name: Latin *camera* = chamber + Greek *sauros* = lizard
Size: At least 18 meters (over 60 feet) long
Period: Late Jurassic, 156 million to 145 million years ago
     Place: Colorado, Utah, Wyoming, Portugal
     Diet: Plants

Camarasaurus is the best known, large, four-legged browser, or sauropod, from North America, and the most abundant of fossils. Its head was short, box-like, and strongly constructed, with large nostrils set above the snout area and in front of the eyes. The head was held at a distinct angle to the neck, which was shorter and thicker than that of most sauropods.

CAMARASAURUS *continued*

The forelimbs and hindlegs of *Camarasaurus* were approximately the same length, making the back of this dinosaur almost horizontal. Its front legs were more robust than those of *Diplodocus*, more slender than *Apatosaurus*, and relatively long.

Its tail was short and somewhat flat, and certainly not the whiplash found on some large sauropods such as *Diplodocus* and *Apatosaurus*.

A wealth of *Camarasaurus* remains have been discovered over the years, much of which has come from immature individuals. This prompted some authors to state, incorrectly, that *Camarasaurus* was small for a sauropod. Adults, however, were quite large, almost as big as *Apatosaurus*. Recently-discovered hatchling specimens indicate that these sauropods, like other dinosaurs, laid eggs and did not give birth to live young.

Camarasaurus agilis (ah-JIL-us) — Doubtful name: This fragmentary find appears to be a cetiosaurid of some sort.

Camarasaurus alenguerensis (al-EN-gwerr-EN-siss) — Doubtful name: This species was originally referred to as *Apatosaurus* and is based on a skeleton, without a head, found in Portugal.

Camarasaurus grandis (GRAN-diss): The smallest known species of *Camarasaurus*, only 7.5 meters (25 feet) long. It had unusually large hind feet, slender toes, and a very large first toe. It was originally thought to be a new species of its contemporary sauropod, *Apatosaurus*.

Camarasaurus lentus (LEN-tus): This is a subadult, which has more massive, shorter vertebrae and shorter legs than the smaller *Camarasaurus grandi*. The most complete sauropod skeleton yet found is that of an immature *Camarasaurus lentus* collected at Dinosaur National Monument in Utah. This skeleton shows the animal in its death pose, with the neck arched back by a constriction of its muscles. A thin layer of carbon found beside the skeleton could be a rare instance of preserved sauropod skin.

CAMELOTIA

(KAM-uh-LOT-ee-uh)

Type Species: *borealis* (BOR-ee-AL-us)
Classification:
   Order: Saurischia
   Suborder: Prosauropoda
   Family: Melanorosauridae
Name: *Camelot* (from Arthurian legend)
Size: Large
Period: Late Triassic, 219 million to 213 million years ago
Place: England
Diet: Plants

    Not much is known of this genus. It is a large member of the melanosaurids, a family of the small-headed, large-bodied, early plant-eaters called prosauropods. Only recently recognized as a new kind of dinosaur, *Camelotia* had previously been referred to *Avalonia, Picrodon,* and *Gresslyosaurus.*

CAMPTONOTUS

(KAMP-tuh-NOH-tus)

Status: Invalid — *See Camptosaurus*

CAMPTOSAURUS

(KAMP-tuh-SAW-rus)

Type Species: *dispar* (DIS-pahr)
Classification:
   Order: Ornithischia
   Suborder: Ornithopoda
   Family: Camptosauridae
Name: Greek *kamptos* = bent + Greek *sauros* = lizard
Size: 6 meters (20 feet) long, 0.9 to 1.2 meters (3 to 4 feet) high at hips
Period: Late Jurassic, 156 million to 145 million years ago
Place: Wyoming, ?South Dakota, Colorado, Utah, England
Diet: Plants

    This bulky plant-eater resembled the more advanced herbivore *Iguanodon*. However, *Camptosaurus* had a more primitive hand, and a first finger that had a short (rather than a sizeable) spike like *Iguanodon*. Also, the ends of its second and third fingers were more curved and less hoof-like than *Iguanodon's*.

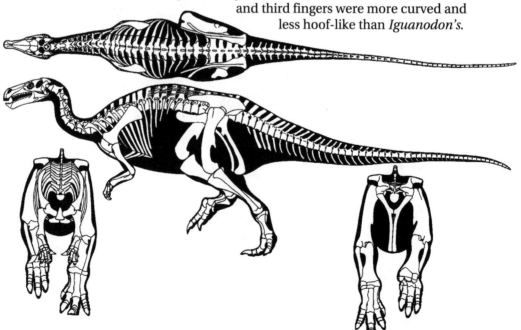

CAMPTOSAURUS *continued*

    Camptosaurus had heavy hindlimbs and short forelimbs, suggesting that it may have moved on two legs. Its large bony wrist, however, indicates that it could also walk on all fours, probably when browsing on low-growing vegetation.

    Since this dinosaur's discovery, much *Camptosaurus* material has been recovered, mostly from Wyoming. Some of these specimens exhibit great individual variation and various growth stages, making this dinosaur particularly well understood.

    Camptosaurus is significant as an intermediate animal. It is more advanced than the smaller plant-eaters, the hypsilophodontids, yet more primitive than the later hadrosaurids, the duckbilled dinosaurs.

    Camptosaurus prestwichii (pres-TWICH-ee-eye) (originally *Cunmoria prestwichii*): *C. prestwichii* represents the only unquestioned *Camptosaurus* remains found outside North America. This species, found near Oxford, England, supports the idea that a land connection existed between North America and Europe during the Late Jurassic Period. This species is more primitive than *Camptosaurus dispar*.

CAMPYLODON

(kam-PYE-loh-don)

Status: Invalid — *See Campylodoniscus*

CAMPYLODONISCUS

(KAM-pye-LOH-duh-NIS-kus)

Type Species: *ameginoi* (AH-mi-JEE-noy)
Status: Doubtful
Classification:
    Order: Saurischia
    Suborder: Sauropoda
    Family: ?
Name: Greek *kampylos* = curved + Greek *odontos* = tooth + *isko* = to make like
Size: Large
Period: Late Cretaceous, 97 million to 85 million years ago
Place: Argentina
Diet: Plants

    This large four-legged browser, or sauropod, is known only from an incomplete upper jaw with a single tooth. Though mysterious, *Campylodoniscus* is especially interesting: it was one of the last surviving sauropods, a group that prospered in South America long after becoming rare in North America.

CARCHARODONTOSAURUS

(kahr-CHAR-uh-DON-tuh-SAW-rus)

Type Species: saharicus (suh-HAYR-i-kus)
Classification:
  Order: Saurischia
  Suborder: Theropoda
  Family: ?Carnosauria
Name: Greek Carcharodon (genus of shark with similar
              teeth) + Greek sauros = lizard
Size: About 8 meters (27 feet) long
Period: Early to Late Cretaceous, 113 million to 91 million
              years ago
Place: Algeria, Egypt, Morocco
Diet: Meat

This large carnivore is known from various remains, which include shark-like teeth, an incomplete skull and torso bones. It seems to have been more advanced than the large primitive meat-eaters, the megalosaurids of the Jurassic Period. This dinosaur's forelimbs were short and had very large claws. The upward-pointing spines on its back vertebrae were unusually high.

The form of its teeth indicate that this dinosaur may not have sliced the flesh of its prey. Perhaps it ate smaller, or softer, animals than the other predators did.

This dinosaur may never be understood, as its remains were destroyed by bombing raids during World War II.

CARDIODON

(KAHR-dee-uh-don)

Type Species: rugolosus (ROO-guh-LOH-sus)
Status: Doubtful
Classification:
   Order: Saurischia
   Suborder: Sauropoda
   Family: Cetiosauridae
Name: Greek kardia = heart + Greek odontos = tooth
Size: Large
Period: Middle Jurassic, 170 million years ago
Place: England
Diet: Meat

This poorly known genus was founded on a single tooth collected in Wiltshire, England. The tooth is heart-shaped, hence the name of this large four-legged browser. It may be the same animal as *Cetiosaurus,* but the fossil evidence for *Cardiodon* is too meager for a definite link to be established.

CARNOTAURUS

(KAHR-nuh-TOR-us)

Type Species: *sastrei* (SAS-tree-eye)

Classification:

  Order: Saurischia

  Suborder: Theropoda

  Family: Abelisauridae

Name: Latin *carnis* = flesh + Greek *tauros* = bull

Size: 7.5 meters (25 feet) long

Period: Middle to Late Cretaceous, 113 million to 91 million years ago

Place: Patagonia, Argentina

Diet: Meat

One of the most unusual meat-eaters ever identified, bulldog-faced *Carnotaurus* had striking features. Its skull was quite large, though shorter and higher than that of later large predators such as *Tyrannosaurus*. Its snout was deep and narrow.

The most remarkable aspect of this skull was the pair of prominent horns above the eyes. These horns projected out toward the sides and upwards. We can only speculate about what these horns were used for. They were probably not weapons, since a carnivore of this size hardly needed such devices. Perhaps they were used for display purposes, or for intimidating another *Carnotaurus*.

CARNOTAURUS *continued*

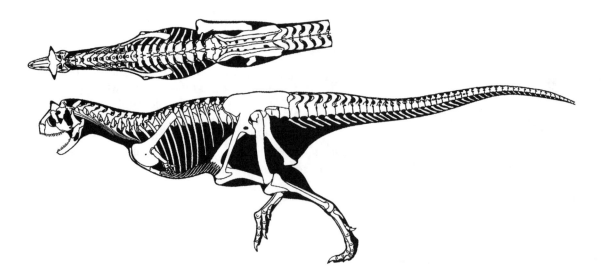

The eyes of this dinosaur were set so they could both focus, at least partially, on the same field of vision at the same time. Our own eyes focus in much the same way, giving us three-dimensional perspectives on the things we look at.

The forelimbs of *Carnotaurus* were unusual; they were remarkably stubby, with especially short lower arm bones.

Found with the skeleton were several fragments of fossilized skin impressions. A rare find among meat-eating dinosaurs, these fragments show that *Carnotaurus's* skin was covered with small bony bumps that were separated from one another by areas of rough skin.

Carnotaurus and the related *Abelisaurus* represent a unique line of carnivores found only in the southern hemisphere, with skull similarities to the Indian meat-eaters, *Indosaurus* and *Indosuchus.*

CATHETOSAURUS

(kuh-THEE-tuh-SAW-rus)

Type Species: *lewisi* (LOO-i-sye)
Status: Doubtful — *See Camarasaurus*
Classification:
    Order: Saurischia
    Suborder: Sauropoda
    Family: Camarasauridae
Name: Greek *kathetos* = sitting upright/perpendicular + Greek *sauros* = lizard
Size: Large
Period: Late Jurassic, 156 million to 145 million years ago
Place: Colorado
Diet: Plants

    The man who collected and named *Cathetosaurus*, the famous "Dinosaur Jim" Jensen, believed it to be the only North American sauropod, or large four-legged plant-eater, capable of rearing up on its hind legs.

    Jensen thought the vertebrae of *Cathetosaurus* had projections where strong ligaments may have attached. Those ligaments, he thought, would help *Cathetosaurus* rear up on its hind legs. The pelvis, too, according to Jensen, was unusually inclined, another perceived adaptation for bipedalism.

    Other scientists think that some of the features that make this genus unique are signs of old age; they argue that *Cathetosaurus* is really a species of *Camarasaurus*.

    Interestingly, the skeleton of *Cathetosaurus* shows deep teeth marks on a pelvic bone, and the front leg bones were displaced. These signs suggest that the carcass had been scavenged before burial, perhaps by a large theropod the size of *Torvosaurus tanneri*, a predator from the same time and place. The carcass was later turned over by the same (or another) meat-eater, which tore off the hind legs. Since the neck and rib cage were intact, the feast seems to have centered on the more heavily muscled pelvic-to-rear limb part of the body.

    Smaller teeth marks show that small scavengers also fed on the carcass. Perhaps when the larger meat-eaters had finished, or between the larger animals' feeding periods, the little flesh-eaters ate what they could.

CAUDOCOELUS
(KAW-duh-SEE-lus)

Status: Doubtful — *See Teinurosaurus*

CAULODON
(KAW-luh-don)

Status: Doubtful — *See Camarasaurus*

CENTROSAURUS
(SEN-truh-SAW-rus)

Status: Doubtful — *See Eucentrosaurus*

CERATOPS

(SER-uh-tops)

Type Species: *montanus* (mon-TAN-us)
Status: Doubtful — *See Chasmosaurus*
Classification:
  Order: Ornithischia
  Suborder: Ceratopsia
  Family: Ceratopsidae
Name: Greek *keratos* = horned + Greek *ops* = face
Size: 7.5 meters (25 feet) long
Period: Late Cretaceous, 80 million to 73 million years ago
Place: Montana
Diet: Plants

Ceratops is a horned dinosaur of considerable size. It is known only from a pair of horn cores and a knoblike bone by which the skull attaches to its first neck vertebra. *Ceratops* was discovered in 1888, but it is still not well understood. It may be the remains of the better known horned dinosaur *Chasmosaurus*, although there is not enough information to make a certain association.

Interestingly, the remains of this dinosaur were found before horned dinosaurs were well known. Consequently, paleontologists believed this genus to be closely related to the plated dinosaur, *Stegosaurus*.

CERATOSAURUS

(si-RAT-uh-SAW-rus)

Type Species: *nasicornis* (NAZ-i-KOR-nis)
Classification:
    Order: Saurischia
    Suborder: Theropoda
    Family: Ceratosauridae
Name: Greek *keratos* = horned + Greek *sauros* = lizard
Size: 6 meters (20 feet) long
Period: Late Jurassic, 156 million to 145 million years ago
Place: Colorado, ?East Africa
Diet: Meat

    Ceratosaurus was a medium-sized, meat-eating dinosaur with a horn above its eyes. The skull of *Ceratosaurus* was lightly built, and was distinguished by a prominent nasal horn with a bony ridge. Just what does a large and frightening carnivore need with a nose horn? Most likely the horn was not used as a weapon. It was delicately constructed, and probably functioned only as a display. The horn may have been a sexual feature; it may have been used by males in contests with others of its kind to establish supremacy; or it may have helped young individuals hatch out of their eggs.

    The brain cavity indicates that *Ceratosaurus's* brain was long and thin, of medium size for a meat-eater, and larger than the brains of plant-eating dinosaurs of the same size. Its eyes may have been large, affording this creature moderately good eyesight.

    Ceratosaurus's hands were equipped with four fingers, a primitive feature. *Tyrannosaurus rex*, the latest and most advanced large carnivore, had just two fingers.

    Ceratosaurus's body plan followed the basic shape of large theropods. Its tail was very long, comprising more than half the entire length of the animal. Its tail was thin, an indication to nineteenth-century dinosaur scientist Othniel Charles Marsh, who named this dinosaur, that *Ceratosaurus* could swim by utilizing its tail.

CERATOSAURUS *continued*

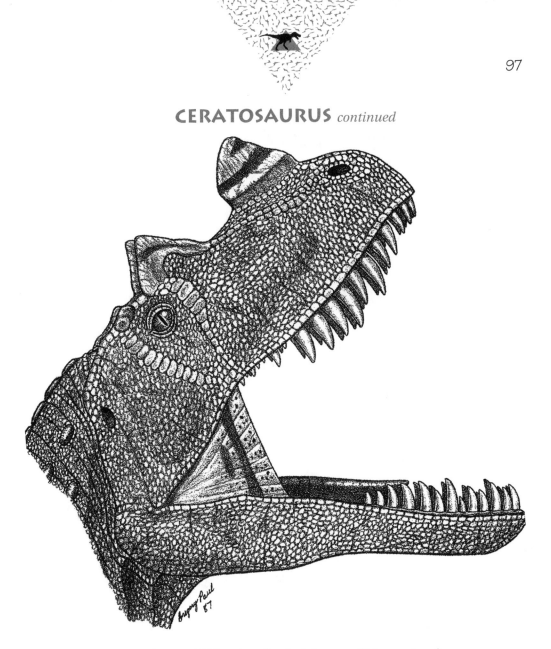

Ceratosaurus ingens (IN-jenz) — Doubtful name: This species, from Tendaguru, Tanzania, was first described as another species of the genus *Megalosaurus*. The flat-bladed teeth of this species are almost 15.5 centimeters (6 inches) long. It is too poorly known to identify positively.

Ceratosaurus roechlingi (ROACH-ling-eye) — Doubtful name: This species is also from Tendaguru, but shows no distinctive characteristics that would single it out as anything other than some sort of theropod, not necessarily *Ceratosaurus*.

CETIOSAURISCUS

(SEE-tee-uh-SAW-ris-kus)

Type Species: stewarti (STOO-ur-tye)

Classification:

    Order: Saurischia

    Suborder: Sauropoda

    Family: Diplodocidae

Name: Greek *ketios* = sea monster (whale) + Greek *sauros* = lizard + *iscus* = like

Size: ?15 meters (50 feet) long

Period: Middle to Late Jurassic, 181 million to 169 million years ago

Place: England

Diet: Plants

This primitive, large four-legged browser had a whip-like tail. It was originally thought to be a *Cetiosaurus,* a larger sauropod with a shorter tail. Instead, *Cetiosauriscus* shares a number of diagnostic characteristics with the diplodocid sauropods, those with whiplash tails.

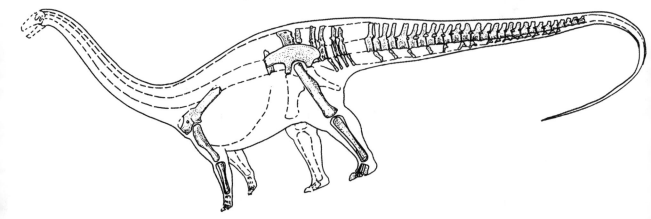

CETIOSAURUS

(SEE-tee-uh-SAW-rus)

Type Species: *medius* (MEE-dee-us)

Classification:

Order:	Saurischia
Suborder:	Sauropoda
Family:	Cetiosauridae
Name:	Greek *ketios* = sea monster (whale) + Greek *sauros* = lizard
Size:	At least 15 meters (over 50 feet) long
Period:	Middle Jurassic, 181 to 169 million years ago
Place:	England, Morocco
Diet:	Plants

The first four-legged plant-eater of the sauropod suborder to be named and described, *Cetiosaurus* is also one of the geologically oldest known sauropods.

This dinosaur typifies the Cetiosauridae family of primitive sauropods. *Cetiosaurus* was a large dinosaur with forelimbs that were moderately long compared to the hindlimb bones.

The genus *Cetiosaurus* was founded on various bones which Sir Richard Owen, the man who invented the term "dinosaur," at first believed represented a huge crocodile. Because its back vertebrae were coarse-textured like that of a whale, Owen believed *Cetiosaurus* was an aquatic animal.

It was, we know now, a land animal. Yet *Cetiosaurus* remains have been found in deposits showing evidence of coastal waters, small lakes and lagoons, so the dinosaur may have lived, or at least died, beside watery areas.

Cetiosaurus mogrebiensis (moh-GREB-ee-EN-sis) — Doubtful name: This species, from Morocco, had longer forelimbs than those of the typical *Cetiosaurus* species. Its relationship to the genus has yet to be established.

"CHANGDUSAURUS"

(CHANG-doo-SAW-rus)

Type Species: *laminaplacodus* (LAM-i-nuh-PLACK-uh-dus)
Status: Unofficial
Classification:
   Order: Ornithischia
   Suborder: Stegosauria
   Family: Stegosauridae
Name: *Chengdu* (basin in Tibet) + Greek *sauros* = lizard
Size: Intermediate
Period: Late Jurassic, 163 million to 144 million years ago
Place: China
Diet: Plants

    There is little to say about this animal other than that it is an intermediate-sized, plate-backed dinosaur, a stegosaurid. Its name has been published, but it has not yet been described.

CHAOYOUNGOSAURUS

(chou-YUNG-uh-SAW-rus)

Type Species: liaosiensis (LEE-ou-see-EN-sis)
Classification:

Order:	Ornithischia
Suborder:	?Pachycephalosauria
Family:	?
Name:	Chaoyoung (city in northeastern China) + Greek sauros = lizard
Size:	?
Period:	Late Jurassic, 163 million to 145 million years ago
Place:	China
Diet:	Plants

Almost nothing is known of this (possible) pachycephalosaur, or bone-headed dinosaur. It seems to be a small dinosaur with weak, canine-like teeth.

CHASMOSAURUS

(KAZ-moh-SAW-rus)

Type Species: *belli* (BEL-eye)
Classification:
  Order: Ornithischia
  Suborder: Ceratopsia
  Family: Ceratopsidae
Name: Latin *chasma* = opening + Greek *sauros* = lizard
Size: 5.8 meters (17 feet) long
Period: Late Cretaceous, 76 million to 70 million years ago
Place: Alberta; Texas
Diet: Plants

Chasmosaurus is one of the geologically-oldest known large, horned dinosaurs. It is also one of the best known, since many specimens have been collected since its discovery in 1901.

Chasmosaurus was a modest-sized horned dinosaur. Its skull measured about 1.5 meters (5 feet) in length; much of it consisted of crest. This crest, or frill, was flat and strikingly long, making up more than half the length of the head. The openings of the crest were especially large. The back edge of the crest was thin, resulting in a neck shield that was probably not effective as a defense. More likely, this crest was used for attachment of the jaw muscles, or as a threatening display.

Chasmosaurus had a long skull. Its brow horns ranged from small and short to large, solid, backward-curving structures. The nose horn was always short and stocky.

This dinosaur had a smaller adult body than other large, horned dinosaurs, and very slender limb bones. Its chest was narrow and straight-sided, its abdomen wide and barrel-shaped. Fossil skin impressions show small, closely-set five- or six-sided bumps that increased in size to larger, rounded knobs.

Of all ceratopsids, *Chasmosaurus* is the most geographically widespread and species-rich.

Chasmosaurus brevicornis (BREE-vi-KOR-nus): This species differs from type species *C. belli* in having a very short, deep muzzle, a larger backward-curving nose horn, and brow horns shaped like the nasal horn, only smaller.

CHASMOSAURUS *continued*

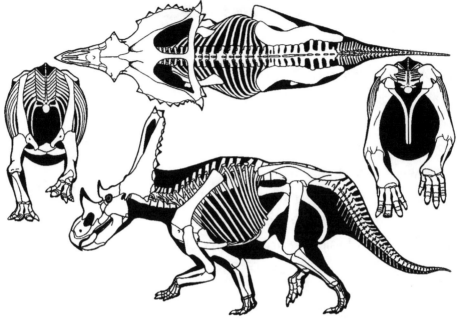

Chasmosaurus mariscalensis (MAR-is-ikuh-LEN-sis): *C. mariscalensis,* which comes from Brewster County, Texas, is the only species discovered outside of Alberta. It differs from other species in various features, especially in having brow horns that are larger in adults than in any other species of *Chasmosaurus.*

Chasmosaurus russelli (RUS-uh-lye): This dinosaur had a large skull, a massive nasal horn, no brow horns, a weakly scalloped crest, and a massive lower jaw.

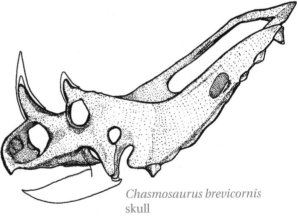

Chasmosaurus brevicornis skull

CHENEOSAURUS

(KEE-nee-uh-SAW-rus)

Status: Invalid — *See Hypacrosaurus*

CHIALINGOSAURUS

(CHEE-uh-LING-uh-SAW-rus)

Type Species: *kuani* (KOO-uh-nye)
Classification:
    Order: Ornithischia
    Suborder: Stegosauria
    Family: Stegosauridae
Name: Chialing (river in China) + Greek *sauros* = lizard
Size: ?4 meters (13 feet) long
Period: Middle or earliest Late Jurassic, 163 million to
                150 million years ago
Place: China
Diet: Plants

    Chialingosaurus was a medium-sized, slender plate-backed dinosaur, or stegosaur. Its skull was narrower than those of other plate-backed dinosaurs such as *Stegosaurus* and *Tuojiangosaurus*.

    The back plates in *Chialingosaurus* seem to be less specialized than in later stegosaurs such as *Kentrosaurus* and *Stegosaurus*. They include rather small, platelike spines, and small plates, arranged in pairs, running in two rows from the neck to the tail.

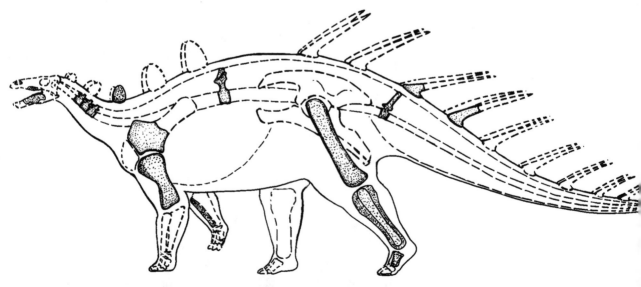

CHIAYUSAURUS

(CHEE-uh-yoo-SAW-rus)

Type Species: *lacustris* (luh-KUS-tris)
Classification:
    Order: Saurischia
    Suborder: Sauropoda
    Family: ?Camarasauridae
Name: Chinese *Chia-yu-kuan* + Greek *sauros* = lizard
Size: ?Large
Period: Late Cretaceous, ?97.5 million to ?65 million
               years ago
Place: Northwestern China
Diet: Plants

    Very little is known about this large, four-legged plant-eater. Possibly a cama-rasaur, it is known only from a single tooth. The tooth is spoon-shaped and about the same size, measuring 27 millimeters around the middle, as teeth of the geologically younger genus *Euhelopus*.

CHILANTAISAURUS

(chee-LAN-tye-SAW-rus)

Type Species: *tashuikouensis* (TASH-oo-EE-koo-EN-sis)
Classification:
    Order: Saurischia
    Suborder: Theropoda
    Family: Allosauridae
Name: Chinese *Chilantai* (lake in Mongolia) + Greek *sauros* = lizard
Size: Large
Period: Early Cretaceous, 113 million to 97 million years ago
Place: Inner Mongolia, ?China, ?Siberia
Diet: Meat

There is considerable puzzlement about this large, carnivorous dinosaur. *Chilantaisaurus* had a long, massive upper arm. The claws of the hand were unusually large, and the first finger had a backward-curving claw. The upper leg bone was longer than the lower leg bone; its toes were short and the toe bones were not fused together. These features suggest that this dinosaur was not as fast a runner as many other theropods.

Chilantaisaurus shared some characteristics with both *Allosaurus*, the large North American Jurassic predator, and to the tyrannosaurids in Asia and North America of the Late Cretaceous Period. *Chilantaisaurus* was most likely an allosaurid, but it may have beeen an intermediate form between allosaurids and tyrannosaurids.

Chilantaisaurus maortuensis (MOU-or-too-EN-sis) — Doubtful name: This species' name was based on a partial skull, twelve teeth, and some other remains discovered in China. This material indicates a theropod with a moderate-sized skull. However, since this species has few bones in common with the type species, the true relationship between them has yet to be understood.

CHILANTAISAURUS *continued*

Chilantaisaurus sibiricus (sye-BEER-i-kus) — Doubtful name: This species is known from part of a fourth toe discovered in Siberia.

Chilantaisaurus zheziangensis (JEE-zee-ang-EN-sis) — Doubtful name: This species was based on a hand claw found in China. It may be one of the segnosaurs, a peculiar group of primitive but late dinosaurs. Its foot and claws are similar to those in *Segnosaurus.*

CHINGKANKOUSAURUS

(ching-KANG-kuh-SAW-rus)

Type Species: *fragilis* (fruh-JIL-is)
Classification:
    Order: Saurischia
    Suborder: Theropoda
    Family: Tyrannosauridae
Name: *Chingkankou* (Chinese village) + Greek *sauros* = lizard
Size: ?Large
Period: Late Cretaceous, ?88.5 million to ?65 million years ago
Place: China
Diet: Meat

This genus was founded on a long, slender piece of bone that seems to be a right shoulder blade. If this bone is, in fact, a scapula, it identifies *Chingkankousaurus* as a tyrannosaurid, a member of the same family of large carnivores as *Tyrannosaurus rex.*

"CHINSAKIANGOSAURUS"

(chin-SACK-ee-ANG-guh-SAW-rus)

Type Species: *zhongheensis* (ZONG-ee-EN-sis)
Status: Unofficial
Classification:
  Order: Saurischia
  Suborder: Sauropodomorpha
  Family: ?Sauropoda
Name: Chinese *Chinshakiang* + Greek *sauros* = lizard
Size: ?
Period: Late Jurassic, ?163 million to 144 million years ago
Place: China
Diet: Plants

    The name of this plant-eater was mentioned, but the animal was not described, in a Chinese article about a Jurassic reptile.

CHIROSTENOTES

(kye-ROSS-tuh-NOH-teez)

Type Species: *pergracilis* (pur-GRAS-i-lis)

Classification:

Order:	Saurischia
Suborder:	Theropoda
Family:	Elmisauridae

Name: Greek *cheir* = hand + Greek *steno* = narrow

Size: 2 meters (7 feet) long

Period: Late Cretaceous, 76 million to 73 million years ago

Place: Alberta

Diet: Meat

Chirostenotes pergracilis hands

This lightly built, bird like theropod was named on the basis of its distinctive narrow hands. The third finger of the hand was longer than the first, and very slender. The toe bones were also long and slender.

What were the functions of these narrow extremities? The hands were suitable for collecting mollusks, other invertebrates, and eggs. The long, slender third finger was somewhat like the fingers in kangaroos and many birds, and was perhaps capable of a wide range of movement. This specialized finger may have been used in prying insects and other invertebrates from crevices in trees or streams, or even used in "grooming." The long hindlimbs and large feet could have been wading adaptations.

Chirostenotes was originally based on a type specimen consisting of bones of the hand. Another dinosaur, *Macrophalangia*, was founded upon material that included a complete foot. Both dinosaurs were discovered in the same formation, and for a long time, scientists suspected that they might be the same kind of animal. When a partial skeleton was found in Alberta in 1979, overlapping parts showed that *Chirostenotes* and *Macrophalangia* were indeed one and the same.

Two kinds of *Chirostenotes* have been recognized. One, with a more delicate foot, seems to be male; the other, with a more robust upper part of foot, female.

CHONDROSTEOSAURUS

(kon-DROH-stee-uh-SAW-rus)

Type Species: *gigas* (JEE-gus)
Status: Doubtful
Classification:
  Order: Saurischia
  Suborder: Sauropoda
  Family: ?Camarasauridae
Name: Greek *chondros* = cartilage + Greek *osteon* = bone + Greek *sauros* = lizard
Size: ?Large
Period: Early Cretaceous, 131 million to 119 million years ago
Place: England
Diet: Plants

This poorly known genus may be a camarasaurid, one of the boxy-headed sauropods. Not enough fossil material has been found to determine if it is indeed one of those enormous plant-eaters. The type specimen consists of only two vertebrae collected on the Isle of Wight.

When this fossil find was first described, Sir Richard Owen believed it came from a sluggish animal best suited to living in watery environments, a notion that has been incorrectly applied to sauropods in general for a century. From that idea, Owen believed that the animal, when on land, must have been supported by "limbs of dinosaurian proportions."

CHUBUTISAURUS

(shoo-BOO-ti-SAW-rus)

Type Species: *insignis* (in-SIG-nis)
Classification:
   Order: Saurischia
   Suborder: Sauropoda
   Family: ?Brachiosauridae
Name: *Chubut* (province in Argentina) + Greek *sauros* = lizard
Size: Large, ?23 meters (75 feet) long
Period: Early Cretaceous, 113 million to 97 million years ago
Place: Argentina
Diet: Plants

   This large, heavily built, and little-known four-legged herbivore had a hump-back or fin-back look.

CHUANDONGOSAURUS

(CHOO-an-DONG-uh-SAW-rus)

Type Species: *primitivus* (PRIM-i-TEE-vus)
Classification:
   Order: Saurischia
   Suborder: Theropoda
   Family: ?
Name: Chinese *Chuandong* (locality of discovery) + Greek
               sauros = lizard
Size: ?
Period: Late Jurassic
Place: China
Diet: ?

   This poorly known genus, based on incomplete skeletal material, may be a juvenile meat-eating dinosaur. Its hind limb suggests theropod affinities, but it also has features similar to an ornithopod, a bird-hipped plant-eater. The lower hind leg bone was longer than the upper leg bone, a feature indicative of a fast-running animal.

CHUNGKINGOSAURUS

(chung-KING-uh-SAW-rus)

Type Species: *jiangbeiensis* (jee-ANG-bay-EN-sis)
Classification:

Order:	Ornithischia
Suborder:	Stegosauria
Family:	Stegosauridae
Name:	Chungking, or Chungqing (Chinese city) + Greek *sauros* = lizard
Size:	3 to 4 meters (10 to 13 feet) long
Period:	Late Jurassic, 163 million to 150 million years ago
Place:	China
Diet:	Plants

This rather small, plate-backed dinosaur, a stegosaur, had a high, narrow skull. Its plates were thick and seem to be intermediate in shape between *Stegosaurus* plates and pointed spikes. This condition could support the theory that, in stegosaurian evolution, spikes evolved into plates. As in the North American genus *Stegosaurus*, *Chungkingosaurus* had four spikes, arranged in pairs. No actual plates of *Chungkingosaurus* have yet been found.

114

CIONODON

(see-OH-nuh-don)

Type Species: *arctatus* (ahrk-TAY-tus)
Status: Doubtful
Classification:
  Order: Ornithischia
  Suborder: Ornithopoda
  Family: ?Hadrosauridae
Name: Greek *kionos* = column + Greek *odontos* = tooth
Size: ?Horse-sized
Period: Late Cretaceous, 97.5 million to 65 million
                years ago
Place: Colorado; Alberta; ?Russia
Diet: Plants

    Cionodon was founded on teeth that Edward Drinker Cope, the great nineteenth-century dinosaur namer, believed were suited for pulverizing vegetation. The pencil-like fossil teeth are too poor to classify with any certainty; they may represent a hadrosaurid. *Cionodon*, named at a time when duckbilled dinosaurs were not well understood, could be synonymous with another duckbill of its time. This name, therefore, should not be used.

CLAORHYNCHUS

(KLAY-uh-RING-kus)

Type Species: *trihedrus* (trye-HEE-drus)
Status: Doubtful
Classification:
  Order: Ornithischia
  Suborder: Ceratopsia
  Family: Ceratopsidae
Name: Greek *klao* = broken + Greek *rhynchus* = beak
Size: ?
Period: Late Cretaceous, 83 million to 73 million
              years ago
Place: Montana
Diet: Plants

    Claorhynchus was founded on the front portion of a jaw bone. It may be identical to another Late Cretaceous horned dinosaur, but the material is too poor to make a correlation.

CLAOSAURUS

(KLAY-uh-SAW-rus)

Type Species: *agilis* (uh-JIL-us)
Classification:

Order:	Ornithischia
Suborder:	Ornithopoda
Family:	Hadrosauridae
Name:	Greek *klaos* = broken + Greek *sauros* = lizard.
Size:	3.5 meters (12 feet) long
Period:	Late Cretaceous, 80 million to 75 million years ago
Place:	Kansas
Diet:	Plants

A so-called "headless wonder," this duckbilled dinosaur was founded upon a skeleton missing the skull. *Claosaurus* is the most primitive known North American hadrosaurid. Its first foot bone was tiny. This bone is entirely absent in more advanced duckbilled dinosaurs, and present in the more primitive iguanodontids. *Claosaurus* may have descended from iguanodontids, and may be ancestral to later North American hadrosaurids. Though smaller, its body proportions superficially resembled those of later duckbills such as the well known *Edmontosaurus*. Without a skull, however, the precise status of *Claosaurus* cannot be known.

Claosaurus affinis (AFF-in-is) — Doubtful name: This species is based on three toe bones from South Dakota, resembling those of *Edmontosaurus*.

CLASMODOSAURUS

(klaz-MOH-duh-SAW-rus)

Type Species: *spatula* (SPAT-yuh-luh)
Status: Doubtful
Classification:
   Order: Saurischia
   Suborder: Sauropoda
   Family: ?
Name: Greek *klasma* = fragment + Latin *modulatus* = measured + Greek *sauros* = lizard
Size: Large
Period: Late Cretaceous, 95 million years ago
Place: Argentina
Diet: Plants

This large four-legged browser, or sauropod, is known only from teeth which measure from 5 to 6 centimeters (about 2 to 2¼ inches) long. Originally, German paleontologist Friedrich von Huene believed these teeth belonged to the crocodile *Teleosaurus*. They were thought to be related to the meat-eating dinosaur *Genyodectes*, but they are now believed to be those of a sauropod.

COELOPHYSIS

(SEE-luh-FYE-sis)

Type Species: *bauri* (BOW-er-eye)
Status: Controversial — *See Rioarribasaurus*
Classification:
   Order: Saurischia
   Suborder: Theropoda
   Family: Podokesauridae
Name: *Greek koilos* = hollow + *Greek physis* = form
Size: About 2.8 meters (approximately 9 feet) long
Period: Late Triassic
Place: New Mexico; ?Utah; ?Arizona
Diet: Meat

This early theropod had a small head, strong jaws, sharp teeth, a long, slender neck, a slim body, and somewhat long front limbs. It belonged to the primitive ceratosaur group of carnivorous dinosaurs, some of which had horns. Hundreds of well-preserved *Rioarribasaurus* skeletons were found by paleontologist Edwin H. Colbert's field party in a "dinosaur graveyard" at Ghost Ranch, New Mexico, in 1947.

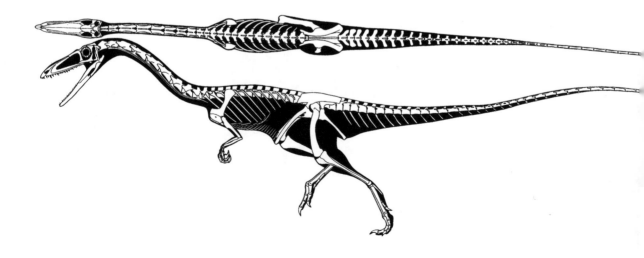

COELOPHYSIS *continued*

The specimen by which *Coelophysis* was named was one that some paleontologists found difficult to distinguish as a distinct genus. A new name has been given to the Ghost Ranch fossils. As of this writing, other paleontologists are attempting to get the name *Coelophysis* reinstated by the committee that determines scientific names.

COELOSAURUS
(SEE-luh-SAW-rus)

Status: Doubtful — *See Ornithomimus*

COELUROIDES
(SEE-luh-ROY-*deez*)

Type Species: *largus* (LAHR-GUS)
Status: Doubtful
Classification:
  Order: Saurischia
  Suborder: Theropoda
  Family: ?
Name: Greek *koilos* = hollow + Greek *oides* = form
Size: Very large
Period: Late Cretaceous, 88.5 million to 83 million
            years ago
Place: India
Diet: Meat

Known only from an incomplete tail, *Coeluroides* seems to have been one of the very large carnivorous dinosaurs, about the size of *Allosaurus*. The vertebrae of the tail are quite large, measuring from 9 to 11 centimeters (3.5 to 4.25 inches) long.

COELURUS

(see-LOOR-us)

Type Species: *fragilis* (fruh-JIL-us)
Status: Doubtful
Classification:
   Order: Saurischia
   Suborder: ?Theropoda
   Family: ?
Name: Greek *koilos* = hollow
Size: 1.8 meters (6 feet) long
Period: Late Jurassic, 156 million to 145 million
               years ago
Place: Wyoming
Diet: Meat

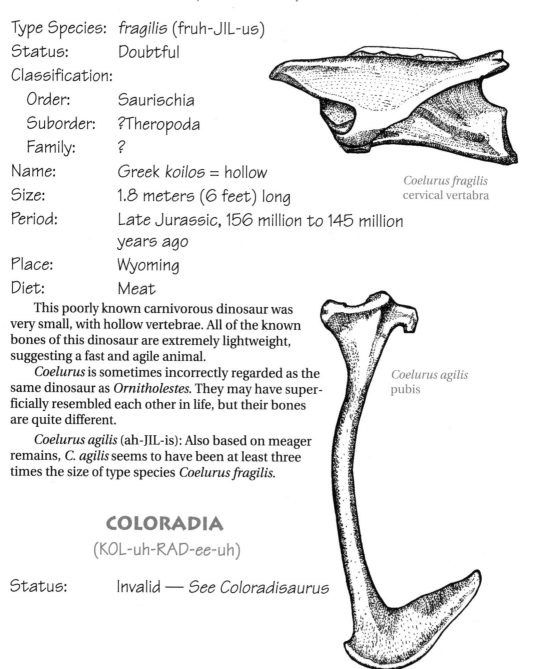

Coelurus fragilis
cervical vertabra

Coelurus agilis
pubis

This poorly known carnivorous dinosaur was very small, with hollow vertebrae. All of the known bones of this dinosaur are extremely lightweight, suggesting a fast and agile animal.

Coelurus is sometimes incorrectly regarded as the same dinosaur as *Ornitholestes*. They may have superficially resembled each other in life, but their bones are quite different.

Coelurus agilis (ah-JIL-is): Also based on meager remains, *C. agilis* seems to have been at least three times the size of type species *Coelurus fragilis*.

COLORADIA
(KOL-uh-RAD-ee-uh)

Status: Invalid — See Coloradisaurus

COLORADISAURUS

(KOL-uh-RAD-i-SAW-rus)

Type Species: *brevis* (BREE-vis)
Classification:
  Order: Saurischia
  Suborder: Prosauropoda
  Family: Plateosauridae
Name: (Los) *Colorados* (Formation) + Greek *sauros*
            = lizard
Size: ?4 Meters (13 feet) long
Period: Late Triassic, 225 million to 219 million years ago
Place: Argentina
Diet: Plants

    Coloradisaurus, while not well known, is related to the well-documented prosauropods *Plateosaurus* and *Lufengosaurus*. These were primitive, early plant-eaters with small heads and large bodies. *Coloradisaurus* had a shorter snout than those dinosaurs; its eyes were apparently relatively large.

COMPSOGNATHUS

(KOMP-sog-NAY-thus)

Type Species: *longipes* (LONG-i-pes)
Classification:

Order:	Saurischia
Suborder:	Theropoda
Family:	Compsognathidae
Name:	Greek *kompsos* = elegant + Greek *gnathos* = jaw
Size:	1 meter (about 40 inches) long; weight approximately 3 to 3.5 kilograms (6.6 to 7.75 pounds)
Period:	Late Jurassic, 156 million to 145 million years ago
Place:	Bavaria, Germany; France
Diet:	Small vertebrates and insects

Compsognathus is one of the smallest of all known dinosaurs. An original estimate of its adult size (70 centimeters, 28 inches) was based on a juvenile skeleton no bigger than a small partridge.

Compsognathus was built like most small carnivorous dinosaurs. Its skull was low and measured 6.5 centimeters (about 2.5 inches) long. Its neck was relatively long; its forelimb was extremely short and seems to have had two fingers with powerful claws. The two-fingered hand (like the hands of the much larger tyrannosaurids of the Late Cretaceous) makes *Compsognathus* unique among Late Jurassic theropods.

The animal's upper leg bone was massively constructed for its size, and measured 76 centimeters (about 2.8 inches) in length. The lower leg bone became slender toward the foot. The foot had a birdlike construction with three functional claws.

With this light and powerful anatomy, *Compsognathus* must have been a fast-running predator. Because of its small size, it probably ate insects, but may also have preyed upon small vertebrates. The latter idea is reinforced by its sharp teeth, and by the discovery of a tiny lizard skeleton in the stomach area of the namesake dinosaur.

COMPSOGNATHUS *continued*

Some modern-day artists have portrayed small theropods with feathers. One strong argument against feathered theropods involves *Compsognathus*. The specimen upon which this genus was founded is one of the most complete dinosaur skeletons ever found. The skeleton is beautifully preserved in the same lithographic limestone that preserved excellent feathered examples of the bird *Archaeopteryx*. Logically, if *Compsognathus* had sported feathers, impressions of them would have been preserved along with the bones.

Compsognathus corallestris (KOR-uh-LES-tris) — Doubtful name: This species, from Canjuers, France, was originally interpreted as having flipper-like appendages that could have been used for swimming. This interpretation has been seriously challenged, and now this species is generally believed to be identical to *Compsognathus longipes*, and that its fossil remains merely represent a larger individual.

COMPSOSUCHUS

(KOMP-soh-SOOK-us)

Type Species: *solus* (SOH-lus)
Status: Doubtful
Classification:
  Order: Saurischia
  Suborder: Theropoda
  Family: ?Allosauridae
Name: Greek *kompsos* = elegant + Greek *souchus* = crocodile
Size: ?Large
Period: Late Cretaceous, 70 million to 65 million years ago
Place: India
Diet: Meat

This poorly known meat-eating dinosaur might be an allosaurid, but it has not even been definitely identified as a carnosaur.

Compsosuchus is known only from a part of the neck. The first vertebra closely resembles the same bone in *Allosaurus*.

CONCHORAPTOR

(KONG-kuh-RAP-tur)

Type Species: *gracilis* (gruh-SIL-is)

Classification:

  Order: Saurischia

  Suborder: Theropoda

  Family: Oviraptoridae

Name: Greek *konche* = shell + Latin *raptor* = robber

Size: 1.5 meters (5 feet) long or less

Period: Late Cretaceous, 80 million to 70 million
               years ago

Place: Mongolia

Diet: Mollusks and other sources of meat

    Conchoraptor was a relatively small member of the oviraptorid family of toothless carnivores. It was originally believed to be a juvenile of the "egg-thief" genus *Oviraptor*. It is known only from a small skull measuring 10 centimeters (about 4 inches) in length. In life, it may have possessed a horny beak, which it could have used to crush mollusks or eggs. Unlike *Oviraptor*, *Conchoraptor* lacked a crest. Crests usually appear as animals grow into maturity.

CORYTHOSAURUS

(kor-ITH-uh-SAW-rus)

Type Species: *casuarius* (KAZ-yoo-AYR-ee-us)

Classification:

Order:	Ornithischia
Suborder:	Ornithopoda
Family:	Hadrosauridae
Name:	Greek *korythos* = Corinthian helmet + Greek *sauros* = lizard
Size:	9 meters (30 feet) long
Period:	Late Cretaceous, 76 million to 72 million years ago
Place:	Alberta
Diet:	Plants

The duckbill *Corythosaurus* is easily distinguished by the feature for which it was named—the helmet-like crest atop its head, resembling the helmet of a Corinthian soldier. The head of *Corythosaurus* is high, narrow, and "compressed" from side to side. The highest part of the crest is directly above the eyes.

The function of *Corythosaurus's* crest has long been a subject of speculation. At one time it was thought that this crest, hollow and connected to the nasal passages, somehow allowed this dinosaur to breathe while under water. Today it is believed that the crest in *Corythosaurus* and other hadrosaurids served other functions, perhaps increasing the animal's sense of smell, or its capacity for sound production. Also, the crest could have served as a visual display for identification purposes. The size and shape of the crest probably varied by age or sex.

Juvenile *Corythosaurus casuarius* skull

CORYTHOSAURUS *continued*

Another feature characteristic of *Corythosaurus's* skull was a muzzle that was short, narrow, and slightly expanded toward the front. The front of the mouth was covered by a horny beak. Inside the mouth, as in other duckbills, was an enormous battery of more than 600 teeth. There were up to 43 rows of teeth in the upper jaw. The lower jaw was deep and massive, and had 37 tooth rows.

Fossilized skin impressions show that *Corythosaurus* had elaborate skin patterns. There were numerous armor plates on *Corythosaurus's* skin; the largest was 38 millimeters (about 1.5 inches) long, 32 millimeters (1.3 inches) wide, and 8 millimeters (about 3.1 inches) high. These armor plates ranged in shape from circular to elliptical to pyramidal.

Some suggest that *Corythosaurus's* body had other decorative features. As on most (or possibly all) other duckbilled dinosaurs, a fleshy frill may have run down its back and tail, and perhaps along its head and neck as well.

Corythosaurus was a sizable animal, weighing perhaps 2 tons or more. It ran on two legs, and balanced itself with its horizontally-held tail.

A number of species have been referred to *Corythosaurus* over the years. All of them are now known to belong to the type species. The differences originally perceived between these species are due to sex, age, or individual variation.

CRASPEDODON

(kras-PEE-duh-don)

Type Species: *lonzeensis* (LON-zee-EN-sis)
Status: Doubtful
Classification:
  Order: Ornithischia
  Suborder: Ornithopoda
  Family: ?Iguanodontidae
Name: Greek *kraspedon* = edge + Greek *odontos* = tooth
Size: ?Large
Period: Late Cretaceous, 87.5 to 83 million years ago
Place: Belgium
Diet: Plants

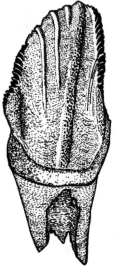

This poorly known herbivore may have resembled the well known and much earlier plant-eater *Iguanodon*. *Craspedodon* is known from two incomplete teeth that are more advanced in the development of their ridges than the teeth in *Iguanodon*. *Craspedodon* may be a descendant of *Iguanodon*.

Craspedodon lonzeensis
tooth

CRATAEOMUS

(KRAY-tay-OH-mus)

Type Species: *lepidophorous* (LEP-i-DOH-fuh-rus)
Status: Doubtful
Classification:
  Order: Ornithischia
  Suborder: Ankylosauria
  Family: Nodosauridae
Name: Greek *krater*/Latin *crater* = bowl + Latin *omasum* = pouch
Size: Possibly about 2 meters (6.8 feet) long
Period: Late Cretaceous, 91 million to 88.5 million years ago
Place: Hungary
Diet: Plants

Poorly known and of doubtful validity, *Crataeomus* was a small, armored dinosaur, similar to *Struthiosaurus* and possibly the same animal.

Crataeomus pawlowitschii (PAW-loh-VIT-shee-eye) — Doubtful name: This species is known from fossils discovered in the same locality. The species is based on various skeleton remains, but no skull.

CRATEROSAURUS

(KRAY-tuh-roh-SAW-rus)

Type Species: *pottonensis* (POT-uh-NEN-sis)
Status: Doubtful
Classification:
  Order: Ornithischia
  Suborder: Stegosauria
  Family: Stegosauridae
Name: Greek *krater*/Latin *crater* = bowl + Greek *sauros* = lizard
Size: ?4 meters (13 feet) long
Period: Early Cretaceous, 138 million to 125 million years ago
Place: England
Diet: Plants

Poorly known and possibly a plate-backed dinosaur, *Craterosaurus* was founded on a single, incomplete vertebra which was first misidentified as a braincase. This bone differs from vertebrae in all other known stegosaurs by having a deep pitting on the top surface.

CREOSAURUS
(KREE-uh-SAW-rus)

Status: Invalid — *See Allosaurus*

CRYPTODRACO

(KRIP-tuh-DRAY-koh)

Type Species: *eumerus* (YOO-mur-us)
Status: Doubtful
Classification:
  Order: Ornithischia
  Suborder: Ankylosauria
  Family: ?Nodosauridae
Name: Greek *kruptos* = hidden + Latin *draco* = dragon
Size: ?
Period: Late Jurassic, 160 million to 156 million years ago
Place: England
Diet: Plants

This nodosaur, or clubless-tailed armored dinosaur, is known only from a right upper leg bone that was originally believed to be that of an iguanodontid. This massive leg bone was 1.1 meters (3.25 feet) long, with a prominent head, suggesting an animal with a thick hind leg. The bone resembles the same bone in the nodosaur, *Hoplitosaurus*.

CRYPTOSAURUS

(KRIP-tuh-SAW-rus)

Status: Invalid — *See Cryptodraco*

CUMNORIA

(kum-NOR-ee-uh)

Status: Invalid — *See Camptosaurus*

DACENTRURUS

(DAY-sen-TROO-rus)

Type Species: *armatus* (ahr-MAY-tus)
Classification:
    Order: Ornithischia
    Suborder: Stegosauria
    Family: Stegosauridae
Name: Greek *da* = very + Greek *kentron* = sharp point +
             Greek *ouros* = tail
Size: 4.4 meters (15 feet) long
Period: Late Jurassic, 163 million to 150 million years ago
Place: England, Portugal, France
Diet: Plants

    Famous as the first stegosaur to be described and named, *Dacentrurus* had the same general proportions as the much larger *Stegosaurus*. It differed mainly in the form and arrangement of its plates and spines, and in having slightly longer front legs.

    Dacentrurus bore two rows of small plates, and two rows of paired spines. Just where the plates ended and the spines began is not known.

    The plates were asymmetrical, and had a slanted base that measured 150 millimeters (about 5.8 inches) across. The only preserved plate seems to have been on the left side of the body. The tail spines were long, with sharp edges. A preserved left tail spine is 45 centimeters (over 1.5 feet) long.

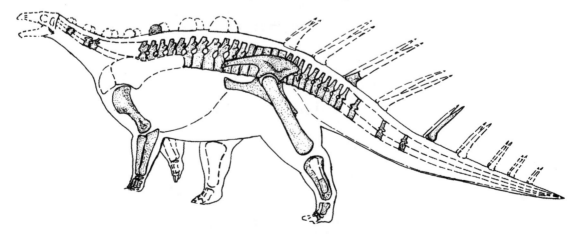

DACENTRURUS *continued*

An egg believed to belong to *Dacentrurus lennieri* was found in Alfeizerao, Portugal. Other species of *Dacentrurus* have been named, all of which were originally referred to the genus *Omosaurus*.

Dacentrurus hastiger (HAS-tig-ger): *D. hastiger* has larger spines with more massive bases than the type species. The length of these spines is over 36 centimeters (14 inches) long.

Dacentrurus phillipsi (PHIL-ipp-sigh) — Doubtful name: This is a tentative species, known only from an incomplete femur.

Dacentrurus lennieri (LENN-ee-er-ee): This animal is known only from incomplete remains from France.

"DACHONGOSAURUS"

(duh-CHONG-uh-SAW-rus)

Type Species: *yunnanensis* (YOO-nan-EN-sis)
Status: Unofficial
Classification:
   Order: Saurischia
   Suborder: ?Sauropodomorpha
   Family: ?
Name: ?Chinese + Greek *sauros* = lizard
Size: ?Large
Period: Jurassic, ?208 million to 145 million years ago
Place: China
Diet: Plants

Hardly anything is known about this big herbivore, which has not yet been formally described. It may be a primitive plant-eater that moved on two or four legs, a prosauropod; or a large, four-legged grazer, a sauropod. "Dachongosaurus" is known from an incomplete skeleton that includes vertebrae, ribs, and limb bones.

133

"DAMALASAURUS"

(DAM-uh-luh-SAW-rus)

Type Species: *magnus* (MAG-nus)
Status: Unofficial
Classification:
    Order: Saurischia
    Subrder: Sauropoda
    Family: ?
Name: ?Chinese or ?Mongolian + Greek *sauros* = lizard
Size: Large
Period: Middle Jurassic, 188 million to 169 million
                    years ago
Place: China
Diet: Plants

    This huge, four-legged plant-eater has not yet been formally described. It was a primitive sauropod.

DANDAKOSAURUS

(dan-DACK-uh-SAW-rus)

Type Species: *indicus* (in-DICK-us)
Status: Unofficial
Classification:
   Order: Saurischia
   Suborder: ?Theropoda
   Family: ?
Name: ?Hindi + Greek *sauros* = lizard
Size: ?Large
Period: Early Jurassic, 213 million to 188 million years ago
Place: Andrah Pradesh, India
Diet: Meat

    Little is known of this dinosaur. It was announced as a new carnosaurian dinosaur, and described as a large carnivore with similarities to *Sinosaurus triassicus*, a primitive meat-eater less than 3 meters (10 feet) long.

DANUBIOSAURUS

(dan-YOO-bee-uh-SAW-rus)

Status: Doubtful — *See Struthiosaurus*

DASPLETOSAURUS

(das-PLEE-tuh-SAW-rus)

Type Species: *torosus* (taw-ROH-sus)
Classification:

Order:	Saurischia
Suborder:	Theropoda
Family:	Tyrannosauridae

Name: Greek *daspletos* = frightful + Greek *sauros* = lizard

Size: 8 to 10 meters (25 to 30 feet) long

Period: Late Cretaceous, 76 million to 72 million years ago

Place: Alberta

Diet: Meat

This enormous carnivorous dinosaur, known only from adult specimens, is similar to such well known tyrannosaurids as *Albertosaurus* and the later *Tyrannosaurus.* It may even have been a direct ancestor of *Tyrannosaurus rex.*

Daspletosaurus had a large head. The triangular bones above its eyes were large, but less prominent than in *Tyrannosaurus rex. Daspletosaurus* had smaller horns above and behind the eyes as well.

Daspletosaurus differed from its contemporary, the well known *Albertosaurus,* in having shorter and higher vertebrae, which would have made its neck and trunk stockier and deeper. Also, its tail was probably thicker. *Daspletosaurus's* forelimbs were longer than

DASPLETOSAURUS *continued*

Albertosaurus's, and the upper part of its foot was slightly shorter. Like other tyrannosaurids, *Daspletosaurus* had a two-fingered hand.

How could two very large, meat-eating dinosaurs have prospered in the same environment? Fewer daspletosaurs and horned dinosaurs are known from about 75 million years ago in western Canada than are albertosaurs and duckbilled dinosaurs. The lighter, more fleet-footed *Albertosaurus* was well-adapted for hunting duckbilled dinosaurs. This may mean that the heavier, more powerful *Daspletosaurus* hunted the horned dinosaurs. *Daspletosaurus* lived in marshlands adjacent to streams, an environment also inhabited by horned dinosaurs like *Centrosaurus*, and duckbills and dome-headed dinosaurs.

DATOUSAURUS

(DAH-too-SAW-rus)

Type Species: *bashanensis* (BASH-uh-NEN-sis)
Classification:
   Order: Saurischia
   Suborder: Sauropoda
   Family: Cetiosauridae
Name: ?Chinese + Greek *sauros* = lizard
Size: 15 meters (over 50 feet) long
Period: Middle Jurassic, 170 million years ago
Place: China
Diet: Plants

    This primitive sauropod was huge and solidly built. Its skull was also large and heavy, with the nostril openings in the front. Its lower jaws were heavily constructed and its teeth were large and spoon-shaped. Sauropod skulls are fragile and very rare, except in the remarkable Zigong quarry which produced *Datousaurus*.

    Since that skull and the skeleton of *Datousaurus* were not found together, they may not belong to the same kind of dinosaur. However, if both elements belong to the same animal, *Datousaurus* could be regarded as a possible ancestor of diplodocids, the whiptailed sauropods. The skull also shows features of the cetiosaurids, a stouter group of sauropods.

    The blocky skull is representative of the entire animal's anatomy. Its limbs were robust, and all four feet had five toes.

    Teeth of a primitive sauropod similar to the teeth of *Datousaurus* were found in the Changdu Basin in Tibet.

DEINOCHEIRUS

(DYE-noh-KYE-rus)

Type Species: *mirificus* (mye-RIF-i-kus)
Classification:
  Order: Saurischia
  Suborder: Theropoda
  Family: ?
Name: Greek *deinos* = terrible + Greek *cheir* = hand
Size: Large
Period: Late Cretaceous, 75 million to 65 million years ago
Place: Mongolia
Diet: Meat and/or insects

Deinocheirus mirificus forelimbs

This bizarre theropod is known mostly from a pair of huge forelimbs. These limbs were spectacularly long and slender, measuring about 240 centimeters (8 feet) long. The length of the lower part of the arm was slightly more than half the length of the upper arm. The hand was slightly longer than the upper arm, and the upper part of the hand was comparatively long. The hand had three fingers of equal length, each bearing claws. In life, the claws were covered by a horny sheath.

Some paleontologists have suggested that these are the claws of a gigantic ornithomimid (ostrich dinosaur); however, *Deinocheirus's* hand was broader than that of the ornithomimid *Ornithomimus*, and unlike *Ornithomimus*, *Deinocheirus's* first finger could not fold inward for effective grasping.

Because the claws also resemble those in both extinct and living sloths, it has been suggested that this dinosaur, like sloths, had a trunk no longer than its forelimbs, and that it could climb some trees.

Without the remains of the rest of the animal, it is impossible to know just what *Deinocheirus* looked like. Clearly, the animal was quite large. For now, this dinosaur remains a mystery, both in its classification and its appearance.

DEINODON

(DYE-nuh-don)

Type Species: *horridus* (HOR-i-dus)
Status: Doubtful
Classification:
   Order: Saurischia
   Suborder: Theropoda
   Family: Tyrannosauridae
Name: Greek *deinos* = terrible + Greek *odontos* = tooth
Size: Large
Period: Late Cretaceous, 75 million to 70 million years ago
Place: Montana
Diet: Meat

   Deinodon was the first tyrannosaurid to be named and described. But it was established only on isolated teeth, and so is questionable as a valid genus.

   The teeth of *Deinodon* are large. In cross-section they are D-shaped, as are the front teeth of other tyrannosaurids.

   Deinodon is usually considered to be the same genus as *Albertosaurus*. Unfortunately, nothing is known of the upper and lower jaws of *Deinodon*, nor of the structure of its other teeth. Without these parts for comparison, *Deinodon* cannot be adequately compared with *Albertosaurus*.

   Whether it is its own genus or synonymous with *Albertosaurus*, *Deinodon* must have been a large theropod, with a huge head and short, two-fingered forelimbs.

DEINONYCHUS

(dye-NON-i-kus)

Type Species: *antirrhopus* (AN-ti-ROH-pus)
Classification:
  Order: Saurischia
  Suborder: Theropoda
  Family: Dromaeosauridae
Name: Greek *deinos* = terrible + Greek *onux* = claw
Size: Almost 3 meters (about 10 feet) long, slightly
             over 1 meter (3.5 feet) high
Period: Early Cretaceous, 119 million to 93 million
             years ago
Place: Montana, Wyoming
Diet: Meat

Deinonychus is a remarkable and important dinosaur, named for the enormous "killer claw" on its foot.

Deinonychus was a relatively small meat-eater, perhaps weighing less than 200 pounds. It had big eyes, a long snout, and sharp serrated teeth. Its forelimbs were long, ending in long, slender hands that had three very long fingers equipped with sharp claws. Its tail was constructed of long vertebrae, and strengthened to the point of stiffness by numerous bony rods. Its feet had four sizeable toes and an almost nonexistent fifth toe.

DEINONYCHUS *continued*

The most distinctive feature of *Deinonychus*'s foot was the second toe, which had a large, curved claw. This claw was extremely long (as much as 13 centimeters (5 inches) long), and had a sharply curved, "sickle," shape. Because of this design, *Deinonychus* probably walked on its third and fourth toes. The second toe, designed for extreme retraction, was carried off the ground and used in attacking prey, rather than in walking.

Deinonychus's teeth were mostly backward-directed (instead of downward), indicating that they were used for slicing, rather than for killing.

The tail was capable of some movement, either from side to side or up and down, but was otherwise inflexible. Its rigidity may have stabilized the animal while it ran. The hands had a remarkable degree of mobility, and could flex and turn toward each other. The claws were perfectly designed for seizing prey.

Altogether, these adaptations created a carnivorous dinosaur that was capable of pursuing its prey at high speed. Seizing its victim with its powerful front claws, *Deinonychus* kicked out, using the sickle claw for disemboweling its prey.

The discovery of *Deinonychus in 1964* drastically altered our conception of dinosaurs. Dinosaurs had been regarded as stupid, slow, sluggish, cold-blooded

DEINONYCHUS *continued*

reptiles. But dinosaurs like *Deinonychus* were designed for living active lives. Like other fast-moving animals, this dinosaur may have been warm-blooded.

Deinonychus offers strong evidence supporting the theory that birds descended from a line of theropods. Because of its resemblance to birds, some artists have made life restorations of *Deinonychus* with feathers, although no feather impressions have yet been found with any dinosaur specimen.

Remains of *Deinonychus* have been found in quarries yielding abundant remains of the large plant-eating dinosaur *Tenontosaurus*. This suggests that *Deinonychus* preyed upon *Tenontosaurus*, Since *Deinonychus* appears to have been too small to bring down one of these large plant-eaters by itself, it may have hunted in packs. The large brain of this theropod suggests that *Deinonychus* was capable of such sophisticated behavior.

DENVERSAURUS

(DEN-vur-SAW-rus)

Status: Doubtful — *See Edmontonia*

DIANCHUNGOSAURUS

(DYE-an-CHUNG-uh-SAW-rus)

Type Species: *elegans* (EL-uh-gans)
Status: Doubtful
Classification:
   Order: Ornithischia
   Suborder: Ornithopoda
   Family: Heterodontosauridae
Name: Dianchung (place in China) + Greek sauros = lizard
Size: ?Small
Period: Early Jurassic, 208 million to 188 million years ago
Place: China
Diet: Plants

   Although poorly known, and described on only fragmentary remains, this plant-eater is classified with the heterodontosaurids, a family of primitive ornithischian (bird-hipped) dinosaurs.

   Dianchungosaurus had an upper jaw that was thin and toothless in the front. Toward the rear of the mouth, it had small, rounded teeth widely separated from one another, and three prominent canine teeth. The nostrils seem to have been large, and were situated low on the upper part of the skull.

   Dianchungosaurus elegans has not yet been formally described.

DICERATOPS

(dye-SER-uh-tops)

Type Species: *hatcheri* (HACH-uh-rye)
Status: ?
Classification:
   Order: Ornithischia
   Suborder: Ceratopsia
   Family: Ceratopsidae
Name: Greek *di* = two + Greek *keratos* = horn + Greek *ops* = face
Size: 9 meters (30 feet) long
Period: Late Cretaceous, 68 million to 65 million years ago
Place: Wyoming
Diet: Plants

Known only from a skull with lower jaws, *Diceratops* is classified as a horned dinosaur, perhaps one and the same as the well-known *Triceratops*. However, recent work by University of Chicago paleontologist Catherine Forster indicates that *Diceratops* is, in fact, a valid genus. *Diceratops* seems to be a rare horned dinosaur, whereas *Triceratops* is known from a wealth of collected specimens.

Like *Triceratops*, *Diceratops* had two large horns over the eyes. However, there was no horn over its snout, not even the blunt knob of bone that is present in those *Triceratops* skulls that lack the nose horn. Also unlike *Triceratops*, the frill of *Diceratops* had openings in the bones. These openings were originally believed to be caused by disease, injury, or bad preservation, but Forster's research indicates that these were natural features of the *Diceratops* skull.

Diceratops hatcheri skull

DICLONIUS

(dye-KLOH-nee-us)

Type Species: *pentagonus* (PEN-tuh-GON-us)
Status: Doubtful
Classification:
  Order: Ornithischia
  Suborder: Ornithopoda
  Family: ?Hadrosauridae
Name: Greek *di* = two + Greek *klon* = stem + Greek *ios* (adjective ending)
Size: ?8 meters (27 feet) long
Period: Late Cretaceous, 83 million to 73 million years ago
Place: Montana
Diet: Plants

Diclonius is one of the least well-known kinds of duckbilled dinosaurs. Hadrosaurs, mostly bipedal plant-eaters, were called duckbills because their bill-like mouths and beaks resembled those of ducks.

All we have of *Diclonius* are fragmentary, detached teeth. These elongated teeth show no features that might distinguish them as representing a valid new kind of dinosaur.

In addition to the type species, two other species were named at the same time: *Diclonius perangulatus* and *Diclonius calamarius*. Like the type species, the details distinguishing these species are no longer considered of any importance.

Even the precise locations in Montana from which these three species were unearthed are uncertain.

DICRAEOSAURUS

(dye-KREE-uh-SAW-rus)

Type Species: *hansemanni* (HANS-muh-nye)
Classification:

Order:	Saurischia
Suborder:	Sauropoda
Family:	Diplodocidae
Name:	Greek *di* = two + Greek *kros* = forked + Greek *sauros* = lizard
Size:	13 meters (about 45 feet) long
Period:	Late Jurassic, 156 million to 150 million years ago
Place:	East Africa
Diet:	Plants

This medium-sized, four-legged browsing dinosaur, or sauropod, is identified by its rather short neck. The vertebrae of *Dicraeosaurus*'s neck, back, and hip area had tall spines. This would have given these areas of the body a kind of hump-backed appearance, perhaps to make the animal seem taller and less vulnerable. The front legs were relatively short, measuring about three-fifths the length of the hind legs.

The skull of *Dicraeosaurus* resembled that of the diplodocid sauropods *Diplodocus* and *Apatosaurus*. It was long and narrow, with nostrils on top of the head and pencil-like teeth. The short forelimbs and high spines of the vertebrae over the hips are other indications that this dinosaur was a diplodocid.

Like other diplodocids, *Dicraeosaurus* had a long tail ending in a whiplash, which may have been used as a weapon against carnivores.

Dicraeosaurus sattleri (SAT-lurr-eye): *D. sattleri* was founded on fragmentary remains that represent-ed several individuals. It was distinguished from the

DICRAEOSAURUS *continued*

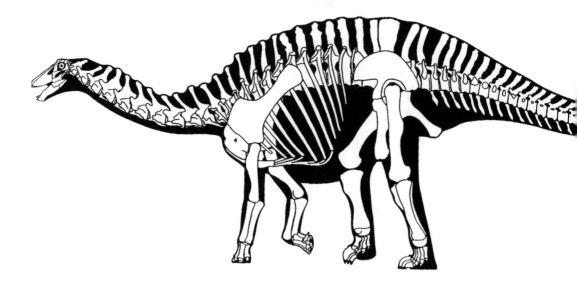

type species by having, among other minor differences, a more slender pelvic bone. Tall spines on its vertebrae would have increased the height of the animal's neck and back. Because these are advanced features, and because this species was found in more recent sediments in Tendaguru, East Africa, *Dicraeosaurus sattleri* may have descended from *Dicraeosaurus hansemanni*.

DIDANODON
(dye-DAN-uh-don)

Status: Invalid — *See Lambeosaurus*

DILOPHOSAURUS

(dye-LOH-fuh-SAW-rus)

Type Species: *wetherilli* (WETH-uh-ri-lye)

Classification:

Order: Saurischia

Suborder: Theropoda

Family: Podokesauridae

Name: Greek *di* = two + Greek *lophos* = crest + Greek *sauros* = lizard

Size: About 6 meters (20 feet) long (juvenile)

Period: Early Jurassic, 208 million to 194 million years ago

Place: Arizona

Diet: Meat

This early and unusual carnivorous dinosaur was distinguished by a pair of highly arched crests adorning the top of its head. Also, its forelimbs were longer than those in later, large carnivores. *Dilophosaurus's* head, though large in relation to its body size, was delicately constructed. Some of the skull bones seem to have been weak, and the teeth were long and slender.

Because of the construction of its skull and form of its

DILOPHOSAURUS *continued*

teeth, some paleontologists suggest that
Dilophosaurus lacked a powerful bite, and was therefore
more of a scavenger than a hunter. It may have plucked at meat with its powerful
grasping hands and feet, rather than tearing into it with its jaws. Other scientists
speculate that *Dilophosaurus*, like many other carnivorous dinosaurs, was an
active predator.

The delicate construction of the animal's high cranial crests implies that these
were used for display purposes, not combat. In life, they may have been brightly
colored, or perhaps decorated with color patterns. There is no evidence to suggest
they spat poison or fanned their necks as the undersized *Dilophosaurs* do in the
film *Jurassic Park*.

Fossil footprints showing multiple tracks of dinosaurs like *Dilophosaurus*, and
the discovery of three skeletons of this genus found close together, hint that
Dilophosaurus may have exhibited complex social behavior, including traveling
in herds.

DIMODOSAURUS
(dye-MOH-duh-SAW-rus)

Status: Invalid — *See Plateosaurus*

DINODOCUS
(DYE-noh-DOH-kus)

Status: Invalid — *See Pelorosaurus*

DINOSAURUS

(DYE-nuh-SAW-rus)

Type Species: ?
Status: Doubtful
Classification:
  Order: ?
  Suborder: ?
  Family: ?
Name: Greek *deinos* = terrible + Greek *sauros* = lizard
Size: Large
Period: Late Cretaceous, 88.5 million to 83 million years ago
Place: India
Diet: Meat

    This carnivore is known only from a large tail vertebra and some fragmentary ribs. The size and shape of the vertebra—13 to 14 centimeters (about 5 inches) long—indicates that *Dinosaurus* was large and may have been heavily built. The vertebra does not have the notches that, in some dinosaurs, lessened the animals' weight.

DIPLODOCUS

(di-PLOH-duh-kus)

Type Species: *longus* (LONG-us)
Classification:
- Order: Saurischia
- Suborder: Sauropoda
- Family: Diplodocidae

Name: Greek *diplax* = double-folded + Greek *dokos* = bearing-beam.

Size: 27 meters (88 feet) long; weighed 10.5 metric tons (under 12 tons)

Period: Late Jurassic, 156 million to 145 million years ago

Place: Colorado, Wyoming, Utah, Montana

Diet: Plants, including conifers, cycads, ginkgoes, ferns

One of the largest of all dinosaurs, *Diplodocus* typifies the sauropod family Diplodocidae, long and rather graceful four-legged plant-eaters that flourished in the middle of dinosaur time.

Diplodocus had an elongated snout, with the nostrils on top of the head and teeth only at the front of the mouth. Its teeth were peglike, and particularly weak. The spines of the animal's vertebrae were divided before the hips, probably for housing a long ligament that worked the neck.

The neck and tail of *Diplodocus* were both extremely long, comprising nearly half of the animal's entire length. Its limbs were very slender, and its hind legs were longer than the front legs, which caused the animal to slope downward toward the front. The toes of its front legs were short and slender. The tail tapered into a whiplash that may have been utilized as a weapon against theropods.

Except for the weak front teeth, *Diplodocus's* jaws were toothless. Some paleontologists believe the weakness and position of these teeth are indications of a diet limited to soft and succulent plants, which could be detached from the floors of lakes and rivers and along shorelines. But these teeth are worn flat at right angles to their length, so such abrasions cannot be attributed to soft vegetation.

More recent studies have shown that *Diplodocus's* teeth were like the cropping teeth of cows and horses, suitable for nipping off a wide variety of plants that could later be broken down by chemicals, bacteria, or "gizzard stones" (called gastroliths). Other studies have shown that peglike teeth were well-suited for eating plants with lesser amounts of grit, in other words, the kinds of plants growing at higher levels.

If *Diplodocus* could rear up on its hind legs, as some paleontologists have suggested, its long giraffe-like neck could have brought its head to a higher feeding level. We can imagine *Diplodocus* probing among the branches of tall trees, nibbling such foods as conifer needles.

Various kinds of giant plant-eaters are found in rocks of the same age and location in the American West. How did these big, hungry animals manage to share the plant resources? Because *Diplodocus's* body was directed downward to the front, it may have had access to both low- and high-growing plants, the kinds of plants usually avoided by its horizontally-directed contemporary, *Camarasaurus*.

The type species of *Diplodocus* was founded upon some vertebrae discovered in 1877 by Samuel Wendell Williston in Fremont County, Colorado. But much of what we know of this genus has resulted from the discovery of the better known species *Diplodocus carnegie*, which is based on some good skeletons collected by O.A. Peterson for the Carnegie Museum of Natural History in 1900. Casts of *Diplodocus carnegie* skeletons were sent to museums all over the world.

Diplodocus carnegii (CAR-negg-eye) — Doubtful name: This was originally recognized as a distinct species, but it may prove to be the same as the type species.

Diplodocus hayi (HAY-eye): Based on a subadult specimen, *D. hayi* differs from the type species in various details of the skull bones.

Diplodocus lacustris (ls-CUSS-triss): This is a smaller species than *D. longus*, with more slender jaws.

DIPLOTOMODON

(DIP-loh-TOH-muh-don)

Type Species: *horrificus* (hor-IF-i-kus)
Status: Doubtful — *See ?Dryptosaurus*
Classification:
   Order: Saurischia
   Suborder: Theropoda
   Family: ?Coeluridae
Name: Greek *diplax* = double-folded + Greek *tome* = cutting + Greek *odontos* = tooth
Size: Large
Period: Late Cretaceous, 97.5 million to 65 million years ago
Place: New Jersey
Diet: Meat

   This meat-eater may have been a member of the coelurosaurs. This group of carnivorous dinosaurs once included only small forms, but it is now being reclassified to include some of the largest of all carnivorous dinosaurs.

   This doubtful genus is described only from a tooth which was originally misidentified as that of a plesiosaur (a non-dinosaurian swimming reptile), and later, as a fish. In fact, the tooth most closely resembles that of the carnivore *Dryptosaurus aquilunguis*, and may belong to that dinosaur species.

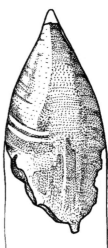

Diplotomodon horrificus tooth

DIRACODON

(dye-RACK-uh-don)

Status: Doubtful — *See Stegosaurus*

DOLICHOSUCHUS

(DOL-i-kuh-SOOK-us)

Type Species: *cristatus* (kris-TAT-us)
Status: Doubtful
Classification:
  Order: Saurischia
  Suborder: Theropoda
  Family: ?
Name: Greek *dolichos* = long + Greek *souchos* = crocodile
Size: Medium-sized
Period: Late Triassic, 223 million to 221 million years ago
Place: Germany
Diet: Meat

Not much is known of this poorly represented dinosaur, which was one of the earliest dinosaurian carnivores. Based only on an imperfect lower hind leg, *Dolichosuchus* may have resembled many of the other early meat-eaters, such as *Podokesaurus* and *Coelophysis*.

Its lower leg bone measures 29 centimeters (about 11 inches) long. It was probably longer than the upper leg bone, a feature which suggests a medium-sized theropod. The tibia is very slender, with a strong growth to the side that has not been seen in any other known Triassic carnivore.

Although *Dolichosuchus* has been classified with the family of small early carnivores called *Podokesauridae*, recent studies have questioned whether this animal was a dinosaur at all.

DORYPHOSAURUS

(dor-IF-uh-SAW-rus)

Status: Invalid — *See Kentrosaurus*

DRACOPELTA

(DRACK-uh-PEL-tuh)

Type Species: *zbyszewskii* (ZIB-i-SOO-skee)
Classification:
    Order: Ornithischia
    Suborder: Ankylosauria
    Family: Nodosauridae
Name: Latin *draco* = dragon + Greek *pelta* = small shield
Size: ?
Period: Late Jurassic, 156 million to 150 million years ago
Place: Portugal
Diet: Plants

   Dracopelta is significant as the first ankylosaur, or armored dinosaur, found from the Late Jurassic Period. Armored dinosaurs were previously known only from the Cretaceous Period. If we imagine a generic nodosaurid—one of the more primitive ankylosaurs—and project those features upon the known armor of *Dracopelta*, we may have some idea of how this dinosaur looked in life: squat, wide, and heavily armored.

   There were at least five distinct types of armor on the chest of this dinosaur, ranging from very small, isolated, flat armor plates to circular, longer plates. The plates ranged in size from 31 millimeters by 21 millimeters (less than 1 inch by 1 inch), to 190 millimeters long by 110 millimeters wide (8 inches by 4 inches).

DRAVIDOSAURUS

(druh-VID-uh-SAW-rus)

Type Species: *blandfordi* (BLAND-fur-dye)

Classification:

Order: Ornithischia

Suborder: Stegosauria

Family: Stegosauridae

Name: Dravidanadu (common name for southern part of Indian peninsula) + Greek *sauros* = lizard

Size: 3 meters (10 feet)

Period: Late Cretaceous, 88.5 million to 87.5 million years ago

Place: India

Diet: Plants

Dravidosaurus is the only stegosaur, or plated dinosaur, that dates from the end of dinosaur time. Most stegosaurs lived in the Late Jurassic Period, more than 50 million years earlier.

Dravidosaurus had much the same body plan as *Stegosaurus*, but it was smaller than other stegosaurs, and had the smallest skull of all the plated dinosaurs. This skull was about 200 millimeters (7.6 inches) long, narrow and depressed, resembling that of *Stegosaurus*, but with a more pointed beak. A preserved tooth of *Dravidosaurus* resembles that of the African stegosaur, *Kentrosaurus*.

The plates on *Dravidosaurus's* back were triangular, measuring about 10 millimeters (1/3 inch) in thickness. The smallest plate was 50 millimeters high (1.5 inches) and 30 millimeters (1 inch) long.

Dravidosaurus had peculiar tail spikes. One preserved tail spike is curved and oddly thickened in the middle. This spike is 150 millimeters (5 inches) long, with the mid-portion bulging to a diameter of 30 millimeters (1 inch). The spine of *Dravidosaurus* tapered near the base to a diameter of 22 millimeters (0.6 inches).

DRINKER

(DRING-kur)

Type Species: *nisti* (NIS-tee)

Classification:

  Order: Ornithischia
  Suborder: Ornithopoda
  Family: ?Hypsilophodontidae

Name: (Edward) Drinker (Cope)

Size: Small

Period: Late Jurassic, 156 million to 145 million years ago

Place: Wyoming

Diet: Plants

   This recently named, poorly understood plant-eater is known from a subadult skeleton that may be related to the better known genus *Othnielia*. It differs in having teeth with more complex crowns. Most likely, *Drinker* resembled *Othnielia* in life.

   Drinker seems to be more advanced than *Othnielia*. As of now, the precise evolutionary placing of *Drinker* cannot be determined.

DROMAEOSAURUS

(DROH-mee-uh-SAW-rus)

Type Species: *albertensis* (AL-bur-TEN-sis)
Classification:
    Order: Saurischia
    Suborder: Theropoda
    Family: Dromaeosauridae
Name: Greek *dromaios* = swift running + Greek *sauros* = lizard
Size: 1.8 meters (6 feet)
Period: Late Cretaceous, 76 million to 72 million years ago
Place: Alberta
Diet: Meat

    Dromaeosaurus was a fleet-footed, carnivorous dinosaur. Like other members of the dromaeosaurid family, this dinosaur had a large head with well-developed, sharply pointed, serrated teeth.

    The top of the *Dromaeosaurus* skull had the same general proportions as the skulls of larger meat-eaters. The brain cavity was relatively large. The jaws were long, but not massive. The skull measured about 21 centimeters (8 inches) long.

    One of the most striking features of *Dromaeosaurus* was its foot, one toe of which was larger than the others (8 centimeters, or 3 inches, long) and bore an oversized claw. This claw was probably used as a weapon to disembowel prey, probably small ornithischian dinosaurs.

    The head was quite birdlike in its construction, and its large brain was more like that of a bird than a reptile. The skull also had bird features, and was similar to the Late Jurassic bird *Archaeopteryx*. These birdlike features show the close resemblance of many later dinosaur carnivores to modern birds.

    With its large brain, big eyes, grasping hands, and specialized toes, *Dromaeosaurus* was probably an intelligent, swift-moving, and skillful hunter that seized its prey with its foreclaws and then disemboweled them with its foot claw. Dinosaurs such as *Dromaeosaurus* may have hunted in packs like wolves.

DROMICEIOMIMUS

(droh-MEE-see-uh-MYE-mus)

Type Species: *brevitertius* (BREV-i-TUR-see-us)
Classification:

Order:	Saurischia
Suborder:	Theropoda
Family:	Ornithomimidae

Name: Latin *Dromiceius* = (generic name for the bird) emu + Latin *mimus* = mimic

Size: 3.6 meters (12 feet) long

Period: Late Cretaceous, 75 million to 70 million years ago

Place: Alberta

Diet: Soft meat, eggs, insects

This large ornithomimid, or ostrich-like dinosaur, may have been the fastest of all dinosaurs.

Its lightly built body and powerful hind limbs indicate that *Dromiceiomimus* may have attained a running speed surpassing that of an ostrich (over 40 mph), but it had less dodging capability. With no adaptations for defense, this dinosaur must have relied on speed to escape large predators like dromaeosaurs or juvenile tyrannosaurids. Its large eyes, which may have been color-sensitive, would have helped alert *Dromiceiomimus* to danger.

Its skull had a remarkably large eye hole, the rim of which was some 72 millimeters (nearly 3 inches) in diameter. The *Dromiceiomimus'* brain was relatively large, comparable in size to that of an ostrich. Its limbs were long, and the hand was not as powerfully developed as that in *Struthiomimus*, another ornithomimid.

The shape of the muzzle, which in life was covered by a horny beak, and other details of the skull indicate that this dinosaur ate insects. The weak jaw muscles suggest that *Dromiceiomimus* and other ornithomimids may also have eaten soft foods, like eggs and soft animal parts. The hands, more suited to uncovering foods than for grasping prey, could have lifted food from the ground. As no gastric stones have ever been found with *Dromiceiomimus* (indicating that it had no mechanism for grinding) it probably did not eat plants.

DROMICEIOMIMUS *continued*

We know that many dinosaurs laid eggs, but we have no evidence of live births among them. However, some researchers have speculated that ornithomimids, especially *Dromiceiomimus*, gave birth to live young. Their pelvic canals are very wide for their small body size. Remains of both adult and half-grown *Dromiceiomimus* at one site suggest these animals maintained a social structure, and that the young relied on parental care.

DROMICOSAURUS

(DROH-mee-kuh-SAW-rus)

Status: Invalid — *See Massospondylus*

DRYOSAURUS

(DRYE-uh-SAW-rus)

Type Species: *altus* (AWL-tus)
Classification:
  Order: Ornithischia
  Suborder: Ornithopoda
  Family: Dryosauridae
Name: Greek *dryos* = oak + Greek *sauros* = lizard
Size: 3 to 3.5 meters (10 to 12 feet) long
Period: Late Jurassic, 156 million to 145 million years ago
Place: Wyoming, Colorado, Utah, East Africa
Diet: Plants, including tough vegetation

Dryosaurus was a slender, primitive, two-footed dinosaur. The forelimbs were long, and the upper leg bone was shorter than the lower, an anatomical feature of swift runners. The toes were long and hollow, another feature of fast-running animals.

We can tell more about *Dryosaurus's* appearance from the bones of its head. Its skull was slim, ending in a horny beak. Its eye holes were large. *Dryosaurus's* cheek teeth were elongated, with coarse cutting edges and vertical ridges adapted for chewing tough vegetation.

The presence of *Dryosaurus* (as well as other Late Jurassic dinosaurs) in both North America and East Africa at about the same time supports the theory that a land route existed during the Late Jurassic Period between Laurasia and Gondwana, the northern and southern supercontinents.

Dryosaurus lettowvorbecki (LET-oh-vor-BECK-eye): Originally the type species of the genus *Dysalotosaurus*, this species was founded on the remains of several individuals discovered in Tendaguru, East Africa. The skulls in this species and *Dryosaurus altus* are almost identical.

DRYPTOSAUROIDES

(DRIP-toh-saw-ROI-deez)

Type Species: *grandis* (GRAN-dis)

Status: Doubtful

Classification:
  Order: Saurischia
  Suborder: Theropoda
  Family: ?

Name: Greek *dryps* = to tear + Greek *sauros* = lizard + Greek *oides* = form

Size: Large

Period: Late Cretaceous, 97.5 million to 65 million years ago

Place: India

Diet: Meat

This carnivore is known only from isolated back vertebrae which were once thought to belong either to a dryptosaurid, a large, slim predator, or a megalosaurid, a stouter meat-eater.

Little else can be said of *Dryptosauroides*. The German paleontologist Friederich von Huene, who first named and described it early in this century, thought that the animal's vertebrae most closely resembled those of the North American genus *Dryptosaurus*. Hence, the name. More modern studies, however, show that this genus is not well enough known to classify.

DRYPTOSAURUS

(DRIP-tuh-SAW-rus)

Type Species: *aquilunguis* (ACK-we-LUNG-gwis)

Classification:

Order: Carnosauria

Suborder: Theropoda

Family: Dryptosauridae

Name: Greek *dryps* = to tear + Greek *sauros* = lizard

Size: 6 meters (20 feet) long

Period: Late Cretaceous, 70 million to 65 million years ago

Place: Eastern North America

Diet: Meat

Dryptosaurus is celebrated as the first meat-eating dinosaur described from North America, and is the only large carnivorous dinosaur known from eastern North America.

Dryptosaurus had the same general body proportions as other large carnivorous dinosaurs. Its most distinctive feature was a very large claw, like an eagle's, on its first finger. This claw was originally thought to belong on the animal's toe. It measured at least 21 centimeters (8 inches) in length, or about 75% of the length of the animal's upper arm bone, and would have been even longer in life because of its horny sheath. Some paleontologists have suggested that this claw may have been used as a tool to cut the blood vessels of prey, or to pry off the armor plates of ankylosaurs.

Originally named *Laelaps* in 1866 (a name that proved to have been taken), *Dryptosaurus* was then perceived to be the most formidable predator of all time, and the natural hunter of the duckbilled dinosaur *Hadrosaurus*. It was depicted pouncing on its prey with huge kangaroo-like leaps, and then ripping into the flesh with its great claws.

Dryptosaurus has usually been depicted as a theropod similar to both megalosaurids and tyrannosaurids. Recent studies indicate that it may actually belong to one of the smaller carnivores, the coelurosaurids, because of its generally slim build and deeply serrated teeth. Its large forelimbs are similar to those in ornithomimids, the ostrich-like dinosaurs.

DRYPTOSAURUS *continued*

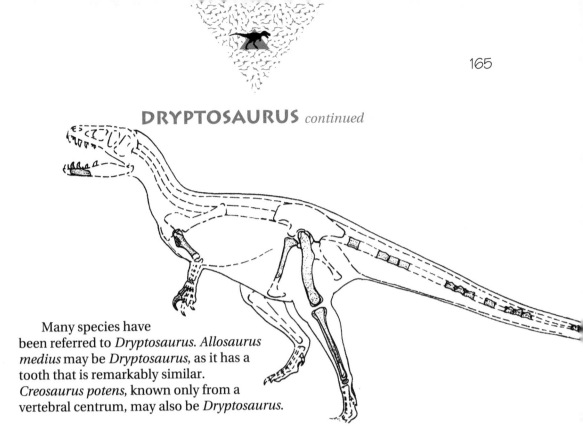

Many species have been referred to *Dryptosaurus*. *Allosaurus medius* may be *Dryptosaurus*, as it has a tooth that is remarkably similar. *Creosaurus potens*, known only from a vertebral centrum, may also be *Dryptosaurus*.

DYNAMOSAURUS
(dye-NAM-uh-SAW-rus)

Status: Invalid — *See Tyrannosaurus*

DYOPLOSAURUS
(dye-OH-pluh-SAW-rus)

Status: Invalid — *See Euoplocephalus*

DYSALOTOSAURUS
(DYE-suh-LOT-uh-SAW-rus)

Status: Invalid — *See Dryosaurus*

DYSGANUS

(dis-GAN-us)

Type Species: *encaustus* (en-KAWS-tus)
Status: Doubtful
Classification:
   Order: Ornithischia
   Suborder: Ceratopsia
   Family: Ceratopsidae
Name: Greek *dys* = bad + Greek *ganos* = brightness
Size: ?
Period: Late Cretaceous, 83 million to 73 million years ago
Place: Montana
Diet: Plants

   Dysganus is a very poorly known horned dinosaur. It is known from various worn and fragmentary teeth originally believed to be those of a duckbilled dinosaur. The teeth are all from the extreme front end of the dental battery of some kind of horned dinosaur of the family Ceratopsidae, to which most horned dinosaurs belong. The teeth were used to establish four doubtful species, none of which can be adequately defined today.

DYSLOCOSAURUS

(diss-SLOH-kuh-SAW-rus)

Type Species: *polyonychius* (POL-ee-oh-NYE-kee-us)

Classification:

Order:	Saurischia
Suborder:	Sauropoda
Family:	Diplodocidae

Name: Greek *dys* = bad + Latin *locus* = place + Greek *sauros* = lizard

Size: 20 meters (about 64.5 feet) long

Period: ?Late Cretaceous, 68 million to 65 million years ago

Place: Wyoming

Diet: Plants

Dyslocosaurus was an unusual, small member of the diplodocid family of long and relatively slender sauropods. All diplodocids had tapering tails ending in a whiplash, among other identifying features.

Dyslocosaurus was distinguished by its particularly big feet. The toes of its hind feet had a greater circumference relative to length than those in any other known diplodocid. The fourth toe of the hind foot ended in a claw, and the fifth may also have had a claw. The presence of four definite claws made *Dyslocosaurus* unique among diplodocids. A nubbin of bone found with the namesake remains—a pair of left legs—may or may not be a fifth claw. If the hind foot does prove to have five claws, this would make it unique among all known sauropods.

Dyslocosaurus is an important dinosaur find, perhaps representing either the last survivor of an otherwise-unknown line of North American diplodocids, or an immigrant evolved from diplodocids from another continent. The latter theory is the more accepted. *Dyslocosaurus* may be a species derived from Late Cretaceous diplodocids, such as the Asian *Nemegtosaurus*.

Another possibility is that, like other North American sauropods, it comes from Late Jurassic sediments, which were improperly dated in the case of *Dyslocosaursus.*

DYSTROPHAEUS

(dis-TROF-ay-us)

Type Species: *viaemalae* (VEE-ay-MAL-ay)
Status: Doubtful
Classification:
  Order: Saurischia
  Suborder: Sauropoda
  Family: Diplodocidae
Name: Greek *dys* = bad + Greek *trepein* = to turn
Size: Large
Period: Late Jurassic, 156 million to 145 million years ago
Place: Utah
Diet: Plants

Dystrophaeus is historically important as the first sauropod, or large, four-legged plant-eater, discovered in the New World.

Dystrophaeus was named and described in 1877, a time when sauropod dinosaurs were not yet well understood. It is founded on scant but well-preserved remains. Its lower front leg bone measures 66 centimeters (about 2.5 feet) long, making it small for a sauropod.

It is possible that *Dystrophaeus* was either *Diplodocus* or *Barosaurus,* two very long members of the Diplodocidae, the family of sauropods with long heads and whiplash tails.

DYSTYLOSAURUS

(die-STYE-luh-SAW-rus)

Type Species: *edwini* (ED-wi-nye)

Classification:

Order:	Saurischia
Suborder:	Sauropoda
Family:	Brachiosauridae
Name:	Greek *di* = two + Greek *stylos* = column + Greek *sauros* = lizard
Size:	Large
Period:	Late Jurassic, 156 million to 145 million years ago
Place:	Colorado
Diet:	Plants

    This is another partial giant four-legged plant-eater, or sauropod, collected by the famous "Dinosaur Jim" Jensen of Brigham Young University. *Dystylosaurus* was a brachiosaurid, one of a family of large sauropods characterized by long front legs. *Dystylosaurus*, founded upon a single back vertebra, is unique among all known North American sauropods for various features of that vertebra. Among these features is a spine that is broad crosswise, but thin and fragile from front to back.

    In life, *Dystylosaurus* may have resembled *Brachiosaurus*, one of the largest of all dinosaurs.

ECHINODON

(eck-EYE-nuh-don)

Type Species: *becklesii* (BECK-uhl-zye)
Classification:

    Order: Ornithischia

    Suborder: Thyreophora

    Family: Scelidosauridae

Name: Greek *echinos* = spiny + Greek *odontos* = tooth

Size: ?

Period: Late Jurassic, 145 million years ago

Place: England, Colorado

Diet: Plants

Echinodon may have been related to *Scutellosaurus*, a plant-eater with small bony armor panels on its back. This little known dinosaur, found in a bay in Dorset, England, was described in 1861 by Sir Richard Owen. Basing his description on parts of the jaw, Owen concluded that *Echinodon* was the most advanced of the small, early, ornithopod plant-eaters, the fabrosaurids. The fabrosaurid family name has now been abandoned, and scientists are uncertain of *Echinodon's* place on the dinosaur family tree.

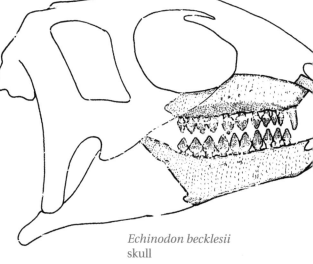

Echinodon becklesii skull

Armor found by Owen in England in 1879 and thought to belong to a lizard, may actually belong to *Echinodon*. *Echinodon* has therefoı ly categorized as one of a suborder of mostly four-legged armorec called *Thyreophora*.

Parts of a jaw and limbs of what may be a new species of *Echinodon* were found in the 1980s near Grand Junction, Colorado, but these finds are too fragmentary to solve the riddle of *Echinodon's* identity.

EDMONTONIA

(ED-mon-TOH-nee-uh)

Type Species: *longiceps* (LONG-i-seps)

Classification:

   Order: Ornithischia

   Suborder: Ankylosauria

   Family: Nodosauridae

Name: *Edmonton* (Formation in Alberta, Canada)

Size: 7 meters (23 feet) long

Period: Late Cretaceous, 76 million to 68 million years ago

Place: Alberta; northwestern Montana

Diet: Plants

   This squat, heavily armored plant-eater grew nearly as large as a tank. Like other nodosaurids (and unlike their close relatives, the ankylosaurids), *Edmontonia* had no tail club. It had a wide, flat head, at least three-fifths as wide as it was long. *Edmontonia* was described in 1928 by the famed dinosaur hunter Charles M. Sternberg. Sternberg described *Edmontonia* from an excellent skeleton found in what was then called the Edmonton (now Horseshoe Canyon) Formation on the Red Deer River in Alberta, Canada.

   Edmontonia rugosidens (ROO-go-see-dens): *Edmontonia rugosidens* had a particularly wide head, (400 millimeters, or about 15.5 inches), and is known from armor, skull, and other parts found in northwestern Montana.

EDMONTOSAURUS

(ed-MON-tuh-SAW-rus)

Type Species: *regalis* (ri-GAY-lis)
Classification:

Order:	Ornithischia
Suborder:	Ornithopoda
Family:	Hadrosauridae

Name: *Edmonton* (Formation in Alberta, Canada) + Greek *sauros* = lizard

Size: 12 meters (about 40 feet)

Period: Late Cretaceous, 73 million to 65 million years ago

Place: Wyoming; Colorado; Montana; South Dakota; Alberta and Saskatchewan

Diet: Plants, including conifer needles, seeds and twigs

Edmontosaurus is the classic duckbilled dinosaur. Often—and wrongly—called *Trachodon*, it is one of the best understood of all dinosaurs, thanks to the discovery of numerous excellent skeletons.

Like most hadrosaurs of this age, *Edmontosaurus* had no crest. And like all other hadrosaurs, it had hundreds of strong teeth that were connected by bony tissue. These batteries formed long grinding surfaces for crushing tough vegetation.

Two mummified specimens of *Edmontosaurus* discovered in Wyoming, (one is now in the American Museum of Natural History in New York), provide a clear

EDMONTOSAURUS *continued*

picture of both the diet and the appearance of *Edmontosaurus*. Its hide was remarkably thin and leathery, and studded with horny bumps, or tubercles, of varying sizes. The tubercles clustered on the throat, neck, and sides were round or oval, and were arranged in definite patterns. Finds show a frill down the spine along the back and tail, a feature that may have been present in all hadrosaurs.

For many years, *Edmontosaurus* was thought to have webbed fingers, a belief based on a mittenlike covering enclosing the hand of the Wyoming mummy. Some paleontologists think the webbed effect occurred during fossilization. Tracks of duckbill feet indicate they were mittenlike in life. The mistaken interpretation of webbed fingers contributed to a long-standing misconception of duckbills as aquatic animals.

In fact, *Edmontosaurus* walked on land, supported by bony tendons in its backbone and thick, pillarlike legs. Its foot, which had three broad, splayed toes, was designed for balance and grip. Powerful ankles supported the animal while it walked.

Edmontosaurus, like other duckbills, varied considerably with age and, apparently, by sex. As a result, many specimens formerly believed to be other kinds of duckbilled dinosaurs are now thought to be different ages and genders of *Edmontosaurus*. For example, *Anatosaurus* was simply a young *Edmontosaurus*, and the two species of *Edmontosaurus*, *regalis* and *annectens*, may represent only different sexes of the same animal. *Edmontosaurus regalis* is the rarer of the two, and has a more robust, higher skull in comparison to its length. Since, for uncertain reasons, female animals are more common among fossils, *Edmontosaurus annectens* may be the female.

ELAPHROSAURUS

(i-LAH-fruh-SAW-rus)

Type Species: *bambergi* (BAM-bur-gye)
Classification:
   Order: Saurischia
   Suborder: Theropoda
   Family: Ornithomimidae
Name: Greek *elaphros* = lightweight + Greek *sauros* = lizard
Size: 5 meters (17 feet) long
Period: Late Jurassic, 155 million years ago
Place: Tanzania, East Africa
Diet: Meat

Elaphrosaurus may have been the earliest member of a family that includes the fastest of all dinosaurs, the ornithomimids. The ornithomimids are best known from the Late Cretaceous Period, 80 million to 65 million years ago, more than 60 million years after the time of *Elaphrosaurus*.

The proportions of *Elaphrosaurus's* limbs resemble those of the ornithomimids, though its shorter pelvic and hindlimb bones, compared to its vertebrae, suggest it was not as fast a runner. Its tail appears to have featured an unusual downward bend.

ELAPHROSAURUS *continued*

Compared to other carnivorous dinosaurs, *Elaphrosaurus* had short forelimbs and long foot and leg bones. Its hands and feet each bore three digits. These are all characteristics of the ornithomimosaurs. However, most conclusions about the identity of *Elaphrosaurus* are guesswork, founded on an incomplete skeleton without a skull, discovered in Tanzania in 1920.

Elaphrosaurus ?gautieri (GOU-ti-rye): Based on vertebrae and fragmentary limb bones from North Africa, this animal was larger than *Elaphrosaurus bambergi*, measuring at least 6 meters (20 feet long). Like *Elaphrosaurus iguidiensis*, it is not well enough known to be conclusively termed a valid species.

Elaphrosaurus iguidiensis (ig-WEE-dee-EN-sis): Named on the basis of teeth and assorted vertebrae and leg bones from southern Tunisia, *Elaphrosaurus iguidiensis* was a Lower Cretaceous animal with a shorter tail vertebrae than *Elaphrosaurus bambergi*.

ELMISAURUS

(EL-mi-SAW-rus)

Type Species: *rarus* (RAYR-us)
Classification:
    Order: Saurischia;
    Suborder: Theropoda
    Family: Elmisauridae
Name: Mongolian *elmyi* = foot + Greek *sauros* = lizard
Size: ?
Period: Late Cretaceous, 80 million to ?70 million
                 years ago
Place: Gobi Desert, Mongolia
Diet: Meat

    This is a rare animal, as its species name suggests. It was named on the basis of its distinctive foot, found in the Gobi Desert of Mongolia in 1970. The bones of the third and fourth toes were completely fused to each other and to the metatarsals, or mid-foot, bones. This "tarsometatarsus" is a birdlike characteristic.

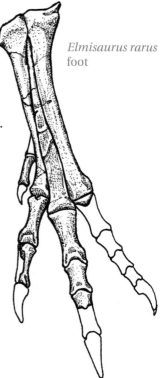

Elmisaurus rarus foot

    The hand of *Elmisaurus* has an upper bone on its first finger that is more than half the length of the second finger. The proportions of its hands indicate a resemblance to *Chirostenotes* ("slender hand"), a dinosaur from the Red Deer River of Alberta known only from fragments of its sharp-clawed hands. The foot of *Elmisaurus* is most like that of *Macrophalangia*, another mysterious animal from the Red Deer River. Like *Macrophalangia*, the slender *Elmisaurus* foot resembles an ornithomimosaur's foot, but has four toes instead of the three toes typical of the ornithomimosaurs. The resemblence of *Elmisaurus* to North American dinosaurs reflects the connection between Asia and North America, and their dinosaurs, in Late Cretaceous times.

ELOSAURUS

(EE-loh-SAW-rus)

Status: Invalid — See Apatosaurus

A young *Apatosaurus,* mistakenly named as new animal in 1902. The name is variously translated as "fish reptile" or "small reptile."

EMAUSAURUS

(EE-mou-SAW-rus)

Type Species: *ernsti* (URN-stye)
Classification:

Order:	Ornithischia
Suborder:	Thyreophora
Family:	Scelidosauridae
Name:	EMAU (Ernst Moritz Arndt Universitat in Germany) + Greek *sauros* = lizard
Size:	About 2 meters (6.6 feet) long
Period:	Early Jurassic, 194 million to 188 million years ago
Place:	Northern Germany
Diet:	Plants

This small dinosaur, identified in 1990, was a primitive example of the early, mostly four-legged, armored plant-eaters. It was named on the basis of an almost complete skull and some associated body bones found in northern Germany.

Emausaurus is distinguished by its relatively small cone- and plate-shaped armor, a broad skull with five teeth on each side of the front of the jaw, and narrow snout.

Emausaurus, Scutellosaurus, and *Scelidosaurus* are all closely related to each other, and to the as-yet-unknown ancestor of the stegosaurs and ankylosaurs.

EMBASAURUS

(EM-buh-SAW-rus)

Type Species: *minax* (MYE-nacks)
Status: Doubtful
Classification:
   Order: Saurischia
   Suborder: Theropoda
   Family: ?
Name: Emba (River in Russia) + Greek *sauros* = lizard
Size: ?
Period: ?Cretaceous, ?145 million to ?65 million years ago
Place: Gruievsk, Siberian Russia
Diet: Meat

    The name *Embasaurus* is in doubt, as the animal is known only from the parts of two vertebrae. The vertebrae have a flat surface, unusual for Early Cretaceous carnivores, which is thought to be a primitive feature.

ENIGMOSAURUS

(i-NIG-muh-SAW-rus)

Type Species: *mongoliensis* (mong-GOH-lee-EN-sis)
Classification:

Order:	Saurischia
Suborder:	Segnosauria
Family:	Segnosauridae

Name: Greek *ainigma* = puzzling + Greek *sauros* = lizard
Size: ? perhaps 6 meters, (20 feet) long
Period: Late Cretaceous, 97 million to 88 million years ago
Place: Mongolia
Diet: ?Plants

Segnosaurs are peculiar animals, and the justly named *Enigmosaurus* is no exception. They measured some 6 meters (20 feet) long, and had small heads and odd jaws. The jaws had no teeth in the front, and short, pointed teeth in the back. Perhaps segnosaurs had a horny beak. Their wide feet and thick legs suggest they were slow-moving, and led some paleontologists to surmise that they ate fish or plants, although they otherwise appear to have been carnivorous dinosaurs.

Enigmosaurus was described on the basis of its pelvis, which is one of the most unusual features of segnosaurs. Though *Enigmosaurus* and other segnosaurs are thought to be lizard-hipped (saurischian) dinosaurs, their hips more closely resemble those of the bird-hipped (ornithischian) dinosaurs.

Segnosaurs were first described in 1979 by the Mongolian paleontologists who named *Enigmosaurus* in 1983. Since only the pelvis is known, this animal may yet prove to be another segnosaur, such as *Erlikosaurus* or *Segnosaurus*.

Enigmosaurus mongoliensis pelvis

EOCERATOPS

(EE-oh-SER-uh-tops)

Type Species: canadensis (KAN-uh-DEN-sis)
Classification:
   Order: Ornithischia
   Suborder: Ceratopsia
   Family: Ceratopsidae
Name: Greek *aeos* = early + Greek *keratos* = horned + Greek *ops* = face
Size: ? 4 meters (13 feet) long
Period: Late Cretaceous, 75 million to 72 million years ago
Place: Alberta
Diet: Plants

    This horned dinosaur had a skull almost one meter (3 feet) long, and a stubby neck frill. Its nose horn curved forward, while its brow horns pointed backwards. It may have been the young or subadult of the ceratopsian, *Chasmosaurus*.

EOLOSAURUS

(ee-OH-luh-SAW-rus)

Status: Invalid — *See Aeolosaurus*

EORAPTOR

(EE-oh-RAP-tur)

Type Species: *lunensis* (loo-NEN-sis)
Classification:

Order:	Saurischia
Suborder:	Theropoda
Family:	?
Name:	Greek *eos* = dawn + Latin *raptor* = plunderer
Size:	1 meter (3 feet) long
Period:	Late Triassic, 228 million years ago
Place:	Argentina
Diet:	Meat

This small predator, named in 1993, may be the most primitive dinosaur yet known. The well-preserved skeleton of *Eoraptor*, lacking only some tail vertebrae, was discovered in 1991 by an American-Argentine expedition to northwestern Argentina. The region is the most productive in the world for finding dinosaurs from the earliest known time of dinosaur life, including the larger carnivore, *Herrerasaurus.*

Eoraptor probably ran on two legs, as its forelimbs are less than half the length of its hind limbs.

Several features of *Eoraptor* reveal its primitive status, including the absence of a hinged lower middle jaw, a feature of other meat-eating dinosaurs. The skull of *Eoraptor* also features a mix of teeth, unique for a dinosaur. While its rear upper teeth are serrated and curved like those of other meat-eating dinosaurs, its front upper teeth are leaf-shaped, more like those of the plant-eating saurischian dinosaurs.

The skeleton of *Eoraptor* has several primitive characteristics, including just three vertebrae supporting its pelvis, the lowest number in any known dinosaur. It also shows the earliest stages of the reduction of fingers in the carnivorous dinosaur's hand, a trend which culminated in the two-fingered hand of *Tyrannosaurus rex* some 163 million years later. On *Eoraptor*, the hand has five fingers, but the fifth digit is greatly reduced in size.

The existence of such a primitive dinosaur as *Eoraptor* at the same time and place as ornithischian dinosaurs such as *Pisanosaurus* and more advanced meat-eaters such as *Herrerasaurus* suggests to scientists that dinosaurs diversified rapidly from a small-sized common ancestor approximately 230 million years ago.

EPACHTOSAURUS

(ee-PACK-tuh-SAW-rus)

Status: Invalid — *See Epachthosaurus*

EPACHTHOSAURUS

(ee-PACK-thuh-SAW-rus)

Type Species: *sciuttoi* (skee-YOO-toy)
Classification:
   Order: Saurischia
   Suborder: Sauropoda
   Family: ?Titanosauridae
Size: ?
Name: Greek *epachthos* = heavy or slow + Greek *sauros* = lizard
Period: Late Cretaceous, ?87.5 million years ago
Place: Argentina
Diet: Plants

    Titanosaurids were huge four-legged plant-eaters, many with armor. They were common in South America throughout the Cretaceous Period. *Epachthosaurus* was named in 1986, but is known only from isolated back vertebrae.

"EPANTERIAS"
(EE-pan-TER-ee-us)

Status: Unofficial — See Allosaurus

This animal may have been the largest, at 15 meters (50 feet) long, of all predatory dinosaurs. It was later identified as an *Allosaurus*, though its name has been informally revived for a large Late Jurassic predator found in the American West.

ERECTOPUS

(i-RECK-tuh-pus)

Type Species: *sauvagei* (SAW-vij-eye)

Classification:

Order:	Saurischia
Suborder:	Theropoda
Family:	Megalosauridae

Name: Latin *erectus* = upright + Greek *pous* = foot

Size: ?

Period: Late Early Cretaceous, 113 million to 97.5 million years ago

Place: France, Egypt, Portugal

Diet: Meat

This moderate-sized theropod was first found in a well in Ardennes, in northern France. Huge teeth, 20 centimeters (more than 8 inches) in diameter at their bases, found in Portugal, may belong to this dinosaur. Leg bones found in Egypt have also been referred to *Erectopus*.

The fingers of *Erectopus*'s hand were quite slender. Its short thumbs sported small claws. The famed German dinosaur scientist Friedrich von Huene, who named *Erectopus*, conjectured that it had a five-fingered hand.

ERLIKOSAURUS

(ur-LICK-uh-SAW-rus)

Type Species: *andrewsi* (AN-droo-zye)
Classification:
  Order: Saurischia
  Suborder: Segnosauria
  Family: Segnosauridae
Name: Mongolian Erlik [Lamaist deity, king of the dead] +
             Greek *sauros* = lizard
Size: ?5 meters (17 feet) long
Period: Late Cretaceous, ?97.5 million to 88.5 million
             years ago
Place: Mongolia
Diet: ?Plants

Erlikosaurus was slightly smaller than *Segnosaurus*, the other well known member of this puzzling group (which also includes *Enigmosaurus*).

Segnosaurs were oddly built animals with long necks and tails, but solid legs and short, four-toed, sharp-clawed feet.

Segnosaurs apppear to have been theropods, but differ from these carnivorous dinosaurs in being largely toothless, unusually stocky, and more bird-hipped (ornithischian) than lizard-hipped (saurischian).

Erlikosaurus, based upon a skull and other bones found in southeastern Mongolia and described in 1980, had a toothless beak with small pointed teeth at the back of the jaw, like *Segnosaurus*. It differed in having more teeth than *Segnosaurus*, and a longer toothless portion of its jaw.

EUCAMEROTUS
(yoo-KAM-uh-ROH-tus)

Status: Doubtful — See Chondrosteosaurus

EUCENTROSAURUS

(yoo-SEN-truh-SAW-rus)

Type Species: *apertus* (uh-PUR-tus)
Classification:
   Order: Ornithischia
   Suborder: Ceratopsia
   Family: Ceratopsidae
   Name: Greek *kentron* = any sharp point + Greek *sauros* = lizard
Size: 5 meters (17 feet) long
Period: Late Cretaceous, 76 million to 72 million years ago
Place: Alberta; ?Montana
Diet: Plants

One of the best known of all horned dinosaurs, *Eucentrosaurus* was characterized by an elaborate frill or crest, featuring a thick border, a pair of hooklike bony processes that project backward, and a pair of horns that projected forward over the openings in the frill. The major part of the crest was relatively broad, the border regularly scalloped, and the outer margin edged with sharp pieces of bone.

This heavily decorated dinosaur had two very small horns above the eyes and one large horn over the snout. This nasal horn, sometimes as long as 47 centimeters (18 inches), varied in curvature between individuals. Sometimes it pointed backward, other times straight up, occasionally even forward.

Eucentrosaurus has been recovered in large numbers from bonebeds in Dinosaur Provincial Park in Alberta, Canada. At one quarry, a herd of *Eucentrosaurus* appears to have died all at the same time, perhaps drowning

while attempting to cross a river in a flood. The animals, crowding together, panicked, and trampled one another before drowning. Their carcasses washed downstream and were scavenged by small carnivorous dinosaurs, whose teeth are also found at the site.

Excellent preservation tells us a great deal about the appearance of this animal. In its general dimensions, *Eucentrosaurus* was smaller and less stoutly constructed than the more famous horned dinosaur, *Triceratops*. Fossil impressions reveal that the skin consisted of small bumps of various sizes. The small bumps were five- or six-sided and set close together. The large ones were round and arranged in rows over the bottom surface of the body.

Eucentrosaurus was renamed from *Centrosaurus*, since scientists found out in 1989 that an obscure lizard already bore the name *Centrosaurus*. It may be identical to the better known genus *Monoclonius*, though that association has not been positively established. However, all the species that were once attributed to *Centrosaurus* and *Monoclonius dawsoni* are now thought to represent individuals that, while they may differ in sex and age, are nevertheless all members of the type species *Eucentrosaurus apertus*.

EUCERCOSAURUS
(yoo-SER-koh-SAW-rus)

Type Species: *tanyspondylus* (TAN-ee-SPON-di-lus)
Status: Doubtful — *See Anoplosaurus*

EUCNEMESAURUS
(yoo-NEE-muh-SAW-rus)

Type Species: *fortis* (FOR-tis)
Status: Doubtful — *See Euskelosaurus*

EUHELOPUS

(YOO-hel-OH-pus)

Type Species: *zdanskyi*
(zuh-DAN-
skee-eye)

Classification:
  Order: Saurischia
  Suborder: Sauropoda
  Family: Camarasauridae
Name: Greek *eu* = good +
Greek *helos* = marsh +
Greek *pous* = foot
Size: About 10 meters (34 feet)
long
Period: Late Jurassic, ?156 million to 150
million years ago
Place: Shandong, China
Diet: Plants

Euhelopus was an extremely long-necked sauropod. Its neck may
have been 5 meters (16 feet) in length. On the other end of its bulky
torso was a long tail.

Euhelopus had spoon-shaped teeth and a small skull like
Camarasaurus, another sauropod, but *Euhelopus's* skull was more
delicately proportioned. Its front legs were almost exactly as long as
its hind legs, giving it longer forelimbs in comparison to its hind
limbs, than any other sauropod
except *Brachiosaurus*.

In size and other respects, *Euhelopus*
more nearly resembled *Omeisaurus*, a Chinese sauropod of the
cetiosaurid family.

EUOPLOCEPHALUS

(YOO-oh-pluh-SEF-uh-lus)

(=Anodontosaurus, Dyoplosaurus, Scolosaurus, Stereocephalus)

Type Species: *tutus* (TOO-tooz)
Classification:
    Order: Ornithischia
    Suborder: Ankylosauria
    Family: Ankylosauridae
Name: Greek *euoplo* = well-protected + Greek *kephale* = head
Size: 5 meters (almost 17 feet); about 1.70 meters (5.8 feet) wide.
Period: Late Cretaceous, 76 million to 70 million years ago
Place: Alberta
Diet: Soft vegetation

Euoplocephalus is the best known of all the armored dinosaurs. The extensive fossil finds of this dinosaur reveal an animal armored from head to tail. Its entire back and sides were covered with bony plates. These plates were smaller at the midsection and back of the animal, and larger on its front and on the sides. Most plates were five- or six-sided, their surfaces marked by raised and irregular criss-cross markings.

EUPLOCEPHALUS *continued*

Euoplocephalus also provided the first evidence of the ankylosaurs' distinctive clubbed tails. *Euoplocephalus's* tail was comprised of ten fused vertebrae, which were strengthened on both sides by additional prongs of bone. The tail club was made of four fused, bony growths.

Euoplocephalus was built low to the ground, like a tank, with massive, short leg bones.

From various specimens referred to *Euoplocephalus*, Denver Museum of Natural History researcher Kenneth Carpenter prepared the first accurate composite-skeletal reconstruction and life restoration ever done for any ankylosaur. Carpenter restored *Euoplocephalus* with its limbs in an upright posture (not splayed out as in earlier depictions), and its tail off the ground. Bands of large, variously shaped plates ran across the body in the back and tail regions. Two bands of armor plates crossed the neck, the first consisting of large, slightly ridged plates, the second of large, blunt spikes. Four bands studded with rows of large, low, keeled plates adorned *Euoplocephalus's* back. Its hips were protected by bands covered with disc-shaped studs. Plates of various sizes were probably present on the forelimbs, shoulders, and thighs.

The function of the tail club is uncertain. Some scientists suggest that it may have been a weapon; others think that the tail was too narrow and stiff for easy movement.

As *Euoplocephalus* skeletons are found in isolation, paleontologists have conjectured that the animals may have been solitary, or that they lived in small groups.

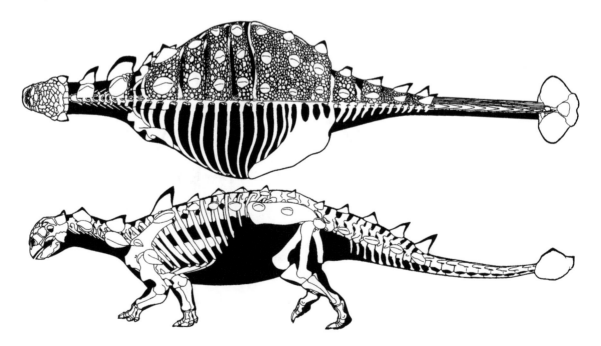

EURONYCHODON

(YOO-roh-NYE-kuh-don)

Type Species: *portucalensis* (POR-choo-kuh-LEN-sis)
Classification:
   Order: Saurischia
   Suborder: Theropoda
   Family: ?Dromaeosauridae
Name: (European form of *Paronychodon*)
Size: ?
Period: Late Cretaceous, 75 million to 65 miillion
                years ago
Place: Portugal
Diet: Meat

   Euronychodon may have been a small predator. Its unserrated teeth suggest it was related to the North American dromaeosaur, *Paronychodon*, a 2-meter-long (6.6 feet) predator.

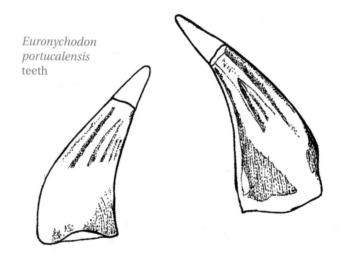

*Euronychodon
portucalensis*
teeth

EUSKELOSAURUS

(yoo-SKEL-uh-SAW-rus)

Type Species: *browni* (BROWN-eye)

Classification:

Order:	Saurischia
Suborder:	Prosauropoda
Family:	Plateosauridae
Name:	Greek *eu* = good + Greek *skelos* = leg + Greek *sauros* = lizard
Size:	9 meters (30 feet) long
Period:	Late Triassic, 220 million to 215 million years ago
Place:	South Africa, Zimbabwe
Diet:	Plants

This four-legged browser was one of the earliest plant-eating dinosaurs. It had a long neck and tail, and a bulky body. Like other Late Triassic prosauropods, such as the more delicately built *Plateosaurus, Euskelosaurus* appears to have been able to walk either on all fours, or on just its hind legs. It also appears to have been relatively plentiful, as its bones (and possible footprints) had been excavated from several localities in southern Africa.

Euskelosaurus africanus (af-ri-KAN-us): This species was found in the Transkei of South Africa and is considered smaller than *Euskelosaurus browni.*

Euskelosaurus capensis (kuh-PEN-sis): Doubtful name.

Euskelosaurus fortis (FOR-tis): Based on a weathered specimen found in South Africa, *Euskelosaurus fortis* is slightly different from *Euskelosaurus browni* in the pubic bone and femur.

Euskelosaurus molengraaffi (MOH-len-GRAF-eye): Doubtful name.

EUSTREPTOSPONDYLUS

(yoo-STREP-toh-spon-DIL-us)

(=Streptospondylus)

Type Species: oxoniensis (ok-soh-nee-EN-sis
Classification:

    Order: Saurischia

    Suborder: Theropoda

    Family: Eustreptospondylidae

Name: Greek *eu* = well + Greek *streptos* = reversed +
                 Greek *spondylos* = vertebrae

Size: 5 to 6 meters (16.5 to 20 feet) long

Period: Middle Jurassic, 165 million years ago

Place: England

Diet: Meat

    Remains of this dinosaur were among the first to be named in 1841 by Sir Richard Owen, the year before he published the term dinosaur for the first time. It resembles the first dinosaur, named *Meglosaurus bucklandi*, though it is slightly smaller and more slender. *Eustreptospondylus* was related to the Later Jurassic carnivore *Allosaurus*, but just where *Eustreptospondylus* fits into the ancestry of the carnosaurs is still uncertain.

    The skeleton of this carnivore at the University Museum in Oxford shows an apparently immature animal, lightly built and less than 6 meters (20 feet) in length. *Eustreptospondylus* may have grown to as much as 7 meters (23 feet) long.

FABROSAURUS

(FAB-ruh-SAW-rus)

Type Species: *australis* (aw-STRAY-lis)

Status: Doubtful

Classification:

   Order: Ornithischia

   Suborder: ?

   Family: ?

Name: *Fabré* (after French geologist Jean Fabré) +
               Greek *sauros* = lizard

Size: ?1 meter (3 feet) long

Period: Early Jurassic, 208 million to 194 million years ago

Place: Lesotho, Africa

Diet: Plants

Fabrosaurus was a primitive member of the ornithischians, small plant-eating dinosaurs, bearing cheek teeth, and perhaps horn-covered beaks. This animal is known only from the back portion of a right lower jaw, which contains three teeth and has sockets for nine more. The teeth are tiny, only 3.3 to 3.5 millimeters (less than a tenth of an inch) long, with narrow crowns and long vertical roots.

Fabrosaurus was first thought to belong to the *Scelidosauridae* family of early armored dinosaurs. It was also considered at one time to be identical to the better known *Lesothosaurus*. More recent studies of the original *Fabrosaurus's* remains indicate only that they are too sketchy to associate with any known dinosaur.

Fabrosaurus australis
lower jaw

FENESTROSAURUS
(fuh-NES-truh-SAW-rus)

STATUS: Invalid — *See Oviraptor*

FRENGUELLISAURUS

(fren-GWEL-uh-SAW-rus)

Type Species: *ischigualastensis* (ISH-ee-gwuh-las-TEN-sis)
Classification:

Order:	Saurischia
Suborder:	?Theropoda
Family:	?

Name: (Joaqun) Frenguelli + Greek *sauros* = lizard
Size: ?Small
Period: Late Triassic, 231 million to 225 million years ago
Place: Argentina
Diet: Meat

This early dinosaur is not well known. A medium-sized meat-eater, it had three hefty canine teeth in its upper jaw, and short teeth in its lower jaw. *Frenguellisaurus* may be closely related to the carnivorous dinosaur *Staurikosaurus*, discovered in Brazil, or to *Herrerasaurus*, a better known early carnivore from the same area in northwestern Argentina.

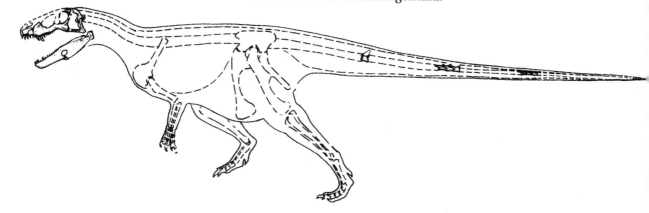

GALLIMIMUS

(GAL-i-MYE-mus)

Type Species: *bullatus* (boo-LAY-tus)
Classification:
  Order: Saurischia
  Suborder: Ornithomimosauria
  Family: Ornithomimidae
Name: Latin *gallus* = chicken + Greek *mimos* = mimic
Size: 5 meters (17 feet) long
Period: Late Cretaceous, 75 million to 70 million years ago
Place: Gobi Desert, Mongolia
Diet: Small vertebrates and insects

The largest of the swift, long-legged ostrich dinosaurs, the ornithomimids, *Gallimimus* is the only one for which a good skull has been found. So it provides the best insight into the appearance of these distinctive dinosaurs.

It had a very long snout, which was shaped like a goose's bill—flattened at the tip from top to bottom. The front part of the lower jaw was shovel-like. Its eyes were positioned on the sides of the head, so the animal may not have had good depth perception. There is no evidence to suggest it was a herding animal, as depicted in *Jurassic Park*.

Gallimimus had a long, mobile neck. Its upper arms were relatively weak; its fingers had little strength for grasping, suggesting that they may have been used for raking the ground, searching for small, live prey, such as mammals and insects. Though *Gallimimus* was the largest of ornithomimids, its hand was the smallest, measuring only one-quarter the length of its forelimb.

With its long legs and light body, *Gallimimus* was probably one of the fastest of all dinosaurs. Ornithomimid-like tracks from Texas suggest this family of dinosaurs was capable of speeds in excess of 25 mph, and some have speculated that they may have achieved more than 50 mph, even faster than the top speed of modern ostriches.

Gallimimus was discovered in the Gobi Desert in the early 1970s.

GARUDIMIMUS

(guh-ROO-di-MYE-mus)

Type Species: *brevipes* (BREV-i-pes)
Classification:
   Order: Saurischia
   Suborder: Ornithomimosauria
   Family: Garudimimidae
Name: Garuda (in Hindu mythology, a heavenly bird, part
                 eagle and part man, symbolic of strength and
                 speed) + Greek *mimos* = mimic
Size: 3.6 meters (12 feet) or more
Period: Late Cretaceous, 97. 5 million to 88.5 million
                 years ago)
Place: Mongolia
Diet: Meat and/or insects

   Garudimimus was a large, primitive ostrich dinosaur. It had shorter toes than
other ornithomimids, and four toes instead of the usual three. It also had unusual
little backward-pointing horns above its eyes. Found in southeastern Mongolia
and named in 1981, it comes from sediments several million years older than that
of *Gallimimus* and other better known ostrich dinosaurs from Mongolia and
western North America.

GASOSAURUS

(GAS-uh-SAW-rus)

Type Species: *constructus* (kun-STRUCK-tus)
Classification:

Order:	Saurischia
Suborder:	Theropoda
Family:	?

Name: gas (company) + Greek *sauros* = lizard
Size: Approximately 3.5 meters (12 feet) long
Period: Middle Jurassic, 175 million to 163 million
              years ago
Place: China
Diet: Meat

Gasosaurus was found in the early 1980s in one of the world's great dinosaur graveyards, the Dashanpu quarry in Sichuan, central China. Though many Dashanpu dinosaurs were found intact and with skulls, *Gasosaurus* is known only from an incomplete skeleton.

Gasosaurus may belong to the carnosaurs, a group of large carnivores that includes a variety of animals from megalosaurs to tyrannosaurs. If it was a carnosaur, *Gasosaurus* was one of the smallest.

Gasosaurus constructus was named by Chinese dinosaur paleontologist Dong Zhiming for the natural gas facility whose construction workers discovered the Dashanpu dinosaurs.

GENYODECTES

(JEN-ee-oh-DECK-teez)

Type Species: serus (SEER-us)
Classification:
   Order: Saurischia
   Suborder: ?Theropoda
   Family: ?
Name: Greek genyos = jaw + Greek dektes = biting
Size: ?
Period: ?Late Cretaceous
Place: Argentina
Diet: Meat

This carnivore, named in 1901, is known only from brittle pieces of a skull found in southeastern Argentina. The teeth in the lower jaw are small. Some features of the skull show similarities to *Carnotaurus,* a large carnivore of the same region that had unusually short arms.

GERANOSAURUS

(juh-RAN-uh-SAW-rus)

Type Species: *atavus* (AT-uh-vus)

Status: Doubtful

Classification:

Order: Ornithischia

Suborder: Genasauria

Family: Heterodontosauridae

Name: Greek *gerabodes* = cranelike + Greek *sauros* = lizard

Size: ?

Period: Early Jurassic, 208 million to 194 million years ago

Place: South Africa

Diet: Plants

This small, long-legged plant-eater probably resembled other, better known heterodontosaurs. We do know that *Geranosaurus* had a horny beak. Its lower jaw was small, only 60 millimeters (2.5 inches) long.

The most distinctive feature of *Geranosaurus* was its teeth. The front teeth of this dinosaur were larger than the rest—five millimeters in diameter, as opposed to three or four millimeters for the back teeth. Both upper and lower jaws had canine-type fangs.

GIGANTOSAURUS

(jye-GAN-tuh-SAW-rus)

Type Species: *megalonyx* (MEG-uh-LON-icks)
Status: Doubtful
Classification:
  Order: Saurischia
  Suborder: Sauropoda
  Family: ?Brachiosauridae
Name: Greek *gigas* = giant + Greek *sauros* = lizard
Period: Late Jurassic, 156 million to 150 million years ago
Size: Large
Place: England
Diet: Plants

From its name and its bones, this dinosaur was clearly imagined as huge. Its fibula, the larger of the two bones of the lower part of the hind limb, measured 70 centimeters (27 inches) long.

Gigantosaurus was one of the first of the giant browsing dinosaurs (sauropods) to be named. Its name, given it by the British paleontologist Harry G. Seeley in 1869, is based on just a few bones, most of them limbs, found in Cambridgeshire, England.

Gigantosaurus may be the same animal as *Pelorosaurus, Brachiosaurus,* or *Ischyrosaurus.* Unfortunately, too little is known of this dinosaur to determine its identity.

To add to the confusion, this animal once bore the same name as a very different, large browser, a titanosaurid now known as *Torneria.*

GIGANTOSCELUS

(jye-GAN-tuh-SKEE-lus)

Status: Doubtful — *See Euskelosaurus*

GILMOREOSAURUS

(gil-MOR-uh-SAW-rus)

Type Species: *mongoliensis* (mong-GOH-lee-EN-sis)
Classification:

Order:	Ornithischia
Suborder:	Ornithopoda
Family:	Hadrosauridae
Name:	(Charles Whitney) Gilmore + Greek *sauros* = lizard
Size:	?
Period:	Late Cretaceous, ?85 million to ?80 million years ago
Place:	Mongolia
Diet:	Plants

    Gilmoreosaurus seems to have been an evolutionary link between two groups of large dinosaurian plant-eaters, the iguanodontids and the later hadrosaurids, or duckbills.

    Several features distinguish *Gilmoreosaurus* as one of the most primitive of all known hadrosaurines; only *Telmatosaurus* from Romania may be more primitive. Most noticeable of these features are the ends of its toes, which are more clawlike, or similar to those found in iguanodontids, than hooflike, or similar to the hadrosaurids.

    Gilmoreosaurus was more lightly built than its hadrosaurine contemporaries, but its limbs were more robust than those of later duckbills. This build suggests *Gilmoreosaurus* may have been agile when running on its hind legs. It also had large muscle attachments to its hind legs, indicating that it could have accelerated to a relatively rapid run.

    Gilmoreosaurus was found in 1923 in the Gobi Desert of Inner Mongolia by an American Museum of Natural History expedition. A second primitive hadrosaur, *Bactrosaurus*, comes from the same region.

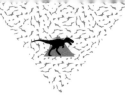

GONGBUSAURUS

(GONG-buh-SAW-rus)

Type Species: shiyii (SHEE-yeye)
Status: Doubtful
Classification:
  Order: Ornithischia
  Suborder: Ornithopoda
  Family: ?
Name: (Yu) Gong (of the Zigong Dinosaur Museum) + Greek sauros = lizard
Size: 1 to 1.5 meters (4 to over 5 feet) long
Period: Late Jurassic, 175 million to 145 million years ago
Place: China
Diet: Plants

This small, primitive plant-eater found in Sichuan, central China, was named on the basis of just two teeth, one from the cheek, the other from the front of the jaw. Its second species, *Gongbusaurus wucaiwanensis*, from northwestern China, is better known.

Gongbusaurus wucaiwanensis (WOO-kye-wah-NEN-sis): An incomplete skeleton indicates this plant-eater grew to 1.5 meters (five feet) in length, with larger and thicker cheek teeth than that of the type species *G. shiyii*. Its long hind limb and narrow foot suggest it was a swift runner.

Gongbusaurus shiyii tooth

GORGOSAURUS

(GOR-guh-SAW-rus)

Type Species: libratus (lye-BRAT-us)
Status: Invalid — See Albertosaurus
Name: Greek gorgos = terrible + Greek sauros = lizard

GOYOCEPHALE

(GOY-uh-SEF-uh-lee)

Type Species: *lattimorei* (LAT-i-MOR-eye)

Classification:

    Order: Ornithischia

    Suborder: Pachycephalosauria

    Family: Homalocephalidae

Name: Mongolian *goyo* = decorated; elegant + Greek *kephale* = head

Size: ?3 meters (10 feet) long

Period: Late Cretaceous, 85 million to 80 million years ago

Place: Mongolia

Diet: Plants

    Goyocephale appears to be the oldest of the "flat-headed" (homalocephalid) group of thick-skulled dinosaurs, the pachycephalosaurs. It is one of the few bone-headed dinosaurs for which parts of the skeleton are known, aside from the thick skull. It is widely believed that all the bone-heads used their thick domes as protection when butting heads in mating and dominance displays.

    Goyocephale is nearly the same size as the less-primitive pachycephalosaur, *Homalocephale*. However, *Goyocephale* had a rough, pitted skull roof, while *Homolocephale's* was smooth and flat. Both *Goyocephale's* upper and lower jaws were fitted with large teeth, which were most likely used for stabbing plant matter.

GRAVITHOLUS

(GRAH-vi-THOH-lus)

Type Species: *albertae* (al-BUR-tye)
Classification:

    Order: Ornithischia
    Suborder: Pachycephalosauria
    Family: Pachycephalosauridae

Name: Latin *gravis* = heavy + Latin *tholus* = dome

Size: ?

Period: Late Cretaceous, 75 million years ago

Place: Alberta

Diet: Plants

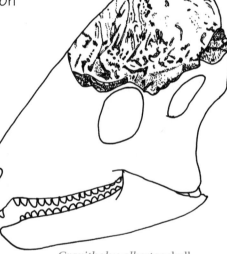

   Gravitholus was a pachycephalosaur, a bone-headed dinosaur distinguished by its particularly large, wide skull. There are no ornamental bumps or nodes on its skull, as there are on some bone-heads. The unique width of *Gravitholus's* skull may be a distortion caused by disease or injury, or by pressure upon the fossil that occurred after the animal died. Since all that is known of this animal is the dome of a skull, its actual appearance remains a mystery.

Gravitholus albertae skull

GRESSLYOSAURUS

(GRES-lee-uh-SAW-rus)

Status: Doubtful — *See Plateosaurus*

GRYPONYX

(grye-PON-icks)

Status: Invalid — *See Massospondylus*

GRYPOSAURUS

(GRYE-puh-SAW-rus)

Type Species: *notabilis* (NOH-tuh-BIL-us)

Classification:

Order:	Ornithischia
Suborder:	Ornithopoda
Family:	Hadrosauridae
Name:	Latin *gryphus* = griffin + Greek *sauros* = lizard
Size:	8 meters (25 feet) long
Period:	Late Cretaceous, 76 million to 72 million years ago
Place:	Alberta
Diet:	Plants

   This duckbilled dinosaur had a large, narrow, deep skull with highly arched nostrils. Its most distinctive feature was its hump of nasal bone. In life, this bony bump was probably covered with skin. It may have been used as a club, and flushed with color or otherwise distinguished during courtship or dominance battles with its own kind.

   Gryposaurus is one of the few dinosaurs for which fossilized skin impressions have been found, giving us a better idea of how this dinosaur looked in life. These skin prints show smooth, polygonal scales less than a half-centimeter (a quarter of an inch) in diameter on the neck, sides, and abdomen. It also appears to have had cone-shaped plates on its tail, about 1.3 centimeters (half an inch) in diameter and spaced 5.2 to 6.8 centimeters (2 to 3 inches) apart.

   For almost half a century, *Gryposaurus* was regarded as being the same animal as the *Kritosaurus* found at the San Juan Basin of New Mexico. They have now been distinguished by their tooth structure as different species, though not all researchers agree with that distinction.

GYPOSAURUS

(JIP-uh-SAW-rus)

Status: Invalid — See *Anchisaurus, Massospondylus*

HADROSAURUS

(HAD-ruh-SAW-rus)

Type Species: *foulkii* (FOH-kye)
Classification:
  Order: Ornithischia
  Suborder: Ornithopoda
  Family: Hadrosauridae
Name: Greek *hadros* = sturdy + Greek *sauros* = lizard
Size: 7 meters (25 feet) long
Period: Late Cretaceous, 76 million to 73 million years ago
Place: Haddonfield, New Jersey
Diet: Plants

Hadrosaurus is a historic, though average-sized hadrosaur, or duckbill. It belongs to the hadrosaurine subfamily of duckbills, those with flat heads. It is not known what type of skull it had, since none was found; it may in fact be a *Kritosaurus*, an animal whose skeleton is nearly identical to *Hadrosaurus's*.

Hadrosaurus was the fifth dinosaur named in North America, and the first dinosaur in the world known from a nearly complete skeleton. In 1858, large bones were excavated from a marl pit on a farm in Haddonfield, New Jersey. The remains were taken to the Philadelphia Academy of Natural Sciences. Scientist Joseph Leidy noted several similarities in the teeth to those of *Iguanodon*, and assumed, correctly, that they were closely related.

At the time, however, *Iguanodon* was incorrectly believed to be a rhinoceros-like animal that ran on all fours. With better skeletal material, Leidy formulated a more accurate reconstruction of a dinosaur.

Leidy believed that *Hadrosaurus* was a mostly amphibious animal that spent some time browsing on land, maintaining a kangaroo-like posture, resting on its hind legs and tail. Leidy's image of *Hadrosaurus*, while inaccurate, pioneered the modern view of most dinosaurs as animals that move on two legs with an upright posture.

HALTICOSAURUS

(HAWL-ti-koh-SAW-rus)

Type Species: *longotarsus* (LONG-uh-TAHR-sis)

Classification:

Order: Saurischia

Suborder: ?Theropoda

Family: ?

Name: Greek *haltikos* = leaping + Greek *sauros* = lizard

Size: About 5.4 meters (18 feet) long

Period: Late Triassic, 222 million years ago

Place: Germany

Diet: Meat

Halticosaurus was an early, lightly built carnivore with a large head and a four- or five-toed foot. Its unusually long, slender foot bones suggest that it was a theropod, perhaps related to *Rioarribasaurus*, a contemporary small carnivore found in Arizona. However, some features of *Halticosaurus's* hip, leg, and vertebral bones indicate it may have been a small plant-eating prosauropod dinosaur. Since it is based on a fragmentary skeleton found almost a century ago (1906), we may never determine *Halticosaurus's* true identity.

Halticosaurus orvitoangulatus skull

HAPLOCANTHOSAURUS

(HAP-loh-KAN-thu-SAW-rus)

Type Species: *priscus* (PRIS-kus)
Classification:
  Order: Saurischia
  Suborder: Sauropoda
  Family: Cetiosauridae
Name: Greek *hoplos* = single + Greek *akantha* = spine +
                 Greek *sauros* = lizard. (*Haplocanthus* was the original
                 name given to this dinosaur by Hatcher, but it was discov-
                 ered to have been previously used to describe a fossil fish.)
Size: Almost 21 meters (70 feet) long
Period: Late Jurassic, 156 milllion to 145 million years ago
Place: Colorado
Diet: Plants

 Haplocanthosaurus is the most primitive sauropod, or giant, four-legged, browsing dinosaur, yet discovered in North America. This animal, the size of two school buses, had solid, single-spined vertebrae, and a short neck and tail. Though *Haplocanthosaurus* has been known for nearly a century, its enormous dimensions were only more recently established.

 Two well-preserved specimens of *Haplocanthosaurus* were discovered in 1901 near Cañon City, Colorado. John Bell Hatcher described the larger of the two. He recognized its primitive nature, including the simple spines on its vertebrae, which did not branch as they did in other North American sauropods. Another, less complete skeleton was found in 1954 in the same area by the Cleveland Museum of Natural History. This animal was from 35 to 50 percent larger than the type species, *Haplocanthosaurus priscus*, but it was not until 1988 that the Cleveland specimen was determined to be a distinct species, and named *Haplocanthosaurus delfsi*.

HARPYMIMUS

(HAHR-pee-MYE-mus)

Type Species: *okladnikovi* (oh-KLAD-ni-KOH-vye)

Classification:

Order:	Saurischia
Suborder:	Theropoda
Family:	Harpymimidae
Name:	Greek *harpya* (mythical bird) + Greek *mimos* = mimic
Size:	3.6 meters (12 feet) long
Period:	Late Early Cretaceous, 119 million to 97.5 million years ago
Place:	Mongolia
Diet:	?Meat, ?Insects, ?Plants

Harpymimus was the earliest and most primitive known "ostrich-mimic," or ornithomimosaurian, dinosaur. Relatives of these large, long-legged dinosaurs have been found in both Mongolia and western North America. Ornithomimosaurs had delicate hands with three long fingers, and their long-shinned, slender legs probably enabled them to run faster than any other dinosaurs. Ornithomimosaurs also had many features resembling those of the large ground birds of today, including beaks and largely toothless jaws.

Harpymimus, however, was an ornithomimosaur with six small, blunt teeth in the front of its jaws. It also had foot bones of uneven length, like toothed theropods and unlike the later ornithomimids. Thus, it appears to be an important transitional animal between the toothy carnivores which preceded it, and the toothless ornithomimids that followed. Because of its teeth, *Harpymimus* has been placed in its own family, distinct from later ornithomimids.

What it ate with those teeth and slim hands is uncertain. Using its speed, it may have trapped and eaten insects and small mammals. It also may have eaten plants and fruits.

210

HECATASAURUS
(HECK-uh-tuh-SAW-rus)

Status: Invalid — *See Telmatosaurus*

HEISHANSAURUS

(HAY-shan-SAW-rus)

Type Species: *pachycephalus* (PACK-i-SEF-uh-lus)
Status: Doubtful
Classification:
  Order: Ornithischia
  Suborder: Ankylosauria
  Family: Ankylosauridae
Name: Chinese Heishan + Greek sauros = lizard
Size: ?
Period: Late Cretaceous, 97.5 million to 65 million
             years ago
Place: China
Diet: Plants

    This animal was an armored dinosaur of some kind, but since its only remains were badly crushed bones that have now disappeared, *Heishansaurus* may never be identified. Its most revealing fossils were flat, thick armor plates, 10 centimeters (4 inches) in diameter, and circular, elongated, or tetragon-shaped. Small bony surface bumps the size of peas were also found, but where they were placed on the animal is unknown. Its partial skull showed teeth resembling those of *Pinacosaurus*, a Mongolian armored dinosaur. *Heishansaurus* was once (wrongly) thought to be related to the thick-headed pachycephalosaurs, hence its species name.

HELOPUS

(HEL-uh-pus)

Status: Invalid — *See Euhelopus*

HEPTASTEORNIS

(hep-TAS-tee-OR-nis)

Type Species: *andrewsi* (AN-droo-zye)
Classification:
    Order: Saurischia
    Suborder: Theropoda
    Family: ?Troodontidae
Name: Greek *hepta* = seven (towns, in reference to
               Siebenburgen, the German name for Transylvania)
               + Greek *asty* = town + Greek *ornis* = bird
Size: Small
Period: Late Cretaceous, ?73 million to 65 million
               years ago
Place: Transylvania, Romania
Diet: Meat

This was almost certainly a small theropod, though it is known only from parts of leg bones. It may be related to *Troodon* or to the dromaeosaurs, but it is definitely not a bird.

This dinosaur has a bird's name because Charles W. Andrews, the scientist who named it (he called it *Elopteryx*) in 1913, thought it was a large bird. Two other scientists, considering it a very large owl, renamed it *Heptasteornis* in 1975.

HERRERASAURUS

(huh-RAYR-uh-SAW-rus)

Type Species: *ischigualestensis* (ISH-ee-gwuh-las-TEN-sis)
Classification:
    Order: Saurischia
    Suborder: Theropoda
    Family: Herrerasauridae
Name: (Victorino) Herrera + Greek *sauros* = lizard
Size: About 5 meters (17 feet) long
Period: Late Triassic, 228 million years ago
Place: Argentina
Diet: Meat

    Herrerasaurus, a large-jawed carnivore, was one of the earliest dinosaurs. Agile and fleet-footed, it weighed about 180 kilograms (400 pounds). Its jaws were double-hinged, allowing it to grip and swallow large hunks of meat, and its 6-centimeter-long (2 inches) serrated teeth were very sharp. *Herrerasaurus* had tiny ear bones, suggesting a keen sense of hearing, and long claws. All of these characteristics may have made it an adept hunter of small mammals and dinosaurs.

    This animal was clearly related to other carnivorous dinosaurs, including *Tyrannosaurus rex*, which lived 160 million years later. However, *Herrerasaurus* had many primitive features, such as long first and fifth toes.

    Herrerasaurus was first collected in 1959 in the Ischigualasto Valley in northwestern Argentina. But, the first complete skull, an unusual and well-preserved specimen, was not found until 1988. It was unearthed by University of Chicago paleontologist Paul Sereno in the same area.

HETERODONTOSAURUS

(HET-ur-uh-DON-tuh-SAW-rus)

Type Species: *tucki* (TUCK-eye)

Classification:

Order:	Ornithischia
Suborder:	Ornithopoda
Family:	Heterodontosauridae

Name: Greek *hetero* = different + Greek *odontos* = tooth + Greek *sauros* = lizard

Size: 1 meter (3.3 feet) long

Period: Early Jurassic, 208 million to 200 million years ago

Place: South Africa

Diet: Plants

Heterodontosaurus was a small, primitive dinosaur capable of moving either on all fours or on just its hind legs. It had large eyes above a short face, and the unusual assortment of teeth that inspired its name. It had three stabbing teeth in the front of its mouth (the third of which was especially large and shaped like a canine tooth), twelve closely set teeth in the upper jaw, grinding molars in the back of its jaw, several ridged teeth, and an upward-pointing canine tooth in each cheek.

Its slender hind legs were well-suited to fast two-legged running. It probably used its long tail as a balance during sprints. When *Heterodontosaurus* was foraging on all fours, it may have adopted a semi-sprawling posture, using its powerful front limbs and large claws to tear up roots or insect nests.

Heterodontosaurus was probably a plant-eater. Its hands, with their long, slender fingers and well-developed claws, may have been used for grasping, tearing, or digging. It may have eaten by using its upper-jaw teeth and lower-jaw beak to nip off leaves. The tall, closely packed cheek teeth probably worked like scissors, cutting up the food and holding it in fleshy cheek pouches. The large canine tusks may have been used as weapons of defense or in social displays. Perhaps only the males had tusks.

HETEROSAURUS

(HET-ur-uh-SAW-rus)

Status: Doubtful — *See Iguanodon*

HIEROSAURUS

(HYE-ur-uh-SAW-rus)

Status: Doubtful — *See Nodosaurus*

HIKANODON

(hye-KAN-uh-don)

Status: Invalid — *See Iguanodon*

"HIRONOSAURUS"

(hye-RON-uh-SAW-rus)

Status: Unofficial
Classification:
   Order: Ornithischia
   Suborder: Ornithopoda
   Family: ?Hadrosauridae
Name: Japanese *Hirono-machi* + Greek *sauros* = lizard
Period: Late Cretaceous, 97.5 million to 65 million
               years ago
Size: Large
Place: Japan
Diet: Plants

This large duckbill is provisionally identified from only fragmentary remains.

"HISANOHAMASAURUS"

(hi-ZAN-uh-HAM-uh-SAW-rus)

Status: Unofficial
Classification:
   Order: Saurischia
   Suborder: Sauropoda
   Family: ?Diplodocidae
Name: Japanese Hisano-hama + Greek sauros = lizard
Period: Late Cretaceous, ?97.5 million to ?65 million years ago
Size: ?
Place: Japan
Diet: Plants

    This animal, an unofficially named large browsing dinosaur, is known only from the pencil-shaped teeth that characteristic of some sauropods.

HOMALOCEPHALE

(HOH-muh-loh-SEF-uh-lee)

Type Species: calathocercos (KAL-uh-THOS-ur-kohs)
Classification:
  Order: Ornithischia
  Suborder: Pachycephalosauria
  Family: Homalocephalidae
Name: Greek homalos = level + Greek kephale = head
Size: ?1.5 meters (5 feet) long
Period: Late Cretaceous, 80 million to 70 million
              years ago
Size: ?
Place: Mongolia
Diet: Plants

Homalocephale was a small, thick-headed pachycephalosaur, and the best known of that entire group. Pachycephalosaurs were small to medium-sized, with short faces and thickened skulls. They had little leaflike teeth, and bony ornaments on their snouts and backs.

The skull of Homalocephale was 138 millimeters (5.5 inches) at its widest, and 118 millimeters (4.5 inches) at its tallest. It had large, deep pits on the roof of its head, and knobs along the edges of the skull. Unlike some pachycephalosaurs, its thick skull was more flat than domed, causing researchers to speculate that pachycephalosaurs butted skulls the way bighorn sheep do, in displays and combat with their own kind.

HOPLITOSAURUS

(huh-PLEE-tuh-SAW-rus)

Type Species: *marshi* (MAHR-shye)
Status: Doubtful
Classification:
  Order: Ornithischia
  Suborder: Ankylosauria
  Family: Nodosauridae
Name: Greek *hoplites* = armed + Greek *sauros* = lizard
Size: 1.2 meters (4 feet) tall at hips
Period: Early Cretaceous, 135 million to 119 million years ago
Place: South Dakota
Diet: Plants

   This squat, armored dinosaur had an impressive array of massive plates and spines that tapered abruptly to sharp edges. At least five different kinds of skin armor have been found on *Hoplitosaurus*: thin, flat rectangles; round and elliptical spikes; thick-keeled spikes shaped like buttons; triangular plates; and spiny scutes. Where these plates were located on the animal's body is uncertain, as they were found scattered. The large triangular plates, which show impressions of blood vessels running through them, may have come from the animal's tail.

   When it was first described in 1901, *Hoplitosaurus* was thought to be a new species of *Stegosaurus*. Later, it was seen as being closer kin to the European armored dinosaur *Polacanthus*, also known as *Hylaeosaurus*.

HOPLOSAURUS

(HOP-loh-SAW-rus)

Status: Doubtful — *See Struthiosaurus*

HORTALOTARSUS

(HOR-tuh-loh-TAHR-sus)

Status: Doubtful — *See Massospondylus*

HUAYANGOSAURUS

(hwye-ANG-guh-SAW-rus)

Type Species: *taibii* (TYE-bee-eye)
Classification:
  Order: Ornithischia
  Suborder: Stegosauria
  Family: Huayangosauridae
Name: *Hua Yang Guo Zhi* [book from Jin Dynasty (A.D. 265- 317); Huayang was an early name for Sichuan] + Greek *sauros* = lizard
Size: 4 meters (13.5 feet) long
Period: Middle Jurassic, 170 million years ago
Place: China
Diet: Plants

   Huayangosaurus was a small, spiky stegosaur. It is distinguished as the earliest and most primitive, and one of the best known, of all stegosaurs.
   Huayangosaurus was adorned with two rows of small, paired, heart-shaped plates that graded into narrow spikes toward the shoulders. The plates were smaller past the hips, and ended halfway down the tail. The tail featured four large spines. This design suggests that large plates in later animals like *Stegosaurus* derived from spikes.
   Another primitive feature of *Huayangosaurus*, in comparison to the later stegosaurs, was the equality of leg lengths between forelimbs and hindlimbs. Later stegosaurs had shorter

HUAYANGOSAURUS *continued*

forelimbs in proportion to the hind legs. And, whereas later stegosaurs had tooth-less snouts, *Huayangosaurus* had seven teeth on each side of the front of its jaw.

This dinosaur was discovered in the rich Dashanpu quarry of Sichuan, central China, in the early 1980s. It was redescribed in 1992, noting previously undocumented features of its skull. These included a small horn near the eye, which appears to have been a sex-linked characteristic. Perhaps only the male *Huayangosaurus* had horns.

HULSANPES

(HOOL-san-pees)

Type Species: perlei (PUR-lee-eye)
Classification:
   Order: Saurischia
   Suborder: Theropoda
   Family: Dromaeosauridae
Name: Khulsan (Mongolian locality) + Latin *pes* = foot
Size: Small
Period: Late Cretaceous, 77 million years ago
Place: Mongolia
Diet: Meat

   Hulsanpes was a small, slender carnivore known only from its three-toed foot, which may have resembled that of the small carnivores, the dromaeosaurids. But *Hulsanpes's* specialized second toe does not appear to have been able to accomodate as large a claw as that on the second toe of dromaeosaurids.

Hulsanpes perlei
foot

HYLAEOSAURUS

(hye-LAY-uh-SAW-rus)

(=Polacanthoides, Polacanthus, Vectensia; =?Acanthopholis, ?Hoplitosaurus)

Type Species: *armatus* (ahr-MAY-tus)
Classification:

Order:	Ornithischia
Suborder:	Ankylosauria
Family:	Nodosauridae
Name:	Greek *hyliaos* = belonging to the forest (Weald) + Greek *sauros* = lizard
Size:	4 meters (13 feet) long
Period:	Early Cretaceous, 135 million to 119 million years ago
Place:	England
Diet:	Plants

Hylaeosaurus was the first armored dinosaur known, and only the third kind of dinosaur to be named. It belonged to the nodosaurid family, the armored dinosaurs without tail clubs. *Hylaeosaurus* was, however, abundantly protected with armor. The plates on its tail were elliptical or circular, and smaller than 8 centimeters (3 inches) in diameter. The plates may have studded the skin in a random arrangement. They do appear to have become smaller as they approached the tip of the tail. The tail featured a double row of rooflike plates with rounded, hollow bases that were shorter toward the tip of the tail. *Hylaeosaurus's* back had paired rows of large spines.

Our image of *Hylaeosaurus's* armored hide has changed considerably since it was named in 1832, based on spines found in Sussex, England. Significant discoveries of this animal and of *Polacanthus* (which may be the same animal) have been made in England as recently as 1979. In recent illustrations, *Hylaeosaurus* has been displayed with spikes protruding almost horizontally from its neck, shoulders, and back, with long spines on the back serving as a frill to protect the animal's flanks and legs.

HYPACROSAURUS

(hye-PACK-ruh-SAW-rus)

Type Species: *?Altispinus* (AWL-tee-SPINE-us)

Classification:
Order:	Ornithischia
Suborder:	Ornithopoda
Family:	Hadrosauridae
Name:	Greek *hy* = very + Greek *akros* = high + Greek *sauros* = lizard
Size:	9 meters (30 feet) long
Period:	Late Cretaceous, 72 million to 70 million years ago
Place:	Alberta; Montana
Diet:	Plants

Hypacrosaurus was a large duckbilled dinosaur of the hollow-crested, or hadrosaurid, family. It featured a helmet-style, tall, narrow crest similar to that of *Corythosaurus*, though *Hypacrosaurus's* was less rounded. Its skull was short and high, with a narrow muzzle. It had nearly forty rows of teeth in dental batteries, and a short, toothless beak.

Aside from its high crest, *Hypacrosaurus's* other distinguishing feature was its ridged back. This was formed of elongated spines on its vertebrae, which in life were surrounded by muscles and bony tendons to make a hump, or fin.

HYPSELOSAURUS

(HIP-sel-uh-SAW-rus)

(=?Magyarosaurus)

Type Species: *priscus* (PRIS-kus)

Classification:

Order:	Saurischia
Suborder:	Sauropoda
Family:	Titanosauridae

Name: Greek *hypsi* = above + Greek *sauros* = lizard

Size: Over 8 meters (27 feet) long

Period: Late Cretaceous, 73 million to 65 million years ago

Place: France and Spain

Diet: Plants

This was a relatively small sauropod, a four-legged browser with weak, slender teeth. *Hypselosaurus* is most famous for its cannonball-shaped eggs. These were the first dinosaur eggs ever found, and the largest yet known. While they are nearly the size of cannonballs, and have a 2-liter (half-gallon) volume, these eggs are far smaller than those of the fossil bird *Aepyornis*.

Fragments of *Hypselosaurus* eggs were found in the 1860s, and were attributed to either a dinosaur or a large bird. In 1930, a French farmer dug up a complete egg in his vineyard. Complete eggs, some in clusters of five, suggest a nest. Thousands of fragments have since been discovered. A *Hypselosaurus* egg was auctioned to an anonymous collector by Christie's in London in 1992 for $11,000.

HYPSIBEMA

(HIP-si-BEE-muh)

Type Species: *crassicauda* (KRAS-i-KAW-duh)
Status: Doubtful
Classification:
   Order: Ornithischia
   Suborder: Ornithopoda
   Family: ?Hadrosauridae
Name: Greek *hypsi* = above + Latin *bema* = platform
                 (stride)
Size: ?
Period: Late Cretaceous, 83 million to 73 million
                 years ago
Place: North Carolina
Diet: Plants

    This dinosaur, named by Edward Drinker Cope in
1869, was identified on the basis of five bones. These
included the partial upper leg of a large theropod,
and two limb bones from duckbills. *Hypsibema*
was probably a duckbill of some sort.

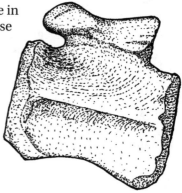

Hypsibema crassicauda
tail vertbra

HYPSILOPHODON

(HIP-suh-LOH-fuh-don)

Type Species: *foxii* (FOCK-sye)
Classification:

   Order: Ornithischia

   Suborder: Ornithopoda

   Family: Hypsilophodontidae

Name: Greek *Hypsilophus* (genus of iguana lizard) +
                Greek *odontos* = tooth

Size: 2.3 meters (7.5 feet) long

Period: Early Cretaceous, 125 million to 115 million years ago

Place: England, Spain,
                Portugal

Diet: Plants

This small, fast-moving dinosaur was lightly built and stood low to the ground. With its body held horizontally, it would have measured only a half meter (2 feet) at the hips.

Hypsilophodon was one of the early dinosaur discoveries, found in 1849 on England's Isle of Wight. Its long fingers and toes led early researchers to speculate that it was a climber, a persistent myth abetted by a scientist's reversal of the proper position of the dinosaur's first toe.

Hypsilophodon had sharp, arched hind claws, and powerful hindlimb muscles. Its tail was long, and kept rigid by bony tendons attached to its tail vertebrae. All these features, once interpreted as adaptations for climbing, are in reality suited to fast running. *Hypsilophodon* was originally believed to have bowed forearms. We now know that this was not true.

One specimen of *Hypsilophodon* was discovered with polygonal bony plates nearby, suggesting the animal may have been armored. But in the absence of other more definitive armor finds, that remains only speculation.

HYPSIROPHUS
(HIP-si-ROH-fus)

Status: Doubtful — See *Allosaurus, Stegosaurus*

IGUANODON

(i-GWAN-uh-don)

Type Species: *anglicus* (ANG-gli-kus)
Classification:

Order:	Ornithischia
Suborder:	Ornithopoda
Family:	Iguanodontidae

Name: Arawak *Iguana* (lizard) + Greek *odontos* = tooth
Size: 10 meters (33 feet) long
Period: Early Cretaceous, 135 million to 110 million
            years ago
Place: England, Belgium, Portugal, Spain, Germany,
            Tunisia, Central Asia, Mongolia, South Dakota,
            ?Utah, ?North Africa
Diet: Plants

Iguanodon, one of the most famous of all dinosaurs, is best known for its distinctive thumb spikes, which projected at a right angle from its other four digits. The spike may have been used to direct tree branches toward *Iguanodon's* mouth, or to defend it against predators. These stout plant-eaters had beaks and powerful tongues to help in cropping and swallowing plants, but had no other spikes or horns for defense.

Iguanodon is legendary among dinosaurs. It was the second dinosaur ever described. Seven of its well-worn teeth were discovered in Sussex, England, in the early 1820s. The familiar (though fictitious) story is that they were discovered by Mary Ann Mantell, wife of family doctor and amateur geologist Gideon Mantell. Mrs. Mantell was accompanying her husband on a doctor's call, as the legend goes, when she spotted fossil teeth in a roadside gravel pile.

In truth, Mantell purchased gravel from quarries in Tilgate Forest and had it delivered to him so that he could search for teeth and bones, which he collected. He described the teeth of *Iguanodon* in 1822, and credited the discovery to his wife. He considered them, correctly, to be suited for cutting plants. *Iguanodon* teeth may have been discovered in Sussex as early as 1808, and also on the Isle of Wight, prior to Mantell's discovery, but Mary Ann Mantell gets the credit.

IGUANODON *continued*

Leading scientists of Mantell's day, Georges Cuvier and William Buckland, speculated that the teeth were from mammals or fish. Mantell insisted the teeth were reptilian, and described them in 1825 as belonging to an extinct, forty-foot-long lizard related to the iguana. Less than a decade later, the first bony spike of *Iguanodon* was discovered in England. It was presumed to have been positioned above the snout. *Iguanodon* was depicted as a rhinoceros-like creature in the first life-sized reconstructions of dinosaurs, which were made in 1851 for London's Crystal Palace, and still stand in London's Sydenham Park.

Iguanodon has now been found in many parts of Europe. The most spectacular find was made 322 meters (1,056 feet) underground in a coal mine in Bernissart, Belgium, where twenty-four nearly complete skeletons, and several less complete individuals, were uncovered in 1878. These were not part of a trapped herd, as was widely reported, but animals that collected over time in a marsh or lake.

Most of the Bernissart skeletons belong to a large *Iguanodon*, species name *Iguanodon bernissartensis*, weighing about three tons. The other species found there is the type species *Iguanodon angelicus*, which weighed less than a ton. They may be different sexes of the same animal, rather than different species, though which was the male and which the female is not clear.

Tracks of *Iguanodon* have been reported throughout Europe. It is estimated that the animals moved at a rate of four kilometers (2.5 miles) an hour, and they may have been capable of much greater speeds.

Iguanodon atherfeldensis (ATH-ur-feld-EN-sis): A small *Iguanodon* found on the Isle of Wight, measuring 6 to 7 meters (20 to 23 feet) in length.

IGUANODON *continued*

Iguanodon bernissartensis (BUR-nis-ahr-TEN-sis): A large *Iguanodon*, 9 meters (30 feet) long and 3 metric tons (almost 3.5 tons) in weight, found in Belgium, England, and possibly France, Portugal, and North Africa. Footprints suggest its distribution may have have extended from Spitzbergen island (north of the Arctic Circle) to South America.

Iguanodon hoggi (HOG-eye): Based on a part of a jaw with teeth, found in Swanage, England, and named in 1874 by Sir Richard Owen, the scientist who coined the term "dinosaur."

Iguanodon lakotaensis (luh-KOH-tuh-EN-sis): An early Cretaceous *Iguanodon* recently identified on the basis of a complete skull that was 550 millimeters (21 inches) long, and a smattering of other bones. These fossils were collected in South Dakota.

Iguanodon orientalis (OR-ee-en-TAL-is): Found in the Gobi Desert of Mongolia, *Iguanodon orientalis* had a large, bulbous snout, a feature not present in other *Iguanodon* specimens. Its body is similar to *Iguanodon bernissartensis*.

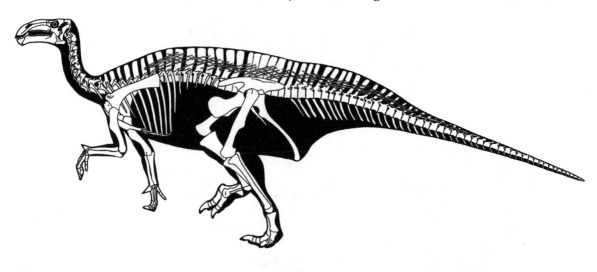

ILIOSUCHUS

(EE-lee-oh-SOOK-us)

Type Species: *incognitus* (IN-cog-NEE-tus)

Classification:

Order:	Saurischia
Suborder:	Theropoda
Family:	?

Name: Latin *ilium* = pelvic bones + Greek *souchos* = crocodile

Size: ?

Period: Middle Jurassic, 172 million years ago

Place: England

Diet: Meat

This carnivore is known only from its small upper hip bone (ilium), which has a prominent ridge. Other carnosaurs from *Stokesosaurus* to *Iliosuchus's* British contemporary, *Megalosaurus*, to the far later *Tyrannosaurus rex*, also have ridges on their hip bones.

Iliosuchus incognitus
hip bone

INDOSAURUS

(IN-duh-SAW-rus)

Type Species: *matleyi* (MAT-lee-eye)
Classification:
  Order: Saurischia
  Suborder: Theropoda
  Family: ?Abelisauridae
Name: *India* + Greek *sauros* = lizard
Size: ?
Period: Late Cretaceous, 70 million to 65 million
            years ago
Place: Jabalpur, India
Diet: Meat

This animal may represent a new and poorly known family of large carnivorous dinosaurs. It is based only on a massive braincase, which was discovered by Charles Matley in central India in 1917. The large skull bones suggest that *Indosaurus* was big and heavily built. The broad skull may have accommodated horns above the eyes. Argentine researchers have noted the close resemblance of the skull of *Indosaurus* to a large South American carnivore of the Late Cretaceous Period, *Abelisaurus*. India and South America were part of the same supercontinent, Gondwana, when Gondwana split into two land masses during the Middle Jurassic Period of dinosaur time.

Indosaurus matleyi
skull

INDOSUCHUS

(IN-doh-SOOK-us)

Type Species: *raptorius* (rap-TOR-ee-us)

Classification:

Order:	Saurischia
Suborder:	Theropoda
Family:	?Abelisauridae

Name: India + Greek *souchos* = crocodile

Size: Large

Period: Late Cretaceous, 70 million to 65 million years ago

Place: India

Diet: Meat

This dinosaur was found at the same time, at the same place, and by the same man who discovered *Indosaurus*, Charles Matley. Like *Indosaurus*, *Indosuchus* was a large carnivore, known only by parts of a skull, and serrated and sharply tapering teeth. Its narrow, crested skull had a flattened roof, suggesting it was closely related to *Tyrannosaurus rex* and *Albertosaurus*. It appears, however, to be smaller and more primitive than *Tyrannosaurus rex*. Recent analysis suggests that, like *Indosaurus*, it is more nearly related to the abelisaurid carnivores of South America.

Indosuchus raptorius skull

INGENIA

(in-JEE-nee-uh)

Type Species: *yanshini* (yan-SHEE-nee)
Classification:

Order:	Saurischia
Suborder:	Theropoda
Family:	Oviraptoridae

Name: *Ingenia* (locality in Mongolia)

Size: ?1.4 meters (4 feet 6 inches) long

Period: Late Cretaceous, 80 million to 70 million years ago

Place: Mongolia

Diet: Meat, ?eggs, ?insects

This small, delicately built predator had a toothless jaw, probably with a beak like other members of the oviraptorid ("egg thief") family. *Ingenia* may have eaten insects, plants, and small mammals as well as eggs. Its hands were more powerfully built than those of other oviraptorids. This may have given it the ability to grasp a greater variety of foods than those consumed by other small, toothless carnivores of its time.

INOSAURUS

(EYE-nuh-SAW-rus)

Type Species: *tedreftensis* (TED-ref-TEN-sis)
Status: Doubtful
Classification:
   Order: Saurischia
   Suborder: ?Theropoda
   Family: ?
Name: Latin *in* = in + Greek *sauros* = lizard
Size: ?2 meters (7 feet) long
Period: Early Cretaceous
Place: Nigeria
Diet: Meat

    This alleged predator is known only from part of a lower leg bone (tibia) and a scattering of vertebrae, found in three places in the Sahara Desert. The small-but-heavy backbones suggest that this animal may have been broad-built, with a strong back. The partial tibia indicates that *Inosaurus* had very short legs. If it was a predator, it was a very strange one.

ISCHISAURUS

(ISH-ee-SAW-rus)

Type Species: *cattoi* (KAT-oy)

Classification:

Order: Saurischia

Suborder: ?

Family: Herrerasauridae

Name: *Ischigualasto* (valley in northwestern Argentina) + Greek *sauros* = lizard

Size: 2+ meters (7 feet) long

Period: Late Triassic, 225 million years ago

Place: Argentina

Diet: Meat

Ischisaurus was one of the earliest and most generalized of dinosaurs. A small carnivore, its skull was only 25 centimeters (9.5 inches) long. It had fifteen or sixteen long, narrow teeth on either side of its mouth, and four elongated teeth in the front of its mouth. It had short arms, and its slender legs had a slight S curve in the upper leg bone (femur).

This animal was very similar to its contemporary from the same region, *Herrerasaurus*. It may represent the same kind of animal.

ISCHYROSAURUS

(ish-CHEE-ruh-SAW-rus)

Type Species: *manseli* (MAN-suh-lye)

Status: Doubtful

Classification:

    Order: Saurischia

    Suborder: Sauropoda

    Family: Brachiosauridae

Name: Greek *isos* = equal + Greek *cheir* = hand + Greek *sauros* = lizard

Size: ?24 meters (80 feet) long

Period: Upper Jurassic, 156 million to 150 million years ago

Place: England

Diet: Plants

    This poorly known herbivore was enormous, and, judging from its few remains, very heavy. It was named from an upper arm bone (humerus) which was smooth and very dense, and almost 13 centimeters (5 inches) thick.

ITEMIRUS

(EYE-ti-MYE-rus)

Type Species: *medullaris* (MED-oo-LAR-us)
Classification:
  Order: Saurischia
  Suborder: Theropoda
  Family: ?
Name: *Itemri* (classical Mongolian name for site)
Size: Small
Period: Late Cretaceous, 90 million years ago
Place: Mongolia
Diet: Meat

This small, little known predator was named from a braincase with unusually high and large semicircular canals of the inner ear, features useful for maintaining equilibrium. The discovery led one scientist to speculate that this and other two-legged carnivores used their ears more for balance than for hearing.

Except that it may have been had good balance and, perhaps, keen vision, there is little we can conclude about *Itemirus* from only its skull bones. It may, in fact, be so distinctive that it belongs to its own family of theropod dinosaurs.

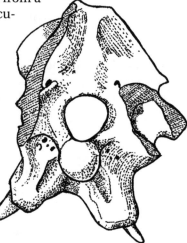

Itemirus medullaris
skull

JANENSCHIA

(yuh-NEN-shee-uh)

Type Species: *robusta* (roh-BUS-tuh)

Classification:

Order:	Saurischia
Suborder:	Sauropoda
Family:	?Titanosauridae

Name: (Werner) Janensch

Size: ?24 meters (80 feet) long or more

Period: Late Jurassic, 156 million to 150 million years ago

Place: Tanzania

Diet: Plants

Janenschia may be the oldest of the titanosaurids, a large group of the giant browsing dinosaurs, the sauropods. Sauropods attained lengths of 40 meters (130 feet) or more. Titanosaurs were relatively small for sauropods, with wide, sloping heads, peglike teeth, and long whiplike tails. They are also distinguished by the armor plates found on at least some of their bodies.

Though little is known of the skeleton of *Janenschia*, it was large and massively built for a titanosaurid, with strong front legs. It may have been twenty percent larger than other titanosaurids, some of which grew to more than 20 meters (66 feet) long. The upper hind leg bone (the femur) alone is longer than the average ten-year-old child, measuring 1.38 meters (approximately 4.75 feet) in length. Cavities in *Janenschia's* bones, such as those found in the neck, may have lessened the weight of this enormous animal.

The hind foot of *Janenschia* was robustly built. The foot had claws on the first three toes, the largest of which was on the first toe. Their function is unknown.

Janenschia dixeyi (DICK-see-eye): A species named in 1928 from remains found in Malawi, Africa. It may represent a new genus of titanosaur.

JAXARTOSAURUS

(jack-SAHR-tuh-SAW-rus)

Type Species: *aralensis* (AHR-uh-LEN-sis)
Status: Doubtful — *See Nipponosaurus*
Classification:
  Order: Ornithischia
  Suborder: Ornithopoda
  Family: Hadrosauridae
Name: Jaxartes (from Yaxart, ancient name for the
    Syr-Daria River, Russia) + Greek *sauros* = lizard
Size: 9 meters (30 feet) long
Period: Late Cretaceous, 91 million to 83 million years ago
Place: Kazakhstan
Diet: Plants

Jaxartosaurus may be an important animal to our understanding of the evolution of the duckbilled dinosaurs. It was an average-sized duckbill, with a wide, low head. Its skull shows features of the both the crested (lambeosaurine) duckbills and the crestless (hadrosaurine) duckbills.

Because the the first fossil finds of *Jaxartosaurus* showed no evidence of a crest, the animal was originally classified as a hadrosaurine. Later finds, however, indicated *Jaxartosaurus* had a helmet-shaped crest, somewhat like that of *Corythosaurus*.

The combination of lambeosaurine and hadrosaurine features suggests that lambeosaurines evolved from the more primitive hadrosaurines, and that *Jaxartosaurus* may have been one of the earliest of the crested dinosaurs.

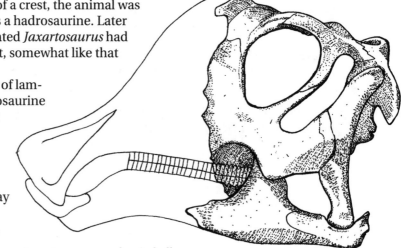

Jaxartosaurus aralensis skull

JAXARTOSAURUS *continued*

The roof of *Jaxartosaurus's* skull had an unusual joint, an anatomical feature that is also found on some other duckbills, carnivorous dinosaurs, and crocodiles. This joint may have worked as shock absorber to protect the animal's braincase from jarring during sudden closing of the jaws.

A questionable species of duckbill from Kazakhstan named *Procheneosaurus convincens* may be a juvenile *Jaxartosaurus.*

"JIANGJUNMIAOSAURUS"

(JANG-JUN-mee-ou-SAW-rus)

Type Species: ?
Status: Unofficial
Classification:
   Order: Saurischia
   Suborder: Theropoda
   Family: Megalosauridae
Name: Chinese *Jiangjunmiao* + Greek *sauros* = lizard
Size: 5 meters (16 feet) long
Period: Middle Jurassic, 170 million years ago
Place: Northwestern China
Diet: Meat

"Jiangjunmiaosaurus" is a provisional name applied by Chinese paleontologists to a large crested predator found in 1984. This primitive carnivore may be related to megalosaurs found in Europe, and an as-yet-unnamed large crested predator discovered in 1991 in Antarctica. It may also be the same animal as *Monolophosaurus,* another as-yet-undescribed Chinese crested carnivore.

JUBBULPURIA

(JUB-ul-POOR-ee-uh)

Type Species: *tenuis* (TEN-yoo-is)
Status: Doubtful
Classification:
  Order: Saurischia
  Suborder: Theropoda
  Family: ?Coeluridae
Name: *Jubbulpore* (former spelling of town in Central India)
Size: ?1.2 meters (4 feet) long
Period: Late Cretaceous, 73 million to 65 million years ago
Place: India
Diet: Meat

    This small meat-eater was originally thought to belong to the family of delicately built theropods, the Coeluridae. But it is so poorly known—only two back vertebrae have been found in central India—that its identity is uncertain.

"JURASSOSAURUS"

(juh-RAS-uh-SAW-rus)

Type Species: *nedegoapeferkimorum* (NED-uh-goh-AY-puh-FUR-ki-MOR-um)

Status: Unofficial — *See "Tianchisaurus"*

Classification:

  Order: Ankylosauridae

  Suborder: Ankylosauria

  Family: ?

Name: Jurassic + Greek *sauros* = lizard

Size: 15 feet long

Period: Middle Jurassic, 170 million years ago

Place: Xinjiang Province, northwestern China

Diet: Plants

"*Jurassosaurus nedegoapeferkimorum*" is the world's oldest well known armored dinosaur and the only species named for the cast of a Hollywood movie. While some ankylosaurs approached the size of tanks, measuring 26 feet long, "*Jurassosaurus*" was relatively small. It may represent not only a new genus and species of ankylosaur, but a new family as well.

Other ankylosaurs are best known from the Late Cretaceous, 100 million years after the time of "Jurassosaurus." Ankylosaurs thrived on every modern continent in the Cretaceous period, both as club-tailed ankylosaurids and clubless, but well-armored, nodosaurids. With the exception of a very fragmentary find from England, *Sarcolestes*, no Jurassic ankylosaurs were well known until "*Jurassosaurus*" was discovered in 1980.

Its remains were uncovered by oil-prospecting geologists close to Lake Tianchi ("Heavenly Lake"), near the Tien Shan Mountains. Chinese paleontologist Dong Zhiming collected the skull, scutes of armor from the shoulders and mid-section, vertebrae, and pelvic bones of the animal. Other remains assigned to "*Jurassosaurus*" were found in two other localities in Xinjiang.

"JURASSOSAURUS" *continued*

Not yet formally named, it may be recognized under its first unofficial name, "Tianchisaurus", with the same species name created from the film's cast.

The bones were not prepared in the laboratory for a decade. The animal was provisionally renamed to commemorate a generous donation to Chinese paleontology by director Steven Spielberg, honoring the cast of his dinosaur film *Jurassic Park*. The new species name is formed from the first letters of the last names of the actors Sam Neill, Laura Dern, Jeff Goldblum, Sir Richard Attenborough, Robert Peck, Martin Ferrero, Wayne Knight, Ariana Richards, and Joseph Mazzello. The name will be formally granted the publication of Dong Zhiming's descriptive paper in a Chinese scientific journal.

KAGASAURUS

(KAH-guh-SAW-rus)

Type Species: ?
Status: Doubtful
Classification:
  Order: Carnosauria
  Suborder: Theropoda
  Family: ?Megalosauridae
Name: Japanese Kaga + Greek sauros = lizard
Size: Large
Period: Early Cretaceous, 135 million to 100 million years ago
Place: Japan
Diet: Meat

A large carnivorous dinosaur which is based, like other dinosaurs named from Japan, on fossils too scrappy for more than an unofficial designation. *Kagasaurus* is known only from large, sharp teeth.

KAIJANGOSAURUS

(kye-JANG-uh-SAW-rus)

Type Species: *lini* (LYE-nye)
Classification:
   Order: Saurischia
   Suborder: Theropoda
   Family: ?Megalosauridae
Name: Chinese Kaijang + Greek sauros = lizard
Size: ?6 meters (20+ feet) long
Period: Middle Jurassic, 175 million to 163 million
             years ago
Place: China
Diet: Meat

    Kaijangosaurus, a little known carnivore with large, sharp teeth and narrow shoulder bones, comes from the same fossil beds that yielded another somewhat mysterious large carnivore, *Gasosaurus*. It is possible that the two are the same kind of animal.

KAKURU

(kah-KOO-roo)

Type Species: *kujani* (koo-JAN-eye)
Status: Doubtful
Classification:
  Order: Saurischia
  Suborder: Theropoda
  Family: ?Coeluridae
Name: *Kakuru* (ancestral "rainbow serpent" of the Guyani tribe)
Size: ?2.4 meters (8 feet) long
Period: Late Cretaceous, 119 million to 113 million years ago
Place: South Australia
Diet: Meat

    Kakuru was a small carnivore with relatively long, slender legs. Its shinbone was 323 millimeters (more than a foot) long; its proportions resembled those of the small theropod *Avimimus*. But *Kakuru* featured a uniquely structured ankle bone, the astragalus, which was higher and narrower than that of other theropods.

    Australian dinosaur finds are rare and fragmentary, and *Kakuru* is no exception. It is known only from the single tibia bone. Discovered in an opal mine, the opalized bone was acquired in 1973 by a local gem shop, along with a slightly crushed and opalized foot claw from what may have been the same theropod.

KANGNASAURUS

(KANG-nuh-SAW-rus)

Type Species: *coetzeei* (koh-ET-see-eye)
Status: Doubtful
Classification:
　Order: Ornithischia
　Suborder: Ornithopoda
　Family: Dryosauridae
Name: Kangnas (Afrikaans farm) + Greek sauros = lizard
Size: Small
Period: Early Cretaceous, ?145 million to ?97.5 million years ago
Place: South Africa
Diet: Plants

Kangnasaurus appears to have been one of the small, primitive plant-eaters, the dryosaurids. It was first thought to be an iguanodontid, but its upper hind leg bone (femur), ankle bone, and three-toed clawed feet resemble those of *Dryosaurus*. Its teeth were long and tapering, and had strong ridges, much like the teeth of *Hypsilophodon*.

Kangnasaurus was named in 1915 on the basis of a tooth found in a farm well in Little Bushmanland, South Africa.

"KATSUYAMASAURUS"

(kat-SOO-yah-muh-SAW-rus)

Type Species: ?
Status: Unofficial
Classification:
  Order: Saurischia
  Suborder: Theropoda
  Family: Allosauridae
Name: Japanese Katsuya + Greek sauros = lizard
Size: Large
Period: Early Cretaceous, ?145 million to ?97.5 million
                years ago
Place: Japan
Diet: Meat

    This large predator is known from only a lower arm bone. Its true identity is in doubt.

KELMAYISAURUS

(kel-MAY-ee-SAW-rus)

Type Species: *petrolicus* (pi-TROH-li-kus)
Status: Doubtful
Classification:
  Order: Saurischia
  Suborder: Theropoda
  Family: ?
Name: Kelmay (petroleum city in China) + Greek
  sauros = lizard
Size: Large
Period: Early Cretaceous, 119 million to 97.5 million
  years ago
Place: China
Diet: Meat

    Kelmayisaurus was a relatively large carnosaur with a high skull similar to that of the smaller North American carnivore *Ceratosaurus*. Just where *Kelmayisaurus* fits into the dinosaur family tree is uncertain. Its lower jaw has features in common with *Megalosaurus bucklandii* from Europe, the first dinosaur described, and to a lesser degree with *Allosaurus fragilis* from North America.

KENTROSAURUS

(KEN-truh-SAW-rus)

Type Species: *aethiopicus* (AY-thee-OH-pi-kus)
Classification:
   Order: Ornithischia
   Suborder: Stegosauria
   Family: Stegosauridae
Name: Greek *kentros* = spiked + Greek *sauros* = lizard
Size: Approximately 5 meters (17 feet) long
Period: Late Jurassic, 156 million to 150 million years ago
Place: Tanzania
Diet: Plants

This spiky, Late Jurassic stegosaur had a paired row of plates on its neck, small in comparison to those of *Stegosaurus,* and continuing only midway down its back. From its midsection to the tip of its tail *Kentrosaurus* sported eight pairs of tall spikes. Another pair of spikes jutted out over the shoulders. For many decades these spikes were thought to have projected from the animal's hips. The discovery of an earlier stegosaur with shoulder spikes, *Huayangosaurus* from China, corrected the error.

Kentrosaurus had hooflike toe claws. It may have weighed more than 2 tons (1.8 metric tons). It appears to be closely related to a British stegosaur, *Lexovisaurus.*

KENTROSAURUS *continued*

It was discovered, nearly entire, by German researchers in Tanzania, East Africa, and named in 1915.

Some kentrosaurs appear to have four sacra ribs, others five. Paleontologist Peter Galton has suggested that this is a sex-linked difference, with females having the additional rib.

Attempts were made to rename *Kentrosaurus* as *Kentrurosaurus*, and later as *Doryphosaurus*, on the incorrect assumption that the similiarity of its name to the horned dinosaur "Centrosaurus" (now *Eucentrosaurus*) would make *Kentrosaurus* an invalid name.

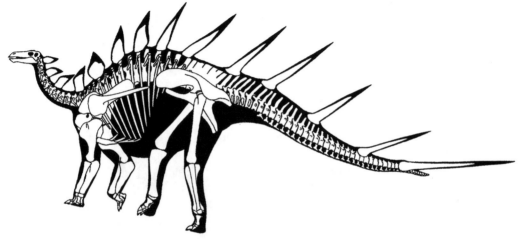

KENTRUROSAURUS
(ken-TROO-ruh-SAW-rus)

Status: Invalid — *See Kentrosaurus*

"KITADANISAURUS"

(KEE-tuh-DAH-ni-SAW-rus)

Type Species: ?
Status: Unofficial
Classification:
  Order: Saurischia
  Suborder: Theropoda
  Family: Coeluridae?
Name: Japanese Kitadani + Greek sauros = lizard
Size: Small
Period: Early Cretaceous, 144 million to 97.5 million
              years ago
Place: Japan
Diet: Meat

This small carnivore, discovered in the same locality as *Katsuyamasaurus* and known only from a single tooth, is also of doubtful validity.

KOREANOSAURUS

(kuh-REE-uh-nuh-SAW-rus)

Type Species: ?
Status: Invalid
Classification:
  Order: Saurischia
  Suborder: Theropoda
  Family: ?
Name: *Korea* + Greek *sauros* = lizard
Size: ?
Period: Late Cretaceous
Place: Korea
Diet: Meat

  A Korean scientist named this animal in 1979 on the basis of a single upper leg bone, or femur. First it was believed to be one of the tyrannosaurids, then one of the small plant-eating hypsilophodontids, and most recently, one of the small North American carnivores, *Deinonychus*. *Koreanosaurus's* true identity is still uncertain.

KOTASAURUS

(KOH-tuh-SAW-rus)

Type Species: *yamanpalliensis* (YAH-mun-PAL-ee-EN-sis)

Classification:

Order:	Saurischia
Suborder:	Sauropoda
Family:	?

Name: Kota (Formation) + Greek *sauros* = lizard

Size: Large

Period: Early Jurassic, 208 million to 188 million years ago

Place: India

Diet: Plants

Kotasaurus was perhaps the most primitive of all known sauropods, the family of huge four-legged, browsing dinosaurs that included the largest animals ever to walk the earth.

Kotasaurus is intermediate in many respects between prosauropods, earlier two- and four-legged plant-eaters, and the larger sauropods. For instance, some of the bones in its hip region were shaped like those of prosauropods, but some pelvic bones are elongated like those in sauropods. Though its size has been not determined, *Kotasaurus* was a much larger animal than any prosauropod. It had weak, spoon-shaped teeth like the sauropod *Camarasaurus*, and vertebrae shaped like those of other sauropods.

KRITOSAURUS

(KRYE-tuh-SAW-rus)

Type Species: *navajovius* (NAH-vuh-HOH-vee-us)
Status: Doubtful — *See Gryposaurus*
Classification:
   Order: Ornithischia
   Suborder: Ornithopoda
   Family: Hadrosauridae
Name: Greek *kritos* = noble + Greek *sauros* = lizard
Size: 9 meters (30 feet) long
Period: Late Cretaceous, 76 million to 65 million
                years ago
Place: New Mexico
Diet: Plants

    Notable for its "Roman nose," this duckbill had a wide, flat head with a distinct bump over its nose. It was named on the basis of a skull found in 1904 by the great American Museum of Natural History collector, Barnum Brown. However, *Kritosaurus* is now considered to be a questionable name. The animal is more likely a *Gryposaurus* specimen.

    What may be another species of *Gryposaurus* was reported from Patagonia, Argentina, and assigned the name *Kritosaurus australis,* but the specimens are too incomplete to determine whether there is any relationship between them.

"KUNMINGOSAURUS"

(kun-MING-uh SAW-rus)

Type Species: *wudingi* (WOO-ding-eye)
Status: Unofficial
Classification:
   Order: Saurischia
   Suborder: Sauropodomorpha
   Family: ?
Name: *Kunming (city in China) + Greek sauros = lizard*
Size: Large
Period: Early Jurassic, 208 million to 170 million years ago
Place: Yunnan Province, China
Diet: Plants

This animal may be a large primitive sauropod with a long neck and tail. It was mentioned in a Chinese scientific paper in 1986, but has not yet been formally described.

LABOCANIA

(LAB-uh-KAN-ee-uh)

Type Species: *anomalis* (uh-NOM-uh-lis)
Classification:
  Order: Saurischia
  Suborder: Theropoda
  Family: ?
Name: Spanish *La Bocana* (Roja Formation)
Size: Large
Period: Late Cretaceous, ?83 million to 73 million
               years ago
Place: Mexico
Diet: Meat

   Labocania was a large carnivorous dinosaur known only from poorly pre-served, incomplete fossils. However, *Labocania* is one of the most unusual of all the known large theropods. Among the few details known about this dinosaur is that the bones at the front of its skull were thick and massive, as were the lower jaws and other cranial bones.

   The skull bones, except for the upper part of the jaw, are larger than in other known meat-eating dinosaurs. They most closely resemble those of various Asian Cretaceous theropods.

   Labocania's resemblance to some Asian carnivores is consistent with the general similarity between Late Cretaceous North American and Asiatic dinosaurs, indicating that the continents were united late in dinosaur times.

LABROSAURUS
(LAB-ruh-SAW-rus)

Status: Invalid — *See Allosaurus*

LAELAPS
(LAY-laps)

Status: Invalid — *See Dryptosaurus*

LAEVISUCHUS

(LAY-vee-SOOK-us)

Type Species: *indicus* (IN-di-kus)

Status: Doubtful

Classification:

   Order: Saurischia

   Suborder: ? Theropoda

   Family: ?

Name: Latin *levis* = smooth + Greek *souchos* = crocodile

Size: 2.1 meters (7 feet) long

Period: Late Cretaceous, 73 million to 65 million years ago

Place: India

Diet: Meat

This small carnivore is known from only three neck vertebrae. The most complete vertebra measures about 3.5 centimeters (about 1.35 inches) in length, indicating the dinosaur's diminutive size. Although *Laevisuchus* was originally thought to be a "coelurid" (a discarded name that lumped together all small theropods), its true affinities are not known. The form of its vertebrae is similar to those of the little known carnivorous dinosaur *Calamospondylus* from England, but *Laevisuchus* is not known well enough to be distinguished from other small theropods of its region.

LAMBEOSAURUS

(LAM-bee-uh-SAW-rus)

Type Species: *lambei* (LAM-bee-eye)
Classification:
  Order: Ornithischia
  Suborder: Ornithopoda
  Family: Hadrosauridae
Name: (Lawrence M.) *Lambe* + Greek *sauros* = lizard
Size: About 9 meters (30 feet) long, almost 2.5
              meters (8 feet) high at the hips
Period: Late Cretaceous, 76 million to 72 million years ago
Place: Alberta; Montana; Mexico
Diet: Plants

Lambeosaurus, a large lambeosaurine (duckbilled dinosaur), was distinguished by a hollow crest atop its head.

The crest had the general shape of a plow, with a long, narrow spike at the back. The shape varied individually by age and sex. The crest housed paired canals that connected with the nostrils. They may have had a function in the animal's sense of smell, or perhaps in sound production. Either sense would have had significant survival value, alerting these almost defenseless animals to danger.

Portions of fossilized skin impressions in some specimens of *Lambeosaurus* show that it had a thin skin. Uniform, polygonal impressions, arranged in no particular order, are present on the neck, sides of the body, and tail areas.

In the past, new species of *Lambeosaurus* have been based on the shape of the crests. For example, *Lambeosaurus clavinitalis*, based on an incomplete skeleton, had a small, rounded crest of medium length. Today we know that variations in crest size and shape may be attributable to age and sex differences. *Lambeosaurus clavinitalis* seems to be a female *Lambeosaurus lambei*.

Tetragonosaurus and *Procheneosaurus*, smaller duckbills with shorter, more rounded skulls, are now known to be juveniles of *Lambeosaurus*.

Lambeosaurus clavinitalis (KLAV-ee-ni-TAL-is) — Invalid: As noted above, this animal was a small-crested female *L. lambei*, and not a separate species. In addition to its crest, bumpy skin impressions have also been found.

LAMBEOSAURUS *continued*

Lambeosaurus laticaudus (LAT-i-KAW-dus) — Doubtful: Found in Baja California, Mexico, this was a large duckbill, possibly measuring some 14 to 15 meters (about 47 to 51 feet) long. This species is distinguished from other lambeosaurines by a long, very high tail, and vertebrae with high spines, some of which were 40 to 50 centimeters (over 15 to 19 inches) long. The spines of the neck vertebrae were smaller. Skin impressions found with this species include large bony bumps that seem to have been randomly placed among large hexagonal and smaller, rounded scales.

Lambeosaurus magnicristatus (MAG-nee-cris-TAT-us): This animal was distinguished by its crest, which was immensely long and high. This crest extended to a point almost over the tip of the beak.

Lambeosaurus paucidens (PAW-sih-dens) — Doubtful: Originally named *Hadrosaurus paucidens*, this species is based on two nearly complete skull bones found in 1888. *L. paucidens* may have been about twenty percent larger than the type species of *Lambeosaurus*.

LAMETASAURUS

(luh-MEE-tuh-SAW-rus)

Type Species: *indicus* (IN-dih-kus)
Status: Doubtful
Classification:
   Order: Ornithischia
   Suborder: Ankylosauria
   Family: ?Nodosauridae
Name: Lameta (Beds) + Greek *sauros* = lizard
Size: ?Large
Period: Late Cretaceous, 73 million to 65 million years ago
Place: India
Diet: Plants

   Lametasaurus, a large, four-legged, poorly understood plant-eater, is based on scrappy remains that include hundreds of bony plates. *Lametasaurus* may have been a nodosaurid, an armored dinosaur with large spikes on its sides and a tail without a club. The plates may have encircled the dinosaur's neck.

   Lametasaurus was originally believed to be a stegosaurid, a plated dinosaur. To add to the confusion about its identity, some of the fossils originally attributed to *Lametasaurus* are actually those of a carnivorous dinosaur or a crocodilian relative.

LANASAURUS

(LAY-nuh-SAW-rus)

Type Species: scalpridens (SKAL-pri-denz)
Classification:

Order:	Ornithischia
Suborder:	Ornithopoda
Family:	Heterodontosauridae
Name:	Latin *lana* = wool (free translation, for Professor A. W. "Fuzz" Crompton) + Greek *sauros* = lizard
Size:	Small
Period:	Early Jurassic, ?208 million to 200 million years ago
Place:	South Africa
Diet:	Plants

Lanasaurus was the most primitive of the known heterodontosaurids, which were small, bipedal, plant-eating dinosaurs.

Lanasaurus differed from other heterodontosaurids in the shape of its teeth. In *Lanasaurus*, the tongue side of the tooth did not have pronounced pits. It had prominent upper "tusk" teeth, and the cheek teeth were very sharp and chisel-shaped.

Lanasaurus scalpridens skull

LANCANGOSAURUS

(LAN-kang-uh-SAW-rus)

Status: Invalid — *See Datousaurus*

LANCANJIANGOSAURUS

(lan-KAN-jee-ANG-guh-SAW-rus)

Type Species: *cachuensis* (KASH-oo-EN-sis)
Status: Doubtful
Classification:
  Order: Saurischia
  Suborder: Sauropoda
                Family: ?
Name: ?Chinese + Greek *sauros* = lizard
Size: Large
Period: Late Jurassic, 163 million to 145 million years ago
Place: China
Diet: Plants

Lancanjiangosaurus was one of the giant sauropods with a long neck, spoon-shaped teeth, and pillarlike legs. Its skeleton was massive and strongly constructed; the vertebrae of its back had cavernous pits that lessened the animal's weight. Its limb bones were long, and its upper hind leg bones were straight and bulky. Too little is known of this dinosaur to say more.

LAOSAURUS

(LAH-oh-SAW-rus)

Type Species: *celer* (SEL-ur)
Status: Doubtful
Classification:
  Order: Ornithischia
  Suborder: Ornithopoda
  Family: Hypsilophodontidae
Name: Greek *laos* (gen. of *laas*) = stone + Greek *sauros* = lizard
Size: Small
Period: Late Jurassic, 156 million to 145 million years ago
Place: Wyoming; Alberta
Diet: Plants

This plant-eater was named from portions of tail vertebrae. With a maximum length of 25 millimeters (about 1 inch), these vertebrae indicated a very small animal. The famed paleontologist, Othniel Charles Marsh, who named *Laosaurus,* thought it was the size of a fox.

Laosaurus backbones appear to be those of a hypsilophodontid, a worldwide group of small, two-legged plant-eaters. The bones are indistinguishable from those of the British dinosaur *Hypsilophodon foxii.* The identity of *Laosaurus* is, therefore, uncertain.

Laosaurus altus (AWL-tus): *Laosaurus altus* is now known as the type species of *Dryosaurus.* Other material referred to *Laosaurus* (including specimens called *Laosaurus gracilis* and *Laosaurus consors*) has been placed in the new genus and species combination, *Othnielia rex.*

Laosaurus minimus (MIN-i-mus): This species is based on a partial left hind limb bone and fragments of vertebrae dating from the Upper Cretaceous, and found in Alberta, Canada. *L. minimus* was similar to *Hypsilophodon,* in that the foot lacked the fifth toe bone. *Laosaurus minimus* may be *Orodromeus.*

LAPLATASAURUS

(luh-PLAT-uh-SAW-rus)

Type Species: *araukanicus* (AHR-aw-KAN-i-kus)
Classification:

Order:	Saurischia
Suborder:	Sauropoda
Family:	Titanosauridae
Name:	La Plata (river in Argentina) + Greek sauros = lizard
Size:	18 meters (60 feet) long
Period:	Late Cretaceous, 83 million to 65 million years ago
Place:	Argentina, Northwest Madagascar, ?India
Diet:	Plants

Laplatasaurus was a large, slender member of the titanosaurids, a group of primitive sauropods, some or all of which were armored. It was far bigger and slimmer than its contemporary titanosaur from South America, *Saltasaurus robustus.*

Laplatasaurus had a long neck for a titanosaurid. Its back vertebrae had deeper grooves for weight reduction than did *Saltasaurus,* and its tail was relatively short.

Included in this species was a large impression of armored skin, constituting the first report of sauropod body armor. At least some South American titanosaurids are now known to have possessed such armor on at least part of their bodies.

Laplatasaurus madagascariensis (MAD-uh-GAS-kuh-ree-EN-sis): *L. madagascariensis* is based on poorly preserved material that includes an upper leg, arm, and two tail vertebrae. It comes from the Late Cretaceous Period in northwest Madagascar. This animal was originally described as another species of *Titanosaurus,* and its identity as a species of *Laplatasaurus* cannot be confirmed.

LAPPARENTOSAURUS

(LAP-uh-REN-tuh-SAW-rus)

Type Species: *madagascariensis* (MAD-uh-GAS-kuh-ree-EN-sis)
Classification:
    Order: Saurischia
    Suborder: Sauropoda
    Family: Brachiosauridae
    Name: (Albert F. de) *Lapparent* + Greek *sauros* = lizard
    Size: Large
    Period: Middle Jurassic, 175 million to 169 million
               years ago
    Place: Madagascar
    Diet: Plants

Lapparentosaurus was named from an almost complete juvenile specimen, which was at first thought to be the English species, *Bothriospondylus*.

Lapparentosaurus was a brachiosaurid, one of a family of gigantic sauropods that had short, low snouts, short tails, and front legs as long or longer than their hind legs. It was distinguished by having primitive, flat spines on its vertebrae that lacked some of the details found in those of *Cetiosaurus*, *Barapasaurus*, and *Patagosaurus*.

Because of the primitive development of these spines, *Lapparentosaurus* may represent an early stage in the development of sauropods.

Lapparentosaurus may have been closely related to, if not the direct ancestor of, the well-known *Brachiosaurus*.

LEAELLYNASAURA

(lay-EL-i-nuh-SAW-ra)

Type Species: *amicagraphica* (uh-MEE-kuh-GRAF-i-kuh)
Classification:

Order:	Ornithischia
Suborder:	Ornithopoda
Family:	Hypsilophodontidae
Name:	Leaellyn (daughter of Thomas and Pat Vickers-Rich) + Greek *saura* (feminine) = lizard
Size:	Adult about 2 to 3 meters (6.5 to 10 feet) long
Period:	Early Cretaceous, 115 million to 110 million years ago
Place:	Australia
Diet:	Plants

This little plant-eater, no bigger than a baby kangaroo, belongs to the Hypsilophodontidae, a family of primitive, bipedal, plant-eating dinosaurs.

Leaellynasaura differs from all other hypsilophodontids in having an upper hind leg bone that narrows, front to back, at its base. And, unlike all hypsilophodontids except *Othnielia*, *Leaellynasaura* has ridges on both sides of its upper cheek teeth.

From a study of part of its braincase, paleontologists determined that this dinosaur was one of the largest-brained (and so perhaps one of the smartest) yet known, and had well-developed optic lobes. Its large eyes would have served it well in winter. Australia was within the Antarctic Circle in *Leaellynasaura*'s time, and so was plunged into darkness every winter.

LEIPSANOSAURUS

(LYEP-san-uh-SAW-rus)

Type Species: *noricus* (NOR-i-kus)

Status: Doubtful — =?Struthiosaurus

Classification:

   Order: Ornithischia

   Suborder: Ankylosauria

   Family: Nodosauridae

Name: Greek *leipein* = to leave behind + Greek *sauros* = lizard

Size: ?

Period: Late Cretaceous, 91 million to 88.5 million years ago

Place: Transylvania, Romania

Diet: Plants

Leipsanosaurus is a poorly known, doubtful genus, established upon only a single, isolated tooth. It is sometimes classified as *Struthiosaurus*, one of a group of armored dinosaurs (ankylosaurs) that lacked tail clubs. However, the fossil evidence of *Leipsanosaurus* is so meager that all that can be said about this dinosaur is that it was probably a nodosaurid.

LEPTOCERATOPS

(LEP-tuh-SER-uh-tops)

Type Species: *gracilis* (GRAS-i-lis)
Classification:
    Order: Ornithischia
    Suborder: Ceratopsia
    Family: Protoceratopsidae
Name: Greek *leptos* = slender + Greek *keratos* = horned
             + Greek *ops* = face
Size: About 181 centimeters (71.5 inches) long; 73
             centimeters (29 inches) high at the hip
Period: Late Cretaceous, 68 million to 65 million
             years ago
Place: Alberta; Wyoming; ?China; ?Mongolia
Diet: Plants

    Leptoceratops was a small horned dinosaur. Though it was one of the last of such dinosaurs, it was also very primitive, having a large head without a nasal horn. (The horned dinosaurs, ceratopsids, were distinguished by their parrot-like beaks. Not all had brow horns.) *Leptoceratops* had a long, moderately low face, a very small solid frill, and a crest with a high, thin ridge and a smooth back.

    Though its teeth had single roots, it was a powerful plant-grinder. Its lower jaw was massive, short, and deep, with fewer than fifteen rows of teeth. The first three digits of its front foot ended in a hoof; its hind foot was clawed; and its tail was long, with high, slender spines.

LEPTOCERATOPS *continued*

Though *Leptoceratops* is usually portrayed as partially bipedal, the concentration of body mass in the front of the pelvis, its broad short "hands," and the straight-shafted upper hind leg bones were adaptations for moving on all fours. Lightly built for a horned dinosaur, it was probably among the swiftest of the four-footed dinosaurs.

Since *Leptoceratops* is the most primitive known protoceratopsid, and yet one whose remains date from near the close of dinosaur time, it seems to be an ancestor that coexisted with its descendants. Well known from North America, it is also reported from Asia, though these finds are vague and somewhat questionable.

LEPTOSPONDYLUS
(LEP-toh-SPON-di-lus)

Status: Invalid — *See Massospondylus*

LESOTHOSAURUS

(li-SOH-thoh-SAW-rus)

Type Species: *diagnosticus* (DYE-ig-NOS-ti-kus)
Classification:
  Order: Ornithischia
  Suborder: [unnamed suborder]
  Family: Fabrosauridae
Name: *Lesotho* (country in southern South Africa) +
             Greek *sauros* = lizard
Size: About 1 meter (39 inches) long
Period: Early Jurassic, 208 million to 200 million
             years ago
Place: South Africa
Diet: Plants

   Lesothosaurus was one of the earliest and most primitive ornithischians, the bird-hipped, plant-eating dinosaurs. Its body was small, lightly built, slender, and without armor. Its head, about 10 centimeters (4 inches) long, was triangular in profile and had large eyes. *Lesothosaurus* had a long snout with a horn-covered tip that probably functioned as a bill to crop vegetation. Its lower jaws were slender, and its varied teeth were arranged in a simple row.
   Lesothosaurus had short forelimbs, less than forty percent of the length of its hindlimbs. Its thumb was partially opposable, suggesting that it may have had some grasping ability. The small thumb spike, which was held well off the ground during walking, may have

LESOTHOSAURUS *continued*

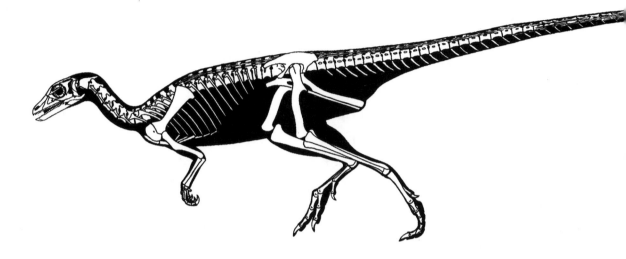

been accompanied by four short fingers ending in small claws. The tail, which was not well preserved, may have been about equal to the combined length of the head, neck, and trunk.

Lesothosaurus was probably an agile, two-legged runner. Virtually every part of *Lesothosaurus's* skeleton was well-adapted to life as a good runner: slender, hollow, thin-walled bones; a pelvis set above the belly to allow freedom of leg movement; a light skull with many openings; a short neck and forelimbs; delicately constructed vertebrae; and the absence of armor.

Lesothosaurus was probably herbivorous, but it may have fed occasionally on insects or carrion. This dinosaur may have chopped and crushed its food by means of simple opening and closing movements of the jaws with help, perhaps, from a horny beak.

LEXOVISAURUS

(lek-SOH-vi-SAW-rus)

Type Species: *durobrivenses* (DOOR-oh-bri-VEN-sis)
Classification:
    Order: Ornithischia
    Suborder: Stegosauria
    Family: Stegosauridae
Name: Latin *Lexovix* = Gallic people from Lyons, France +
             Greek *sauros* = lizard
Size: 5 meters (17 feet)
Period: Middle Jurassic, 169 million to 156 million
             years ago
Place: England
Diet: Plants

    Lexovisaurus was a stegosaurid, or plated, dinosaur, which had large, thin plates more than twice as high as they were wide, and a pair of shoulder spines. These plates resembled those of the African stegosaurid, *Kentrosaurus*, which was closely related but less ornamented.

    Lexovisaurus had at least one pair of tail spines or spikes, and its shoulder spines were particularly large. In one specimen, the broad spine had a maximum width of 275 millimeters (about 10.5 inches). If complete, it would have had a length of 1.1 meters (3 feet, 9 inches).

    Given the size, grooves, and thinness of *Lexovisaurus*'s plates, they may have functioned either as display ornaments, or radiators for body temperature regulation.

LIKHOELESAURUS

(LICK-hoh-li-SAW-rus)

Type Species: *ingens* (IN-jenz)
Classification:
    Order: Saurischia
    Suborder: ?Theropoda
    Family: ?
Size: ?
Name: *Li Khoele* (town in Lesotho, South Africa) + Greek *sauros* = lizard
Period: Late Triassic, 225 million to 208 million years ago
Place: South Africa
Diet: ?

    Little can be said about this early dinosaur. It is represented only by some teeth that resemble those of the carnivorous dinosaur *Basutodon,* and are about 70 millimeters (2.7 inches) in length. First thought to be a theropod, *Likhoelesaurus* may in fact have been a plant-eater.

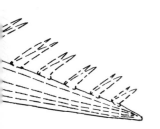

LILIENSTERNUS

(LIL-ee-en-STUR-nus)

Type Species: *liliensterni* (LIL-ee-en-STUR-nye)
Classification:

    Order: Saurischia

    Suborder: Theropoda

    Family: Podokesauridae

Name: Named after (Ruhle von) *Lilienstern*

Size: 5 meters (16 feet) long

Period: Late Triassic, 222 million to 219 million years ago

Place: Germany

Diet: Meat

    Liliensternus is a recently named carnivore (1984) whose features resembled the early two-legged dinosaurs *Dilophosaurus* and *Coelophysis*. Its skull had a large triangular opening in front of the eye hole. Its neck was long, judging by the nine elongated neck vertebrae, as was its tail. *Liliensternus's* forelimbs, by contrast, were very short. Its hand had five digits, the first and fifth of which were small.

    Liliensternus was originally described as a third species of genus *Halticosaurus*, based upon two incomplete skeletons from lightly built subadults.

LIMNOSAURUS
(LIM-noh-SAW-rus)

Status: Invalid — *See Telmatosaurus*

LISBOASAURUS

(liz-BOH-uh-SAW-rus)

Type Species: *estesi* (ES-ti-sye)
Classification:
 Order: Saurischia
 Suborder: Theropoda
 Family: ?Troodontidae
Name: Portuguese *Lisboa* = Lisbon (capital city of
     Portugal) + Greek *sauros* = lizard
Size: Small
Period: Late Jurassic, 163 million to 156 million years ago
Place: Portugal
Diet: Meat

  This birdlike, meat-eating dinosaur was originally described as a lizard, but its upper jaw bones have some similarities to those of the saurischian dinosaurs. Furthermore, various features of the teeth suggest that *Lisboasaurus* belongs to the troodontids, a family of small carnivorous dinosaurs related to birds.

Lisboasaurus estesi
skull

LONCOSAURUS

(LONG-kuh-SAW-rus)

Status: Invalid = ?*Genyodectes*

LONGOSAURUS

(LONG-uh-SAW-rus)

Status: Invalid — See *Rioarribasaurus*

LOPHORHOTHON

(LOF-ur-HOH-thon)

Type Species: *atopus* (ay-TOH-pus)
Classification:

Order: Ornithischia
Suborder: Ornithopoda
Family: Hadrosauridae

Name: Greek *lophos* = crested + Greek *rhothon* = nose
Size: Almost 4.5 meters (about 15 feet) long
Period: Late Cretaceous, 83 million to 73 million
              years ago
Place: Alabama
Diet: Plants

    This flat-headed, duckbilled dinosaur, or hadrosaurine, had a deep skull, short snout, and broad eye holes. Above the nose was a pyramid-shaped crest similar to that in the better known duckbills, *Prosaurolophus* and *Maiasaura*, though on *Lophorhothon* the crest was placed well in front of the eyes.

    Lophorhothon seems to be geologically older than *Kritosaurus* and its nearer relative, *Prosaurolophus*.

LORICOSAURUS

(LOR-i-kuh-SAW-rus)

Type Species: scutatus (skoo-TAT-us)

Classification:

Order:	Saurischia
Suborder:	Sauropoda
Family:	Titanosauridae

Name: Latin *lorica* = corselet + Greek *sauros* = lizard

Size: Large

Period: Late Cretaceous, 95 million to 90 million years ago

Place: Argentina

Diet: Plants

This big, four-legged plant-eater is now known to be a member of the titanosaurid family of armored sauropods, which were common in South America during the Late Cretaceous Period.

Twenty-six armor plates and small armor pieces of *Loricosaurus* were collected from one Argentine site. Originally, these fossils were thought to belong to a nodosaurid (armored dinosaur). They are more similar to the armor of *Saltasaurus*, a titanosaurid whose remains have been found at the same locality.

LUFENGOSAURUS

(loo-FUNG-guh-SAW-rus)

Type Species: *hueni* (HOO-nye)
Classification:

Order:	Saurischia
Suborder:	Prosauropoda
Family:	Plateosauridae

Name: Chinese Lufeng (Series) + Greek *sauros* = lizard
Size: 6 meters (20 feet) long
Period: Early Jurassic, 208 million to 200 million
           years ago
Place: China
Diet: Plants

   Lufengosaurus was a large, early plant-eater, a prosauropod, and closely related to *Plateosaurus*. Its skull was small, with a large, circular eye hole. Its jaw had serrated teeth. Its neck was long, its spine strongly constructed, its back legs stubby, and its tail massive. The first claws of both its front and hind feet were especially strong.

LUKOUSAURUS

(LOO-kuh-SAW-rus)

Type Species: *yini* (YEE-nee)
Status: Doubtful
Classification:
   Order: Saurischia
   Suborder: ?Theropoda
   Family: ?
Name: Chinese *Lukou* (bridge) + Greek *sauros* = lizard
Size: 2 meters (6.6 feet) long
Period: Early Jurassic, 200 million to ?194 million
   years ago
Place: China
Diet: Meat

   This poorly known little carnivore was named from the front part of a small skull that had well-rounded eye holes and a nasal opening close to the front of the snout. The muzzle seems to have been slender. The lower jaw was slender, with a straight lower margin. Its fifteen teeth, all of them sharply compressed and directed backwards, had fine short serrations on their backs for tearing meat.

   Lukousaurus was originally regarded as one of the Coelurosauria (a term formerly meaning nearly all small theropods), though it was larger than such Jurassic-Period "coelurosaurian" dinosaurs as *Procompsognathus* and *Podokesaurus.*

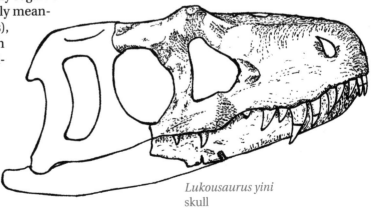

Lukousaurus yini
skull

LUSITANOSAURUS

(LOO-si-TAN-uh-SAW-rus)

Type Species: *liasicus* (lye-AS-i-kus)
Status: Doubtful
Classification:
  Order: Ornithischia
  Suborder: Thyreophora
  Family: ?
Name: Lusitanian (age) + Greek *sauros* =lizard
Size: ?
Period: Early Jurassic, 200 million to 194 million years ago
Place: Portugal
Diet: Plants

    This dinosaur, known only from parts of an upper jaw and teeth, may be a thyreophoran, a group of dinosaurs that included the plated stegosaurs and armored ankylosaurs.

    The jawbone fragment measures about 10.5 centimeters (4 inches) long and 4.5 centimeters (1.75 inches) high. It is quite similar to that of the primitive armored dinosaur *Scelidosaurus*, differing mainly in its teeth: the eight teeth in the *Lusitanosaurus* specimen are taller than those of *Scelidosaurus*, and lack scalloped edges at the point.

LYCORHINUS

(LYE-koh-RYE-nus)

Type Species: angustidens (ang-GUS-ti-denz)
Classification:

Order:	Ornithischia
Suborder:	Ornithopoda
Family:	Heterodontosauridae

Name: Greek lykos = wolf + Greek rhinos = nose
Size: Small
Period: Early Jurassic, 208 million to 200 million
           years ago
Place: South Africa
Diet: Plants

Lycorhinus is now known to belong to the heterodontosaurids, a group of primitive, two-legged plant-eaters distinguished by their large canine teeth. Since Lycorhinus is known only from a portion of a left lower jawbone with teeth, this dinosaur was originally believed to be a cynodont, a nondinosaurian reptile. The jaw is distinguished by a large, pointed, stabbing canine tooth.

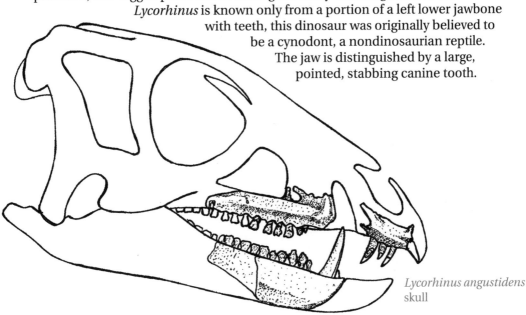

Lycorhinus angustidens
skull

MACRODONTOPHION

(MACK-roh-DON-tuh-FEE-on)

Type Species: (No specific name designated)
Status: Doubtful
Classification: ?
Name: Greek *makros* = long + Greek *odontos* = tooth + Greek *ophis* = snake
Size: ?
Period: Late Jurassic or Early Cretaceous, ?170 million to ?97 million years ago
Place: Ukraine
Diet: ?Meat

This questionable genus was founded upon a single large, slender, recurved tooth thought to belong to a megalosaurid meat-eater. But the tooth, unlike most theropod teeth, seems to taper only slightly, if at all, from neck to tip.

MACROPHALANGIA

(MACK-roh-fuh-LAN-jee-uh)

Status: Invalid — *See Chirostenotes*

MACRUROSAURUS

(mack-ROOR-uh-SAW-rus)

Type Species: *semnus* (SEMM-nuss)

Classification:

    Order: Saurischia

    Suborder: Sauropoda

    Family: Titanosauridae

Name: Greek *makros* = long + Greek *oura* = tail + Greek *sauros* = lizard

Size: 12 meters (40 feet) long

Period: Early Cretaceous, 138 million to 95 million years ago

Place: England

Diet: Plants

This was one of the first titanosaurids discovered. Titanosaurs were a group of large four-legged plant-eaters that may all have had armored skin.

This sauropod is known mostly from tail vertebrae. The 19th century paleontologist Harry Govier Seeley estimated the tail included 50 vertebrae, and may have been almost 4.5 meters (15 feet) long.

MAGNOSAURUS

(MAG-nuh-SAW-rus)

Type Species: *nethercombensis* (NETH-ur-koh-MEN-sis)
Classification:

Order:	Saurischia
Suborder:	Theropoda
Family:	Megalosauridae

Name: Latin *magnus* = great + Greek *sauros* = lizard
Size: Large
Period: Late Jurassic, 188 million to 175 million years ago
Place: England
Diet: Meat

    Magnosaurus, a large meat-eater, is poorly known. It may belong to the Megalosauridae, a family of large, carnivorous dinosaurs.

MAGYAROSAURUS

(MAG-yahr-uh-SAW-rus)

Type Species: *dacus* (DAY-kus)
Status: Doubtful
Classification:
  Order: Saurischia
  Suborder: Sauropoda
  Family: Titanosauridae
Name: Magyar (ethnic group of Hungary) + Greek
                sauros = lizard
Size: Large
Period: Late Cretaceous, 70 million to 65 million
                years ago
Place: Hungary, Romania
Diet: Plants

    Magyarosaurus was a titanosaurid, a group of armor-skinned, plant-eating sauropods known mostly from South America. *Magyarosaurus* is distinguished by its slender limbs; however, much of its appearance remains unknown. Its name, given it by the early 20th century paleontologist Baron von Nopcsa, was intended to embrace various remains from the Upper Cretaceous Period found in Transylvania that were originally referred to the somewhat better known dinosaur *Titanosaurus.* These fossils may in fact belong to several kinds of dinosaurs that are now under review by Romanian, British, and American paleontologists.

    Magyarosaurus hungaricus: *M. hungaricus* was based on a left lower leg bone that measures 47 centimeters (about 18.5 inches) long. The wider leg bone and differences in the upper arm bone distinguished *Magyarosaurus hungaricus* from the type species.

    Magyarosaurus transylvanicus (TRAN-sil-VAN-i-kus): This animal was named from vertebrae, with the shorter ones thought to belong to a male, others to a female.

MAIASAURA

(MYE-uh-SAW-ruh)

Type Species: *peeblesorum* (PEE-bool-SAW-rum)
Classification:

Order:	Ornithischia
Suborder:	Ornithopoda
Family:	Hadrosauridae
Name:	Greek *maia* = good mother + Greek *saura* (feminine) = lizard
Size:	9 meters (30 feet) long
Period:	Late Cretaceous, 77 million to 73 million years ago
Place:	Montana
Diet:	Plants

One of the most important dinosaur discoveries in recent years, *Maiasaura* was one of the so-called "flat-headed" hadrosaurids. This was a diverse subfamily of duckbilled dinosaurs that flourished during the Late Cretaceous Period.

The remarkable details we know about this animal's appearance, behavior, and development are the result of extensive work done by paleontologist John R. Horner.

Maiasaura had a long, wide face with a short, wide bill. Above and between the eyes was a small, solid crest resembling that of *Lophorhothon* and *Prosaurolophus*. Its skull was large, measuring 820 millimeters (about 32 inches) long, and about 350 millimeters (about 13.5 inches) high. The massive muzzle shows primitive characteristics common to both iguanodonts and early hadrosaurs, including the skull's most significant features, the small nostril opening and the long, broad nasal bones at the front end of the muzzle.

At the site of the original discovery, Horner found skeletal remains of eleven *Maiasaura* babies, each about 1 meter (3.3 feet) long, and clustered in a nestlike structure. The remains of four more babies were found no more than 2 meters (about 7 feet) from the nest. These juveniles had short snouts and relatively large feet, but otherwise resembled the adult maiasaurs.

Found with these skeletons were numerous pieces of fossilized eggshell. The eggs were ovoid, and lay in an oval, concave nest that was about 2 meters (approximately 7 feet) in diameter, and .75 meters (approximately 2.5 feet) deep near the center.

MAIASAURA *continued*

Horner's later discovery of an egg containing a *Maiasaura* embryo, the first dinosaur embryo found in the United States, proved that these eggs belonged to this genus.

Maiasaura, like some modern crocodiles and birds, may have nested in colonies and returned to the same nesting area annually. During the dry season, the mother made her nest on the flood plains, using fine-grained silts, then laid her eggs in a spiral pattern. The nests were then covered with reeds and other vegetation for incubation. Babies may have been 35 centimeters (13 inches) long when they hatched, growing to 3 meters (10 feet) by the end of their first year. Such rapid growth requires a high metabolism, and may support the theory that at least some dinosaurs were warm-blooded at some point in their lives.

Until the discovery of *Maiasaura*, it was usually believed that dinosaurs, like most reptiles, abandoned their eggs. The babies hatched out on their own, and were forced to survive—or not—alone and unattended. But according to the evidence gathered and interpreted at these nests, *Maiasaura* babies must have stayed together in the nest, where they were fed and given parental care for an extended period of time. During their time in the nest, they grew from approximately 35 centimeters (13 inches) to almost 90 centimeters (3 feet) long. Trampled eggshells and regurgitated plant matter provided clues to this extended nest stay and to parental feeding of the young. Babies may have been fed on berries and seeds regurgitated by the mother. Soft, unfinished cartilage on the joint surfaces of the very young dinosaurs would have prohibited them from much activity. Like modern altricial birds, such as robins, these dinosaur hatchlings would have been helpless.

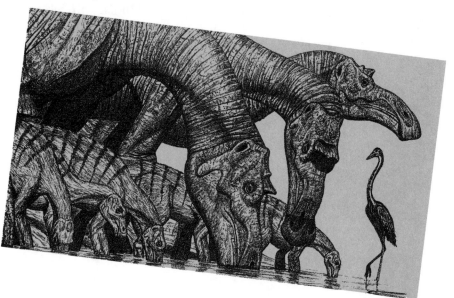

MAJUNGASAURUS

(mah-JUNG-uh-SAW-rus)

Type Species: *crenatissimus* (KREN-uh-TIS-i-mus)

Classification:

Order:	Saurischia
Suborder:	Theropoda
Family:	?Abelisauridae

Name: *Majunga* (District of Madagascar) + Greek
            sauros = lizard

Size: Large

Period: Late Cretaceous, 83 million to 73 million
            years ago

Place: Madagascar, Egypt, ?India

Diet: Meat

Not much is known about this large meat-eater, which was founded on an incomplete jaw bone with teeth.

The curved lower jaw is known in the abelisaurid *Carnotaurus sastrei*, suggesting that *Majungasaurus* may belong to the Abelisauridae, a family of short-faced theropods known from South America and India. Through much of early dinosaur time, these regions, as well as southern Africa and Madagascar, had been united as part of the world's then-single land mass, which explains the presence of similar dinosaurs in regions now so widely spaced.

MAJUNGATHOLUS

(mah-JUNG-uh-THOH-lus)

Type Species: *atopus* (uh-TOH-pus)

Classification:

Order:	Ornithischia
Suborder:	Pachycephalosauria
Family:	Pachycephalosauridae
Name:	Majunga (District of Madagascar) + Latin *tholus* = dome
Size:	3 meters (10 feet) or more
Period:	Late Cretaceous, ?83 million to 73 million years ago
Place:	Madagascar
Diet:	Plants

Majungatholus atopus skull

This relatively large bone-headed dinosaur, or pachycephalosaur, had a skull with a single, domelike thickening that was irregularly ornamented by furrows and nodes. *Majungatholus's* single dome and large openings in the skull bone are unique among pachycephalosaurs.

This dinosaur may have had a powerful sense of smell, for its braincase had a long olfactory portion, with the olfactory lobes enclosed on the bottom by bone.

Among bone-headed dinosaurs, *Majungatholus* was surpassed in size only by *Pachycephalosaurus*. It was similar to the slightly more primitive British *Yaverlandia bitholus*, the oldest known pachycephalosaurid. *Majungatholus* seems to have derived from a *Yaverlandia*-like ancestor, probably representing a pachycephalosaurid lineage that evolved independently of those in the Northern Hemisphere.

The occurrence of *Majungatholus* in Madagascar, and the presence of other "Laurasian" dinosaur families in the Southern Hemisphere, supports the theory that a land connection existed between the two supercontinents, Laurasia and Gondwana, at least during the first half of the Cretaceous Period, and possibly later.

MALEEVOSAURUS

(MAH-lee-AY-vuh-SAW-rus)

Type Species: *novojilovi* (NOH-voh-yee-LOH-vye)
Classification:
   Order: Saurischia
   Suborder: Theropoda
   Family: Tyrannosauridae
Name: (Eugene Alexandrovich) *Maleev* + Greek *sauros* = lizard
Size: Small for a tyrannosaurid
Period: Late Cretaceous, ?75 million to 70 million years ago
Place: Mongolia
Diet: Meat

    Maleevosaurus was a member of the tyrannosaurid family, the large theropods that flourished during the Late Cretaceous Period in both Asia and North America. *Maleevosaurus* was distinguished from other tyrannosaurids by various features, including a small opening in its upper jaw, and a moderate-sized and nonbumpy horn above its eye sockets. This dinosaur had large eye sockets, a slender lower jaw and, unlike other tyrannosaurids, tall spines on its neck vertebrae.

    Originally named *Gorgosaurus novojilovi*, it was later thought to be a juvenile *Tyrannosaurus*. Now this animal is considered to be a distinct genus.

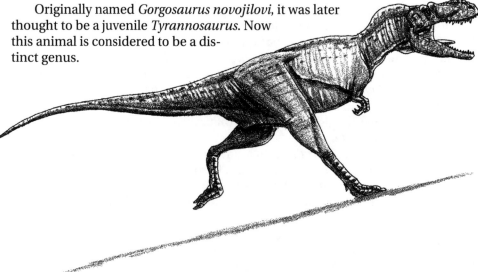

MALEEVUS

(MAH-lee-AY-vus)

Type Species: *disparoserratus* (dis-PAR-oh-suh-RAY-tus)
Classification:
  Order: Ornithischia
  Suborder: Ankylosauria
  Family: Ankylosauridae
Name: (Eugene Alexandrovich) *Maleev*
Size: 6 meters (20 feet) long
Period: Late Cretaceous, 97.5 million to 88.5 million
  years ago
Place: Mongolia
Diet: Plants

A poorly known ankylosaurid, *Maleevus* was a heavily armored dinosaur, identified by large lateral spikes and no tail club. It was based on fragmentary fossils that were originally described as *Syrmosaurus disparoserratus*, a now-invalid name for *Pinacosaurus*, a 5.5-meter-long (18 feet) ankylosaur.

Maleevus is distinguished from *Pinacosaurus* by two anatomical details: a down- and backwardly oriented bone at the back of the head that attached the skull to the neck, and aspects of its tooth structure.

MAMENCHISAURUS

(mah-MEN-chi-SAW-rus)

Type Species: *constructus* (kuhn-STRUCK-tus)
Classification:
   Order: Saurischia
   Suborder: Sauropoda
   Family: Diplodocidae
Name: Chinese Mamenchi (Ferry; from *Chi* = brook +
                Mamen, the name of that brook) + Greek
                sauros = lizard
Size: 21 meters (70 feet) long
Period: Late Jurassic, 156 million to 145 million years ago
Place: China
Diet: Plants

Mamenchisaurus, the largest known dinosaur from Asia, was distinguished by its remarkably long neck, which had nineteen cervical vertebrae and made up half the animal's length. This nearly eleven-meter-long (35 foot) neck was the longest of any animal ever known.

Because the neck was not well preserved in the type specimen, it was originally, and incorrectly, reconstructed as a relatively short neck when the skeleton, supplemented with plaster, was mounted at the Institute of Vertebrate Paleontology and Paleoanthropology, in Beijing.

Mamenchisaurus may belong to the Diplodocidae, a family of giant sauropods with tapering, whiplike tails. *Mamenchisaurus's* vertebrae were similar in size and structure to those in *Omeisaurus* and *Tienshanosaurus*. The limb, foot, and ankle bones resembled those of the diplodocid *Apatosaurus*. However, the recent discovery of an as-yet-undescribed skull, which superficially resembles the boxy skull of the camarasaurid *Euhelopus*, may indicate that *Mamenchisaurus* was not a diplodocid.

MAMENCHISAURUS *continued*

Mamenchisaurus hochuanensis (HOCH-yoo-an-EN-sis): This species had a neck with nineteen elongated vertebrae that extended to 9.8 meters (33 feet). The total skeleton measured some 18.5 meters (62 feet) long; if the tail were complete, it may have been as much as 23.5 meters (80 feet) long. In life, this animal may have weighed approximately 36 metric tons (40 tons).

MANDSCHUROSAURUS

(mand-SHOO-ruh-SAW-rus)

Type Species: *amurensis* (AM-yoo-REN-sis)
Status: Doubtful
Classification:
   Order: Ornithischia
   Suborder: Ornithopoda
   Family: ?Hadrosauridae
Name: Manchuria + Greek *sauros* = lizard
Size: 8 meters (almost 27 feet) long
Period: Late Cretaceous, ?70 million years ago
Place: Manchuria, China
Diet: Plants

Mandschurosaurus was a large hadrosaurid, or duckbilled, dinosaur. Whether it was flat-headed (hadrosaurine), as it has been classed, or crested (lambeosaurine), is uncertain, since its remains do not include a complete skull. Much of the mounted skeleton of *Mandschurosaurus* displayed at the Central Geological and Prospecting Museum in Leningrad, Russia, is heavily restored in plaster.

The first Chinese dinosaur named (it was originally called *Trachodon amurensis*), *Mandschurosaurus* was founded on an incomplete, poorly preserved skeleton discovered in 1914 by Russian scientists on the bank of the Amur River.

Mandschurosaurus laoensis (LAH-oh-EN-sis): This species, based on incomplete remains from China, may or may not belong to *Mandschurosaurus*.

Mandschurosaurus mongoliensis (mong-GOH-lee-EN-sis) — Invalid name: *M. mongoliensis* became the type species of *Gilmoreosaurus*.

MANOSPONDYLUS

(MAN-oh-SPON-di-lus)

Status: Doubtful — *See Tyrannosaurus*

MARMAROSPONDYLUS

(mahr-oh-SPON-di-lus)

Status: Invalid — *See Bothriospondylus*

MARSHOSAURUS

(MAHR-shuh-SAWR-us)

Type Species: *bicentessimus* (BYE-sen-TES-i-mus)
Status: Doubtful
Classification:
   Order: Saurischia
   Suborder: Theropoda
   Family: ?
Name: (Othniel Charles) *Marsh* + Greek *sauros* = lizard
Size: Approximately 5 meters (17 feet) long
Period: Late Jurassic, 156 million years to 145 million
      years ago
Place: Utah, Colorado
Diet: Meat

   Marshosaurus was a small- to medium-sized carnivorous dinosaur. The pelvis and slender pubic bone distinguish it from other large theropods of the Late Jurassic Period. Unless more complete skeletal remains can be found, *Marshosaurus* cannot be compared with other theropods, or assigned to a particular theropod family.

MASSOSPONDYLUS

(MAS-oh-SPON-di-lus)

Type Species: *carinatus* (KAR-i-NAY-tus)
Classification:

   Order: Saurischia
   Suborder: Prosauropoda
   Family: Massospondylidae
Name: Greek *masson* = greater +
                 Greek *spondylos* = vertebra
Size: 4 to 6 meters (12 to 20
                 feet) long
Period: Early Jurassic, 208
                 million to 194 mil-
                 lion years ago
Place: South Africa,
                 Arizona
Diet: Plants

   This moderate-sized, slender, and
lightly built animal was a prosauropod, a
group of long-necked, plant-eating
dinosaurs that included the first large
dinosaurs. *Massospondylus* is mostly known
from fossils found in South Africa, though some
remains have been discovered in Arizona.

   Massospondylus's small head was narrow, with
large, almost circular eye holes, large nostrils, and
relatively large teeth. Some of its teeth were serrated, others flat. Its body resembled that of the other
large Prosauropoda, with its long neck, front legs
long enough to allow for some movement on all fours,
and long tail.

MEGACERVIXOSAURUS

(MEG-uh-SUR-vik-suh-SAW-rus)

Type Species: *tibetensis* (ti-BET-EN-sis)
Status: Doubtful
Classification:
  Order: Saurischia
  Suborder: Sauropoda
  Family: ?Diplodocidae
Name: Greek *megas* = large + Latin *cervix* = neck + Greek *sauros* = lizard
Size: Large
Period: Late Cretaceous, ?97.5 million to ?65 million years ago
Place: China
Diet: Plants

    This large four-legged browser's peglike teeth had long, thin crowns, no serrations, and cylindrical roots. Aside from some large vertebra, these teeth are all that is known of this animal. *Megacervixosaurus* may belong to the Diplodocidae, a family of sauropods with small, but relatively long, heads and whiplike tails.

MEGADACTYLUS

(MEG-uh-DACK-ti-lus)

Status: Invalid — *See Anchisaurus*

MEGALOSAURUS

(MEG-uh-luh-SAW-rus)

Type Species: *bucklandi* (BUCK-lan-dye)
Classification:

Order:	Saurischia
Suborder:	Theropoda
Family:	Megalosauridae
Name:	Greek *megalos* = big + Greek *sauros* = lizard
Size:	7 to 8 meters (23 to 26 feet) long
Period:	Middle Jurassic, 175 million to ?155 million years ago
Place:	England, France, ?Portugal
Diet:	Plants

    Megalosaurus was a large carnivore, and among the first dinosaurs to be named and described. It was a key member of the Megalosauridae, a family of large theropods with massive heads, long jaws, double-edged teeth, very short forelimbs, three-fingered hands, strong hind legs, and feet with large-taloned claws.

    Megalosaurus may have resembled the better known *Allosaurus* from western North America. It was thick-necked, and had a robust upper arm. The lower arm bones were stout, and slightly more than half the length of the upper arm.

    Early conceptions of the dinosaur's appearance were dramatically misguided. It was pictured as a giant, an elephantine, lizardlike, humpbacked monster, and estimated as 21 meters (about 70 feet) long. Since its naming in 1824, much material—most of it unfounded—has been referred to *Megalosaurus*, so that this genus has become, over the years, a "junk basket" category for any large, little known carnivorous dinosaur. Indeed, after more than a century and a half, more species have been referred to *Megalosaurus* than to any other dinosaur. Many of those have now been placed in other genera. Most were based on material too poor to be positively identified.

    As *Megalosaurus* itself was founded on fragmentary remains, comparing it with other dinosaurs is difficult at best.

MELANOROSAURUS

(muh-LAN-oh-ruh-SAW-rus)

Type Species: *readi* (REE-dye)
Classification:
- Order: Saurischia
- Suborder: Prosauropoda
- Family: Melanorosauridae

Name: Greek *melas* = black + Greek *oros* = mountain + Greek *sauros* = lizard

Size: 12 meters (40 feet) long

Period: Late Triassic, 228 million to 219 million years ago

Place: South Africa

Diet: Plants

This large, early plant-eater established the family of melanorosaurids, a group of large prosauropods that tended to walk on all fours. *Melanorosaurus* is the largest and heaviest of the known prosauropods. It bears some resemblance to the later sauropods, which were the largest of all dinosaurs. It had a small head, long neck, long tail, powerful legs, and sturdy bones. Although some melanorosaurids were at least partially bipedal, this heavily built dinosaur probably walked on all fours.

METRIACANTHOSAURUS

(MET-ree-uh-KAN-thuh-SAW-rus)

Type Species: *parkeri* (PAHR-kuh-rye)
Classification:
    Order: Saurischia
    Suborder: Theropoda
    Family: ?Megalosauridae
Name: Greek *metrios* = of moderate measure + Greek *akanthos* = spine + Greek *sauros* = lizard
Size: Large
Period: Late Jurassic, 160 million years ago
Place: England
Diet: Meat

    Metriacanthosaurus, a large carnivore with a humped back, was so closely related to *Megalosaurus* (also from England), that it was originally believed to be a new species of *Megalosaurus*.

    Metriacanthosaurus was distinguished by the high spines of its dorsal vertebrae. These spines were about 25 centimeters (almost 10 inches) long, twice the length of the vertebrae. With the accompanying back muscles, they would have created a kind of humpback.

MICROCERATOPS

(MYE-kroh-SER-uh-tops)

Type Species: *gobiensis* (GOH-bee-EN-sis)
Classification:

Order:	Ornithischia
Suborder:	Ceratopsia
Family:	Protoceratopsidae

Name: Greek *mikros* = small + Greek *keratos* = horned + Greek *ops* = face

Size: 76 centimeters (30 inches) long

Period: Late Cretaceous, 83 million to 65 million years ago

Place: China

Diet: Plants

This child-sized plant-eater is one of the tiniest known dinosaurs. *Microceratops* was a lightly built, small-sized protoceratopsid, or horned dinosaur, with a short frill and slender forelimbs.

Microceratops probably resembled the better known primitive horned dinosaurs *Protoceratops* and *Leptoceratops*. Though more slender, the upper forelimb bone in *Microceratops* resembles that in *Leptoceratops*, and measures 10 centimeters (4 inches) long. The upper hindlimb bone of *Microceratops* is more slender than that in both *Leptoceratops* and *Protoceratops*. The entire hind limb of *Microceratops* is exceptionally long, compared with the length of its trunk, for the bird-hipped dinosaurs, suggesting that this animal was capable of running well on its hind legs. Its unusually long forelimbs may have been used when walking, perhaps at a slower pace, on all fours.

MICROCOELUS
(MYE-kroh-SEE-lus)

Status: Doubtful — *See Saltasaurus*

"MICRODONTOSAURUS"

(MYE-kroh-DON-tuh-SAW-rus)

Type Species: *dayensis* (day-EN-sis)
Status: Unofficial
Classification:
  Order: Saurischia
  Suborder: Sauropoda
  Family: ?
Name: Greek *mikros* = small + Greek *odontos* = tooth +
                Greek *sauros* = lizard
Size: Relatively small for the large sauropods
Period: Late Cretaceous, 98 million to 65 million
                years ago
Place: China
Diet: Plants

    "Microdontosaurus" was a sauropod, one of the very large dinosaurs with small heads, long necks, and pillarlike legs. Named for its tiny teeth, it has not yet been formally described.

MICROHADROSAURUS

(MYE-kroh-HAD-ruh-SAW-rus)

Type Species: *nanshiungensis* (NAN-shee-ung-EN-sis)
Status: Doubtful
Classification:
  Order: Ornithischia
  Suborder: Ornithopoda
  Family: ?Hadrosauridae
Name: Greek *mikros* = small + Greek *hadros* = large + Greek *sauros* = lizard
Size: 2.6 meters (8.75 feet) long
Period: Late Cretaceous, ?97.5 million to ?65 million years ago
Place: China
Diet: Plants

Microhadrosaurus was a flat-headed duckbill known only from a partial lower jaw with teeth belonging to a juvenile dinosaur. This tiny animal's jaw was quite similar to the large, well known hadrosaurine genus *Edmontosaurus*, and may represent a young member of a known genus and species.

MICROPACHYCEPHALOSAURUS

(MYE-kroh-PACK-i-SEF-uh-loh-SAW-rus)

Type Species: *hongtuyanensis* (HONG-too-yuh-NEN-sis)

Classification:

Order: Ornithischia

Suborder: Marginocephalia

Family: Pachycephalosauridae

Name: Greek *mikros* = small + Greek *pachy* = thick + Greek *kephalos* = head + *sauros* = lizard

Size: Very small

Period: Late Cretaceous, 83 million to 73 million years ago

Place: China

Diet: Plants

Micropachycephalosaurus is one of only two bone-headed (pachycephalosaur) dinosaurs discovered in China. The other is *Wannanosaurus*. Other than to note that it was a relatively small pachycephalosaur, it has not been formally described.

The species differs from all other known Asian pachycephalosaurians in various details of the upper hindlimb bone and the upper bone of the pelvic girdle.

Though it is small, *Micropachycephalosaurus* has the longest name of any known dinosaur.

MICROSAUROPS

(MYE-kruh-SAW-rops)

Type Species: None designated
Status: Invalid
Classification:
  Order: Saurischia
  Suborder: Sauropoda
  Family: ?Titanosauridae
Name: Greek *mikros* = small + Greek *sauros* = lizard +
  Greek *ops* = face
Size: Relatively small
Period: Late Cretaceous, ?97.5 million to ?65 million
  years ago
Place: Argentina
Diet: Plants

   This four-legged, plant-eating dinosaur is very poorly known. It was apparently a small, odd titanosaurid, one of the sauropod family, some or all of which had skin armor. Since the fossil material from which it was named is missing or unavailable, little can be known of its true identity.

MICROVENATOR

(MYE-kroh-vi-NAY-tor)

Type Species: *celer* (CHEL-ur)
Classification:

Order:	Saurischia
Suborder:	Theropoda
Family:	?

Name: Greek *mikros* = small + Latin *venator* = hunter

Size: 1.2 meters (4 feet) long; weight 6.4 kilograms (14 pounds)

Period: Early Cretaceous, 119 million to 113 million years ago

Place: Montana

Diet: Meat

Microvenator is one of the smallest known carnivorous dinosaurs. Though twice the size of *Compsognathus*, it was still no bigger than a turkey. Since its bones were well formed, it is clear they were not those of a juvenile individual.

Microvenator may have been most closely related to *Compsognathus, Ornitholestes*, and *Coelurus*. However, it had features that suggest it might have had affinities with the Caenagnathidae, a family of birdlike theropods. Perhaps *Microvenator* was a primitive caenagnathid, or even a relative of the ostrich dinosaurs, the Ornithomimidae.

Microvenator chagyabi (CHAG-yuh-bye) — Doubtful name: A possible second species, this animal has not yet been described.

MINMI

(MIN-mee)

Type Species: *paravertebra* (PAR-uh-VUR-ti-bruh)
Classification:

Order:	Ornithischia
Suborder:	Ankylosauria
Family:	Nodosauridae

Name: *Minmi* (Crossing) Australia

Size: 3 meters (10 feet) long

Period: Early Cretaceous, 119 million to 113 million years ago

Place: Australia

Diet: Plants

    Minmi was a nodosaurid, an armored ankylosaur without a clubbed tail. It was unique in comparison with nodosaurs from other continents: *Minmi* was small, with unusual plated structures upon its body. A new word, "paravertebra," was coined by its describer, paleontologist Ralph Molnar, in response to these structures.

    Well-preserved dinosaur skeletons from Australia are unusual, yet much of *Minmi* was found in good shape, including small bony armor on its underside. Belly armor is not known on other armored dinosaurs.

    Flat platelike structures alongside the arches of the back vertebrae also make *Minmi* unique not only among ankylosaurs, but among all other backboned dinosaurs. Originally, these structures were thought to have been attached to armor, serving either to move the armor as a threatening or defensive display, or else attached to the ribs, presumably as an aid in breathing. Now, however, some paleontologists have reinterpreted these plates as buttresses for the spinal column, especially at the pelvis. Others suggest these structures may be modified bony tendons.

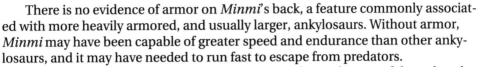

There is no evidence of armor on *Minmi*'s back, a feature commonly associated with more heavily armored, and usually larger, ankylosaurs. Without armor, *Minmi* may have been capable of greater speed and endurance than other ankylosaurs, and it may have needed to run fast to escape from predators.

Minmi was the first ankylosaur found in Australia, and is one of the only ankylosaurs known from the Southern Hemisphere. Its presence there in the Early Cretaceous Period offers evidence supporting the existence of a land route into Australia via South America. It also reflects the widespread distribution of ankylosaurs shortly after their original appearance in the Late Jurassic Period.

Minmi is also distinguished for having the shortest dinosaur name.

MOCHLODON

(MOCK-luh-don)

Status: Doubtful — *See Rhabdodon*

MONGOLOSAURUS

(mong-GOH-luh-SAW-rus)

Type Species: *haplodon* (HAP-luh-don)
Status: Doubtful
Classification:
  Order: Saurischia
  Suborder: Sauropoda
  Family: ?
Name: Mongolia + Greek *sauros* = lizard
Size: Large
Period: Early Cretaceous, ?144 million to ?97.5 million
                years ago
Place: Mongolia
Diet: Plants

Mongolosaurus is another poorly known, large, four-legged browser of uncertain family classification. Most of what we know about this dinosaur is based on its teeth. They are unlike those of any previously known sauropod: tapered and set at an obtuse angle, somewhat flattened on the inner side, and rounded on the outer side. These teeth resemble those in *Diplodocus* and *Pleurocoelus*, but differ in the faintly serrated borders of the crown.

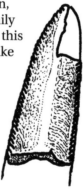

Mongolosaurus haplodon teeth

MONKONOSAURUS

(mong-KON-uh-SAW-rus)

Type Species: *Iawulacus* (LAW-wuh-LAH-kus)
Classification:

Order:	Ornithischia
Suborder:	Stegosauria
Family:	Stegosauridae

Name: *Monko* (county in eastern part of Tibet) + Greek *sauros* = lizard

Size: 5 meters (approximately 16.75 feet) long

Period: Late Jurassic or Early Cretaceous, ?150 million to 138 million years ago

Place: Tibet

Diet: Plants

    The first dinosaur known from Tibet, *Monkonosaurus* was originally thought to be a pachycephalosaur, or bone-headed dinosaur. In fact, *Monkonosaurus* was a medium-sized stegosaur, with large, thin plates similar in shape to those in *Stegosaurus.*

MONOCLONIUS

(MON-uh-KLOH-nee-us)

Type Species: *crassus* (KRAS-us)

Classification:

Order:	Ornithischia
Suborder:	Ceratopsia
Family:	Ceratopsidae

Name: Greek *monos* = single + Greek *klon* = twig

Size: 5 meters (17 feet) long

Period: Late Cretaceous, 76 million to 73 million years ago

Place: Montana; Alberta

Diet: Plants

Monoclonius was one of the larger horned dinosaurs. It had comparatively small brow horns that pointed upwards, and a prominent single horn on the nose.

The only complete skull of *Monoclonius* seems large enough to have been that of an adult, though the open sutures between the bones suggest that it was a younger individual.

In the past, *Monoclonius* has been regarded as the same genus as "Centrosaurus" (now *Eucentrosaurus*). In fact, most life restorations of *Monoclonius* have been based upon the better-preserved fossil remains of *Centrosaurus*, from Alberta. Some paleontologists now regard the two genera as distinct, one of the main differences being the lack of hooks on the edge of *Monoclonius*'s. Current research may finally clarify our understanding of *Monoclonius* and its relationship to other horned dinosaurs.

Monoclonius dawsoni (DAW-suh-nye): This species was based upon a skull that lacked much of its back end. It had a large, backward-curving nasal horn, and small horn cores near the eyes.

"MONOLOPHOSAURUS"

(MON-uh-LOH-fuh-SAW-rus)

Type Species: *jiangjiunmiaoi* (jee-ANG-jee-un-mee-OU-eye)
Status: Unofficial
Classification:
   Order: Saurischia
   Suborder: Theropoda
   Family: ?Megalosauridae
Name: Greek *monos* = single + Greek *lophos* = crest + Greek *sauros* = lizard
Size: Large
Period: Late Jurassic, 170 million years ago
Place: China
Diet: Meat

   "Monolophosaurus," a large theropod, had a big head which was distinguished by a crest above the snout and eyes. The crest may have had some display function, perhaps used by males to attract females, or to establish territory.

   This carnivore, discovered in the far northwest of China in 1984, has yet to be formally described. It may be a megalosaurid, or a member of another large predator family, an eustreptospondylid, or an allosaurid.

MONTANOCERATOPS

(mon-TAN-uh-SER-uh-tops)

Type Species: *cerorhynchus* (SER-uh-RIN-chus)
Classification:

Order:	Ornithischia
Suborder:	Ceratopsia
Family:	Protoceratopsidae
Name:	Montana + Greek *keratos* = horned + Greek *ops* = face
Size:	1.8 meters (6 feet) long
Period:	Late Cretaceous, 73 million to 70 million years ago
Place:	Montana
Diet:	Plants

Montanoceratops was a small horned dinosaur. It bore a superficial resemblance to its slightly more primitive Asian relative, *Protoceratops*. However, *Montanoceratops* had a proportionately larger, deeper, heavier snout with a well-developed horn core. It was more developed than *Protoceratops*, since it had a pronounced nose horn, comparatively longer forelimbs, a higher back, and generally more robust bones.

Montanoceratops seems to have been the most advanced member of the protoceratopsid family, since it shared many features with their more sophisticated cousins, the ceratopsids (true horned dinosaurs). These features include a broader-based nose horn.

The namesake skeleton of *Montanoceratops*, which was displayed at the American Museum of Natural History in New York, was approximately the size of larger individual *Protoceratops*.

MORINOSAURUS

(muh-REE-noh-SAW-rus)

Type Species: *typus* (TYE-pus)
Status: Doubtful
Classification:
  Order: Saurischia
  Suborder: Sauropoda
  Family: Brachiosauridae
Name: Indo-European *mori* (from the Latin *mare*, referring to the French *mer*) = sea + Greek *sauros* = lizard
Size: Very large
Period: Late Jurassic, 153 million to 150 million years ago
Place: France
Diet: Plants

    Morinosaurus is a poorly known member of the brachiosaurids, a family of giant sauropods of which *Brachiosasurus* is representative. *Morinosaurus* was named by a very worn tooth, and a partial upper arm bone which may have belonged to the same animal. The tooth was characterized by an internal edge with a strong peak, similar to that of another sauropod from France, *Hypselosaurus.*

MOROSAURUS

(MOR-uh-SAW-rus)

Type Species: *impar* (IM-pahr)
Status: Invalid — *See Camarasaurus*
Name: Greek *moros* = doom + Greek *sauros* = lizard

MUSSAURUS

(MOO-SAW-rus)

Type Species: *patagonicus* (PAT-uh-GON-i-kus)
Classification:
  Order: Saurischia
  Suborder: Prosauropoda
  Family: Plateosauridae
Name: Latin *mus* = mouse + Greek *sauros* = lizard
Size: Tiny [baby about 37 centimeters (16 inches) long;
              adult size unknown]
Period: Late Triassic, 215 million years ago
Place: Argentina
Diet: Plants

The almost complete skeleton of *Mussaurus*, which fits in a man's cupped hands, is the smallest dinosaur skeleton, excluding embryos, yet found.

The skeleton belonged to a very young prosauropod. It had a short, high skull and a very short snout. The skull measured just 3.2 centimeters (about 1¼ inches) in length; its upper leg bone only 30 millimeters (about 1.2 inches) long, and its lower leg bone just 27 millimeters (about 1 inch) long.

MUTTABURRASAURUS

(MUT-uh-BUR-uh-SAW-rus)

Type Species: *langdoni* (LANG-don-eye)
Classification:

    Order: Ornithischia

    Suborder: Ornithopoda

    Family: Iguanodontidae

Name: Muttaburra (township in central Queensland) + Greek *sauros* = lizard

Size: About 7 meters (24 feet) long

Period: Lower Cretaceous, 113 million to 97.5 million years ago

Place: Australia

Diet: Plants

    Muttaburrasaurus was a large plant-eater with a flat snout. Its head was distinguished by a bumplike rise between its snout and eyes. This swelling may have enhanced the animal's sense of smell or amplified sound. This dinosaur's teeth, unlike those of *Iguanodon* and *Camptosaurus*, seem to have worked like a pair of shears, leading to speculation that, unlike all other known bird-hipped dinosaurs, *Muttaburrasaurus* may have been partially carnivorous.

    Muttaburrasaurus also may have had a spike-shaped thumb that was larger, relative to the size of its other digits, than the thumb spike in *Iguanodon*. *Muttaburrasaurus*, originally classified as an iguanodontid, is now thought to be more similar to the camptosaurid, *Camptosaurus*.

NANOSAURUS

(NAN-uh-SAW-rus)

Type Species: *agilis* (uh-JIL-is)
Status: Doubtful
Classification:
   Order: Ornithischia
   Suborder: Ornithopoda
   Family: Hypsilophodontidae
Name: Greek *nanos* = dwarf + Greek *sauros* = lizard
Size: 60-120 centimeters (2-4 feet) long; 30-46
             centimeters (12-18 inches) high at hips
Period: Late Jurassic, 156 million to 145 million years ago
Place: Utah, Colorado
Diet: Plants

   Nanosaurus was the first of the Late Jurassic North American ornithischian (plant-eating dinosaurs) to be described. A small animal, it was established on an incomplete jaw bone found in a slab of very fine sandstone. The poorly preserved fossil had indistinct impressions of fifteen teeth. Since the fossil evidence is so scant, *Nanosaurus* is difficult to classify with certainty.

NANOTYRANNUS

(NAN-uh-tye-RAN-us)

Type Species: *lancensis* (lan-SEN-sis)
Classification:
    Order: Saurischia
    Suborder: Theropoda
    Family: Tyrannosauridae
Name: Greek *nanos* = dwarf + Greek *tyrannos* = absolute
                  sovereign
Size: ?Relatively small; weighed about 250-450
                  kilograms (600 to 1,000 pounds)
Period: Late Cretaceous, 68 million to 65 million
                  years ago
Place: Montana
Diet: Meat

Nanotyrannus was the smallest known, and one of the last, of the tyrannosaurids, a family of large carnivores. *Nanotyrannus* was classified in 1988 upon a well-preserved, almost complete skull found in 1942. The skull, which had languished in the basement of the Cleveland Museum of Natural History, had been affixed with gorgosaur-style horns that were a preparer's plaster invention. It had originally been named *Gorgosaurus lancensis*, a third species of *Gorgosaurus*.

In addition to its relatively small size, this so-called "pygmy" tyrannosaur was distinguished by several features of its long, low skull. It more closely resembled a miniature *Tyrannosaurus* than *Gorgosaurus*. Its snout was particularly long and narrow; the back of its skull was wide; and its eyes were forwardly directed for binocular vision, instead of the more lizardlike eye orientation of *Gorgosaurus*.

Although the skull seems to be that of an adult individual, it is only half the size of an adult *Albertosaurus libratus*. The skull is the smallest of any known adult tyrannosaurid, measuring just 572 millimeters (approximately 22 inches) long.

Some paleontologists have questioned the validity of *Nanotyrannus*, regarding it as a juvenile specimen of *Tyrannosaurus*.

NANSHIUNGOSAURUS

(NAN-shee-UNG-guh-SAW-rus)

Type Species: *brevispinus* (BREV-i-SPYE-nus)
Classification:

    Order: Saurischia

    Suborder: Segnosauria

    Family: Segnosauridae

Name: Nanshiung (province of China) + Greek *sauros* = lizard

Size: ?4 meters (13 feet) long

Period: Late Cretaceous, 75 million years ago

Place: Nanshiung, China

Diet: Plants

Nanshiungosaurus was originally believed to be a peculiar, relatively small, sauropod. It is now known to be a segnosaur, one of the recently discovered lizard-hipped dinosaurs resembling prosauropods. Segnosaurs had horny beaks, followed by a toothless front-of-the-jaw, then by cheek teeth. These odd animals had hands like the carnivorous theropods, stout hind legs, and broad clawed feet.

NEMEGTOSAURUS

(ni-MEG-tuh-SAW-rus)

Type Species: *mongoliensis* (mong-GOH-lee-EN-sis)

Classification:

   Order: Saurischia

   Suborder: Sauropoda

   Family: Diplodocidae

Name: *Nemegt* (Formation) + Greek *sauros* = lizard

Size: ?Large

Period: Late Cretaceous, ?75 million to 70 million years ago

Place: Gobi Desert, Mongolia

Diet: Plants

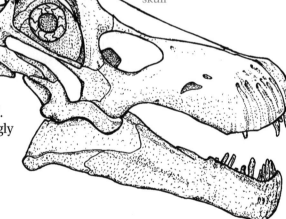

*Nemegtosaurus
mongoliensis
skull*

   Nemegtosaurus may have been one of the diplodocids, a family of large, whiptailed, four-legged plant-eaters. It appears to have been an intermediate form between *Dicraeosaurus* and *Diplodocus.*

   Nemegtosaurus's is the only nearly complete skull found in the world for any sauropod from the Late Cretaceous Period. It was long, lightly constructed, and strongly elongated, with a long, downwardly bent snout. The eye holes were large, the lower jaw was light, and the teeth were lance-shaped.

NEOSAURUS

(NEE-uh-SAW-rus)

Status: Invalid — *See Parrosaurus*

NEOSODON

(NEE-oh-suh-don)

Type Species: [None designated]
Classification:
    Order: Saurischia
    Suborder: Sauropoda
    Family: Brachiosauridae
Name: Greek *neos* = new + Greek *odontos* = tooth
Size: ?Very large
Period: Late Jurassic, 160 million to 148 million years ago
Place: France
Diet: Plants

This was a very large brachiosaurid, and so one of the largest dinosaurs known. Brachiosaurids were one of the giraffe-necked, four-legged browsing dinosaurs, of which *Brachiosaurus* is the most famous. *Neosodon*, named from a large, well-worn tooth with a broken point and root, is very poorly known. The tooth, originally thought to come from a carnivorous dinosaur, *Megalosaurus*, is 60 millimeters (more than 2.3 inches) high, blackish in color, smooth, and rather flat. It resembles the head of a spear.

Some researchers regard *Neosodon* as the same genus as *Pelorosaurus*.

NEUQUENSAURUS

(NOY-kwen-SAW-rus)

Type Species: *australis* (aw-STRAL-is)
Classification:
  Order: Saurischia
  Suborder: Sauropoda
  Family: Titanosauridae
Name: Neuquen (city in Argentina) + Greek *sauros* = lizard
Size: ?Large
Period: Late Cretaceous, ?97.5 million to 65 million years ago
Place: Argentina
Diet: Plants

  Neuquensaurus was originally described as a species of *Titanosaurus*, a large four-legged browser of the armor-skinned titanosaur family. It differs from other known North American sauropods in lacking grooves in its back vertebrae, which probably made for a more solidly built back and (possibly) neck. This dinosaur had long, slender upper limbs. It also had armor, round-to-oval plates, and small, irregularly shaped bumps. These armor patches were at first believed to belong to an ankylosaur. However, a more recent discovery of similar plates and bumps, referred to the titanosaurid *Saltasaurus loricatus*, has raised the possibility that other—or even all—titanosaurids were similarly armored. *Neuquensaurus* may even be a species of *Saltasaurus*.

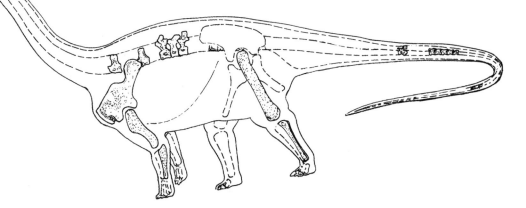

"NGEXISAURUS"

(nuh-GEK-si-SAW-rus)

Type Species: *dapukaensis* (duh-POO-kay-EN-sis)
Status: Unofficial
Classification:
   Order: Saurischia
   Suborder: Theropoda
   Family: ?
Name: ? + Greek *sauros* = lizard
Size: ?Small
Period: Jurassic, ?200 million to ?145 million years ago
Place: China
Diet: Meat

    It is almost as difficult to determine what *Ngexisaurus* was as it is to spell it. Apparently it was a small theropod. It belonged to the large group Coelurosauria, which was made up of very primitive forms with relatively large heads. If so, "*Ngexisaurus*" probably had three-toed feet, and was capable of running fast. Since it has never been described, nothing can be said about it with any assurance.

NIPPONOSAURUS

(ni-PON-uh-SAW-rus)

Type Species: *sachalinensis* (SACK-uh-li-NEN-sis)
Classification:
    Order: Ornithischia
    Suborder: Ornithopoda
    Family: Hadrosauridae
Name: Japanese Nippon = Japan + Greek sauros = lizard
Size: Small for a duckbilled dinosaur
Period: Late Cretaceous, 88 million to 86 million
           years ago
Place: Sakhalin Island
Diet: Plants

    Nipponosaurus was a relatively small lambeosaurine, a hollow-crested, duck-billed dinosaur with a short, deep, and somewhat broad skull. A low "swelling" on the skull may represent the just-beginning growth of a domelike crest, and can be attributed to the individual's immaturity.

    Nipponosaurus was founded on an incomplete juvenile skeleton that has yet to be fully studied. It is one of the very rare dinosaur finds on Asian islands. It may be the same genus as *Jaxartosaurus,* but no adult specimens of *Nipponosaurus* have been found.

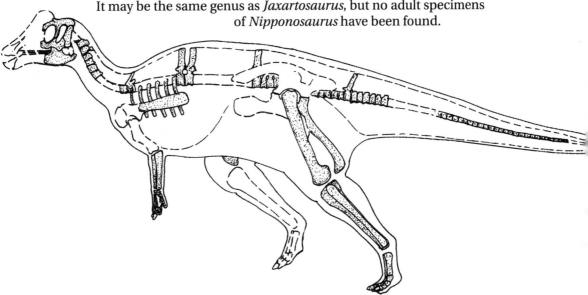

NOASAURUS

(NOH-uh-SAW-rus)

Type Species: *leali* (LEE-uh-lye)
Classification:

Order:	Saurischia
Suborder:	Theropoda
Family:	Noasauridae
Name:	Spanish (abbreviation) *Noa* or *NOA* (Northwestern Argentina) + Greek *sauros* = lizard
Size:	1.8 meters (6 feet) long
Period:	Late Cretaceous, ?75 million to 65 million years ago
Place:	Argentina
Diet:	Meat, possibly birds and young sauropods

Noasaurus was a small carnivorous dinosaur distinguished by its "killer claw." The second toe of its foot had a sickle claw, larger and capable of a wider angle of movement than *Deinonychus*, another clawed animal. As indicated by its different anatomical structure, *Noasaurus's* claw evolved independently from that of *Deinonychus*.

Noasaurus was slender, and probably agile. The structure of its teeth and hind foot suggests it preyed on small animals such as birds and young sauropods.

It was the first "coelurosaur," one of a questionable grouping of small carnivores, to be discovered in South America. Because it is known only by partial remains, it is difficult to assess its relationship to other coelurosaurs. Since so few skulls of Cretaceous coelurosaurs are known, *Noasaurus* was put into its own family, the Noasauridae.

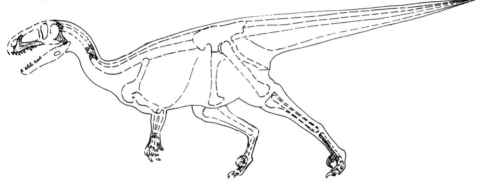

NODOSAURUS

(NOH-duh-SAW-rus)
(=Hierosaurus, Stegopelta)

Type Species: *textilis* (TEX-ti-lus)
Classification:
   Order: Ornithischia
   Suborder: Ankylosauria
   Family: Nodosauridae
Name: Latin *nodus* = knob + Greek *sauros* = lizard
Size: 6 meters (20 feet) long
Period: Early Cretaceous, 113 million to 98.5 million
             years ago
Place: Wyoming, Kansas
Diet: Plants

    Nodosaurus was the first dinosaur to be named in the nodosaurid family, a group of armored dinosaurs without tail clubs. Its remains were originally thought to belong to a new genus of stegosaur. *Nodosaurus's* armor covered its sides. As some armor was found in its original position, we know that these plates were arranged in a series of rows. The external surface of the armor was marked by a pattern that appears interwoven.

    This was a bulky creature with massive, powerful front limbs, which had five well-developed digits. As *Nodosaurus* remains are not complete, it is not known whether it had spikes projecting from its sides like other nodosaurids. Its tail seems to have been slender, flexible, and about half the length of the trunk.

    Now considered to be *Nodosaurus* are the fossils of ankylosaurs once named *Stegopelta* and *Hierosaurus*. *Stegopelta* was founded upon incomplete material from Benton, Wyoming. *Hierosaurus* was named from a pair of armored plates, perhaps from its tail, and six scutes, found in Logan County, Kansas.

NOTOCERATOPS

(NOH-toh-SER-uh-tops)

Type Species: *bonarelli* (BON-uh-REL-eye)

Status: Doubtful

Classification:

    Order: Ornithischia

    Suborder: ?

    Family: ?

Name: Greek *noton* = back + Greek *keratos* = horned + Greek *ops* = face

Size: ?Small

Period: Late Cretaceous, ?83 million to 73 million years ago

Place: Patagonia, Argentina

Diet: Plants

This is a poorly understood dinosaur of uncertain classification. *Notoceratops* was founded upon the fragment of a left jaw bone, discovered in 1917. It was originally believed to belong to the ceratopsians, the horned, plant-eating dinosaurs.

The specimen was distinguished by its small size, measuring only 24.5 centimeters (about 9.5 inches) in length, with an estimated complete length of 30 centimeters (about 11.5 inches). These remains were first attributed to the comparably sized *Protoceratops*.

Because no other horned dinosaurs were reported from South America, Australian paleontologist Ralph E. Molnar speculated that *Notoceratops* was actually a duckbilled dinosaur. Just what *Notoceratops* was has yet to be determined.

NUROSAURUS

(NOOR-uh-SAW-rus)

Type Species: *qaganensis* (KWAG-uh-NEN-sis)
Status: Invalid
Classification:
   Order: Saurischia
   Suborder: Sauropoda
   Family: Camarasauridae
Name: ? + Greek *sauros* = lizard
Size: 25 meters (85 feet) long
Period: ?
Place: China
Diet: Plants

   Nurosaurus has not yet been described, although it has been called an unusual sauropod by its discoverer, Chinese paleontologist Dong Zhiming. It is believed to have been a camarasaurid, but its skeleton superficially resembles that of *Brachiosaurus*, with front legs that are longer than its hind legs. This dinosaur was first mentioned in a Japanese book as *Nuoerosaurus chaganensis*.

OHMDENOSAURUS

(ohm-DEN-uh-SAW-rus)

Type Species: *liasicus* (lye-AS-i-kus)
Classification:
    Order: Saurischia
    Suborder: Sauropoda
    Family: ?Vulcanodontidae
Name: Ohmden (discovery site) + Greek *sauros* = lizard
Size: 3 to 4 meters (10 to 13.5+ feet) long
Period: Early Jurassic, 191 million years ago
Place: Germany
Diet: Plants

    Ohmdenosaurus was one of the earliest sauropods, or giant browsing dinosaurs. The first fossil found, a lower-leg bone, was initially mistaken for the upper arm of a plesiosaur, a marine reptile. *Ohmdenosaurus's* tibia was massive, indicating that this dinosaur had powerful hind limbs.

    Ohmdenosaurus has been tentatively referred to the vulcanodontid sauropods, an "intermediate" family between the more primitive two- and four-legged prosauropods and their later, larger four-legged cousins, sauropods. Some paleontologists have suggested that vulcanodontids are advanced prosauropods, while others think that *Ohmdenosaurus* and other vulcanodonts were primitive sauropods.

OLIGOSAURUS

(oh-LIG-uh-SAW-rus)

Status: Doubtful — *See Rhabdodon*

OMEISAURUS

(OH-may-SAW-rus)

Type Species: *junghsienensis* (JOONG-see-en-EN-sis)

Classification:

Order: Saurischia

Suborder: Sauropoda

Family: Cetiosauridae

Name: Omeishan (sacred mountain) + Greek sauros = lizard

Size: 16 to 20 meters (54 to 68 feet) long

Period: Late Jurassic, 156 million to 145 million years ago

Place: China

Diet: Plants

Omeisaurus was a medium-sized, slow-moving sauropod, the family of four-legged herbivores that included the largest of all land animals. Its skull was placed high on an extremely long neck. It had a moderately developed snout, with the nostrils placed toward the front, and it had spoon-shaped teeth. Judging by the large number of *Omeisaurus* individuals found in one area of less than 3,000 square meters, it may have been a sociable dinosaur.

Omeisaurus may be closely allied with *Datousaurus*. Because of the abundance and completeness of its remains, when fully described it will be among the best-known sauropods.

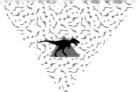

OMEISAURUS *continued*

This animal is already considered to be the same animal as the dinosaur originally named *Zigongsaurus fuxiensis*. That small sauropod was first described as a large brachiosaurid which may have reached as much as 15 meters (50 feet) in length.

Omeisaurus changshouensis (CHANG-shoo-EN-sis): This somewhat larger species is based on remains from Moutzenshan, in the Changshouhsien county of China. The tibia and fibula (lower hindlimb bones) were proportionately quite long. This species was similar to *O. junghsienensis*, and also to another exceptionally long-necked sauropod, *Mamenchisaurus*. *O. changshouensis* is therefore a problematic species that may or may not belong in the genus *Omeisaurus*.

Omeisaurus luoquanensis (LOO-kwuh-NEN-sis): Based on two partial skeletons from Luoquan, a village in the Szechuan province of China, *O. luoquanensis* was very similar in size and shape to *Omeisaurus tianfuensis*. *Omeisaurus luoquanensis* differs in various details, including a remarkably straight upper forelimb bone with a long, slender shaft.

Omeisaurus tianfuensis (TEE-an-FUN-sis): This better known species is based on an incomplete skeleton, including the skull, of a large animal from a quarry near Zigong. Skulls from sauropods are extremely rare: scarcely two dozen of them have been found in the world. This skull was wedge-shaped in side view, with robust, spoon-shaped teeth.

The basic outline of the species' skeleton resembled *Mamenchisaurus hochuanensis*, especially its elongated neck, relatively short trunk, and the short fore- and hind limbs for its body length. Because of those similarities, it was assumed that a close affinity existed between the two species. However, the first four dorsal spines in *Mamenchisaurus* are divided, while those in the *Omeisaurus* species are not.

OMOSAURUS

(OH-muh-SAW-rus)

Type Species: armatus (ahr-MAY-tus)
Status: Invalid — *See Dacentrus*

ONYCHOSAURUS

(ON-i-kuh-SAW-rus)

Type Species: hungaricus (hung-GAR-i-kus)
Status: Doubtful — *See Rhabdodon*

OPISTHOCOELICAUDIA

(oh-PIS-thuh-SEE-li-KAW-dee-uh)

Type Species: *skarzynskii* (skahr-ZIN-skee-eye)

Classification:

    Order: Saurischia

    Suborder: Sauropoda

    Family: ?Camarasauridae

Name: Greek *opisthen* = behind + Greek *koilas* = valley + Latin *cauda* = tail

Size: 12 meters (40 feet) long

Period: Late Cretaceous, ?75 million to 70 million years ago

Place: Mongolia

Diet: Plants

This large browser was the latest of the known sauropods from Asia. It may have been one of the Camarasauridae, a family with boxy heads, and front and hind legs of about equal length. Among sauropods, it was only midsized, with an unusually straight, streamlined back.

Its tail was shorter than that of *Camarasaurus*, with vertebrae aligned in a manner that shows the tail was carried off the ground in a horizontal position. The tail may have been used as a prop, forming a tripod that allowed the animal to rear up to a bipedal position while feeding on high branches. The animal's massive pelvis could have helped support such a posture.

In *Opisthocoelicaudia*, walking was apparently powered by exceptionally strong muscles attached to the rear of a pelvic bone, the ilium. It probably carried its neck low to the ground.

Opisthocoelicaudia was discovered in 1965 during a Polish-Mongolian Expedition to the Gobi Desert. The type specimen was an unusually complete skeleton, perhaps because the animal was buried in sand before its soft parts decayed completely. Traces of gnaw marks found on the bones suggest that the remains were scavenged by meat-eaters.

OPLOSAURUS

(OH-pluh-SAW-rus)

Type Species: armatus (ahr-MAY-tus)
Status: Doubtful = ?Brachiosaurus, ?Pelorosaurus
Classification:
  Order: Saurischia
  Suborder: Sauropod
  Family: Brachiosauridae
Name: Greek oplon = large shield + Greek sauros = lizard
Size: ?Large
Period: Early Cretaceous, 138 million to 125 million years ago
Place: Isle of Wight, England
Diet: Plants

   This poorly known sauropod was founded on a single, large spoon-shaped tooth similar to that of *Brachiosaurus*, although from a relatively smaller individual.
   Oplosaurus has generally been considered a junior synonym of *Pelorosaurus*. It is probably the same animal as *Pelorosaurus* or *Brachiosaurus*, although its type material is inadequate for a positive match.
   Its name has sometimes been misspelled as *Hoplosaurus*.

ORINOSAURUS

(OR-i-noh-SAW-rus)

Type Species: capensis (kay-PEN-sis)
Status: Doubtful — See Euskelosaurus

ORNATOTHOLUS

(or-NAT-uh-THOH-lus)

Type Species: *browni* (BROW-nye)

Classification:

Order:	Ornithischia
Suborder:	Pachycephalosauria
Family:	Pachycephalosauridae

Name:	Latin *ornatus* = adorned + Latin *tholus* = dome
Size:	Small, 2.5 meters (6.6 feet) long
Period:	Late Cretaceous, 75 million years ago
Place:	Alberta
Diet:	Plants

This primitive bone-headed dinosaur, a pachycephalosaur, was first described as a possible female of the better known *Stegoceras validus*. The pachycephalosaurs were a rare group of small bird-hipped dinosaurs whose heads were thickened on top, sometimes into a prominent dome.

Ornatotholus had a low dome, with several bony knobs and a groove running across it. Its flat skull-roof differentiates it from the domed *Stegoceras*, although the skulls of both forms are almost the same length.

This genus is important as the first recorded North American flat-headed pachycephalosaurid.

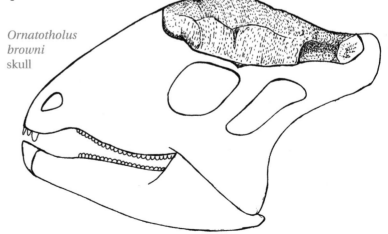

Ornatotholus browni skull

ORNITHODESMUS

(or-NITH-uh-DEZ-mus)

Type Species: *cluniculus* (kloo-NICK-yuh-lus)
Classification:
  Order: Saurischia
  Suborder: Theropoda
  Family: ?
Name: Greek *ornis* = bird + Greek *desmos* = bond
Size: ?Small
Period: Lower Cretaceous, 125 million to 119 million
             years ago
Place: England
Diet: Meat

   Ornithodesmus was known only from a sacrum (the lower part of the vertebral column) with six sacral vertebrae. These lower-back bones, which have been lost, were originally described as being more similar to those of birds than to those of dinosaurs. *Ornithodesmus* was therefore believed to be a primitive bird which was more closely related to dinosaurs than any other then-known fossil birds. Later, its bones were believed to be that of a pterosaur, one of the flying reptiles. *Ornithodesmus* is now regarded as a small theropod, or meat-eating dinosaur, of uncertain classification.

ORNITHOIDES

(OR-ni-THOY-deez)

Type Species: *oshiensis* (OH-shee-EN-sis)
Status: Invalid — *See Saurornithoides*

ORNITHOLESTES

(OR-ni-thuh-LES-teez)

Type Species: *hermanni* (HUR-muh-nye)
Classification:

Order:	Saurischia
Suborder:	Theropoda
Family:	?

Name: Greek *ornis* = bird + Greek *lestes* = robber

Size: 1 to 2 meters (about 3.4 to 6.8 feet) long

Period: Late Jurassic, 156 million to 145 million years ago

Place: Wyoming, Utah

Diet: Meat

This well known meat-eater had a small head with large nostrils. Its skull also seems to show the base of a prominent nose horn or crest.

Another of *Ornitholestes*'s distinguishing features was its narrow four-fingered hand on which there were three elongated fingers and the vestige of a fourth.

The extreme lightness of its skeleton, its long legs, and the possible balancing function of its tail indicate that this was a fast-runnning dinosaur. Early paleontologists thought *Ornitholestes* may have been adapted to hunt Jurassic birds.

ORNITHOMERUS
(or-NITH-uh-MEE-rus)

Type Species: gracilis (GRAS-i-lis)
Status: Doubtful — See Rhabdodon

ORNITHOMIMIDORUM
(or-NITH-uh-MYE-mi-DOR-um)

Status: Invalid — See Betasuchus, Ornithomimus

ORNITHOMIMOIDES

(or-NITH-uh-mye-MOY-deez)

Type Species:	*mobilis* (moh-BIL-is)
Status:	Doubtful
Classification:	
Order:	Saurischia
Suborder:	Theropoda
Family:	?
Name:	Greek *ornis* = bird + Greek *mimos* = mimic + Greek *oides* = appears like
Size:	Large ?2.1 meters (7 feet) long
Period:	Late Cretaceous, 88.5 milllion to 83 million years ago
Place:	India
Diet:	Meat

This large carnivorous dinosaur was named on just five large backbones, each measuring about 9 centimeters (almost 3.5 inches) long. *Ornithomimoides* may be one of the Carnosauria, a group of large meat-eaters that included *Allosaurus*. However, its fossils are too few for this relationship to be demonstrated.

Ornithomimoides barasimiensis (BAR-uh-SEE-mee-EN-sis) — Doubtful name: This species was based on four backbones. These are smaller, shorter, fuller, and more constricted in the middle than in *Ornithomimoides mobilis*. Each measures about 5 centimeters (approximately 1.95 inches) long.

ORNITHOMIMUS

(OR-ni-thuh-MYE-mus)

Type Species: *velox* (VEL-ocks)
Classification:

    Order: Saurischia
    Suborder: Theropoda
    Family: Ornithomimidae

Name: Greek *ornis* = bird + Greek *mimos* = mimic
Size: 3.5 meters (12 feet) long, 2 meters (7 feet) tall
Period: Late Cretaceous, 76 million to 65 million
            years ago
Place: Colorado, Utah, Montana, Wyoming; Alberta
Diet: Meat, ?insects, ?eggs

The discovery of this long-legged dinosaur in 1889 established an entire family of so-called "ostrich-mimic dinosaurs," the ornithomimids, which superficially resembled the modern ostrich.

Like its close relative *Struthiomimus*, *Ornithomimus* had a small head, toothless mouth, long neck, and long-fingered forelimbs.

Long hind limbs, lightly built skeletons, and rod-like tails (used for balance) suggest that *Ornithomimus* and related animals were the fastest of all dinosaurs, attaining speeds of at least 25 mph.

Some paleontologists thought that ornithomimids were herbivorous, or even omnivorous. These ideas were rejected by later researchers on the basis of the close relation of the ornithomimids to the carnivorous theropods. The ornithomimid muzzle was shaped like the beak of insectivorous birds, suggesting it may have eaten insects. The weakly developed jaw muscles suggest they may have subsisted on a diet of eggs or soft-bodied animals. And the complete absence of grinding teeth or gastric stones for crushing vegetable matter indicates that ornithomimids did not eat plants. *Ornithomimus's* large, nimble hands may have been used to clean off foodstuffs found on the ground, or for digging.

Ornithomimus was regarded as the same animal as *Struthiomimus*. However, *Ornithomimus* lived later than *Struthiomimus*, and had lost the remnant of the

ORNITHOMIMUS *continued*

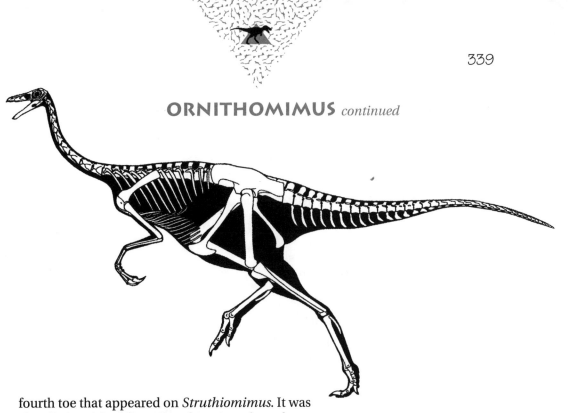

fourth toe that appeared on *Struthiomimus*. It was
also distinguished from *Struthiomimus* by a shorter
back, longer forelimbs with the form of the hand, and shorter hind limbs.

    Ornithomimus edmontonicus (ED-mun-TON-i-kus): A better known species,
O. edmontonicus was based on an almost complete skeleton found in western
Canada. This was a larger, more slender animal than *Ornithomimus velox*. It is
regarded as a distinct species mainly because of its geographic separation from
Ornithomimus velox.

ORNITHOPSIS
(OR-ni-THOP-sis)

Type Species: *hulkei* (HUL-kee-eye)
Status: Doubtful — *See Pelorosaurus*

ORNITHOTARSUS

(OR-ni-thuh-TAHR-sus)

Type Species: *immanis* (IM-uh-nis)
Status: Doubtful — *See Hadrosaurus*
Classification:
  Order: Ornithischia
  Suborder: Ornithopoda
  Family: Hadrosauridae
Name: Greek *ornis* = bird + Greek *tarsos* = the flat of the foot
Size: Large
Period: Late Cretaceous, 83 million to 73 million years ago
Place: New Jersey
Diet: Plants

    Ornithotarsus is one of the many now-doubtful names for duckbilled dinosaurs, names that originated in the early days of dinosaur discoveries. It was founded on fossils consisting of parts of leg bones. These bones were originally thought to belong to a meat-eater related to *Compsognathus*. In fact, they correspond to the same elements of the flat-headed duckbill, *Hadrosaurus,* differing mainly in size and proportions.

ORODROMEUS

(OR-uh-DROH-mee-us)

Type Species: *makelai* (MACK-uh-lye)
Classification:

Order:	Ornithischia
Suborder:	Ornithopoda
Family:	Hypsilophodontidae
Name:	Greek *oros* = (Egg) Mountain + Greek *dromos* = running race
Size:	Small, 2.5 meters (8 feet) long
Period:	Late Cretaceous, 77 to 73 million years ago
Place:	Montana
Diet:	Plants, ?insects

Embryonic remains are among the rarest of dinosaur fossils, but scientists have found several embryos, as well as eggs and babies, of *Orodromeus*. So this member of the family of small plant-eaters, the hypsilophodontids, gives us some of our best insights into dinosaur behavior and development. As it was found at the Egg Mountain site in north-central Montana and was slightly built with long legs, (features advantageous for fast running), John R. Horner and David Weishampel named the animal *Orodromeus*, or "mountain runner."

Orodromeus was named from an almost complete, tiny skull and skeleton discovered by Robert Makela. Fossils found at the same remarkable site included skeletal remains and a clutch of nineteen eggs with embryos. The eggs of *Orodromeus*, and the eggs and nests of the large duckbill, *Maiasaura*, found at Egg Mountain by Makela, Horner, and associates are the first dinosaur eggs and nests discovered in North America.

Orodromeus, like other hypsilophodontids, was a primitive plant-eating dinosaur. It had a small head, and it walked on its hind legs. The proportions of its hind limbs suggest that *Orodromeus* was among the fastest of all hypsilophodontids.

The Egg Mountain hypsilophodontid eggs were identified by embryonic skeletons. The eggs are elongated, averaging about 17 centimeters (6.3 inches) long and 7 centimeters (about 2.75 inches) at their greatest diameter. Under magnification, the surfaces of the eggs show numerous parallel, low-relief, grooves and ridges.

ORODROMEUS *continued*

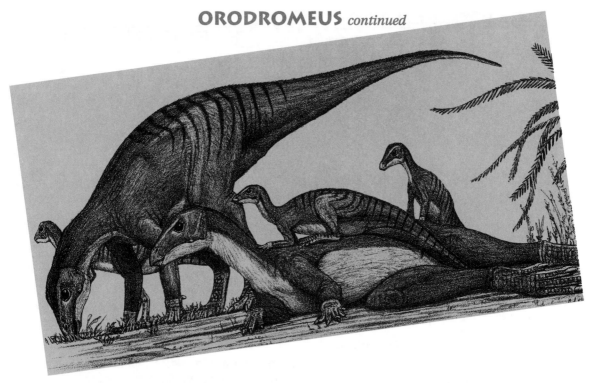

The eggs were laid in a spiral pattern, and the clutches apparently numbered either twelve or twenty-four eggs. As most clutches contained a total of twelve, those with double that number may have represented communal nests.

Because the limbs in the embryos were sufficiently formed to have calcified cartilage, we think this dinosaur may have been developed enough in the egg to be able to seek out its own food almost immediately after hatching. While the contemporary *Maiasaura* babies' bone surfaces are unfinished, suggesting that these young could not fend for themselves shortly after birth, *Orodromeus* young appear to have been hatched "up and running."

Adult hypsilophodonts may have removed vegetation and sediment from the top portions of the eggs, letting the (relatively large) babies hatch themselves out by popping off these tops.

The young at first fed on regurgitated plant matter, then proceeded to eat small plants and insects. They remained under the protection of the adults (whose fossils were also discovered) until they became large and swift enough to fend for themselves.

OROSAURUS

(OR-uh-SAW-rus)

Status: Doubtful — *See Orinosaurus, Euskelosaurus*
Type Species: *capensis* (kuh-PEN-sis)

ORTHOGONIOSAURUS

(OR-thuh-GOH-nee-uh-SAW-rus)

Type Species: *matleyi* (MAT-lee-eye)
Status: Doubtful
Classification:
   Order: Saurischia
   Suborder: Theropoda
   Family: ?
Name: Greek *orthos* = upright + Greek *genea* = family + Greek *sauros* = lizard
Size: ?
Period: Late Cretaceous, ?95 million to 65 million years ago
Place: India
Diet: Meat

Orthogoniosaurus is known from only one incompletely preserved tooth. The tooth is small; the preserved portion measures only 27 millimeters (about 1.1 inches) long.

This serrated tooth may belong to one of the meat-eating carnosaurs (a group of large theropods), but it cannot be identified with certainty.

Orthogoniosaurus
matleyi
tooth

ORTHOMERUS

(or-THOM-uh-rus)

Type Species: *dolloi* (DOH-loh-eye)
Status: Doubtful = *?Telmatosaurus*
Classification:
   Order: Ornithischia
   Suborder: Ornithopoda
   Family: ?Hadrosauridae
Name: Greek *orthos* = upright + Greek *meros* = part or heritage
Size: ?Relatively small (but a juvenile)
Period: Late Cretaceous, 72 million to 65 million years ago
Place: The Netherlands
Diet: Plants

   Orthomerus was the first European dinosaur to be classified as a duckbill. If it was a hadrosaurid (duckbill), it cannot be determined if it was flat-headed (hadrosaurine) or crested (lambeosaurine). The genus *Orthomerus,* founded upon the remains of a juvenile individual, is usually regarded as the junior synonym of *Telmatosaurus,* but it is too poorly known for a positive match.

"OSHANOSAURUS"

(oh-SHAN-uh-SAW-rus)

Type Species: *youngi* (YUNG-eye)
Status: Unofficial
Classification:
   Order: Ornithischia
   Suborder: Ornithopoda
   Family: ?Heterodontosauridae
Name: ?Chinese + Greek *sauros* = lizard
Size: ?Small
Period: Early Jurassic, 208 million to 180 million
               years ago
Place: China
Diet: Plants

   Not yet described scientifically, this animal may have been a heterodontosaurid, a small primitive plant-eater with canine teeth.

OTHNIELIA

(oth-NEE-lee-uh)

(=?Laosaurus)

Type Species: rex (recks)
Classification:
    Order: Ornithischia
    Suborder: Ornithopoda
    Family: Hypsilophodontidae
Name: Othniel (Charles Marsh)
Size: Small, 1.4 meters (4.6 feet) long
Period: Late Jurassic, 156 million to 145 million years ago
Place: Colorado, Utah, Wyoming
Diet: Plants

Othnielia was a member of the Hypsilophodontidae, a family of primitive,
    plant-eating dinosaurs. Hypsilophodontids had small skulls, and walked
    on their hind legs.
        Othnielia closely resembled the better known Hypsilophodon, but
    differed in the shape of its vertebrae. Also, Othnielia had a hind foot
    with more slender digits, and a functional first digit.

OURANOSAURUS

(oo-RAN-uh-SAW-rus)

Type Species: *nigeriensis* (NYE-jur-ee-EN-sis)
Classification:
    Order: Ornithischia
    Suborder: Ornithopoda
    Family: Iguanodontidae
Name: Touareg *ourane* = valiant + Greek *sauros* = lizard
Size: About 7 meters (24 feet) long
Period: Early Cretaceous, 115 million years ago
Place: Niger, Africa
Diet: Plants

   Ouranosaurus was a large bipedal plant-eater of the iguanodont family. Its head was long, large, and relatively deep, and had what resembled the beginnings of a crest near its nose.

OURANOSAURUS *continued*

Its muzzle was long and slender, ending in a beak. But the most distinctive feature of *Ouranosaurus* was its long-spined backbone, suggesting that this animal had a sail-like shape to its back. This finned back appears to have been shared by a large carnivore of the same time and habitat, *Spinosaurus*. Perhaps these North African dinosaurs used their sails as radiators, cooling themselves in the equatorial heat. The sail may also have served as a display feature, making the animal appear to be larger. Perhaps the fin was brightly colored, or marked by decorative lines or patterns.

Ouranosaurus's hand was very delicately constructed. The fifth digit had a small spur, something like the spiked thumb in *Iguanodon*.

OVIRAPTOR

(OH-vi-RAP-tor)

Type Species: *philoceratops* (FYE-loh-SER-uh-tops)

Classification:

    Order: Saurischia

    Suborder: Theropoda

    Family: Oviraptoridae

Name: Latin *ovum* = egg + Latin *raptor* = robber

Size: 1.8 meters (6 feet) long

Period: Late Cretaceous, ?88 million to 70 million years ago

Place: Gobi Desert in Mongolia

Diet: Meat, ?eggs, ?mollusks, ?plants

The unusual theropod *Oviraptor* had an extremely light skull with no teeth, large eye holes, and other perforations in the skull.

Oviraptor was named "egg thief" because the first remains to be found were atop a clutch of eggs allegedly belonging to the horned dinosaur *Protoceratops*. More recently, specimens have been found with a clavicle, or collar bone, a feature of birds once thought to be absent in dinosaurs. Recent discoveries have also shown a considerable degree of variation in *Oviraptor* skulls, especially in the shape of the snout. One specimen features a large, blunt, rounded nasal crest with a prominent, hornlike, prong. These variations may reflect different species, or different male and female forms within a species.

OVIRAPTOR *continued*

A horny sheath probably covered the front of *Oviraptor's* jaws. This "beak" suggests that this dinosaur might have been omnivorous. The form of the jaws and its large-clawed hands indicate that it was a rapacious hunter.

It has been theorized that *Oviraptor* was amphibious; that the strong jaws were adapted for crushing much harder food than eggs (like mollusks); and that the muscular tail may have been used for propulsion, a conclusion which has been disputed in recent years.

Oviraptor mongoliensis (mong-GOH-lee-EN-sis): *Oviraptor mongoliensis* was based on an incomplete skull from Mongolia, originally identified as belonging to genus *Ingenia*. This species was distinguished from the type species by a thick, extremely tall, "cupola-shaped" crest. The high point of the crest was above the eye instead of at the front of the skull, as in the type species. This crest may have served as a display structure, or been used to aid the animal in passing through obstructions such as vegetation. The skull was approximately 16 centimeters (6.2 inches) long. The skeleton was somewhat smaller than that of the type species.

PACHYCEPHALOSAURUS

(PACK-i-SEF-uh-luh-SAW-rus)

Type Species: *wyomingensis* (wye-OH-ming-EN-sis)
Classification:
  Order: Ornithischia
  Suborder: Pachycephalosauria
  Family: Pachycephalosauridae
Name: Greek *pachos* = thick + Greek *kephale* = head +
             Greek *sauros* = lizard
Size: ?4.5 meters (15 feet) long
Period: Late Cretaceous, 68 million to 65 million years ago
Place: Montana, Wyoming, South Dakota, ?Alaska
Diet: Plants

Pachycephalosaurus was the largest and most advanced of the bone-heads, or pachycephalosaurs. This was a rare group of plant-eating, short-faced, bipedal dinosaurs. Its members were called bone-headed because of their thickened skull roofs.

Pachycephalosaurus had a narrow face, leaf-shaped teeth, and an extremely thickened skull roof liberally studded with bumps. Its skull cap was decorated with various- sized spikes.

The skull of this animal measures 62 centimeters (almost 25 inches) in length, and may have belonged to a sub-adult. The bony spikes on its snout may have been used for digging up vegetation, and its thick skull may have been used in head-butting contests between rival males.

Remains now known to belong to *Pachycephalosaurus* were discovered in southeastern Montana more than seventy years before the genus was named and misidentified as part of the armor of a giant armadillo-like reptile, named *Tylosteus*. Today, however, we know that bone-heads are closer to ceratopsians, the horned dinosaurs.

Various *Pachycephalosaurus* specimens, including *Pachycephalosaurus grangeri* and *Pachycephalosaurus reinheimeri*, that were once considered different species are now thought to represent different sexes of the same species.

Pachycephalosaurus grangeri
skull

PACHYRHINOSAURUS

(PACK-i-RYE-nuh-SAW-rus)

Type Species: *canadensis* (KAN-uh-DEN-sis)

Classification:

Order:	Ornithischia
Suborder:	Ceratopsia
Family:	Ceratopsidae
Name:	Greek *pachos* = thick + Greek *rhinos* = nose + Greek *sauros* = lizard
Size:	7 meters (23 feet) long
Period:	Late Cretaceous, 72 million to 68 million years ago
Place:	Alberta; Alaska
Diet:	Plants

    Pachyrhinosaurus was the largest of all the short-frilled horned dinosaurs, the centrosaurines. *Pachyrhinosaurus* had a large, rectangular skull that narrowed rapidly to a beak. Above its snout was a large knob of bone; its eye holes were small and circular; and its crest was low, thin, and rounded. Its jaws and teeth were short, massive, and thick.

    The presence of a low bump (instead of the usual nasal horn of the horned dinosaurs) was an unusual feature in *Pachyrhinosaurus*. This bump may have been utilized in shoving matches with rival individuals.

    In 1987, a quantity of new *Pachyrhinosaurus* material, including two and a half skulls and 278 other bones, was collected at Pipestone Creek in northern Alberta. The animals represented here seem to have been the victims of a flood. The most surprising discovery from this site was that *Pachyrhinosaurus* bore from one to three straight, unicorn-like horns on the midline of its frill. The Pipestone Creek site continues to produce intriguing information about how these animals' frills varied with age and sex.

    Pachyrhinosaurus remains have also been reported recently from the North Slope of Alaska. The wide distribution of this horned dinosaur suggests that it may have migrated widely in large herds, perhaps summering in the High Arctic.

PACHYSAURISCUS

(PACK-i-saw-RIS-kus)

Type Species: *ajax* (AY-jacks)

Status: Doubtful — *Pachysaurus, =?Plateosaurus*

Classification:

   Order: Saurischia

   Suborder: Sauropoda

   Family: Plateosauridae

Name: Greek *pachos* = thick + Greek *sauros* = lizard + *isko* = like

Size: ?Medium-sized

Period: Late Triassic, 225 million to 208 million years ago

Place: Germany

Diet: Plants

Pachysauriscus was one of the plateosaurid family of long-necked prosauropods, a group of heavily built, primitive plant-eaters with thick limbs. It had stout arms and long fingers. It was founded upon fossils originally named *Pachysaurus.*

Pachysauriscus giganteus (gye-GAN-tee-us): *Pachysauriscus giganteus* was based on three long, slender foot bones from Trossingen.

Pachysauriscus magnus (MAG-nus): This German dinosaur is known from fragmentary remains and appears to have been slightly smaller than *P. ajax.*

Pachysauriscus wetzelianus (WET-zell-ee-an-us): This animal, also from Trossingen, had slender toe bones and a claw corresponding to that of *Plateosaurus reinigeri,* an animal which is now considered to be *Pachysauriscus.*

PACHYSAURUS

(PACK-i-SAW-rus)

Type Species: *ajax* (AY-jacks)
Status: Doubtful — *See Pachysauriscus*
Name: Greek *pachos* = thick + Greek *sauros* = lizard

PACHYSPONDYLUS

(PACK-i-SPON-di-lus)

Type Species: *orpenii* (or-PEN-ee-eye)
Status: Doubtful — *See Massospondylus*
Name: Greek *pachos* = thick + Greek *spondylos* = vertebra

PALAEOSAURISCUS

(PAY-lee-oh-saw-RIS-kus)

Type Species: *cylindrodon* (si-LIN-droh-don)
Status: Doubtful — *See Paleosaurus*
Classification:
    Order: Saurischia
    Suborder: Prosauropoda
    Family: Plateosauridae
Name: Greek *palaios* = ancient + Greek *sauros* = lizard + *isko* = like
Size: Relatively small
Period: Late Triassic, 225 million to 208 million years ago
Place: England
Diet: Plants

    Palaeosauriscus was a prosauropod of the family Plateosauridae, which includes heavily built plant-eaters of medium to large size, with stout limbs. It is little known, as it was named for a single worn tooth, and was originally called *Palaeosaurus*. Associated with the tooth were fragments that included limb bone portions. The tooth was described as broadly lance-shaped and measuring 14 millimeters in length (½ an inch).

    Paleosauriscus fraserianus (FRAY-zhur-ee-AN-us) — Invalid name: Its remains were referred to *Anchisaurus polyzelus*.

PALAEOSAURUS

(PAY-lee-oh-SAW-rus)

Type Species: *platyodon* (PLAT-ee-uh-don)
Status: Doubtful — *See Palaeosauriscus, Plateosaurus*
Name: Greek *palaios* = ancient + Greek *sauros* = lizard

PALAEOSCINCUS

(PAY-lee-uh-SKING-kus)

Type Species: costatus (kos-TAY-tus)
Status: Doubtful — See ?Panoplosaurus
Classification:
  Order: Ornithischia
  Suborder: Ankylosauria
  Family: Nodosauridae
Name: Greek palaios = ancient + Greek skincus =
              (generic name for modern skinks)
Size: ±5.5 meters (18 feet) long
Period: Late Cretaceous, 83 million to 73 million
              years ago
Place: Montana
Diet: Plants

    Palaeoscincus is one of the first North American ankylosaurs, or armored dinosaurs, to be discovered. Founded upon a single tooth, *Palaeoscincus* cannot be associated for certain with any particular genus. This animal has been depicted as a squat dinosaur with armor plates, lateral spikes, and a clubbed tail similar to that of the better known armored dinosaur *Panoplosaurus*. Today, we know that this image is a fiction. As one of the nodosaurid family of armored dinosaurs, *Palaeoscincus* would not have possessed a tail club. The tooth could possibly represent a valid genus, or it could be that of *Edmontonia* or *Panoplosaurus*.

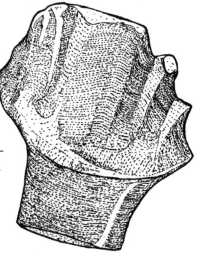

Palaeoscincus costatus
tooth

PANOPLOSAURUS

(PAN-oh-pluh-SAW-rus)

(=?Palaeoscincus)

Type Species: *mirus* (MYE-rus)

Classification:

Order:	Ornithischia
Suborder:	Ankylosauria
Family:	Nodosauridae

Name: Greek *panoplos* = armored + Greek *sauros* = lizard

Size: 5.5 meters (18 feet) long

Period: Late Cretaceous, 76 million to 73 million years ago

Place: Alberta; Montana

Diet: Plants

Panoplosaurus is a well known armored dinosaur. It belonged to the nodosaurid family, none of which had tail clubs. Its pear-shaped head, and its neck, back, and tail were covered with thick bony plates in differing sizes and shapes. Its sides were adorned with prominent spikes, completing an imposing defense. *Panoplosaurus* was discovered in 1917 in the most productive dinosaur-bearing rocks in the world, the Judith River Formation of Alberta, Canada.

PARANTHODON

(puh-RAN-thuh-don)

Type Species: *africanum* (AF-ri-KAN-um)

Classification:

Order:	Ornithischia
Suborder:	Stegosauria
Family:	Stegosauridae
Name:	Greek *para* = by + Greek *anthos* = flower + Greek *odontos* = tooth
Size:	?5 meters (17 feet) long
Period:	Early Cretaceous, 145 million to 138 million years ago
Place:	South Africa
Diet:	Plants

 Paranthodon was one of the stegosaurs, the plant-eating, quadrupedal dinosaurs distinguished by armor plates and spikes on their necks, backs, and tails. But *Paranthodon*, known only from a partial skull, has some confusion over its identity. *Paranthodon* was first thought to be a non-dinosaurian reptile. Later, it was considered to be a species of the ankylosaur, *Palaeoscincus*. Now it is known to be a unique, broad-snouted stegosaur, most closely resembling *Kentrosaurus*, an African plated dinosaur.

Paranthodon africanus skull

PARASAUROLOPHUS

(PAR-uh-SAW-ruh-LOH-fus)

Type Species: *walkeri* (WAW-kuh-rye)

Classification:

   Order: Ornithischia

   Suborder: Ornithopoda

   Family: Hadrosauridae

Name: Greek *para* = by + Greek *sauros* = lizard + Greek *lophos* = crest

Size: 9 meters (30 feet) long

Period: Late Cretaceous, 76 million to ?65 million years ago

Place: Alberta; Utah, New Mexico

Diet: Plants

Parasaurolophus, the most highly derived member of the lambeosaurine group of duckbilled dinosaurs, is one of the least commonly found.

Parasaurolophus may have weighed more than two tons. It was built to walk on all fours as well as on two legs. It is distinguished by its skull crest, an elongated, curved structure longer than the entire skull. Housed within the crest were two hollow tubes that ran to the far end and looped back again.

The function of this elaborate crest has long been a source of speculation and controversy. One notion, now discarded, was that the hollow crests had external nostril openings to accommodate an aquatic life style, allowing the animal to breathe while the head was submerged. This, however, was an impossibility, since there was no nostril at the tip of the crest. Also,

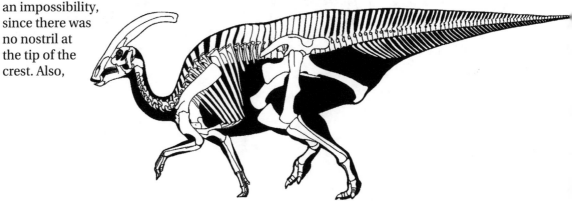

PARASAUROLOPHUS *continued*

since hadrosaurs are now known to have been terrestrial animals, the snorkel function has been discredited. One current theory is that these tubes might have produced low-frequency sounds that could have travelled long distances. Such sounds would have been similar to those used by elephants and whales for communication with other herd members.

The *Parasaurolophus* crest may also have housed nasal chambers that heightened the animal's sense of smell. A keen sense of smell would have been an important survival adaptation in an animal otherwise lacking defensive weapons. Also, the crest may have provided a visual means of recognizing another *Parasaurolopus.*

PARKSOSAURUS

(PAHRK-suh-SAW-rus)

Type Species: *warreni* (WAHR-uh-nye)
Classification:
  Order: Ornithischia
  Suborder: Ornithopoda
  Family: Hypsilophodontidae
Name: (William) *Parks* + Greek *sauros* = lizard
Size: 2 meters (7 feet) long
Period: Late Cretaceous, 68 million to 65 million
            years ago
Place: Alberta; Montana
Diet: Plants

    Parksosaurus was a hypsilophodontid, a small, primitive plant-eater. It had a little head on a long neck. *Parksosaurus* walked on its stubby-toed hind legs, leaving its short, strong front limbs free, perhaps for manipulating the plants that it ate.

    This animal's wide jaw and the shape of its teeth, which had low, rounded ridges, are unique among all known bird-hipped dinosaurs.

    Parksosaurus, the first North American hypsilophodont known from a specimen that included a skull, was originally described as *Thescelosaurus warreni.*

PARONYCHODON

(PAR-uh-NYE-kuh-don)

Type Species: *lacustris* (luh-KUS-tris)
Status: Doubtful — *See Tripriodon, Zapsalis*
Classification:
  Order: Saurischia
  Suborder: Theropoda
  Family: Dromaeosauridae
Name: Greek *para* = by or near + Greek *onux* = claw + Greek *odontos* = tooth
Size: ?Small
Period: Late Cretaceous, 73 million to 65 million years ago
Place: Montana
Diet: ?Meat

    This dinosaur is known only from an incisor-like tooth that was originally thought to belong to a mammal. A dinosaur named *Zapsalis abradens,* based on a worn tooth, is thought to be another example of *Paronychodon lacustris.* Other teeth previously called *Paronychodon* can now be referred to other kinds of dinosaurs. The name *Paronychodon lacustris* is used only for non-serrated teeth from the Late Cretaceous Period that may belong to an undiscovered animal.

PARROSAURUS

(PAR-uh-SAW-rus)

Type Species: *missouriensis* (mus-ZURE-ee-EN-sis)
Status: Invalid — *See Hypsibema*
Name: (Albert) Parr + Greek *sauros* = lizard

PATAGOSAURUS

(PAT-uh-guh-SAW-rus)

Type Species: *fariasi* (fuh-REE-uh-see)
Classification:
  Order: Saurischia
  Suborder: Sauropoda
  Family: Cetiosauridae
  Name: *Patagonia* (area in Argentina) + Greek *sauros* =
              lizard
  Size: Very large, ?20 meters (65 feet) long
  Period: Middle Jurassic, 169 million to 163 million
              years ago
  Place: Argentina
  Diet: Plants

  Patagosaurus was a huge four-legged, South American plant-eater, about the size of the European sauropod, *Cetiosaurus leedsi*. It was similar to *C. leedsi* in having neck vertebrae with nondivided spines, shallow cavities in its back vertebrae, and in the structure of its hip. Because of these similarities, *Patagosaurus* is grouped with the cetiosaurid family of primitive, unspecialized sauropods.

  The presence of *Patagosaurus*, the sauropod *Volkheimeria*, and the theropod *Piatnitzkysaurus*, was significant in providing the first record of a group of large South American dinosaurs from the Jurassic Period. This supported the theory that during the Jurassic, dinosaurs were able to travel between South America and other continents.

PECTINODON

(peck-TIN-uh-don)

Type Species: *bakkeri* (BAH-kuh-rye)
Status: Invalid — *See Troodon*
Name: Latin *pectin* = comb + Greek *odontos* = tooth

PEISHANSAURUS

(PYE-shan-SAW-rus)

Type Species: *philemys* (FIL-i-mees)
Status: Doubtful
Classification:
    Order: Ornithischia
    Suborder: Ankylosauria
    Family: ?Ankylosauridae
Name: *Peishan* (Chinese place name) + Greek *sauros* = lizard
Size: ?
Period: Late Cretaceous, ?97.5 million to ?65 million years ago
Place: China
Diet: Plants

    Peishansaurus is a poorly known, possibly armored, dinosaur, founded on the front end of a right lower jawbone that has since disintegrated. It may be a member of the family Ankylosauridae, armored dinosaurs distinguished by small lateral spikes and bony tail clubs. The specimen may have belonged to a very young individual.

PELOROSAURUS

(PEL-or-uh-SAW-rus)

Type Species: conybeari (KOH-ni-BAYR-eye)
Status: Doubtful — See Dinodocus, Ornithopsis; ?Brachiosaurus, ?Ischyrosaurus, ?Morinosaurus, ?Neosodon, ?Oplosaurus

Classification:
Order: Saurischia
Suborder: Sauropoda
Family: Brachiosauridae
Name: Greek pelorios = gigantic + Greek sauros = lizard
Size: Very large, ?25 meters (80 feet) long
Period: Early Cretaceous, 138 million to 97 million years ago
Place: England, Portugal, France
Diet: Plants

Though poorly known, *Pelorosaurus* is historically important as one of the first sauropods, or large four-legged browsing dinosaurs, to be described from Great Britain. It was named in 1847 by Dr. Gideon Mantell.

Its vertebrae and pelvis are similar to those in the better known sauropod, *Brachiosaurus*. In fact, *Pelorosaurus* and *Brachiosaurus* cannot be separated with certainty, especially given the fragmentary nature of the *Pelorosaurus* material. That *Pelorosaurus* was younger and smaller suggests that the two were different animals, but a final verdict depends on future discoveries.

Pelorosaurus becklesii (BECK-ul-zye): This species was based on Wealden Formation fossils from England. Associated with this specimen was a fossilized skin impression that revealed a series of convex, contiguous hexagonal plates ranging from 9 to 26 millimeters in diameter. This species is sometimes regarded as a junior synonym of the brachiosaur *Chondrosteosaurus gigas*, although no evidence supports referring it to any brachiosaur. In fact, this animal differs from known brachiosaurids in the proportions of the forelimb bones.

Pelorosaurus humerocristatus (HYOO-muh-roh-kris-TAT-us): This animal was based on a large upper arm bone from Fervenca, Portugal. This material established the presence of large sauropods in that country during the Late Jurassic Period.

PENTACERATOPS

(PEN-tuh-SER-uh-tops)

Type Species: *sternbergii* (STURN-bur-gee-eye)
Classification:

Order:	Ornithischia
Suborder:	Ceratopsia
Family:	Ceratopsidae
Name:	Greek *pente* = five + Greek *keratos* = horned + Greek *ops* = face
Size:	7 to 8 meters (23 to 28 feet) long
Period:	Late Cretaceous, ?75 million to 65 million years ago
Place:	New Mexico
Diet:	Plants

Pentaceratops was a very large dinosaur named for its five horns. Actually, *Pentaceratops* had only three horns—two forward-directed horns above the eyes, and a smaller one on the snout. The two additional horns were actually protuberant cheek bones, present in all horned dinosaurs but particularly elongated in *Pentaceratops*.

Pentaceratops's striking crest had a sculpted border and narrow, elongated openings. The elaborate crest may have been used as a threatening display, with the animals inclining their heads forwards, and perhaps shaking them from side to side. The crest certainly added to the imposing appearance of a head that was 2.3 meters (7.5 feet) long.

PENTACERATOPS *continued*

Pentaceratops's frill may have served as an expanded frame for large jaw muscles. Those muscles would have allowed it to chew many forms of vegetation. One skull was found surrounded by fossilized vegetation that included grape leaves, figs, cottonwoods, viburnum, palms, and pines, all possible elements in this dinosaur's diet.

Pentaceratops was one of several kinds of large horned dinosaurs found in the American West from near the end of dinosaur time. It resembled another large ceratopsian, *Chasmosaurus.*

Pentaceratops fenestratus (FEN-is-TRAT-us) — Doubtful name: This animal was discovered in San Juan, New Mexico. It was distinguished from *Pentaceratops sternbergi* on the grounds that they were found in two different formations.

PHAEDROLOSAURUS

(fay-DROH-luh-SAW-rus)

Type Species: *ilikensis* (IL-i-KEN-sis)
Status: Doubtful
Classification:
  Order: Saurischia
  Suborder: Theropoda
  Family: ?Dromaeosauridae
Name: *Phaedrus* = Roman creator of fables + Greek *sauros* = lizard
Size: Small
Period: Early Cretaceous, ?145 million to ?97.5 million years ago
Place: China
Diet: Meat

    Phaedrolosaurus was a small meat-eater known only from short, thick, solid teeth with small, dense serrations. *Phaedrolosaurus's* teeth were similar in outline and form to those in the earlier and somewhat smaller North American killer-claw carnivore, *Deinonychus*. The teeth in *Phaedrolosaurus* are thicker, shorter, and more solid. *Phaedrolosaurus* was probably lightly built, with long legs.

PHYLLODON

(FYE-luh-don)

Type Species: *henkeli* (HENG-kuh-lye)
Status: Doubtful
Classification:
  Order: Ornithischia
  Suborder: Ornithopoda
  Family: Hypsilophodontidae
Name: Greek *phyllon* = leaf + Greek *odontos* = tooth
Size: ?Small
Period: Late Jurassic, 156 million to 150 million years ago
Place: Portugal
Diet: Plants

    Phyllodon was a small hypsilophodontid, a primitive, bipedal, plant-eating dinosaur. It is known only from a single tooth.

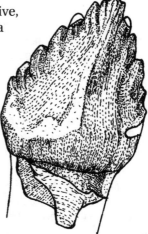

Phyllodon henkeli
tooth

PIATNITZKYSAURUS

(PEE-at-NIT-skee-SAW-rus)

Type Species: *floresi* (FLOR-i-sye)
Classification:

Order:	Saurischia
Suborder:	Theropoda
Family:	Allosauridae

Name: (A.) *Piatnitzky* + Greek *sauros* = lizard
Size: 4.3 meters (14 feet) long
Period: Middle Jurassic, 169 million to 163 million years ago
Place: Argentina
Diet: Meat

This was the earliest known true member of the carnosaurs, a worldwide group. Carnosaurs were large carnivorous dinosaurs with huge heads, short necks, barrel-like trunks, small forelimbs, and clawed toes. The carnosaurs endured for another 100 million years after *Piatnitzkysaurus*, ending with *Tyrannosaurus*.

Piatnitzkysaurus was distinguished from its later North American relative *Allosaurus* by its more primitive pelvis, longer upper arm bone, and features of the shoulder and backbones. Yet in overall design, *Piatnitzkysaurus's* body was very similar to that of *Allosaurus*. It was not as massive as the earlier North American carnivore, *Dilophosaurus*.

The discovery of *Piatnitzkysaurus*, along with two sauropods, *Patagosaurus* and *Volkheimeria*, is the first evidence that South America was populated by relatives of well-known North American dinosaurs during the Middle Jurassic Period. This discovery supports the idea that animals moved between South America and other continents during that time.

PICRODON

(PYE-kruh-don)

Type Species: *herveyi* (HUR-vee-eye)
Status: Doubtful — *See ?Avalonianus, ?Plateosaurus*
Classification:
  Order: Saurischia
  Suborder: Sauropoda
  Family: ?
Name: Greek *pikros* = sharp + Greek *odontos* = tooth
Size: ?
Period: Late Triassic, 225 million to 208 million years ago
Place: England
Diet: Plants

Picrodon was a prosauropod named on a single, sharply-pointed, serrated tooth that measured 20 millimeters (about .75 inches) long. Some vertebrae and a tooth found near Warwick, England, have since been referred to this animal. This herbivorous dinosaur had a small head and a long neck.

PINACOSAURUS

(pi-NACK-uh-SAW-rus)

Type Species: *grangeri* (GRAYN-juh-rye)
Classification:

   Order: Ornithischia

   Suborder: Ankylosauria

   Family: Ankylosauridae

Name: Greek *pinakos* = broad + Greek *sauros* = lizard

Size: 3.5 meters (12 feet) long

Period: Late Cretaceous, ?85 million to 81 million
               years ago

Place: Mongolia, China

Diet: Plants

   Pinacosaurus was a small armored dinosaur found in the Gobi Desert. It was one of the ankylosaurids, a group of advanced armored dinosaurs distinguished from the more primitive group by having clubbed tails.

   Ankylosaurs have been regarded as solitary animals. That notion was challenged by the discoveries made by a joint Chinese and Canadian paleontological expedition to the Gobi Desert in 1988. More than a dozen young *Pinacosaurus* skeletons were found under a dune, suggesting that the baby dinosaurs were smothered in a sandstorm. One skeleton was found curled up.

   Pinacosaurus was slender, so it may have been faster-moving than other ankylosaurs. Its tail could move both up and down and side-

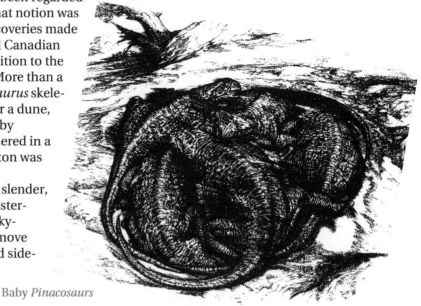

Baby *Pinacosaurs*

PINACOSAURUS *continued*

ways, although the tail club may have been locked in place by fused vertebrae. This dinosaur was also distinguished by large oval nostrils. Its sinuses may have been used as a chamber in which sounds were resonated for increased volume; for housing a variety of glands; or for strengthening the skull.

Pinacosaurus seems to have been an intermediate form between two other Asian armored dinosaurs, the more primitive *Talarurus* and the more evolved *Saichania*. *Pinacosaurus* was characterized by its relatively light skeleton, and by its relatively few openings (compared to other armored dinosaurs) for nerves and blood vessels in the back part of the skull.

The genus *Syrmosaurus*, founded on an incomplete skeleton found in Mongolia, is now known to be *Pinacosaurus*.

PISANOSAURUS

(pye-SAN-uh-SAW-rus)

Type Species: *mertii* (MUR-tee-eye)
Classification:

Order:	Ornithischia
Suborder:	?
Family:	?
Name:	*Pisano* + Greek *sauros* = lizard
Size:	Small
Period:	Late Triassic, 231 million to 225 million years ago
Place:	Argentina
Diet:	Plants

Pisanosaurus is the oldest known member of the ornithischians, a diverse group of plant-eating dinosaurs. It was a small, two-legged, and probably fast-running dinosaur with a small head.

Classification of *Pisanosaurus* has not been easy. It was allied with the Ornithischia on the basis of its lower back and jaw. It is separated from the more advanced ornithischians by various details, and is regarded as a very primitive member of that group.

Pisanosaurus seems to have played a role in an environment dominated by large, now-extinct reptiles, not by early dinosaurs like itself.

PIVETEAUSAURUS

(PEEV-toh-SAW-rus)

Type Species: *divesensis* (deev-ZEN-sis)
Classification:

Order:	Saurischia
Suborder:	Theropoda
Family:	?Eustreptospondylidae

Name: (Jean) *Piveteau* + Greek *sauros* = lizard
Size: Large, ?11 meters (36 feet) long
Period: Middle Jurassic, 166 million to 163 million years ago
Place: France
Diet: Meat

This large carnivore is known from a partial skull. It was originally designated as a second species of *Eustreptospondylus*, distinguished on the basis of the contraction of certain of *Piveteausaurus*'s skull bones. It was later recognized as a new genus of dinosaur.

Piveteausaurus and *Eustreptospondylus* may have been close relatives and early representatives of the Carnosauria, a broad grouping of very large theropods with very large heads, short necks and forelimbs, stout hind limbs and sharp claws.

Piveteausaurus divesensis skull

PLATEOSAURAVUS

(PLAY-tee-oh-saw-RAV-us)

Status: Invalid — *See Euskelosaurus*

PLATEOSAURUS

(PLAY-tee-uh-SAW-rus)
(See Dimodosaurus, Dinosaurus,
Gresslyosaurus, ?Pachysauriscus)

Type Species: engelhardti (ENG-gul-HAHR-tye)
Classification:

    Order: Saurischia

    Suborder: Sauropoda

    Family: Plateosauridae

Name: Greek *platus* = flat or broad + Greek *sauros* = lizard

Size: 8 meters (27.5 feet) long

Period: Late Triassic, 222 million to 219 million years ago

Place: Germany, France, Switzerland

Diet: Plants

    This genus was one of the earliest large dinosaurs. It established the prosauropod family Plateosauridae, a grouping of medium- to large-sized, sometimes heavily built animals with stout limbs.

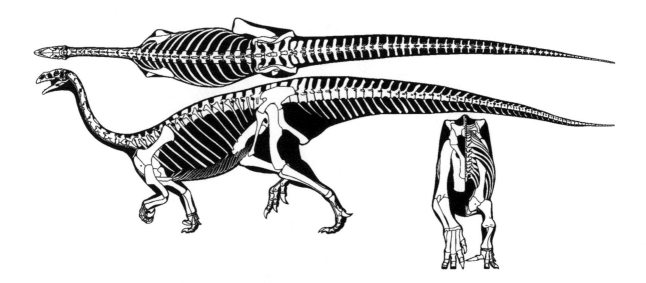

PLATEOSAURUS *continued*

Plateosaurus was one of the largest prosauropods. Like others of its family, it had a small head, long neck, heavily built torso, relatively long forelimbs, grasping hands, and strongly developed hind limbs. Its skull was high and narrow, with an elongated snout. Its teeth were somewhat spoon-shaped. Its lower jaw was not very flexible.

Plateosaurus, and possibly all other prosauropods, probably walked on all fours. The hand was constructed so as to allow the second through fourth fingers to rest on the ground like toes, while the scythe-like claw of the first finger was held clear of the ground. This raised claw could have been utilized in raking at vegetation, or as a weapon.

Plateosaurus was among the most common of all European dinosaurs and the best known of all prosauropods. Its remains have been found in more than fifty European localities. The abundance of skeletons suggests that *Plateosaurus* may have been a herding creature, and may have migrated over this arid part of Europe during the Late Triassic Period. An accumulation of adult and subadult remains found in Trossingen, Germany, may have been the result of a catastrophe inflicted upon a herd during migration. However, other evidence suggests that the fossil finds were an accumulation, over time, of solitary individuals and small groups. Or, perhaps herding was a seasonal, rather than a permanent, feature of *Plateosaurus*'s life.

PLEUROCOELUS

(PLOOR-uh-SEE-lus)

Type Species: *nanus* (NAN-us)
Status: See *?Astrodon*
Classification:
   Order: Saurischia
   Suborder: Sauropoda
   Family: Brachiosauridae
Name: Greek *pleura* = side + Greek *koilos* = hollow
Size: 8.8 meters (30 feet) long
Period: Early Cretaceous, 131 million to 119 million
        years ago
Place: Maryland, Texas; ?England; ?Portugal
Diet: Plants

Pleurocoelus was a brachiosaurid, a four-legged browser with front limbs as long or longer than its hind limbs. According to the type specimen, which may have been a juvenile, it was relatively small for a brachiosaur,

Pleurocoelus had a small, narrow skull. Its teeth were similar to those in *Camarasaurus*, but thinner. Its limbs resembled those of the sauropod *Camarasaurus*, but *Pleurocoelus's* toes were more slender than those of other sauropods. The fourth toe of the hind foot may have had a small claw, an uncommon feature in sauropods. Apparently, this claw was small and may have been mostly buried in the tissue of the sole of the foot.

Pleurocoelus is sometimes identified as *Brontopodus*, a footprint genus name for the trackmaker of the famous sauropod footprints at the Paluxy River in Glen Rose, Texas.

Pleurocoelus altus (AWL-tus) — Invalid name: This was thought to be a larger species of *Pleurocoelus*, but is now thought to represent an adult of the type species. It was distinguished by elongated hindlimb bones, resembling—but proportionately longer than—those of *Camarasaurus*.

PLEUROCOELUS *continued*

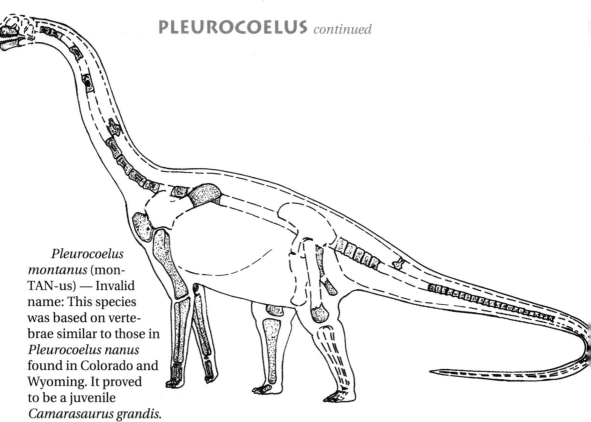

Pleurocoelus montanus (mon-TAN-us) — Invalid name: This species was based on vertebrae similar to those in *Pleurocoelus nanus* found in Colorado and Wyoming. It proved to be a juvenile *Camarasaurus grandis*.

Pleurocoelus valdensis (val-DEN-sis): This species was based on two imperfect vertebrae and two teeth from Sussex and the Isle of Wight. Three teeth from Boca do Chapin, Portugal, were referred to this species. Two of them are about 22 centimeters (over 8 inches) long; the third was much smaller.

PLEUROPELTUS
(PLOOR-uh-PEL-tus)

Type Species: *suessii* (SOO-see-eye)
Status: Doubtful — *See Danubiosaurus*

PODOKESAURUS

(POH-doh-kuh-SAW-rus)

Type Species:	*holyokensis* (HOH-lee-oh-KEN-sis)
Status:	Doubtful — *See Coelophysis, Rioarribasaurus*
Classification:	
Order:	Saurischia
Suborder:	Theropoda
Family:	Podokesauridae
Name:	Greek *podokes* = swiftfooted + Greek *sauros* = lizard
Size:	About 1 meter (about 3.5 feet) long
Period:	Early Jurassic, 200 million to 188 million years ago
Place:	Massachusetts
Diet:	Meat

This poorly known small carnivore established a family of podokesaurids, various-sized meat eaters with lightly built bodies and hollow bones. They had elongated heads, and some had crests. These dinosaurs had long necks, short, slender forelimbs, four-fingered hands, and birdlike feet with three functional toes.

Podokesaurus had a small body, typical of this group. It was comparable in size and in the proportions of its hip and leg bones to some of the smaller specimens of the Late Triassic carnivore, *Rioarribasaurus colberti*, also known as *Coelophysis bauri*. *Podokesaurus* might represent an immature *Rioarribasaurus*, though a different species.

The type specimen was discovered on the campus of Mount Holyoke College in Massachusetts, and was destroyed in a fire. However, casts exist at the Yale Peabody Museum and the American Museum of Natural History. Connecticut Valley dinosaur fossil tracks, the first dinosaur tracks ever identified (named as the footprint genus *Grallator*), could belong to *Podokesaurus*.

POEKILOPLEURON

(POY-ki-loh-PLOOR-on)

Type Species: *bucklandii* (buck-LAN-dee-eye)
Classification:

Order: Saurischia

Suborder: Theropoda

Family: Megalosauridae

Name: Greek *poikilos* = spotted or dappled + Greek *pleura* = side

Size: Large, ?9 meters (30 feet) long

Period: Middle Jurassic, 175 million to 172 million years ago

Place: France, ?Russia

Diet: Meat

Poekilopleuron, one of the earliest giant carnivores, is based on fragmentary remains that were destroyed in World War II. This dinosaur was a megalosaurid, one of the large carnivores with big heads, long jaws, double-edged teeth, very short forelimbs, three-fingered hands, powerful hind limbs, and taloned toes.

Poekilopleuron was distinguished by its forelimb, which was extraordinarily short and heavy. Its upper arm bone was stout, and 38 to 40 centimeters (15 inches) long, about half the length of the lower hindlimb bone. The forearm shows evidence of the attachment of powerful muscles in life, and its hand was relatively large.

Poikilopleuron was somewhat similar to the large North American carnivore *Torvosaurus*, especially in the forelimb and pelvic girdle.

Poikilopleuron schmidtii (SHMIT-ee-eye) — Doubtful name: This animal is represented by pieces of ribs and a poorly preserved shinbone found at Kursk, in the former U.S.S.R. It could belong to any large Late Cretaceous meat-eater.

POLACANTHOIDES
(POH-luh-kan-THOY-deez)

Status: Doubtful — *See Hylaeosaurus*

POLACANTHUS
(POH-luh-KAN-thus)

Status: Invalid — *See Hylaeosaurus*

POLYODONTOSAURUS
(POL-ee-oh-DON-tuh-SAW-rus)

Status: Invalid — *See Troodon*

POLYONAX

(POL-ee-OH-nacks)

Type Species: *mortuarius* (MOR-choo-AYR-ee-us)
Status: Doubtful — *See Torosaurus, Triceratops*
Classification:
   Order: Ornithischia
   Suborder: Ceratopsia
   Family: Ceratopsidae
Name: Greek *poly* = many + Greek *anax* = master
Size: Large, 7 meters (23 feet) long
Period: Late Cretaceous, 70 million to 65 million
                years ago
Place: Colorado
Diet: Plants

    Polyonax was established on three vertebrae, limb-bone fragments, and horn core fragments that represented a young horned dinosaur. It was named during the early days of North American dinosaur discoveries, when horned dinosaurs were not yet a well known or well established group.

PRENOCEPHALE

(PREE-noh-SEF-uh-lee)

Type Species: *prenes* (PREN-is)
Classification:

Order:	Ornithischia
Suborder:	Pachycephalosauria
Family:	Pachycephalosauridae

Name: Greek *prenes* = face downwards + Greek *kephale* = head

Size: 2 meters (7 feet) long

Period: Late Cretaceous, ?77 million to ?69 million years ago

Place: Mongolia

Diet: Plants

   Prenocephale was a bone-headed dinosaur of the pachycephalosaurid family. These small- to medium-sized plant-eaters had domed skulls of various shapes. Its skull was particularly high and slightly roughened, and measured about 218 millimeters (8 inches) long. *Prenocephale* had big, forward-directed eyes. This rare dinosaur may have had excellent vision, as well as a head well equipped for butting its rivals.

PRICONODON

(prye-KOH-nuh-don)

Type Species: crassus (KRAS-us)
Status: Doubtful
Classification:
  Order: Ornithischia
  Suborder: Ankylosauria
  Family: Nodosauridae
Name: Old English *prica* = punctured + Greek *odontos* = tooth
Size: ?
Period: Early Cretaceous, 113 million to 98 million years ago
Place: Maryland
Diet: Plants

Priconodon was a large plant-eater known only from a single tooth. This tooth had a narrow neck, swollen base, and flattened crown, and was first regarded as resembling that of the plate-backed dinosaur, *Stegosaurus*. It is now known to belong to one of the nodosauridae, a family of armored dinosaurs distinguished by large lateral spikes and no tail clubs.

Priconodon crassus
tooth

PRIODONTOGNATHUS

(PRYE-uh-DON-toh-guh-NAY-thus)

Type Species: *phillipsii* (FIL-ip-see-eye)
Status: Doubtful
Classification:
   Order: Ornithischia
   Suborder: Ankylosauria
   Family: ?Nodosauridae
Name: Greek *prion* = saw + Greek *odontos* = tooth +
              Greek *gnathos* = jaw
Size: ?
Period: Late Jurassic, ?163 million to 156 million
              years ago
Place: England
Diet: Plants

    Priodontognathus was based on a single upper jaw bone that was at first thought to belong to an iguanodontid. It was later classified as a stegosaur, but it is now known to be an ankylosaur. It may belong to the Nodosauridae, the family of armored dinosaurs without tail clubs. The teeth in this jaw resemble those of the nodosaurids *Pricodon* and *Sauropelta*.

PROBACTROSAURUS

(proh-BACK-truh-SAW-rus)

Type Species: *gobiensis* (GOH-bee-EN-sis)
Classification:
    Order: Ornithischia
    Suborder: Ornithopoda
    Family: Iguanodontidae
Name: Greek *pro* = before + *Bactria* (ancient southwest Asian country) + Greek *sauros* = lizard
Size: 5-6 meters (17 to 20+ feet) long
Period: Late Cretaceous, ?97.5 million to ?91 million years ago
Place: China
Diet: Plants

    Probactrosaurus was a medium- to large-sized plant-eater. This was a transitional animal that may have been a predecessor of duckbills. *Probactrosaurus* displayed some of the primitive characteristics typical of iguanodontids, such as the narrow snout, double-layer tooth row structure, elongated lower jaw, and crestless skull. *Probactrosaurus* also exhibited some similarities to the hadrosaurids. *Probactrosaurus* is now placed in its own unnamed family, one closely related to the duckbills, or hadrosaurids.

    Probactrosaurus alashanicus (al-ah-SHAN-ick-us)— Doubtful name: This species was based on the back of a skull found in the same locality as the type species. It looks the same but for minor distinctions and may represent another individual of the type species.

Probactrosaurus alashanicus skull

PROCERATOSAURUS

(PROH-suh-RAT-uh-SAW-rus)

Type Species: bradleyi (BRAD-lee-eye)
Classification:
    Order: Saurischia
    Suborder: Theropoda
    Family: ?
Name: Greek pro = before + Greek keratos = horned +
               Greek sauros = lizard
Size: Small
Period: Middle Jurassic, 175 million to 169 million
               years ago
Place: England
Diet: Meat

This very small carnivore is known from only a partial skull, the chief distinction of which was its bony nose horn. The skull was lightly built and measured 26 centimeters (about 10 inches) in length. The teeth of this meat-eater were cone-shaped, large-rooted, and poorly serrated.

Proceratosaurus may be related to *Ornitholestes*.

PROCHENEOSAURUS

(proh-CHEE-nee-uh-SAW-rus)

Status: Invalid — *See Lambeosaurus*

PROCOMPSOGNATHUS

(proh-KOMP-soh-guh-NAY-thus)

Type Species: *triassicus* (trye-AS-i-kus)
Status: *See Pterospondylus*
Classification:
  Order: Saurischia
  Suborder: Theropoda
  Family: ?Segisauridae
Name: *Greek pro = before + Greek kompsos = elegant + Greek gnathos = jaw*
Size: Small
Period: Late Triassic, 222 million to 219 million years ago
Place: Württemberg, Germany
Diet: Plants

   Procompsognathus represents one of the major dinosaur misidentifications in the history of paleontology. This animal was known only from a fragmentary skeleton and was long thought to be a small, birdlike dinosaur that resembled *Compsognathus*. However, it was recently discovered that the skull of this purported dinosaur actually belonged to a primitive relative of crocodiles. The rest of the skeleton is now known to be that of one of the ceratosaurians, a group of primitive, carnivorous dinosaurs, some with crests or horns. It seems to have been an advanced ceratosaur quite similar to *Rioarribasaurus*, and particularly *Segisaurus*.

PRODEINODON

(proh-DYE-nuh-don)

Type Species: *mongoliensis* (mong-GOH-lee-EN-sis)

Status: Doubtful

Classification:

   Order: Saurischia

   Suborder: ?Theropoda

   Family: ?

Name: Greek *pro* = before + Greek *deinos* = terrible + Greek *odontos* = tooth

Size: Large

Period: Early Cretaceous, 119 million to 113 million years ago

Place: Mongolia, China

Diet: Meat

    Prodeinodon established the presence of large carnivorous dinosaurs in Mongolia during the Early Cretaceous Period. It was based on the upper part of one tooth that most closely resembled the teeth of the dinosaur *Aublysodon*.

    Prodeinodon kwangshiensis (KWANG-shee-EN-sis) — Doubtful name: This dinosaur is based on four nondistinctive teeth from the Early Cretaceous Period, found in China. The tooth is quite different from that of *Prodeinodon mongoliensis*, but similar to the tooth of the Japanese species *Wakinosaurus satoi*.

    Future studies may show that identification based only on teeth results in a multiplicity of useless names.

PROSAUROLOPHUS

(PROH-saw-ROL-uh-fus)

Type Species: *maximus* (MACK-si-mus)

Classification:

    Order: Ornithischia

    Suborder: Ornithopoda

    Family: Hadrosauridae

Name: Greek *pro* = before + Greek *sauros* = lizard + Greek *lophos* = crest

Size: 8 meters (26 feet) long

Period: Late Cretaceous, 77 million to 73 million years ago

Place: Alberta

Diet: Plants

    Prosaurolophus was a flat-headed, or crestless, duckbilled dinosaur. Like other flat-heads of this subfamily of large plant-eaters, it belonged to the hadrosaurines, and was one of the earliest of that group.

    Superficially, *Prosaurolophus* resembled the spike-headed *Saurolophus*, though it had a smaller, shorter bill, and no crest. *Prosaurolophus* had a large, tall, elongated skull.

PROTIGUANODON

(PROH-ti-GWAH-nuh-don)

Status: Invalid — *See Psittacosaurus*

PROCERATOPS

(proh-SER-uh-tops)

Status: Invalid — *See Ceratops*

PROTOCERATOPS

(PROH-tuh-SER-uh-tops)

Type Species: *andrewsi* (AN-droo-zye)
Classification:
   Order: Ornithischia
   Suborder: Ceratopsia
   Family: Protoceratopsidae
Name: Greek *protos* = first + Greek *keratos* = horned +
            Greek *ops* = face
Size: 2.4 meters (8 feet) long, 177 kilograms (389
            pounds) weight
Period: Late Cretaceous, 85 million to 77 million years ago
Place: Mongolia
Diet: Plants

   This primitive horned dinosaur was discovered in the 1920s in the Gobi Desert by the Roy Chapman Andrews expedition for the American Museum of Natural History.

PROTOCERATOPS *continued*

Protoceratops was one of the first of a new family of horned dinosaurs, the protoceratopsids. These animals were characterized by the lack of large brow horns, and the presence of very large eye holes. *Protoceratops* was a small horned dinosaur with a triangular head, long tail, and feet adapted to walking on all fours. Yet this dinosaur was capable of at least some bipedal movement. In fact, *Protoceratops* and its more primitive cousin, *Leptoceratops*, may have been the swiftest of all known ceratopsian dinosaurs.

Sex-linked variations have been determined in *Protoceratops* skulls. In one adult sex (perhaps the female) there is no nasal horn, while a low bump is present in the other sex. The frills also vary by sex, with one sex (perhaps the male) having a more erect frill and prominent snout bump.

Protoceratops is one of the most common and best known of all dinosaurs, with more than one hundred specimens collected. At first regarded as one of the most primitive of the horned dinosaurs, *Protoceratops* is now known to be the largest and most advanced of a series of early horned dinosaurs that included *Psittacosaurus*, *Bagaceratops*, and *Leptoceratops*.

The Andrews expedition also collected nests of eggs at the Flaming Cliffs of Mongolia. These were presumed to have been laid by *Protoceratops*. Andrews claimed that fossilized embryos found within the eggs offered positive identification with *Protoceratops*. However, no positively identifiable embryonic remains have been found in any of these eggs.

Protoceratops kozlowskii (koz-LOU-skee-eye) — Doubtful name: This species was based on material collected in the Gobi Desert during the 1964-71 Polish-Mongolian Paleontological Expeditions. This species had a skull with a backward-sloping profile, a short, stout upper arm bone, and other distinguishing details. *Protoceratops kozlowskii* represents a new genus named *Breviceratops kozlowskii*, in 1990.

PROTOGNATHOSAURUS

(PROH-toh-guh-NAY-thuh-SAW-rus)

Type Species: oxyodon (OK-see-uh-don)
Classification:
   Order: Saurischia
   Suborder: Sauropoda
   Family: ?Cetiosauridae
Name: Greek *protos* = first + Greek *gnathos* = jaw +
               Greek *sauros* = lizard
Size: Large
Period: Middle Jurassic, 188 million to 163 million
               years ago
Place: China
Diet: Plants

    Protognathosaurus may have been a member of the Cetiosauridae, a family of primitive four-legged browsers with front and hind legs of nearly equal length.

    Protognathosaurus is known from a portion of its thick, heavy jaw bone, which contained nineteen or twenty teeth (more than in other sauropods). The teeth were similar to those in the more primitive, smaller plant-eaters, the prosauropods, and, along with the shape of the jawbone itself, suggest that *Protognathosaurus* was a primitive sauropod.

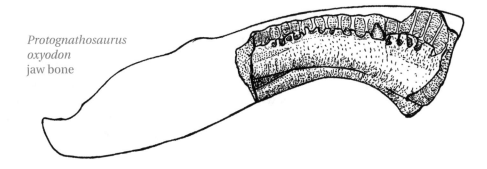

Protognathosaurus
oxyodon
jaw bone

PROTOGNATHUS

(PROH-toh-guh-NAY-thus)

Status: Invalid — *See Protognathosaurus*

PROTOROSAURUS

(PROH-tuh-roh-SAW-rus)

Status: Invalid — *See Chasmosaurus*

PSITTACOSAURUS

(si-TACK-uh-SAW-rus)

Type Species: *mongoliensis* (mong-GOH-lee-EN-sis)
Classification:
    Order: Ornithischia
    Suborder: Ceratopsia
    Family: Psittacosauridae
Name: Greek *psittakos* = parrot + Greek *sauros* = lizard
Size: 2 meters (6.6 feet) long
Period: Early Cretaceous, 119 million to 97.5 million
            years ago
Place: Mongolia, China, Thailand
Diet: Plants

   This little plant-eater is the most primitive known horned dinosaur. It was a small, two-legged runner with a short, deep skull and a narrow face. The face was distinguished by a prominent parrot-like beak. The bone that supported that beak, a key feature of all the horned dinosaurs, was first seen in *Psittacosaurus*.

PSITTACOSAURUS *continued*

Psittacosaurus may have run either on four legs or on two. Its diverging first digit suggests that its hands could do a limited degree of grasping, perhaps to hold vegetation. In the very young specimens of *Psittacosaurus* that have been found, the teeth show wear. This suggests they ate abrasive vegetation at an early age, and that hatchlings may not have required much parental care.

Psittacosaurus guyangensis (GYE-ang-EN-sis): Founded on a skull fragment and other remains from Chinese Mongolia, *Psittacosaurus guyangensis* was an intermediate-sized psittacosaur.

Psittacosaurus meileyingensis (MAY-lay-ing-EN-sis): This dinosaur was based on remains found in northeastern China that included an almost complete skull and three vertebrae. The skull was unusually high, and had a short snout.

Psittacosaurus osborni (oz-BOR-nye) — Doubtful name: This species from Gansu, China, was approximately half the size of *Psittacosaurus mongoliensis*. It may have been an immature individual.

Psittacosaurus sattayaraki (SAT-tay-a-RAK-eye): Based on a lower-jaw bone from Chaiyaphum Province, Thailand, less developed than that of *Psittacosaurus mongoliensis* and *Psittacosaurus meileyingensis*.

Psittacosaurus sinensis (sye-NEN-sis): *P. sinensis* was based on an almost complete skeleton with a well preserved skull found at Shandong, China. It was the smallest known species of psittacosaur. The skull was short and broad, and measured just 120 millimeters (over 4.6 inches) long.

Psittacosaurus tingi (TING-eye) — Invalid name: This species was based on two lower jaws and seven teeth from the same locality as *P. sinensis*. It was subsequently referred to *P. osborni*.

Psittacosaurus xinjiangensis (ZIN-jee-ang-EN-sis): This small species was based on an almost complete skeleton found in northwestern China.

PTEROPELYX

(TER-uh-PEL-icks)

Status: Doubtful — *See Corythosaurus*

PTEROSPONDYLUS

(TER-uh-SPON-di-lus)

Type Species: *trielbae* (TREE-el-bye)
Status: Doubtful — *See Procompsognathus*
Classification:
   Order: Saurischia
   Suborder: Theropoda
   Family: ?
Name: Greek *pteron* = feathers + Greek *spondylos* = vertebrae
Size: Small
Period: Late Triassic, 231 million to 208 million years ago
Place: Halbertstadt, Germany
Diet: Meat

    Pterospondylus was a small meat-eating dinosaur. Beyond that, little else can be said of it, since it was based on a single backbone found within the shell of a more than 200-million year-old turtle.

    Pterospondylus is sometimes regarded as synonymous with *Procompsognathus*, a doubtful dinosaur. But *Pterospondylus's* vertebra is twice the size of a comparable bone in *Procompsognathus*.

QUAESITOSAURUS

(kway-SEE-tuh-SAW-rus)

Type Species: *orientalis* (OR-ee-en-TAL-is)
Classification:

Order:	Saurischia
Suborder:	Sauropoda
Family:	Diplodocidae
Name:	Latin *quaesitus* = abnormal + Greek *sauros* = lizard
Size:	Large
Period:	Late Cretaceous, ?85 million to 80 million years ago
Place:	Southeastern Gobi region, Mongolia
Diet:	Meat

Quaesitosaurus was a diplodocid, one of a group of long-necked sauropods with tapering, whiplike tails.

Quaesitosaurus is known only from a short, high skull with a wide snout. The skull most closely resembles that of another Mongolian sauropod, *Nemegtosaurus*, though *Nemegtosaurus* had a much narrower snout.

There are some distinctive features of *Quaesitosaurus's* skull that separate it from all other sauropods—or at least the few for which skulls have been found. Below the rounded skull bone that connected the head to the first vertebra of

Quaesitosaurus orientalis skull

the neck was a canal, a feature of unknown function. An abnormally large "resonator" opening of the middle ear suggests that *Quaesitosaurus* had very sensitive hearing.

The musculature and bone structure of *Quaesitosaurus's* jaw, with its long face and little, worn teeth, were adaptations for taking in large volumes of soft vegetation. These features suggested to some researchers that the animal fed with its head partially submerged in water. However, its environment was semi-arid, not watery. It may also have carried stomach stones (gastroliths) in its gut to aid in digesting the coarse land plants its jaws were not equipped to process.

RAPATOR

(ruh-PAY-tur)

Type Species: *ornitholestoides* (or-NITH-uh-les-TOY-deez)
Status: Doubtful = *?Walgettosuchus*
Classification:
    Order: Saurischia
    Suborder: Theropoda
    Family: ?
Name: Latin *rapere* = to seize + Latin suffix *-ator* = one performing
Size: 9 meters (30 feet) long
Period: Early Cretaceous, 113 million to 97.5 million years ago
Place: Australia
Diet: Meat

    Rapator, a poorly known carnivore from Australia, cannot be related to any particular group of meat-eating dinosaurs. It is known only from a toe bone with a knob on the back, which is unlike that of any other carnivorous dinosaur. All that can be concluded from this bone is that it belonged to a meat-eater about the size of *Allosaurus*.

REBBACHISAURUS

(ruh-BACH-i-SAW-rus)

Type Species: *garasbae* (GAR-us-bay)

Classification:

Order:	Saurischia
Suborder:	Sauropoda
Family:	Diplodocidae

Name: Rebbach (territory) + Greek *sauros* = lizard

Size: 20 meters (about 68 feet) long

Period: Early Cretaceous, 113 million to 97.5 million years ago

Place: Morocco, Niger

Diet: Plants

Rebbachisaurus was a huge plant-eater which belonged to the diplodocid family of large to giant sauropods. Among dinosaurs of this family, the front limbs were usually shorter than the hindlimbs. The diplodocids had long tapering heads and whiplike tails. Like many other diplodocids, *Rebbachisaurus* had broad, spoon-shaped teeth, and powerfully built hind legs that ended in large claws.

Rebbachisaurus had a high-arched back that made it distinct from other diplocids and all known sauropods. This arch, and perhaps a sail, were created by back vertebrae with large, upward-pointing spines.

Rebbachisaurus tamesnensis (TAM-es-NEN-sis): This species, based on teeth and skeletal parts found in the central Sahara Desert, is distinguished from *R. garasbae* by the different shape of its shoulder blade and its shorter spines. Enormous fossil footprints that are possibly related to *R. tamesnensis* have been reported from Niger.

REGNOSAURUS

(REG-nuh-SAW-rus)

Type Species: *northamptoni* (north-HAMP-tuh-nye)
Status: Doubtful = *?Chondrosteosaurus*
Classification:
  Order: Saurischia
  Suborder: Sauropoda
  Family: Camarasauridae
Name: Latin *regnum* = reign + Greek *sauros* = lizard
Size: ?Large
Period: Early Cretaceous, 131 million to 119 million
                years ago
Place: England
Diet: Plants

    Regnosaurus, a big browser known only from a lower right jaw fragment, was first thought to be an ankylosaur, or armored dinosaur. Now it is believed to be a sauropod. It has been placed in the camarasaurid family of medium- to giant-sized sauropods with short boxy heads, heavy spoon-shaped teeth, and front and back legs of nearly equal length.

REVUELTOSAURUS

(REV-yoo-EL-tuh-SAW-rus)

Type Species: *callenderi* (KAL-en-duh-rye)
Status: Doubtful
Classification:
   Order: ?Ornithischia
   Suborder: ?
   Family: ?
Name: *Revuelto* (Creek) + Greek *sauros* = lizard
Size: ?
Period: Late Triassic, 225 million to 219 million years ago
Place: New Mexico, ?Arizona
Diet: Plants

   Revueltosaurus was a mysterious herbivore named from a single and unrevealing incisor-like tooth. The low tooth, triangular in side view, is typical of that of one of the small ornithischians, a large, diverse group of plant-eating dinosaurs.

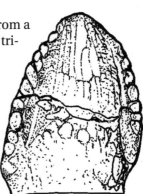

*Revueltosaurus
callenderi*
tooth

RHABDODON

(RAB-duh-don)

Type Species: *priscus* (PRIS-kus)
Classification:
   Order: Ornithischia
   Suborder: Ornithopoda
   Family: ?
Name: Greek *rhabdos* = rod + Greek *odontos* = tooth
Size: 4 meters (14.5 feet) long
Period: Late Cretaceous, 83 million to 65 million
              years ago
Place: France, Romania, Austria, Hungary
Diet: Plants

    Rhabdodon was one of a small, solidly built, primitive group of dinosaurs that lived in island and archipelago regions of central Europe at the end of dinosaur time. *Rhabdodon* has long been considered one of the latest of the iguanodontians, a group of bipedal plant-eaters that includes the iguanodontids and the hadrosaurids.

    Rhabdodon probably looked something like *Camptosaurus*, although its remains are too incomplete to derive a strong impression of its appearance in life.

    Rhabdodon robustum (roh-BUS-tum): Found in Siedenburgen, Transylvania, *R. robustum*, originally called *Mochlodon*, was based on a lower jaw of stout proportions.

RHODANOSAURUS

(ron-DAN-uh-SAW-rus)

Type Species: *ludgunensis* (LUJ-yoo-NEN-sis)
Status: Doubtful — ?*Struthiosaurus*
Classification:
   Order: Ornithischia
   Suborder: Ankylosauria
   Family: Nodosauridae
Name: Latin *rhodanos* for Rhone River + Greek *sauros* = lizard
Size: ?2 meters (6 feet) long
Period: Late Cretaceous, 73 million to 65 million years ago
Place: France
Diet: Plants

    A poorly known armored dinosaur, *Rhodanosaurus* was named from a series of tail vertebrae, portions of limb bones, and some well preserved spines and plates. These fossils were originally thought to belong to *Crataeomus*, a small armored dinosaur. *Rhodanosaurus* was a nodosaurid, armored dinosaurs without tail clubs. Like *Danubiosaurus*, *Struthiosaurus*, and *Craterosaurus*, it was a dwarf ankylosaur that lived in the final dinosaur days, when Europe was a series of islands and archipelagos.

RHOETOSAURUS

(ROH-tuh-SAW-rus)

Type Species: *brownei* (BROU-nye)
Classification:

Order:	Saurischia
Suborder:	Sauropoda
Family:	Cetiosauridae

Name: Latin *Rhoeteus* = Trojan + Greek *sauros* = lizard

Size: More than 11.5 meters (40 feet) long

Period: Early Jurassic, ?181 million to 175 million years ago

Place: Queensland, Australia

Diet: Plants

    Rhoetosaurus was a cetiosaurid, one of the sauropods with boxy heads, robust, spoon-shaped teeth, and front and back legs of almost equal length. It was the first large dinosaur found in Australia. Like almost all Australian finds, it is known only from incomplete fossils.

    Rhoetosaurus had a somewhat rigid tail, especially large at its base. It also had enormous legs: its huge thigh bone would have been almost 1.5 meters (about 5 feet) long.

RICARDOESTESIA

(ri-KAHR-doh-es-TEE-zee-uh)

Type Species: *gilmorei* (GIL-mor-eye)
Status: Doubtful — *See Chirostenotes*
Classification:
  Order: Saurischia
  Suborder: Theropoda
  Family: ?
Name: Latinized Richard Estes
Size: Small
Period: Late Cretaceous, 83 million to 70 million
               years ago
Place: Alberta; ?eastern Wyoming
Diet: Meat

   Ricardoestesia, known only from a long, slender lower jaw with teeth, was a small carnivorous dinosaur. This fossil was originally thought to belong to the little flesh-eater, *Chirostenotes pergracilis*. It may prove, with new discoveries, to be *Chirostenotes*, or another small carnivore, *Elmisaurus*. Isolated teeth, including baby teeth found in Wyoming, that were identified as those of *Paronychodon lacustris*, may belong to *Ricardoestesia*.

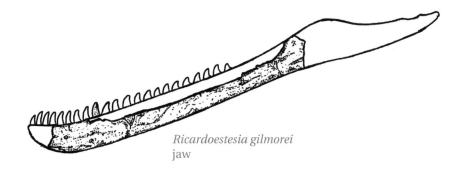

Ricardoestesia gilmorei
jaw

RIOARRIBASAURUS

(REE-oh-uh-REE-buh-SAW-rus)

Type Species: *colberti* (KOL-bur-tye)
Status: Controversial — *See Coelophysis*
Classification:
  Order: Saurischia
  Suborder: Theropoda
  Family: Podokesauridae
Name: Rio Arriba (County) + Greek *sauros* = lizard
Size: About 3 meters (approximately 9 feet) long
Period: Late Triassic
Place: Ghost Ranch, New Mexico; ?Utah; ?Arizona
Diet: Meat

Rioarribasaurus is among the best known of the small carnivorous dinosaurs. It is famous under its former name, *Coelophysis*, with its new name currently under scientific protest. The specimen by which *Coelophysis* was named was one that some paleontologists found difficult to recognize as a distinct genus. Thus, the new name, *Rioarribasaurus*, was given to the Ghost Ranch fossils. Other paleontologists are now attempting to get the original name, *Coelophysis*, reinstated.

This early theropod had a small head, strong jaws, sharp teeth, a long, slender neck, a slim body, and long front limbs. It belonged to the primitive ceratosaur group of carnivorous dinosaurs, some of which had horns.

Hundreds of well preserved *Rioarribasaurus* skeletons were found by paleontologist Edwin H. Colbert's field party in a "dinosaur graveyard" at Ghost Ranch, New Mexico, in 1947. The skeletons were found piled one on top of another. Some of the complete specimens were among the most perfect ever collected, and represented both juveniles and adults. Such a great concentration suggested that these dinosaurs were victims of a local catastrophe, most likely a flood. Whatever caused this mass burial, its discovery makes *Rioarribasaurus* the best known of all Triassic theropods.

The smallest Ghost Ranch skull was 8 centimeters (about 3.1 inches) long, though some hatchling skulls may have been only 2.5 centimeters (one inch) long. Among the most surprising discoveries were two adult skeletons with tiny *Rioarribasaurus* skeletons in their body cavities. This may mean that

RIOARRIBASAURUS *continued*

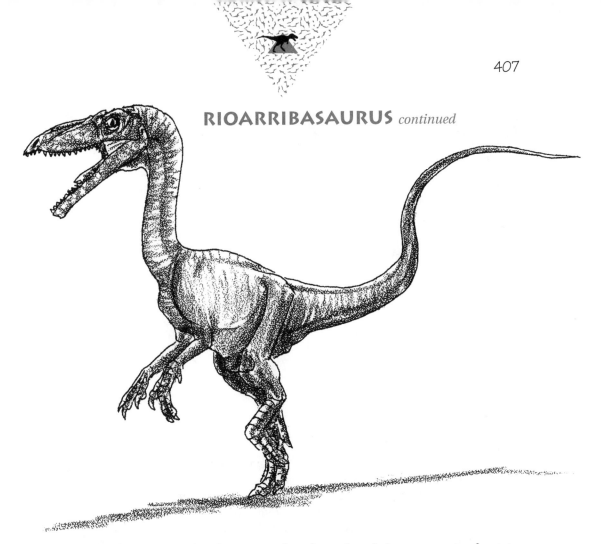

Rioarribasaurus gave birth to live young, but these tiny skeletons were too large to be embryos and had fully turned to bone. More likely, the tiny remains show that *Rioarribasaurus* was a cannibal. Since the bones were uninjured, *Rioarribasaurus* may have swallowed these young whole.

Rioarribasaurus lived in upland environments and probably fed upon whatever prey it could catch, including lizard-like creatures. Its strong forelimbs may have been used extensively in feeding. Its large hands and clawed digits were well adapted for grasping prey. Its strong, supple neck allowed the dinosaur to dart its head about while making its attack.

Although carnivores do not usually live in groups, the concentration of *Rioarribasaurus* skeletons found at Ghost Ranch, because it included animals ranging from very young to large adults, seems indicative of herding. However, it could represent a gradual accumulation of many smaller feeding groups, or solitary individuals. Tracks of solitary carnivorous dinosaurs, possibly made by *Rioarribasaurus*, have been found in southwestern Utah and in Petrified Forest National Monument, Arizona.

RIOJASAURUS

(ree-OH-hah-SAW-rus)

Type Species: *incertis* (in-SUR-tis)
Classification:
    Order: Saurischia
    Suborder: Prosauropoda
    Family: Melanorosauridae
Name: (La) *Rioja* (province, Argentina) + Greek
                   sauros = lizard
Size: 11 meters (36 feet) long
Period: Late Triassic, 225 million to 219 million years ago
Place: Argentina
Diet: Plants

    Riojasaurus was one of the first large, heavily built plant-eating dinosaurs. It is known from Argentina, where the earliest of all dinosaurs have been found. It belonged to the melanorosaurid family of large, more advanced prosauropods that had a tendency to walk on all fours. *Riojasaurus* had a long, slender neck, implying that its skull was small. Its forelimbs were relatively large and robust.

"ROCCOSAURUS"

(ROH-kuh-SAW-rus)

Type Species: *tetrasacralis* (TET-ruh-SACK-ruh-lis)
Status: Unofficial
Classification:
  Order: Saurischia
  Suborder: Sauropoda
  Family: ?Melanorosauridae
Name: *Rocco* + Greek *sauros* = lizard
Size: ?
Period: Late Triassic, 225 million to 208 million years ago
Place: Africa
Diet: Plants

    "*Roccosaurus*" reportedly was a large, four-legged, early browser with sharp teeth. It may belong to the melanosaurid family of small-headed, long-tailed prosauropods. It has not yet been formally described.

SAICHANIA

(sye-CHAN-ee-uh)

Type Species: *chulsanensis* (HUL-suh-NEN-sis)
Classification:
  Order: Ornithischia
  Suborder: Ankylosauria
  Family: Ankylosauridae
Name: Mongolian *saichan* = beautiful
Size: 7 meters (about 24 feet) long
Period: Late Cretaceous, 79 million to 75 million years ago
Place: Mongolia
Diet: Plants

Saichania was an ankylosaurid, an armored dinosaur with small spikes on its flanks, and a clubbed tail. It was unique among armored dinosaurs in that both its back and its belly armor were discovered. Others may have had such extensive protection, but their armor was not preserved.

Saichania and *Pinacosaurus* differed from most of the other known Mongolian ankylosaurs in the structure of their nostrils and nasal cavities. The nasal cavity was divided into right and left passages. Within these passages were thin, spiralling bones. In living mammals, similar bones are covered with membranes that warm, moisten, and filter the incoming air. Similar nasal bones were recently discovered in *Nanotyrannus*, a newly named tyrannosaurid.

If *Saichania* had a keenly developed sense of smell, it could have compensated for its slowness by warning it of approaching predators, and by helping it locate food sources in the semi-arid environment of the ancient Gobi.

SALTASAURUS

(SAWL-tuh-SAW-rus)

Type Species: *loricatus* (LOR-i-KAY-tus)

Classification:

Order:	Saurischia
Suborder:	Sauropoda
Family:	Titanosauridae

Size: 12 meters (40 feet) long

Period: Late Cretaceous, ?83 million to 79 million years ago

Name: Salta (province of Northwestern Argentina) + Greek *sauros* = lizard

Place: Argentina

Diet: Plants

This big plant-eater was the first sauropod known to have had armor. *Saltasaurus* was one of the titanosaurids, primitive four-legged browsers, some or all of which were armored. It was closely related to another South American sauropod, *Neuquensaurus*. A few plates and thousands of bony bumps belonging to this animal have been found.

Because only eight pieces of plate were found, some scientists suggested that the animal had only a few such plates, and that they were scattered over its back. Each plate was circular or oval in shape, and averaged 10 to 12 centimeters (about 3.8 to 4.5 inches) in diameter. The surface was roughened, suggesting that spikes or horns might have been attached. The small, shapeless bumps were 6 to 7 millimeters (.25 inch) or less, and numbered approximately 540. They covered the back and sides of the body.

Saltasaurus robustus (roh-BUS-tus)—Doubtful name: This species was based on vertebrae and limb elements from several individuals. Originally named a species of *Titanosaurus*, it might belong to *Titanosaurus* or to *Saltasaurus*.

SALTOPUS

(SAWL-tuh-puss)

Type Species: *elginensis* (EL-ji-NEN-sis)
Status: Doubtful
Classification:
   Order: Saurischia
   Suborder: Theropoda
   Family: ?
Name: Latin *saltus* = leaping + Greek *pous* = foot
Size: Approximately 60 centimeters (about 23 inches) long
Period: Late Triassic, 225 million to 222 million years ago
Place: Scotland
Diet: Meat

Saltopus was a tiny, very primitive carnivore weighing less than 2 kilograms (4 pounds). It had a long tail and long fingers, but is so poorly preserved that it cannot definitely be called a dinosaur.

"?SANGONGHESAURUS"

(SANG-ong-hi-SAW-rus)

Type Species: No species designated
Status: Unofficial
Classification:
   Order: Ornithischia
   Suborder: Ankylosauria
   Family: Ankylosauridae
Name: Chinese Sangonghe + Greek saurus = lizard
Size: ?
Period: ?
Place: China
Diet: Plants

   "*Sangonghesaurus*" was an ankylosaur with small lateral spikes and a clubbed tail. It had well-developed armor on the back of its neck and trunk, and around the tail. Its back armor consisted of large plates and smaller bony bumps. Spikes projected from the animal's sides.

SANPASAURUS

(SAN-puh-SAW-rus)

Type Species: *yaoi* (YOU-eye)
Classification:
    Order: ?
    Suborder: ?
    Family: ?
Name: Sanpa (ancient name of Szechuan province) +
             Greek sauros = lizard
Size: ?Large
Period: Late Jurassic, 150 million to 145 million years ago
Place: China
Diet: Plants

    This little known dinosaur had massive vertebrae and long front legs. From these and other features, scientists concluded that *Sanpasaurus* was either an iguanodontid or another large plant-eater, such as *Camptosaurus*. It was larger than both, however.

    If *Sanpasaurus* was an iguanodontid, it represents the first certain occurrence of this family in China. But various noniguanodontid features have been seen among the fossils of *Sanpasaurus*, suggesting that it was a juvenile sauropod. Or perhaps the fossils represent a hodge-podge of assorted dinosaur parts. This would not be surprising, as the original remains, unearthed in 1939, reached the laboratory in a jumbled state.

SARCOLESTES

(SAHR-koh-LES-teez)

Type Species: *leedsi* (LEED-zye)

Classification:

    Order: Ornithischia

    Suborder: Ankylosauria

    Family: Nodosauridae

Name: Greek *sarkos* = flesh + Greek *lestes* = robber

Size: ?

Period: Middle Jurassic, 161 million to 157 million years ago

Place: England

Diet: Plants

    Prior to the discovery of the 170-million-year-old *Jurassosaurus*, *Sarcolestes* was the earliest known nodosaurid, an armored dinosaur with large spikes on its sides and a tail without a club. It is known from the left half of a lower jaw with teeth, similar to that of the nodososaur *Sauropelta*.

    Sarcolestes had a skull plate similar to that of the bone-headed pachycephalosaur, *Stegoceras*. This skull feature may have served a head-butting function for *Sarcolestes*.

Sarcolestes leedsi tooth

SARCOSAURUS

(SAHR-kuh-SAW-rus)

Type Species: *woodi* (WOOD-eye)
Classification:
  Order: Saurischia
  Suborder: Theropoda
  Family: ?
Name: Greek *sarkos* = flesh + Greek *sauros* = lizard
Size: ?3.5 meters (12 feet) long
Period: Early Jurassic, ?206 million to 200 million
              years ago
Place: England
Diet: Meat

   Sarcosaurus was an early carnivorous dinosaur. It belonged to the group Ceratosauria, which includes small-to-large meat-eaters, some of which had crests or horns on their heads. Like many European dinosaurs, *Sarcosaurus* is based on fragmentary fossils, and is too poorly known to place in a family.

   Sarcosaurus andrewsi (AN-droo-zye)—Doubtful name: This animal is based upon an isolated right leg bone.

SAURECHINODON

(SAWR-i-KYE-nuh-don)

Status: Invalid—See Echinodon

SAUROLOPHUS

(SAW-ruh-LOH-fus)

Type Species: *osborni* (OZ-bor-nye)
Classification:
    Order: Ornithischia
    Suborder: Ornithopoda
    Family: Hadrosauridae
Name: Greek *sauros* = lizard + Greek *lophos* = crest
Size: About 9.7 meters (32 feet) long
Period: Late Cretaceous, 72 million to 68 million
              years ago
Place: Alberta; Mongolia, China
Diet: Plants

    Saurolophus, a large duckbill, was the first Canadian dinosaur known from nearly complete remains. The first skeleton discovered was so complete that it even included fossilized skin impressions.

    Saurolophus belonged to the hadrosaurine family of duckbills, which did not have hollow head crests like other duckbills. *Saurolophus*, however, did have a distinguishing solid crest that was raised above the face in a spikelike growth. This crest could have been significant in sexual identification. Found with the dinosaur was a sclerotic ring, a bone from inside the eye socket, and the first known in any duckbilled dinosaur. The ring revealed that the eye was considerably smaller than the eye hole.

    The close relationship between this species and a Mongolian form (see below) provides compelling evidence that dinosaurs moved between Asia and North America near the end of dinosaur time, when the continents were joined.

    Saurolophus angustirostris (ang-GUS-ti-ROS-tris): This animal, based on a skeleton found in Mongolia, was larger than the type species. There are reports that an an even larger specimen exists from the same region. *S. angustirostris* was the most abundant Asian hadrosaur discovered, and may have been the dominant plant-eater in its world. The primary differences between this species and *Saurolophus osborni* were that the skull of the former was narrower and the crest probably longer.

SAUROPELTA

(SAW-ruh-PEL-tuh)

Type Species: *edwardsorum* (ED-wurd-ZOR-um)

Classification:

    Order: Ornithischia

    Suborder: Ankylosauria

    Family: Nodosauridae

Name: Greek *sauros* = lizard + Greek *pelta* = small shield

Size: 6 meters (19 feet) long

Period: Early Cretaceous, 116 million to 91 million years ago

Place: Montana, Wyoming

Diet: Plants

    Sauropelta was one of the earliest known nodosaurs, or clubless armored dinosaurs, from North America. *Sauropelta* was medium-sized, with stout legs. Its tail was stiff and nearly half its length. Its hind legs were longer than its forelimbs, and its back was arched. Its neck was short, its shoulders and limbs massive, and its feet were short and broad.

    This squat animal was well protected. Its neck armor was made up of oval plates. Flanking these plates were large triangular spikes with sharp front edges. The largest spikes were placed just in front of the shoulders. Hollow triangular plates comprised the animal's remaining armor.

SAUROPELTA *continued*

Sauropelta was a relatively abundant dinosaur. Many specimens were collected in Wyoming and Montana during the 1930s by the American Museum of Natural History and during the 1960s by the Peabody Museum of Natural History at Yale University.

Footprints attributed to *Tetrapodosaurus borealis* may have been made by *Sauropelta.*

SAUROPHAGUS
(SAW-ruh-FAY-jus)

Status: Invalid—*See Allosaurus*

SAUROPLITES

(SAW-ruh-PLYE-teez)

Type Species: *scutiger* (SKOO-ti-jur)
Status: Doubtful
Classification:
  Order: Ornithischia
  Suborder: Ankylosauria
  Family: ?
Name: Greek *sauros* = lizard + Greek *hoplites* = hoplite, an armed foot soldier of ancient Greece
Size: ?Large
Period: Early Cretaceous, ?145 million to ?97.5 million years ago
Place: China, ?Mongolia
Diet: Plants

    Sauroplites was an armored dinosaur, known only from fragmentary remains. These included several complete plates from its back and many plate fragments. *Sauroplites*'s ribs suggest that the animal's girth was about 5 meters (almost 17 feet), making it very stout indeed.

SAURORNITHOIDES

(SAWR-or-ni-THOY-deez)

Type Species: *mongoliensis* (mong-GOH-lee-EN-sis)

Classification:

    Order: Saurischia

    Suborder: Theropoda

    Family: Troodontidae

Name: Greek *sauros* = lizard + *ornithoides* = birdlike

Size: 1.9 meters (6.5 feet) long

Period: Late Cretaceous, ?85 million to 77 million years ago

Place: Mongolia

Diet: Meat

This small, intelligent, carnivorous theropod from the Gobi Desert was among the most birdlike of dinosaurs. Originally mistaken for a bird, it was most likely a fleet-footed hunter of small mammals and reptiles. *Troodon*, which lived in western North America during the same time period, appears to be closely related to *Saurornithoides*, providing further evidence of the connection between these continents near the end of the Cretaceous Period.

S. "asiamericanus" (AY-zee-uh-uh-MER-i-KAN-us)—Unofficial name. This species has not yet been described.

Saurornithoides junior (JOO-nee-ur): A relatively large animal based on an incomplete skull and skeleton from the Gobi Desert. It differed from *S. mongoliensis* in being about 1.3 times larger, with a different tooth count.

SAURORNITHOLESTES

(SAWR-or-NITH-uh-LES-teez)

Type Species: *langstoni* (LANG-stoh-nye)
Classification:
> **Order:** Saurischia
> **Suborder:** Theropoda
> **Family:** ?Dromaeosauridae

Name: Greek *sauros* = lizard + Greek *ornithos* = bird + Greek *lestes* = robber

Size: 1.8 meters (6 feet) long

Period: Late Cretaceous, 76 million to 73 million years ago

Place: Alberta

Diet: Meat

Saurornitholestes was a small, lightly built carnivore, probably of the dromaeosaurid family. This group of small meat-eaters had large heads with narrow snouts; long forelimbs with mobile wrists; "hands" that had three long fingers with large curved claws; feet with a sickle claw on the second toe; and a long stiff tail.

The skull, teeth, and other skeletal parts of this dinosaur are almost identical to those of the Asian dromaeosaurid, *Velociraptor mongoliensis,* and the North American dromaeosaurid, *Deinonychus.* This is yet another piece of evidence that the two continents were closely linked in the Late Cretaceous Period.

SCELIDOSAURUS

(SKEL-eye-duh-SAW-rus)

Type Species: harrisoni (HAR-i-suh-nye)
Classification:

Order:	Ornithischia
Suborder:	Scelidosauria
Family:	Scelidosauridae
Name:	Greek *skelos* = leg + Greek *sauros* = lizard
Size:	4 meters (13.5 feet) long
Period:	Early Jurassic, 208 million to 200 million years ago
Place:	England
Diet:	Plants

Scelidosaurus was one of the oldest and first known bird-hipped, or ornithischian, dinosaurs. It was named in 1859 by the scientist who coined the name dinosaur, Sir Richard Owen.

Scelidosaurus, a primitive armored dinosaur that moved on four legs, belonged to the Thyreophora, as did stegosaurs and ankylosaurs. The armor on its back included numerous oval plates and unique three-pointed plates just behind the skull. Skin impressions indicate that the skin was covered with a mosaic of small rounded scales.

Scelidosaurus was probably a slow-moving creature that relied mostly on its armor for protection. But with its long tail counterbalancing its body, it might have been able to make short, two-legged runs.

SCOLOSAURUS

(SKOH-luh-SAW-rus)

Status: Invalid—*See Euoplocephalus*

SCUTELLOSAURUS

(SKOO-tuh-luh-SAW-rus)

Type Species: *lawleri* (LAW-luh-RYE)
Classification:

Order:	Ornithischia
Suborder:	?Thyreophora
Family:	?
Name:	Latin *scutellum* = little shield + Greek *sauros* = lizard
Size:	1.2 meters (4 feet) long
Period:	Early Jurassic, 208 million to 200 million years ago
Place:	Arizona
Diet:	Plants

Scutellosaurus was a small plant-eater of the Thyreophora group, which included stegosaurs and ankylosaurs. It was distinguished by a very long tail, short hind limbs, and an abundance of armor plates.

Armor in *Scutellosaurus* was more fully developed than in any other known primitive dinosaur. There were at least 304 armor plates found with the namesake skeleton, indicating that the total number in the living animal may have been even more extensive. Six types of plates were found, ranging from stegosaur-like, large plates to little nubbins.

This armored dinosaur may have been mostly bipedal, as shown by the long slender hind limbs, compact hind foot, and very long tail. But other features of *Scutellosaurus*, such as its disproportionately long trunk and forelimbs, large front foot, and wide pelvis, suggest it also moved about on all fours.

Scutellosaurus may have been a remote ancestor to the Jurassic and Cretaceous plated and armored dinosaurs.

SECERNOSAURUS

(suh-KUR-nuh-SAW-rus)

Type Species: *koerneri* (KUR-nuh-rye)
Classification:
    Order: Ornithischia
    Suborder: Ornithopoda
    Family: Hadrosauridae
Name: Latin *secerno* = severed/divided + Greek *sauros* = lizard
Size: 3 meters (10 feet) long
Period: Late Cretaceous, ?73 million to 65 million years ago
Place: Argentina
Diet: Plants

    Secernosaurus was a small duckbill, known only from part of its braincase and a few other pelvic bones. Without a skull, it is impossible to tell if it was crested or crestless.

    Secernosaurus was the first certain hadrosaurid to be found in the Southern Hemisphere. Duckbills and their iguanodontid ancestors were dominant in the Northern Hemisphere in the Cretaceous Period. The discovery of *Secernosaurus* indicates that, by the Late Cretaceous, hadrosaurs had established themselves in the Southern Hemisphere as well.

SEGISAURUS

(SEG-i-SAW-rus)

Type Species: *halli* (HAW-lye)
Classification:
   Order: Saurischia
   Suborder: Theropoda
   Family: Segisauridae
Name: Segi (Canyon) + Greek *sauros* = lizard
Size: Very small
Period: Early Jurassic, ?206 million to ?200 million
                years ago
Place: Arizona
Diet: Meat, ?Insects

The mistaken belief that this small carnivore had solid bones, unlike other meat-eating dinosaurs, led to its definition as the first of the segisaurid family, primitive, lightly built meat-eaters with long necks. *Segisaurus* had some very birdlike characteristics, including three-toed feet, and a well-developed collar bone, a feature once thought to distinguish birds from dinosaurs.

Because of the way the skeleton was found, with hind limbs and feet flexed closely underneath the body, and the way in which the knee and ankle joints were aligned, scientists think *Segisaurus* may have been able to squat like a hen. The forefoot seems to have been adapted for clawing and grasping. The fingers may have raked burrowing insects or small animals out of the loose sand. The light construction of the vertebrae, hip bones and feet, along with short body, long tail, and powerful leg bones, indicate that *Segisaurus* was also adapted for rapid running and leaping.

SEGNOSAURUS

(SEG-nuh-SAW-rus)

Type Species: *galbinensis* (GAL-bi-NEN-sis)
Classification:

Order:	Saurischia
Suborder:	Segnosauria
Family:	Segnosauridae

Name: Latin *segnis* = slow + Greek *sauros* = lizard
Size: 6.5 meters (20 feet) long
Period: Late Cretaceous. ?97.5 million to ?88.5 million years ago
Place: Mongolia; ?Alberta
Diet: ?Meat, ?Plants ?Insects

This was the first dinosaur to be discovered from the Segnosauridae, a peculiar and puzzling family. The segnosaurids were medium- to large, two- and four-legged meat- and plant-eating dinosaurs. They may have been omnivorous.

Segnosaurs were distinguished by a series of cheek teeth, followed by a toothless area in the jaw, and then a horny beak. Their hands were like those of meat-eating dinosaurs, but their stout hind limbs, broad clawed feet, and hips were features of bird-hipped dinosaurs.

Segnosaurus, a large member of this odd family, was perhaps a slow-moving plant-eater with a bulky trunk and short, broad feet. It was first thought to be a strange kind of theropod, with its small cheek teeth and a horny beak. Now it is believed to be equally related to the broad-footed sauropodomorphs, a group of large, lizard-hipped plant-eaters that includes prosauropods and sauropods.

SEISMOSAURUS

(SYEZ-muh-SAW-rus)

Type Species: *halli* (HAW-lye)
Classification:
    Order: Saurischia
    Suborder: Sauropoda
    Family: Diplodocidae
Name: Greek *seismos* = earthquake + Greek *sauros* = lizard
Size: 39 to 52 meters (about 128 to 170 feet) long
Period: Late Jurassic, 156 million to 145 million years ago
Place: New Mexico
Diet: Plants

    Seismosaurus, which was half the length of a football field, may have been the longest dinosaur known. It was a member of the diplodocid family, long sauropods with whiplash tails. Although *Seismosaurus* was extremely long, it also seems to have been low-slung, making it known popularly as the "dachshund" of giant dinosaurs. Good limb bone fossils have yet to be found, but scientists think the legs of *Seismosaurus* were short. Reduced leg length would have helped stabilize this enormous animal. *Seismosaurus* looked a lot like *Barosaurus* and *Diplodocus*, and some scientists have speculated that it was a particularly large specimen of *Diplodocus*.

Seismosaurus   *Ultrasauros*   *Supersaurus*

Numerous polished gizzard stones, like those swallowed by some modern animals for grinding up food, have been found in the middle region of this skeleton. One very large stone, too big to be swallowed, was discovered. Scientists have speculated that *Seismosaurus* may have choked to death on it.

Because the rock in which this dinosaur's partial remains were found is very hard, high-tech devices for sound, radiation, and magnetic detection are being tried out to locate the remaining bones.

SELLOSAURUS

(SEL-uh-SAW-rus)

Type Species: *gracilis* (GRAS-i-lis)
Classification:

Order:	Saurischia
Suborder:	Prosauropoda
Family:	Plateosauridae
Name:	Latin *sella* = saddle + Greek *sauros* = lizard
Size:	6 meters (20 feet) long
Period:	Late Triassic, 219 million to 208 million years ago
Place:	Germany
Diet:	Plants

Sellosaurus was a slender-footed plant-eater belonging to the plateosaurid family of prosauropods. These were medium- to large-sized herbivores with stout limbs and small heads. *Sellosaurus* was quite primitive in its anatomy, and may have been an ancestor to the prosauropod, *Anchisaurus*. A juvenile specimen of this animal was once incorrectly named as a new genus, *Efraasia*.

SHAMOSAURUS

(SHAM-uh-SAW-rus)

Type Species: *scutatus* (skoo-TAT-us)
Classification:
    Order: Ornithischia
    Suborder: Ankylosauria
    Family: Ankylosauridae
Name: Mongolian *Shamo* (Gobi) + Greek *sauros* = lizard
Size: ?
Period: Early Cretaceous, 119 million to 97.5 million
               years ago
Place: Mongolia
Diet: Plants

    Shamosaurus was an ankylosaurid, the earliest Asian armored dinosaur with a clubbed tail. It had an armored head ornamented with little pimply bumps. Its skull most closely resembled that of *Saichania*, another Mongolian ankylosaur. *Shamosaurus* may have been intermediate between the clubless nodosaurids and club-tailed ankylosaurids.

SHANSHANOSAURUS

(shan-SHAN-uh-SAW-rus)

Type Species: huoyanshanensis (HOY-an-sha-NEN-sis)

Classification:

Order: Saurischia

Suborder: Theropoda

Family: ?

Name: Shanshan (County) + Greek sauros = lizard

Size: 2.5 meters (approximately 8.5 feet) long

Period: Late Cretaceous, ?83 million to 65 million years ago

Place: China

Diet: Meat

Shanshanosaurus was a small, bipedal, carnivorous dinosaur of uncertain classification. It was originally assigned to its own family and then reassigned as a species of Aublysodon. Shanshanosaurus showed similarities in bone structure to both big South American carnivores, the abelisaurids, and to small Asian and North American carnivores, the dromaeosaurids. Its relationship to other dinosaurs is a puzzle. It may have been an active, agile animal.

SHANTUNGOSAURUS

(shan-TUNG-uh-SAW-rus)

Type Species: *giganteus* (jye-GAN-tee-us)
Classification:

Order:	Ornithischia
Suborder:	Ornithopoda
Family:	Hadrosauridae
Name:	Shantung (Province, China) + Greek sauros = lizard
Size:	At least 15 meters (about 51 feet) long
Period:	Late Cretaceous, ?83 million to 73 million years ago
Place:	China
Diet:	Plants

    Shantungosaurus, the largest of all known duckbills, was perhaps the largest animal ever to walk on two legs. A member of the subfamily of flat-headed hadrosaurids, it had a long, broad skull. Except for some features related to its size, *Shantungosaurus* cannot be distinguished from the better known North American *Edmontosaurus*.

    Since only one specimen of *Shantungosaurus* has been scientifically described, a positive link cannot be made.

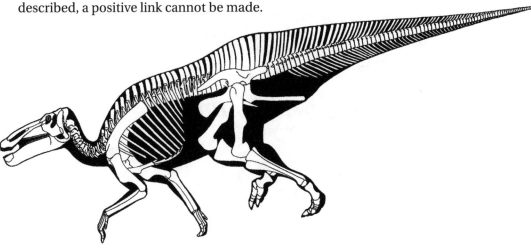

SHUNOSAURUS

(SHOO-nuh-SAW-rus)

Type Species: *Iii* (LEE-eye)

Classification:

Order: Saurischia

Suborder: Sauropoda

Family: Cetiosauridae

Name: Shuo (old Chinese spelling of Sichuan) + Greek sauros = lizard

Size: Up to 12 meters (40 feet) long

Period: Middle Jurassic, 175 million to 163 million years ago

Place: China

Diet: Plants

Shunosaurus was a large, four-legged browser that brought a surprise to dinosaur paleontology. When *Shunosaurus* was discovered, it was revealed that this dinosaur carried a tail club, a feature previously unknown among sauropods. Its tail vertebrae were swollen to form a tail "mace," which resembled those in some armored dinosaurs. The club had two pairs of small spines, similar to the tail spines in the stegosaurs. This club may have been used as a weapon.

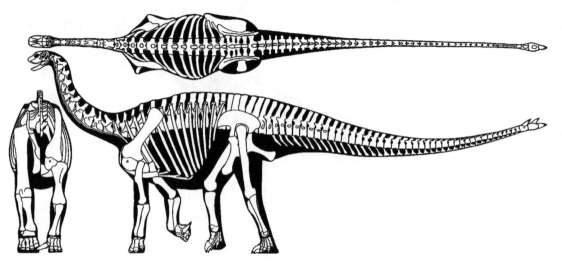

SHUNOSAURUS *continued*

Scientists have suggested that *Shunosaurus* was intermediate between the primitive prosauropods of ealy dinosaur time and the more advanced sauropods of the Late Jurassic to Late Cretaceous Periods.

Because of the spectacular condition of the specimens found, *Shunosaurus lii* may be the best known of all Chinese dinosaurs. It is one of the few sauropods found anywhere in the world for which complete skulls are known. It also appears to have been a very common dinosaur and perhaps was the most abundant in China.

Shunosaurus "ziliujingensis" (ZEE-lee-YOO-jing-EN-sis)—Unofficial name. This not-yet-described dinosaur may have come from the Lower Jurassic Period within the Sichuan Basin.

SHUOSAURUS
(SHOO-uh-SAW-rus)

Status: Invalid—See Shunosaurus

SIAMOSAURUS

(sye-AM-uh-SAW-rus)

Type Species: suteethorni (SOO-tee-THOR-nye)
Classification:
    Order: Saurischia
    Suborder: Theropoda
    Family: ?Spinosauridae
Name: Siam (nineteenth century name of Thailand) +
               Greek sauros = lizard
Size: Large
Period: Late Jurassic, 163 million to 145 million years ago
Place: Thailand
Diet: Meat, ?Fish

This genus is known only from teeth that resembled those of *Spinosaurus*, a huge carnivore from North Africa. *Siamosaurus* was assigned to the spinosaurids, an unusual group of large meat-eaters distinguished by three-fingered hands, and sails on their backs which were supported by long back spines.

Because of the compressed, non-serrated form of *Siamosaurus's* teeth, researchers suggested that they were used for piercing instead of slicing prey. Similiar teeth were found in crocodilians and plesiosaurs, so *Siamosaurus* may have been a fish-eater as well. *Baryonyx*, another of *Spinosaurus's* relatives, may also have been a fish-eater.

SILVISAURUS

(SIL-vi-SAW-rus)

Type Species: *condrayi* (kon-DRAY-eye)
Classification:

    Order: Ornithischia

    Suborder: Ankylosauria

    Family: Nodosauridae

Name: Latin *silva* = forest + Greek *sauros* = lizard

Size: About 3.25 meters (11 feet) long

Period: Early Cretaceous, 116 million to 113 million
              years ago

Place: Kansas

Diet: Plants

    Silvisaurus was a nodosaurid, one of the primitive armored dinosaurs with large spikes on their sides and no tail clubs. It had a pear-shaped skull that was about three-fourths as wide as it was long.

    A number of *Silvisaurus's* features, including its unusually long neck, indicate that it was a primitive armored dinosaur. It may have been ancestral to *Edmontonia*, a North American armored dinosaur of the Late Cretaceous Period.

    Silvisaurus may have been a honker. The sinus chambers of its skull formed almost balloon-like inflations. These chambers may have allowed the passage of air and amplified sound vibrations in the manner of a voice-box.

SINOCOELURUS

(SYE-noh-si-LOOR-us)

Type Species: *fragilis* (fruh-JIL-is)
Status: Doubtful
Classification:
  Order: Saurischia
  Suborder: Theropoda
  Family: ?
Name: Latin *sino* = eastern + Greek *koilos* = hollow
Size: ?Small
Period: Early or Middle Jurassic, 208 million to 180 million years ago
Place: China
Diet: Meat

This carnivorous dinosaur was founded upon four isolated long, slender teeth. Unlike the teeth of most meat-eating dinosaurs, these lacked serrations. With so little evidence, it is impossible to say what dinosaur yielded these teeth, if indeed it was a dinosaur. *Sinocoelurus* marked the first record of a coelurosaur (a small carnivorous dinosaur) in China during Jurassic times.

SINOSAURUS

(SYE-nuh-SAW-rus)

Type Species: *triassicus* (trye-AS-i-kus)
Status: Doubtful
Classification:
  Order: Saurischia
  Suborder: ?Theropoda
  Family: ?
Name: Latin *sino* = eastern + Greek *sauros* = lizard
Size: Possibly 2.4 meters (8 feet) long
Period: Early Jurassic, 208 million to 188 million
               years ago
Place: China
Diet: Meat

    This is yet another poorly known meat-eater. Apparently, *Sinosaurus* was a carnivore with long serrated, sharply pointed teeth. However, the teeth may not belong to a dinosaur at all, but to a more primitive "thecodontian" reptile.

SPHENOSPONDYLUS

(SFEE-noh-SPON-di-lus)

Status: Doubtful—*See Iguanodon*

SPINOSAURUS

(SPYE-nuh-SAW-rus)

Type Species: *aegypticus* (i-JIP-ti-kus)

Classification:

    Order: Saurischia

    Suborder: Theropoda

    Family: Spinosauridae

Name: Latin *spina* = spine + Greek *sauros* = lizard

Size: Over 12 meters (40 feet) long

Period: Late Cretaceous, ?97.5 million to 95 million years ago

Place: Egypt

Diet: Meat

This unusual giant carnivore may have been the largest meat-eater ever to walk the earth. *Spinosaurus* is known from fragmentary North African fossils collected by German scientists. Much of its remains were destroyed in bombing raids on Munich in World War II, but those remains suggested that this was an enormous creature. The vertebrae in *Tyrannosaurus*, often called the largest carnivore, measure about 16 centimeters (over 6 inches) long, while those of *Spinosaurus* measure 19 to 21 centimeters (7.1 to 7.8 inches) long.

Spinosaurus's most striking feature were the very long spines on its back vertebrae. The spines may have

SPINOSAURUS *continued*

supported a sail-like membrane similar to the so-called finbacks of the synapsid reptiles, *Dimetrodon* and *Edaphosaurus*. Though this sail could have served as an identification signal or a sexual display, it may also have functioned as a heat-regulating device, allowing the animal to increase heat loss during vigorous exercise in its hot environment. With the body turned so that the sail could receive solar rays, the blood circulating through the sail would be warmed to increase body temperature. Away from the sun, the sail could dissipate heat.

Ouranosaurus, a large plant-eater found in rocks of the same age and region, had a similar series of spines, suggesting that climate was a factor in the evolution of the sail fins. The belief that these spines were solar panels or radiators may be evidence that not all dinosaurs were warm-blooded.

SPONDYLOSOMA

(SPON-di-luh-SOH-muh)

Type Species: *absconditum* (AB-skon-DEE-tum)
Status: Doubtful
Classification:
   Order: ?
   Suborder: ?
   Family: ?
Name: Greek *spondulios* = vertebral + Greek *soma* = body
Size: ?
Period: Late Triassic, 231 million to 225 million years ago
Place: Brazil
Diet: ?

This dinosaur of doubtful status was named from fragmentary remains which included two teeth. *Spondlyosoma* differed from *Staurikosaurus*, a small early meat-eater from the same area, in the structure of the vertebrae. There were also differences in the form of its pubic bone. Whether *Spondylosoma* was another primitive meat-eating dinosaur, or even a dinosaur at all, remains a mystery.

STAURIKOSAURUS

(STAW-ri-kuh-SAW-rus)

Type Species: *pricei* (PRYE-sye)

Classification:

Order: ?

Suborder: ?

Family: ?

Name: Greek *staurikos* = stake-like + Greek *sauros* = lizard

Size: 2 meters (about 7 feet) long

Period: Late Triassic, 231 million to 225 million years ago

Place: Brazil; Argentina

Diet: Meat

This very primitive carnivore was one of the earliest of all dinosaurs. It was, in fact, so primitive it might not be neither ornithischian nor saurischian, but more primitive than both. Like the related theropod *Herrerasaurus*, *Staurikosaurus* was slender, had a medium-length neck, and ran on two legs. Its forelimbs were small and may have had a four-fingered hand. (Carnivorous dinosaurs advanced from four fingers to two by the end of dinosaur time.) The hind limbs had five-toed feet (later carnivorous dinosaurs had three toes). *Staurikosaurus's* long body, legs, and tail suggest that it was a swift runner.

STEGOCERAS

(ste-GOS-uh-rus)

Type Species: *validum* (VAL-i-dum)

Classification:

Order:	Ornithischia
Suborder:	Pachycephalosauria
Family:	Pachycephalosauridae

Name: Greek *stegos* = roof + Greek *keras* = horn

Size: 2 meters (about 7 feet) long

Period: Late Cretaceous, 76 million to 65 million years ago

Place: Alberta; Montana

Diet: Plants

Stegoceras was a small two-legged, thick-headed plant-eater. It was small- to medium-sized for a pachycephalosaurid.

The dense dome on top of its head may have been used in head-butting contests for sexual and/or social dominance. The anatomy of *Stegoceras* supports this idea. The skull was thick enough to protect the brain against such clashes. Bony tendons held the vertebrae together tightly, and specialized links between the vertebrae prevented twisting. The skeleton seemed designed so that an individual might position its head face down, while keeping its neck, back, and tail in a horizontal line. The impact of butting would have been absorbed by its spine.

Much of this combat may have been flank-butting, not head-to-head ramming. *Stegoceras's* curved skull did not allow for easy head-to-head confrontation.

Stegoceras, the best known of all North American pachycephalosaurids, has been known since the early 1900s. It was originally thought to be a horned dinosaur.

STEGOPELTA
(STEG-uh-PEL-tuh)

Status: Invalid—See Nodosaurus

STEGOSAURIDES

(STEG-uh-SAW-ri-deez)

Type Species: *excavatus* (ECKS-kuh-VAY-tus)
Status: Doubtful
Classification:
   Order: Ornithischia
   Suborder: ?Ankylosauria
   Family: ?
Name: Greek *stegos* = roof + Greek *sauros* = lizard +
                     Greek *oides* = appearing like
Size: ?
Period: Late Cretaceous, ?97.5 million to ?65 million
                     years ago
Place: Northwestern China
Diet: Plants

   This is a poorly known ankylosaur, or armored dinosaur, of unknown family affiliation. *Stegosaurides* was founded on a fragmentary specimen that included two vertebrae and the base of an armor spine. Other bones nearby were thought to belong to a stegosaur, a plate-backed dinosaur, hence its name.

STEGOSAURUS

(STEG-uh-SAW-rus)

Type Species: *armatus* (ahr-MAY-tus)

Classification:

Order:	Ornithischia
Suborder:	Stegosauria
Family:	Stegosauridae
Name:	Greek *stegos* = roof + *sauros* = lizard
Size:	7 meters (25 feet) long
Period:	Late Jurassic, 156 million to 145 million years ago
Place:	Colorado, Utah, Wyoming
Diet:	Plants

One of the best known dinosaurs, the plate-backed *Stegosaurus* was the first plate-backed dinosaur found. These stegosaurid dinosaurs were a nearly world-wide group of plated, spiked plant-eaters that thrived in the Late Jurassic Period and beyond. All of these were four-legged, small-headed, heavy-limbed dinosaurs. *Stegosaurus* itself was named from a specimen that had still not been adequately described more than a century after its discovery. The animal we know as *Stegosaurus* was based upon a well preserved skeleton of another species, *Stegosaurus stenops.*

Stegosaurus had short front legs and a narrow snout. Its most identifiable feature was an array of thin, vertically oriented plates along its back. These were roughly tri-angular in shape. The plates on *Stegosaurus's* back were small. The plates became larger at the middle of the back, then smaller again down the tail, stopping halfway down the tail. The placement of the plates has remained controversial to this day. At first they were believed to have been arranged in a single row down the neck, back, and tail. They have also been shown in two rows of paired plates, although no two plates on *S. stenops* had an opposite counterpart, or "mirror image."

The first skeleton of *S. stenops* was found with the plates in two alternating rows, an arrangement that most paleontologists agreed on for many decades. Then the old notion of a single row of plates was reintroduced and became quite popular. However, several newer discoveries of still-undescribed specimens indicate that the two-alternating-row arrangement was basically correct. Earlier stegosaurs also appear to have had a double row of plates, which would support

STEGOSAURUS *continued*

the theory of double row arrangement in *Stegosaurus*. Plates weren't the only ornaments on *Stegosaurus*. At the end of its tail were four tall spines, arranged in pairs and angled toward the rear. The spines varied in size and shape with the individual animal.

Also scattered along the body were numerous small, flattened, irregular-sized armor plates, some just 35 millimeters (1¼ inches) in diameter.

The tail spikes in *Stegosaurus* were almost certainly used as weapons. A swing of the tail could have caused serious damage to attacking predators like *Allosaurus* and *Ceratosaurus*. The function of the plates, however, may involve more than simple defense.

Originally, the plates were regarded as armor, although they would have protected only the top of the animal. They certainly made the animal appear bigger than it really was, perhaps creating a deterrent to hungry meat-eaters. They may also have served as a display to attract mates or intimidate rivals.

A newer explanation is that the plates helped control body temperature. Dissection of a *Stegosaurus* plate showed that it was not solid bone, as we might expect of armor plating, but honeycombed with small, tubelike passages that could have housed blood vessels. The presence of blood vessels within the plates suggested that they may have served a heat regulating function. If they were arranged in two alternating rows, the plates were ideally shaped to dissipate heat and cool the animal. Acting as solar panels, they could also absorb heat from the sun to warm *Stegosaurus*. Just like organs of our own bodies, the plates may have served more than just one function.

STEGOSAURUS *continued*

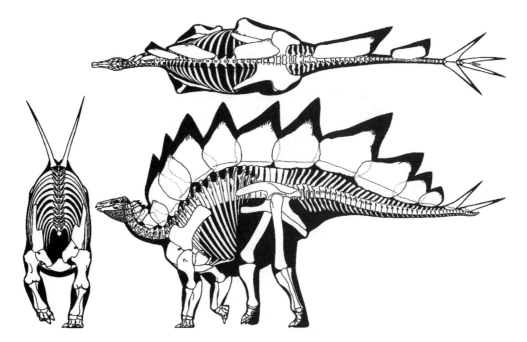

Much has been said about the tiny size of the *Stegosaurus* brain. Judging from a crushed skull, its brain seems to have been very small relative to its body size. It was smaller than a ping-pong ball and weighed only about 70 grams (2.5 ounces).

It has also been said that this dinosaur had two or even three "brains," or enlargements in the spinal cord, for controlling the rear parts of the body. However, recent studies have shown that these so-called extra brains were energy stores for muscles, not nerve tissue or secondary brains.

Stegosaurus longispinus (LONG-i-SPYE-nus): This species was characterized by two pairs of very long tail spines. These spines were the longest known in any specimen: one was estimated at 86 centimeters (almost 3 feet) long.

Stegosaurus stenops (STEN-ops): This is the species, several specimens of which have been discovered over the last century, from which the popular image of *Stegosaurus* has been derived.

Stegosaurus ungulatus (UNG-gyoo-LAT-us): This large, robust species may have been the same as *Stegosaurus armatus*. The plates in this species were smaller and more pointed than in *Stegosaurus stenops*, and seem to have been arranged in pairs, two being mirror images of each other. The legs were longer than those of *Stegosaurus stenops*. There may have been four pairs of tail spines.

STENONYCHOSAURUS
(ste-NON-i-kuh-SAW-rus)

Status: Invalid—See Troodon

STENOPELIX

(STEN-uh-PEL-icks)

Type Species: *valdensis* (val-DEN-sis)
Classification:
   Order: Ornithischia
   Suborder: Marginocephalia
   Family: ?
Name: Greek *stenos* = narrow + Greek *pelike* = pitcher
Size: 1.5 meters (5 feet) long
Period: Early Cretaceous, 144 million to 138 million years ago
Place: Germany
Diet: Plants

Though *Stenopelix* is the most completely known dinosaur from Germany in the Cretaceous Period, this little herbivore is still poorly understood. Just what this dinosaur was and to what group it belongs has yet to be determined.

Stenopelix was established on a partial skeleton discovered in 1877 in northwestern Germany. Since its discovery, its name has been tossed back and forth between dinosaur groups as scientists speculated over its identity. Over a century ago, *Stenopelix* was thought to be related to the small two-legged plant-eater, *Hypsilophodon*. Later it was classified with the most primitive family of horned dinosaurs, the parrot-beaked psittacosaurs. Then it was transferred to the pachycephalosaurs, the bone-headed dinosaurs. Just what it was still remains unclear. However, since *Stenopelix* exhibited aspects of both bone-heads and horned dinosaurs, it is now regarded as a member of a group ancestral to both.

STENOTHOLUS

(STEN-uh-THOL-us)

Status: Invalid—*See Stygimoloch*

STEPHANOSAURUS

(stuh-FAN-uh-SAW-rus)

Status: Doubtful—*See Lambeosaurus*

STEREOCEPHALUS

(STER-ee-uh-SEF-uh-lus)

Status: Invalid—*See Euoplocephalus*

STERRHOLOPHUS

(STUR-huh-loh-fus)

Status: Invalid—*See Triceratops*

STOKESOSAURUS

(STOHK-suh-SAW-rus)

Type Species: *clevelandi* (KLEEV-lan-dye)
Classification:

Order:	Saurischia
Suborder:	Theropoda
Family:	?

Name: (William Lee) *Stokes* + Greek *sauros* = lizard
Size: 4 meters (about 13.5 feet) long
Period: Late Jurassic, 156 million to 145 million years ago
Place: Utah
Diet: Meat

   This small carnivore has an uncertain family status. Its distinguishing characteristic was a pelvic bone with a vertical ridge down the middle, a rare feature in meat-eating dinosaurs. It may also have had a peculiarly short snout.

   Some features of this fragmentary dinosaur resemble those of advanced carnivores of the Late Cretaceous Period. If *Stokesosaurus* was a tyrannosaurid, it would have been the earliest known by tens of millions of years. For now, it is not certain whether or not this genus was even a member of the Carnosauria, a group to which tyrannosaurids and many other large meat-eaters belong.

STRENUSAURUS

(STREN-yuh-SAW-rus)

Status: Invalid—See Riojasaurus

STREPTOSPONDYLUS

(STREP-tuh-SPON-di-lus)

Status: Invalid—See Eustreptospondylus

STRUTHIOMIMUS

(STROO-thee-uh-MYE-mus)

Type Species: *altus* (AWL-tus)

Classification:

Order: Saurischia

Suborder: Theropoda

Family: Ornithomimidae

Name: Latin *struthio* = ostrich + Greek *mimos* = mimic

Size: About 4 meters (13 feet) long; about 2.3 meters (8 feet) high

Period: Late Cretaceous, 76 million to 70 million years ago

Place: Alberta

Diet: Meat, insects

Struthiomimus is the best known of all the so-called ostrich dinosaurs, or ornithomimosaurs. Like other ostrich dinosaurs, *Struthiomimus* had a small head, long neck, relatively long forelimbs with long fingers, and long legs. It was average-sized for an ornithomimid and entirely toothless.

Without teeth, this dinosaur must have relied on speed, strong hands, and a beak to locate food. Its hands were large and powerful, equal in length to its upper arm. Three fingers of equal length ended in elongated, slightly recurved claws.

Struthiomimus's anatomy, from its long shins to its light body, suggests that it was a fast-running dinosaur. The stiff tail counterbalanced the body and helped stabilize the animal when it ran or changed direction. While it was among the swiftest of dinosaurs, the shorter vertebrae near the hips indicate that *Struthiomimus* was less of a speedster than other ostrich-mimic dinosaurs such as *Ornithomimus* and *Dromiceiomimus*.

STRUTHIOSAURUS

(STROO-thee-uh-SAW-rus)

Type Species: *austriacus* (AW-stree-ACK-us)
Status: Doubtful
Classification:
  Order: Ornithischia
  Suborder: Ankylosauria
  Family: Nodosauridae
Name: Latin *struthio* = ostrich + Greek *sauros* = lizard
Size: 2 meters (about 7 feet) long
Period: Late Cretaceous, 83 million to 65 million
                years ago
Place: Austria, Romania
Diet: Plants

    Struthiosaurus was the smallest known ankylosaur, or armored dinosaur. It belonged to the nodosaur family of bird-hipped dinosaurs, all of which were plant-eaters. *Struthiosaurus* and other nodosaurs were distinguished from other armored dinosaurs by large lateral spines and clubless tails.

    Struthiosaurus was a primitive dinosaur. Like several other dwarfish central European dinosaurs of the Late Cretaceous, it was a survivor of that continent's isolation as a series of islands and archipelagos.

    This dinosaur may have been the end of the European line of nodosaurids. Known from the Early Cretaceous animals called *Hylaeosaurus*, these armored dinosaurs were characterized by their relatively small size, about one-fourth the size of North American nodosaurids.

    Struthiosaurus transilvanicus (TRAN-sil-VAN-i-kus): This is a better understood species. It was based on the posterior portion of a skull and other bones found in Transylvania.

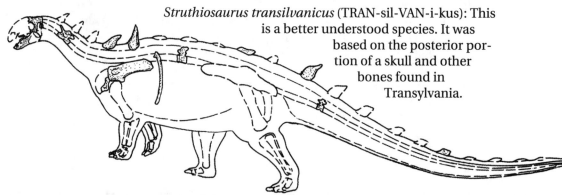

STYGIMOLOCH

(STIG-i-MOL-uck)

Type Species: *spinifer* (SPIN-i-fur)

Classification:

Order: Ornithischia

Suborder: Pachycephalosauria

Family: Pachycephalosauridae

Name: *Styx* (Greek mythology, a river of the underworld along which the dead passed to Hades) + *Moloch* (Old Testament god of the Ammonites and Phoenicians)

Size: 2 meters (7 feet) long

Period: Late Cretaceous, 68 million to 65 million years ago

Place: Montana

Diet: Plants

This bone-headed dinosaur, known only from partial skulls, was distinguished by having three or four massive spikes surrounded by a cluster of bony bumps. These bizarre skull features inspired its demonic name. The biggest of its horns was about 100 millimeters (4 inches) long—a large ornament for a relatively small dinosaur.

Like other pachycephalosaurs, *Stygimoloch* may have brandished its thick-domed skull in defense or for butting contests with rivals.

STYRACOSAURUS

(stye-RACK-uh-SAW-rus)

Type Species: *albertensis* (AL-bur-TEN-sis)
Classification:
  Order: Ornithischia
  Suborder: Ceratopsia
  Family: Ceratopsidae
Name: Greek *styrax* = the spike at the lower end of a
               spear shaft + Greek *sauros* = lizard
Size: About 5.25 meters (18 feet) long
Period: Late Cretaceous, 77 million to 73 million years ago
Place: Alberta; Montana
Diet: Plants

    Styracosaurus was a relatively small horned dinosaur, a four-legged browser weighing "only" two or three tons. Its massive, elongated skull was pointed at the front and greatly extended behind to form a distinctive neck frill. This frill was ornamented with long, large, tapering spikes.

    Various theories have been offered as to the function of this elaborate frill. The spikes made the head appear larger, and may have intimidated predators such as *Albertosaurus* or *Daspletosaurus*. The fear caused by this spiked head could have eliminated the need for direct physical combat during contests for sex or territory.

    Styracosaurus "*makeli*" (MACK-uh-lye)—Unofficial name. This species, which has a forward- and downward-turned nasal horn, has not yet been formally described.

    Styracosaurus "*ovatus*" (oh-VAY-tus): Based on the posterior portion of a crest and numerous fragments from Glacier County, Montana, *Styracosaurus ovatus* was distinguished from *Styracosaurus albertensis* by features of its crest.

SUPERSAURUS

(SOO-pur-SAW-rus)

Type Species: *vivianae* (VIV-ee-AN-eye)
Classification:
   Order: Saurischia
   Suborder: Sauropoda
   Family: Diplodocidae
Name: Latin *super* = high, ruling + Greek *sauros* = lizard
Size: About 30 meters (98 feet) long
Period: Late Jurassic, 156 million to 145 million years ago
Place: Colorado
Diet: Plants

Supersaurus, one of the largest known land animals of all time, was a building-sized four-legged plant-eater. Known from very incomplete material, and based on a shoulder bone nearly 2.3 meters (8 feet) long. *Supersaurus* was a diplodocid, one of the sauropods with long, narrow heads, very long necks, and tails that ended in a tapering whiplash. Its remains were collected by the famous "Dinosaur Jim" Jensen in 1973.

SYMPHYROPHUS
(SIM-fi-ROH-fus)

Status: Doubtful—*See Camptosaurus*

SYNGONOSAURUS
(sing-GOH-nuh-SAW-rus)

Status: Doubtful—*See Anoplosaurus*

SYNTARSUS

(sin-TAHR-sus)

Type Species: *rhodesiensis* (roh-DEE-see-EN-sis)
Classification:
   Order: Saurischia
   Suborder: Theropoda
   Family: Podokesauridae
Name: Greek *syn* = with + Greek *tarsus* = flat of the foot
Size: 3 meters (10 feet) long
Period: Early Jurassic, 208 million to 194 million
               years ago
Place: Zimbabwe; Arizona
Diet: Meat

   Syntarsus was a small, early, two-legged meat-eater. Like the closely related *Rioarribasaurus* from New Mexico, it had a small head, relatively long neck and a lightly built body. Its hands were large and well developed, and had three functional and somewhat opposable fingers fixed with sharp claws.

SYNTARSUS *continued*

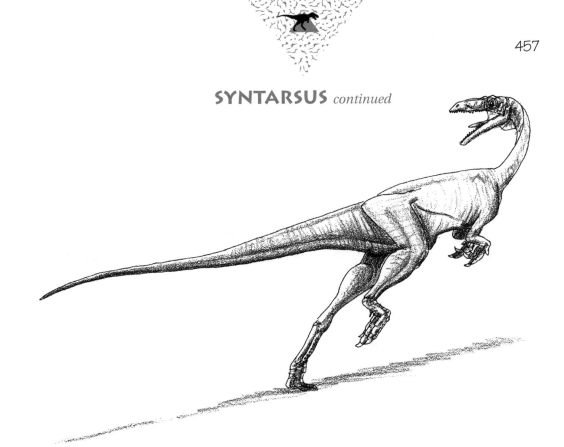

Remains of thirty *Syntarsus* individuals of both sexes were recovered from a single bone bed in Zimbabwe. Using modern predatory birds as a model, it was presumed that the more numerous and more robust forms were female, and the less abundant, lighter individuals were male. The robust forms were about 15 percent larger than the slender ones. Discovery of these animals together suggests that they were a social group killed by a catastrophic event.

Scientists concluded from its stomach contents that *Syntarsus* preyed on smaller vertebrates. Some researchers have speculated, without evidence, that this dinosaur had feathers for insulation and for reflecting the hot sun in this desert environment.

Copious remains of a large plant-eater, the prosauropod *Massospondylus carinatus*, were found with the *Syntarsus* skeletons. The discovery of these animals in what was an arid environment suggested that *Syntarsus* was a desert-dwelling dinosaur, capable (like *Massospondylus*) of tolerating a wide ecological range.

Syntarsus kayentakatae (KYE-en-tuh-KAY-tay): This species was the first North American *Syntarsus*, founded on a skull and partial skeleton. It had a paired crest, while no crest was found on the species from southern Africa.

SYRMOSAURUS

(SUR-moh-SAW-rus)

Status: Invalid—*See Pinacosaurus*

SZECHUANOSAURUS

(SECH-oo-WAN-nuh-SAW-rus)

Type Species: *campi* (KAM-pye)
Status: Doubtful
Classification:
   Order: Saurischia
   Suborder: Theropoda
   Family: Allosauridae
Name: Szechuan (province in China) + Greek *sauros* = lizard
Size: 6 meters (20 feet) long
Period: Late Jurassic, 156 million to 145 million years ago
Place: China
Diet: Meat

   Szechuanosaurus, a medium-sized meat-eater, was thought to be a member of the allosaurid family. These large carnivores had big heads, short necks, and short arms. Their three-fingered hands had large, sharp claws.

   Szechuanosaurus is not well known. We do know that it had teeth like the large, early carnivore *Megalosaurus*, which were pointed and moderately curved.

TALARURUS

(TAL-uh-ROOR-us)

Type Species: *plicatospineus* (PLYE-kat-uh-SPYE-nee-us)
Classification:
  Order: Ornithischia
  Suborder: Ankylosauria
  Family: Ankylosauridae
Name: Greek *talaros* = basket + Greek *oura*/Latin *urus* = tail
Size: 4 to 5 meters (about 13.5 to 16.5 feet) long
Period: Late Cretaceous, 97.5 million to 88.5 million years ago
Place: Mongolia
Diet: Plants

  Talarurus was an ankylosaurid, a mid-sized member of the armored dinosaurs that had small spikes on their sides, and clubbed tails. *Talarurus* was a squat animal with a long, narrow skull, ribbed armor plates, and a small tail club. It was one of the earliest known Mongolian ankylosaurids, and was similar to the clubless armored dinosaurs.

TANIUS

(TAN-ee-us)

Type Species: sinensis (si-NEN-sis)
Classification:
    Order: Ornithischia
    Suborder: Ornithopoda
    Family: Hadrosauridae
Name: Tan (people in southern China, also called "Tanka")
              + Greek *idion* = of their own
Size: Large
Period: Late Cretaceous, ?88.5 million to ?65 million
              years ago
Place: China
Diet: Plants

   Tanius was a large duckbilled dinosaur with a low, flat skull. Since it showed no evidence of a crest, it may have belonged to the crestless hadrosaurine group of duckbills.

   Tanius may well have been the same animal as *Tsintaosaurus*, a familiar duckbill in dinosaur books because of its unicorn-like spike.

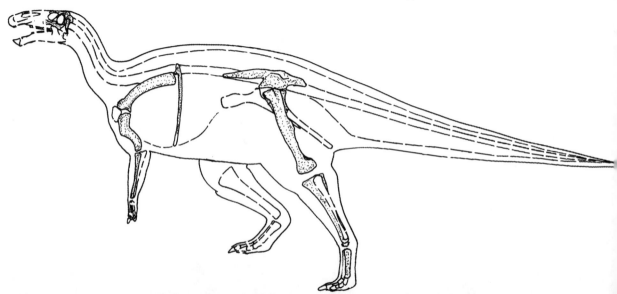

TANYSTROSUCHUS

(TAN-i-stroh-SOOK-us)

Type Species: *posthumus* (POS-thoo-mus)
Status: Doubtful
Classification:
   Order: ?Saurischia
   Suborder: ?Theropoda
   Family: ?
Name: Greek *tanaos* = long + Greek *stropheus* = a pivot
               + Greek *souchos* = crocodile
Size: Small
Period: Late Triassic, 231 million to 225 million years ago
Place: Germany
Diet: Meat

This poorly known animal was named from a tail vertebra which may have belonged to the small carnivorous dinosaur *Halticosaurus,* or to another early, non-dinosaur reptile.

TARASCOSAURUS

(tuh-RAS-kuh-SAW-rus)

Type Species: salluvicus (suh-LOO-vi-kus)
Classification:
    Order: Saurischia
    Suborder: Theropoda
    Family: Abelisauridae
Name: Tarasque (legendary Basque dragon-like animal) +
             Greek sauros = lizard
Size: Medium
Period: Late Cretaceous, 83 million to 80 million
             years ago
Place: France
Diet: Meat

Tarascosaurus was a small member of a group of large predators, the abelisaurids. These ceratosaurs had large heads with long jaws, double-edged teeth, very short front limbs, three-fingered hands, strong hind limbs, and large-taloned toes.

The occurrence of an abelisaurid—a kind of theropod known from South America, India and Africa—in Europe suggests that other dinosaurs from the southern supercontinent, Gondwana, might also have lived in Europe during *Tarascosaurus's* time.

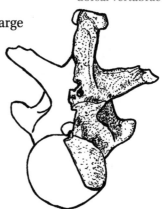

Tarascosaurus salluvicus dorsal vertabrae

TARBOSAURUS BATAAR

(TAHR-buh-SAW-rus buh-TAHR)

Status: Invalid — *See Tyrannosaurus bataar*

TARCHIA

(TAR-chee-uh)

Type Species: *gigantea* (jye-GAN-tee-uh)
Classification:

Order:	Ornithischia
Suborder:	Ankylosauria
Family:	Ankylosauridae
Name:	Mongolian *tarchi* = brain
Size:	About 5.5 meters (18 feet) long
Period:	Late Cretaceous, 78 million to 69 million years ago
Place:	Mongolia
Diet:	Plants

   Tarchia was a Mongolian armored dinosaur of the ankylosaurid family. These dinosaurs were distinguished by the small spikes on their sides and their clubbed tails. *Tarchia* had a high skull, spikes at the corners of its mouth, and a particularly large tail club. It was the largest and geologically most recent of known Mongolian armored dinosaurs. At least seven specimens have been discovered.

TATISAURUS

(TAT-i-SAW-rus)

Type Species: *oehleri* (oh-LAYR-eye)

Status: Doubtful

Classification:

  Order: Ornithischia

  Suborder: ?Thyreophora

  Family: ?

Name: Tati (village in the Lufeng Basin) + Greek *sauros* = lizard

Size: Small

Period: Early Jurassic, 208 million to 188 million years ago

Place: China

Diet: Plants

Tatisaurus was a small plant-eater named from a fragment of a left-jaw bone with teeth. It had a slender jaw with simple teeth, and may have had cheek pouches. *Tatisaurus* was one of a diverse group of bird-hipped dinosaurs. First thought to belong to a hypsilophodontid, its jaw was recently identified as perhaps belonging to one of the thyreophorans, a group of plant-eaters that included the plated stegosaurs and armored ankylosaurs.

Tatisaurus oehleri jawbone

TAVEIROSAURUS

(tuh-VYE-ruh-SAW-rus)

Type Species: *costai* (KOS-tye)

Status: Doubtful

Classification:

   Order: Ornithischia

   Suborder: Pachycephalosauria

   Family: ?Homalocephalidae

Name: *Taveiro* (village of the District of Coimbra, Portugal) + Greek *sauros* = lizard

Size: Small

Period: Late Cretaceous, 73 million to 65 million years ago

Place: Portugal

Diet: Plants

    This doubtful genus was founded upon teeth similar to those of *Wannanosaurus*, a Chinese bone-headed dinosaur. *Taveirosaurus* was therefore referred to the group of bone-headed dinosaurs, the Pachycephalosauria, and tentatively to the family of small- to medium-sized flat-headed forms, the homalocephalosaurids. *Taveirosaurus* was small, even for a flat-head.

Taveirosaurus costai teeth

TAWASAURUS

(TAH-wuh-SAW-rus)

Type Species: *minor* (MYE-nur)
Status: Doubtful — See ?Lufengosaurus
Classification:
   Order: Saurischia
   Suborder: ?Prosauropoda
   Family: ?
Name: Tawa (now spelled "Dawa," in China) + Greek
                sauros = lizard
Size: ?
Period: Late Jurassic, 208 million to 194 million years ago
Place: China
Diet: Plants

   Tawasaurus was a prosauropod, a long-necked, small-headed, early plant-eater. The family of prosauropods to which it belonged is unknown. *Tawasaurus* is known from a skull that was no longer than 35 millimeters (about 1.5 inches), and had a short snout. This tiny skull may have been that of a juvenile: its eye holes were comparatively large and circular, as young animals' eyes tend to be.

   Tawasaurus was first thought to be a primitive ornithischian, or bird-hipped dinosaur. Now, however, features have been seen in its fossils that resemble the lizard-hipped saurischians.

TECHNOSAURUS

(TECK-nuh-SAW-rus)

Type Species: smalli (SMAW-lye)
Status: Doubtful
Classification:
  Order: Ornithischia
  Suborder: ?
  Family: ?
Name: (Texas) Tech (University) + Greek sauros = lizard
Size: Small
Period: Late Triassic, 231 million to 225 million years ago
Place: Texas
Diet: Plants

    Technosaurus was proposed as the oldest, most primitive of the small bird-hipped plant-eaters formerly known as "fabrosaurids." It is now known that *Technosaurus* was named from remains of at least two different kinds of animals, one a lizard-hipped prosauropod, the other a bird-hipped ornithischian.

Technosaurus smalli
jawbone

TEINCHISAURUS

(TAYN-chi-SAW-rus)

Status: Invalid — *See "Tianchisaurus"*

TEINUROSAURUS

(TAYN-yoor-uh-SAW-rus)

Type Species: *sauvagei* (SO-vizh-i)
Status: Doubtful
Classification:
  Order: Saurischia
  Suborder: Theropoda
  Family: ?
Name: Greek *teino* = to stretch + Greek *uro* = tail +
               Greek *sauros* = lizard
Size: Small
Period: Late Jurassic, 156 million to 150 million years ago
Place: France
Diet: Meat

Teinurosaurus was a small carnivore named from a single elongated vertebra that was destroyed during World War II. It was originally referred to *Iguanodon*, then to *Camptosaurus*. However, it most closely resembled the small carnivore, *Elaphrosaurus*.

TELMATOSAURUS

(tel-MAT-uh-SAW-rus)

Type Species: *transylvanicus* (TRAN-sil-VAN-i-kus)
Classification:
  Order: Ornithischia
  Suborder: Ornithopoda
  Family: Hadrosauridae
Name: Greek *telmatos* = marsh + Greek *sauros* = lizard
Size: Less than 5 meters (16 feet) long
Period: Late Cretaceous, 83 million to 65 million years ago
Place: Romania, France
Diet: Plants

This primitive, but late, duckbill is the best known Transylvanian dinosaur, and one of only two known European duckbills. *Telmatosaurus* is regarded as the most primitive hadrosaurid, though it is not known whether it was flat-headed (hadrosaurine) or crested (lambeosaurine), or more primitive than both.

Fossil eggs, possibly belonging to *Telmatosaurus*, were also discovered in Transylvania. Originally believed to belong to the sauropod *Magyarosaurus*, these eggs were later recognized as duckbills' when embryonic remains were discovered nearby.

TENCHISAURUS

(TEN-chi-SAW-rus)

Status: Invalid — *See "Tianchisaurus"*

TENONTOSAURUS

(te-NON-tuh-SAW-rus)

Type Species: *tilletti* (TIL-i-tye)
Classification:

Order:	Ornithischia
Suborder:	Ornithopoda
Family:	?

Name: Greek *tenon* = sinew + Greek *sauros* = lizard
Size: 7 meters (23 feet) long
Period: Early Cretaceous, 116 million to 113 million
          years ago
Place: Montana, Wyoming, Utah, Texas, Oklahoma
Diet: Plants

Tenontosaurus was a large plant-eater that not only moved on two legs, but also on all four. It had an *Iguanodon*-like skull with large nostrils; relatively long and robust forearms; and an extremely long tail. This tail, stiffened by ossified tendons, was apparently designed to counterbalance the trunk.

Tenontosaurus probably utilized a bipedal stance for rapid walking, and came down onto all four legs to stand, walk at a slower pace, or browse on low vegetation.

The killer-clawed theropod *Deinonychus* is known from the same rock formation as *Tenontosaurus*, and scientists speculated that *Tenontosaurus* was *Deinonychus's* prey. This idea was supported by the presence of isolated *Deinonychus* teeth often found near *Tenontosaurus* remains. Since the adult

TENONTOSAURUS *continued*

Tenontosaurus was four or five times larger than *Deinonychus*, it suggests that the smaller meat-eater either hunted in packs, or if it were alone, hunted only half-grown individuals.

Since well preserved *Tenontosaurus* skeletons occur in ancient swampy environments along with the remains of turtles and crocodilians, this dinosaur may have preferred a wet environment.

Based upon its general resemblance to *Iguanodon* and *Camptosaurus*, *Tenontosaurus* was originally assigned to the iguanodontid family. It was later regarded as a member of the smaller bird-hipped plant-eaters, the hypsilophodontids. Today, the consensus is that *Tenontosaurus* occupies an intermediate, basal position between the hypsilophodontids and the iguanodontids.

TETRAGONOSAURUS
(TET-ruh-GON-uh-SAW-rus)

Status: Invalid — *See Lambeosaurus*

THECOCOELURUS

(THEE-koh-si-LOOR-us)

Type Species: *daviesi* (DAY-vee-zye)
Status: Doubtful — *See ?Calamospondylus*
Classification:
  Order: Saurischia
  Suborder: ?Theropoda
  Family: ?
Name: Greek *thekion* = small case + Greek *koilos* = hollow
Size: Small
Period: Early Cretaceous, ?144 million to ?97.5 million years ago
Place: England
Diet: Meat

   This small meat-eating dinosaur is poorly known and of uncertain status. *Thecocoelurus* was founded on a neck vertebra resembling that of *Calamospondylus,* another small carnivore found in England.

THECODONTOSAURUS

(THEE-koh-DON-tuh-SAW-rus)

Type Species: *antiquus* (an-TICK-wus)
Classification:

Order:	Saurischia
Suborder:	Prosauropoda
Family:	Thecodontosauridae
Name:	Greek *thekion* = small case + Greek *odontos* = tooth + Greek *sauros* = lizard
Size:	3 meters (10 feet) long
Period:	Late Triassic, ?225 million years ago
Place:	England
Diet:	Plants

Thecodontosaurus antiquus tooth

This was the name bearer of a family of prosauropods, the first large plant-eating dinosaurs, all of whom had small heads. Thecodontosaurids were the only prosauropods to be entirely bipedal.

Thecodontosaurus was the earliest and most primitive known prosauropod. It had a small head, long neck and tail, and slender limbs. Its hind legs were particularly long.

Thecodontosaurus appears to be closer than any other prosauropod to the imagined ancestor of all lizard-hipped dinosaurs: small, carnivorous, erect-postured, bipedal, and fast-running.

Thecodontosaurus-like fossils have also been found in North America, Africa, and Australia, though only the English fossils can be referred to this genus with certainty.

THECOSPONDYLUS

(THEE-koh-SPON-di-lus)

Status: Doubtful — *See ?Calamospondylus*

THERIZINOSAURUS

(THER-i-ZEE-nuh-SAW-rus)

Type Species: *cheloniformis* (che-LOH-ni-FOR-mis)
Classification:
  Order: Saurischia
  Suborder: Theropoda
  Family: ?
Name: Greek *therizo* = to reap + Greek *sauros* = lizard
Size: Large
Period: Late Cretaceous, ?77 million to 69 million
            years ago
Place: Mongolia
Diet: Meat, ?insects

   One of the most bizarre and perplexing of all dinosaurs, *Therizinosaurus* was named for its enormous sickle-shaped claws. What kind of creature those enormous claws were attached to is a mystery.

   Therizinosaurus was a carnivorous dinosaur, but to which family it belonged is unknown. Most meat-eating dinosaurs had small to very small foreclaws, but on this animal the claws were more than one-quarter the length of the arm: more-than-2-foot-long claws on 8-foot-long arms. It has been suggested that this dinosaur fed on insects, using its huge claws to tear into large anthills. Originally, *Therizinosaurus* was described as a giant turtle.

   Therizinosaurus was discovered during the 1948 Soviet-Mongolian paleontological expedition to the Gobi Desert.

THEROSAURUS

(THER-uh-SAW-rus)

Status: Invalid — *See Iguanodon*

THESCELOSAURUS

(THES-ki-luh-SAW-rus)

Type Species: *neglectus* (ne-GLECK-tus)
Classification:

Order:	Ornithischia
Suborder:	Ornithopoda
Family:	Hypsilophodontidae
Name:	Greek *theskelos* = marvelous + Greek *sauros* = lizard
Size:	About 3.5 meters (12 feet) long, and about .9 meters (3 feet) high at the hips
Period:	Late Cretaceous, ?77 million to 65 million years ago
Place:	Wyoming, Montana, South Dakota; Alberta and Saskatchewan
Diet:	Plants

Thescelosaurus was one of the hypsilophodontids, the small plant-eaters. It was medium-sized with a massive body. *Thescelosaurus* had a small head, medium-length neck, heavy body, short legs, and a long tail. It may have moved on all fours rather than hind legs, which was unusual for a hypsilophodontid.

Portions of *Thescelosaurus's* skin may have been discovered. A small, dark-colored area was found outside the ribs, and a second patch was found along the chest vertebrae. This carbonized skin was described as "punctured" rather than scaled, a condition that probably occurred after death.

Thescolosaurus garbanii (GAHR-buh-nye) — Doubtful name. This species is based on cranial and postcranial remains from both Montana and South Dakota, and may not refer to *Thescelosaurus*.

THESPESIUS

(thes-PEE-see-us)

Type Species: *occidentalis* (OCK-si-DEN-tuh-lis)
Status: Doubtful — *See ?Edmontosaurus*
Classification:
  Order: Ornithischia
  Suborder: Ornithopoda
  Family: Hadrosauridae
Name: Greek *thespesios* = awful
Size: Large
Period: Late Cretaceous, 73 million to 65 million
                years ago
Place: South Dakota
Diet: Plants

   Thespesius was one of the first dinosaurs described from North America. It was a hadrosaurid, but we do not know if it was a flat-headed (hadrosaurine) or crested (lambeosaurine) duckbill.

THOTOBOLOSAURUS

(THOH-tuh-BOH-luh-SAW-rus)

Type Species: *mabeatae* (MAY-bee-tye)
Status: Doubtful
Classification:
   Order: Saurischia
   Suborder: ?Sauropodomorpha
   Family: ?
Name: *Thobol* + Greek *sauros* = lizard
Size: ?
Period: Late Triassic, 231 million to 219 million years ago
Place: Africa
Diet: Plants

   This little known dinosaur belonged to a group of long-necked dinosaurs that included both prosauropods and the later sauropods. *Thotobolosaurus* may have been a four-legged melanorosaurid, a large, more advanced prosauropod. If so, it was very much like a true sauropod.

"TIANCHISAURUS"

(tee-AN-chi-SAW-rus)

Status: Informal — *See "Jurassosaurus"*

"TIANCHUNGOSAURUS"

(TEE-an-CHUNG-uh-SAW-rus)

Type Species: ?
Status: Unofficial
Classification:
  Order: Ornithischia
  Suborder: ?Pachycephalosauria
  Family: ?
Name: Chinese location name + Greek sauros = lizard
Size: ?
Period: Jurassic, ?208 million to ?144 million years ago
Place: China
Diet: Plants

"*Tianchungosaurus*" may have been a bone-headed dinosaur that walked on two legs and ate plants. However, it is still not formally described. "*Tianchungosaurus*" may have been a primitive Jurassic pachycephalosaur. If that assessment is correct, "*Tianchungosaurus*" was many millions of years older than *Yaverlandia,* the most primitive known member of the Pachycephalosauria.

TICHOSTEUS

(tye-KOH-stee-us)

Type Species: *lucasanus* (LOO-kuh-SAN-us)
Status: Doubtful
Classification:
  Order: ?
  Suborder: ?
  Family: ?
Name: Greek *teichos* = protective wall + Greek *osteon* = bone
Size: ?
Period: Late Jurassic, 156 million to 145 million years ago
Place: Colorado
Diet: Plants

    Tichosteus is named from vertebrae of some sort of dinosaur, perhaps a plant-eater, collected near Cañon City, Colorado.

TIENSHANOSAURUS

(TEE-an-SHAN-uh-SAW-rus)

Type Species: *chitaiensis* (KYE-tye-EN-sis)
Classification:

Order: Saurischia

Suborder: Sauropoda

Family: ?Camarasauridae

Name: Tien Shan (mountain system in Asia) + Greek sauros = lizard

Size: About 10 meters (approximately 33 feet) long

Period: Late Jurassic, 163 million to 156 million years ago

Place: China

Diet: Plants

    Tienshanosaurus may have been a modest-sized titanosaurid, primitive and relatively small-sized sauropods. Titanosaurs, *Tienshanosaurus* included, had sloping heads and peglike teeth. Some or all had armor, though no armor is yet known for *Tienshanosaurus*. This dinosaur was distinguished by its unusually short front limbs.

    It remains uncertain whether *Tienshanosaurus* was a titanosaurid, a more boxy-headed camarasaurid, or a whip-tailed diplodocid.

TITANOSAURUS

(tye-TAN-uh-SAW-rus)

Type Species: *indicus* (in-DICK-us)
Classification:

Order:	Saurischia
Suborder:	Sauropoda
Family:	Titanosauridae
Name:	Titan ("gigantic," after one of the Titans, a family of primordial Greek gods) + Greek sauros = lizard
Size:	18 to 20 meters (60 to 66 feet) long
Period:	Late Cretaceous, 83 million to 65 million years ago
Place:	India, Argentina, ?England
Diet:	Plants

Titanosaurus was a sauropod, a four-legged browser with a sloping head. Incompletely known, it has become a "junkbasket" name to which many fragmentary fossils have been referred.

Despite the name, *Titanosaurus* was not one of the largest sauropods. Though it was heavily constructed, *Titanosaurus* had limb bones that were more slender than those of other titanosaurids such as *Alamosaurus* and *Saltasaurus*. Cannonball-like dinosaur eggs found in India may belong to *Titanosaurus*.

TOCHISAURUS

(TOH-chee-SAW-rus)

Type Species: *nemegtensis* (NEM-ig-TEN-sis)
Classification:
  Order: Saurischia
  Suborder: Theropoda
  Family: Troodontidae
Name: Mongolian *toch* = ostrich + Greek *sauros* = lizard
Size: Small
Period: Late Cretaceous, 77 million to 69 million years ago
Place: Mongolia
Diet: Meat

Tochisaurus was a troodontid, one of a family of small meat-eating dinosaurs with long, narrow heads and slender, delicate jaws. Judging by their relatively large brains, troodontids may have been the smartest of all dinosaurs. They may also have been able to manipulate their hands with good dexterity, and to run well on their long hind limbs. *Tochisaurus* had a slender foot well-suited for sprinting.

Tochisaurus nemegtensis foot

TOMODON

(TOM-uh-don)

Status: Doubtful — *See Diplotomodon*

TORNIERIA

(tor-NEE-ree-uh)

Status: Invalid — *See Barosaurus*

TOROSAURUS

(TOR-uh-SAW-rus)

Type Species: *latus* (LAT-us)

Classification:

    Order: Ornithischia

    Suborder: Ceratopsia

    Family: Ceratopsidae

Name: Latin *torus* = protuberance + Greek *sauros* = lizard

Size: 6.2 meters (21 feet) long

Period: Late Cretaceous, 70 million to 65 million years ago

Place: Wyoming, Utah, South Dakota, Montana, New Mexico, Texas; Saskatchewan

Diet: Plants

    Torosaurus was an uncommon but very large horned dinosaur distinguished by having the largest skull of any animal that ever lived on land. It was one of the last and most advanced of all ceratopsids, the large horned dinosaurs. Its skull was wedge-shaped in top view, with a short, pointed facial portion. Its nose horn and large brow horns were forward-pointing. The skull measured nearly 2.8 meters (8.5 feet) in length, with the huge, smooth crest accounting for more than half its area.

Torosaurus latus skull

TORVOSAURUS

(TOR-voh-SAW-rus)

Type Species: *tanneri* (TAN-uh-rye)

Classification:

    Order: Saurischia

    Suborder: Theropoda

    Family: Megalosauridae

Name: Latin *torvus* = savage, cruel + Greek *sauros* = lizard

Size: Approximately 9 meters (31 feet) long

Period: Late Jurassic, 156 million to 145 million years ago

Place: Colorado, Wyoming

Diet: Meat

    Torvosaurus was a large, robust predator with very short forearms. It differed from other theropods of the same period and region, among them *Allosaurus* and *Ceratosaurus*, in the structure of its forelimbs and pelvis. Those features were more like those of the large, primitive European carnivores *Megalosaurus*, *Poekilopleuron*, and *Erectopus*.

TRACHODON

(TRACK-uh-don)

Type Species: *mirabilis* (mi-RAB-i-lis)
Status: Doubtful — *See Edmontosaurus*
Classification:
   Order: Ornithischia
   Suborder: ?
   Family: ?
Name: Greek *trachys* = rough + Greek *odontos* = tooth
Size: Large
Period: Late Cretaceous, 77 million to 73 million years ago
Place: Montana
Diet: Plants

   Trachodon is usually (but incorrectly) considered to be the same animal as *Edmontosaurus*, a large duckbilled dinosaur. *Trachodon* was named by its teeth, some of which, with single roots, are now thought to belong to *Hadrosaurus*. The rest, with double roots, may belong to a horned dinosaur. Technically, *Trachodon* must now be regarded as a ceratopsian, a horned dinosaur. No matter what kind of plant-eater it was, *Trachodon's* status remains in doubt.

TRICERATOPS

(trye-SER-uh-tops)

Type Species: *horridus* (HOR-i-dus)
Classification:
  Order: Ornithischia
  Suborder: Ceratopsia
  Family: Ceratopsidae
Name: Greek *tri* = three + Greek *keratos* = horn + Greek
             ops = face
Size: At least 8 meters (25 feet) long
Period: Late Cretaceous, 68 million to 65 million years ago
Place: Colorado, Wyoming, Montana, South Dakota;
             Alberta, Saskatchewan
Diet: Fibrous plants

The three-horned plant-eater *Triceratops* is the largest, most common, and best known of the horned dinosaurs. It may have weighed 4.5 metric tons (5 tons). Curiously, the first certain *Triceratops* remains that were collected, a pair of horn cores, were given the name *Bison alticornis*. The man who named them, the famous dinosaur scientist Othniel Charles Marsh, believed they were those of a mammal.

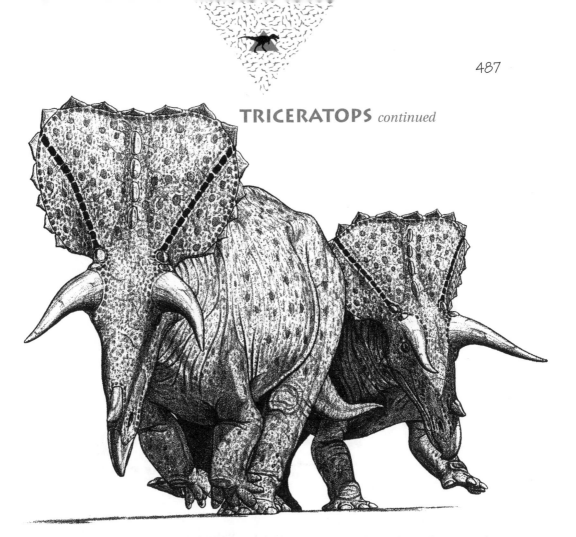

TRICERATOPS *continued*

Triceratops's skull was indeed distinctive, with a pair of long brow horns and a nasal horn. The brow horns could have been as long as 90 centimeters (3 feet), and material covering them may have added considerably to their length. Its frill had no holes, as some horned dinosaur frills did, though it could have had knobs or other ornamentations. The frill was enormous, up to 2.5 meters (7 feet) wide in some individuals.

The teeth of *Triceratops* were elongated blades, with no ability to crush or grind. The jaws and muscles were structured to work these teeth as shears. Apparently these specialized teeth and extremely strong jaws were not designed for chewing ordinary leafy plant tissues, seeds, and fruits. These foods would have required crushing and grinding abilities that this dinosaur did not possess. Instead, *Triceratops* may have eaten more fibrous plants, like cycad or palm fronds.

Using its bulk and horns, *Triceratops* may have charged predators, like its contemporary, *Tyrannosaurus*, in the same manner as an enraged rhinoceros. One skull had a brow horn that had broken off and begun to heal, perhaps after a

TRICERATOPS *continued*

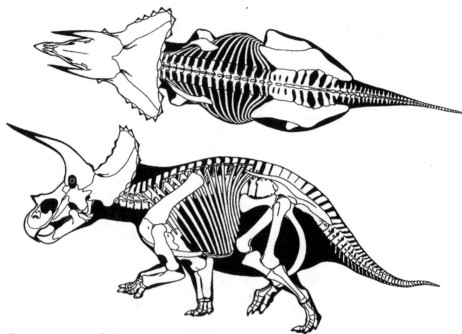

battle. Puncture wounds in some
skulls imply conflicts between *Triceratops* individuals,
possibly to win mates or establish territory. Rivals may have engaged in such
contests by locking horns, shoving and twisting, protecting themselves with
their frills.

    Triceratops remains were quite common in Late Cretaceous sediments of
western North America. Duckbill dinosaurs, *Triceratops* and other horned
dinosaurs, and *Tyrannosaurus rex* are among the last of all dinosaurs known
from the Late Cretaceous Period.

    A grand total of sixteen species were assigned to *Triceratops* over the years.
In 1986, paleontologists concluded that there was but one valid species of
Triceratops, the type species *Triceratops horridus.* The differences between the
sixteen different species were attributed to individual variation. Current studies,
however, indicate that there are maybe two valid species, the second of which is
as yet unnamed.

TRIMUCRODON

(trye-MYOO-kruh-don)

Type Species: *cuneatus* (KYOO-nee-AT-us)
Status: Doubtful
Classification:
  Order: ?Ornithischia
  Suborder: ?
  Family: ?
Name: Greek *tri* = three + Latin *mucro* = point + Greek *odontos* = tooth
Size: Small
Period: Late Jurassic, 153 million to 150 million years ago
Place: Portugal
Diet: Plants

This poorly known ornithischian was one of a diverse group of plant-eating, bird-hipped dinosaurs. It was named from the crown of a single tooth.

Trimucrodon cuneatus tooth

TRIPRIODON

(trye-PRYE-uh-don)

Status: Doubtful — *See Paronychodon*

TROODON

(TROH-uh-don)

Type Species: *formosus* (for-MOH-sus)

Classification:

Order: Saurischia

Suborder: Theropoda

Family: Troodontidae

Name: Greek *trogein* = to gnaw + Greek *odontos* = tooth

Size: About 1.75 meters (6 feet) long

Period: Late Cretaceous, 76 million to 70 million years ago

Place: Montana, Wyoming; Alberta

Diet: Meat

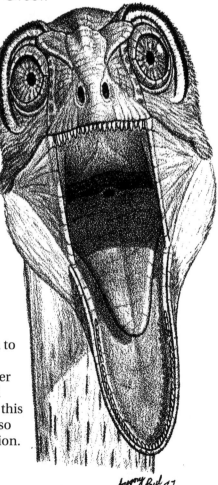

Perhaps the smartest of all dinosaurs, *Troodon* was the basis for the theropod family Troodontidae, man-sized carnivores with large brains, long, narrow heads, delicate jaws, closely spaced teeth, long slender hind limbs, and enlarged toes.

Much of what we know today about *Troodon* stems from studies of the skeletons of the dinosaur once called *Stenonychosaurus*, which is now known to be the same genus.

Aside from its large brain, *Troodon* had a number of special qualities. Its large eyes, with an estimated diameter of 44 millimeters (1¾ inches), suggest that this dinosaur had a nocturnal lifestyle. Their position also suggests that *Troodon* may have had depth perception.

TROODON *continued*

It may also have had a keen sense of hearing, though its sense of smell was not well developed.

Troodon may have been able to rotate its forearms. Its frame was lightly constructed and its legs were long, suggesting agility. Its thin tail was flexible at its base, which would have controlled the angular momentum of the animal's body during quick turns. Each foot had two sharp claws, the largest and most formidable of which was on the second digit. Dromaeosaurids used these to eviscerate prey. *Troodon* may not have been able to apply much force with its toe claws. However, the toe claws in troodontids may have been associated with quite long and delicate toe bones. Rather, it may have used its long fingers to snare small mammals and reptiles.

Troodon's brain was enormous by the standards of other animals of its time. This dinosaur may have weighed only 22.7 kilograms (50 pounds), but its brain weight is estimated at 37 to 45 grams (1.3 to 1.6 ounces), as large, compared to body weight, as the brains of many modern birds.

TSINTAOSAURUS
(sin-TOU-SAW-rus)

Status: Doubtful — *See Tanius*

TUGULUSAURUS

(too-GOO-luh-SAW-rus)

Type Species: *faciles* (fuh-SIL-is)
Status: Doubtful
Classification:
   Order: Saurischia
   Suborder: ?Theropoda
   Family: ?
Name: *Tugulo* (Geologic group of formations) + Greek *sauros* = lizard
Size: ?
Period: ?Early Cretaceous, 145 million to 97.5 million years ago
Place: China
Diet: Meat

This carnivore is known only from various bones, which were discovered without a skull.

TUOJIANGOSAURUS

(TOO-oh-jee-ANG-guh-SAW-rus)

Type Species: *multispinus* (MUL-ti-SPYE-nus)

Classification:

Order: Ornithischia

Suborder: Stegosauria

Family: Stegosauridae

Name: Tuojiang (River, tributary of the Yangtzi in the Sichuan Basin) + Greek *sauros* = lizard

Size: 7 meters (about 23.5 feet) long

Period: Late Jurassic, 163 million to 150 million years ago

Place: China

Diet: Plants

This was the first Asian stegosaur, or plate-backed plant-eater, known from a nearly complete skeleton. *Tuojiangosaurus* had a typical stegosaurian skull, with an elongated face and overlapping spoon-shaped teeth.

It had two rows of triangular plates sticking up from its neck, spikes on both shoulders, and four spikes protruding from the tip of its tail.

TURANOCERATOPS

(tuh-RAN-uh-SER-uh-tops)

Type Species: *tardabilis (tahr-DAB-i-lis)*
Classification:
   Order: Ornithischia
   Suborder: Ceratopsidae
   Family: Protoceratopsidae
Name: Persian *Turan* (region) + Greek *keratos* = horn + Greek *ops* = face
Size: Small
Period: Late Cretaceous, ?97.5 million to ?65 million years ago
Place: Russia
Diet: Plants

    This plant-eater has been described in Russian papers which have yet to be translated into English. If it was a small horned dinosaur, it is notable because true horned dinosaurs are not known from Asia. They may not have favored Asia's dry habitats during Cretaceous times.

TYLOCEPHALE

(TYE-luh-SEF-uh-lee)

Type Species: *gilmorei* (GIL-mor-eye)
Classification:
    Order: Ornithischia
    Suborder: Pachycephalosauria
    Family: Pachycephalosauridae
Name: Greek *tyle* = swelling on the skin + Greek *kephale* = head
Size: Small, 2.5 meters (7 feet) long
Period: Late Cretaceous, 80 million to 75 million years ago
Place: Mongolia
Diet: Plants

    Based on a damaged skull, *Tylocephale* was a bone-headed dinosaur. *Tylocephale's* skull was unique among known pachycephalosaurids in that its domed front is so elevated that it can be seen when the skull is viewed from behind. The skull had a height of 133 millimeters (over 5 inches) and width of 99 millimeters (about 3.8 inches).

TYLOSTEUS

(tye-LOH-stee-us)

Status: Invalid — *See Pachycephalosaurus*

TYRANNOSAURUS

(tye-RAN-uh-SAW-rus)

Type Species: *rex* (RECKS)

Classification:

Order:	Saurischia
Suborder:	Theropoda
Family:	Tyrannosauridae

Name: Greek *tyrannos* = ruler + Greek *sauros* = lizard

Size: 11.75 meters (40 feet) long

Period: Late Cretaceous, 68 million to 65 million years ago

Place: Montana, Wyoming, Colorado, New Mexico, South Dakota; western Canada; ?Mongolia; ?China

Diet: Meat

Tyrannosaurus is the most famous of all theropods, and perhaps the most popular dinosaur of all. It may not have been the biggest carnivorous dinosaur, but it was certainly among the largest and most powerful land carnivores that ever lived.

This dinosaur epitomized the sophisticated family named for it, the tyrannosaurids. *Tyrannosaurus* was typical of its family, but on a grand scale—huge, with a large head, a short, muscular neck, barrel-like body, powerful hind legs with three-taloned feet, and short forelimbs equipped with small, two-fingered hands.

Tyrannosaurus rex's skull was enormous—more than 1.35 meters (4.5 feet) long, with dagger-shaped, banana-sized teeth measuring from nearly 8 to almost 16 centimeters (3 to 6 inches) long, and about 2.5 centimeters (1 inch) wide. These serrated teeth were able to saw through meat and puncture bone. The jaw, with its powerful muscles, could rip off as much as 500 pounds of meat at one time.

T. rex appears to have had keen senses. Brain casts indicate it had a long olfactory tract and perhaps a strong sense of smell. The skull had a long, narrow muzzle, allowing for well-developed stereoscopic vision. The ear structure in *Tyrannosaurus* was similar to that in crocodiles, which have a well-developed sense of hearing. The presence of an efficient ear implies the possibility of some vocal ability, presumably used to recognize others of its species or to give warning.

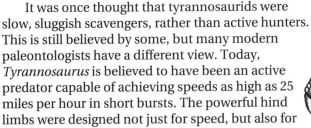

TYRANNOSAURUS *continued*

It was once thought that tyrannosaurids were slow, sluggish scavengers, rather than active hunters. This is still believed by some, but many modern paleontologists have a different view. Today, *Tyrannosaurus* is believed to have been an active predator capable of achieving speeds as high as 25 miles per hour in short bursts. The powerful hind limbs were designed not just for speed, but also for bearing great weight and perhaps for holding down large prey. Regardless of actual speed, dinosaurs like *Tyrannosaurus* were probably as fast or faster than the animals they preyed upon. One can envision this dinosaur charging its prey, holding it down with its claws, and lowering its cavernous mouth to feed. Still, some of the most effective hunters are primarily scavengers, and *T. rex*, even if it was a skillful killer, may have fed largely on already dead animals.

Tyrannosaurus seems to have been designed for dynamic action. The most complete *Tyrannosaurus rex* skeleton, "Sue," found in South Dakota in 1990, shows evidence of healed-over facial grooves and other injuries inflicted by another *Tyrannosaurus rex*.

Forearm and hand bones of *Tyrannosaurus rex* were not found until 1989 and 1990, in Montana. The arm and hand had an estimated length of 90 centimeters (about 34.5 inches), and were probably strong enough to lift over 450 pounds.

Dynamosaurus imperiosus, originally believed to be another large theropod, is now known to be a *T. rex*. It was thought to be distinct because of numerous

TYRANNOSAURUS *continued*

plates found with its type specimen. These armor plates were later shown to belong to an ankylosaur. An Asian cousin of *Tyrannosaurus rex, T. bataar*, originally described as *Tarbosaurus*, lived at the same time. Its fossil remains indicate that dinosaurs moved freely between the continents in Late Cretaceous times.

Tyrannosaurus bataar (buh-TAHR): Until recently, this Asian species of *Tyrannosaurus* was regarded as a separate genus of tyrannosaurid called *Tarbosaurus*. This species is known from many good specimens, both adult and juvenile, discovered in Mongolia. *Tyrannosaurus bataar* was smaller than *Tyrannosaurus rex*, and had a less massive skull, more compressed teeth, and comparatively shorter forelimbs. Three other Mongolian species, *Tarbosaurus efremovi, Gorgosaurus lancinator,* and *Gorgosaurus novojilovi*, have all been referred to *Tyrannosaurus bataar*.

UGROSAURUS

(OO-groh-SAW-rus)

(=?Triceratops)

Type Species: olsoni (OHL-suh-nye)
Status: Doubtful
Classification:
  Order: Ornithischia
  Suborder: Ceratopsia
  Family: Ceratopsidae
Name: Scandinavian *ugro* = ugly + Greek *sauros* = lizard
Size: Large
Period: Late Cretaceous, 68 million to 65 million years ago
Place: Montana
Diet: Plants

All that we know of this large horned dinosaur is based on part of a snout and other bits of skeleton.

Ugrosaurus was distinguished from other horned dinosaurs, (except some specimens of *Triceratops*), by its stout, flattened nose horn. This animal was probably *Triceratops*, but it is too poorly known to say with certainty.

Ugrosaurus olsoni
nose and beak

UINTASAURUS
(yoo-WIN-tuh-SAW-rus)

Status: Invalid — *See Camarasaurus*

ULTRASAUROS
(UL-truh-SAW-rohs)

Status: Doubtful — *See Brachiosaurus*

Ultrasauros, originally *Ultrasaurus*, was named by Brigham Young University dinosaur digger Jim Jensen for fossils of a gigantic animal found in Colorado. Jensen's specimen, which represents another sauropod, may be the largest known dinosaur, weighing 50 tons or more. Since the name had been claimed previously by the South Korean specimen, Jensen's animal has been renamed *Ultrasauros*. However, Jensen's giant may be a particularly large specimen of the well known genus *Brachiosaurus*.

ULTRASAURUS

(UL-truh-SAW-rus)

Type Species: *tabriensis* (TAB-ree-EN-sis)
Status: Doubtful
Classification:
  Order: Saurischia
  Suborder: Sauropoda
  Family: ?
Name: Latin *ultra* = beyond + Greek *sauros* = lizard
Size: Large
Period: Early Cretaceous, 145 million to 113 million
               years ago
Place: South Korea
Diet: Plants

   Ultrasaurus, a large, four-legged browser, is known only from a few bones found in South Korea.

UNQUILLOSAURUS

(UNG-kwi-luh-SAW-rus)

Type Species: *ceibalii* (see-BAW-lee-eye)

Classification:

    Order: Saurischia

    Suborder: Theropoda

    Family: ?

Name: *Unquillo* (river) + Greek *sauros* = lizard

Size: 11 meters (36 feet) long

Period: Late Cretaceous, ?83 million to 73 million years ago

Place: Argentina

Diet: Meat

    Unquillosaurus was the first of the large theropods discovered in South America. It may have been one of the carnosaurs, enormous meat-eaters with large heads, big teeth, short necks, barrel-like trunks, very short forelimbs, and toe talons. *Unquillosaurus* was identified by its pubic bone, which differs from those found in most other theropods by the presence of a deep furrow.

UTAHRAPTOR

(YOO-tah-RAP-tor)

Type Species: *ostrommaysi*

Classification:

Order: Saurischia

Suborder: Theropoda

Family: ?Dromaeosauridae

Name: Utah (state) + Latin *raptor* = robber

Size: 6.5 meters (20 feet) long

Period: Early Cretaceous, 125 million years ago

Place: Eastern Utah

Diet: Meat

Utahraptor may be the deadliest dinosaur yet known. It appears to have been a large, early member of the dromaeosaur family. Dromaeosaurs were small, swift, smart carnivores. Like its smaller and somewhat later relative, *Deinonychus* (literally, "killer claw"), *Utahraptor* was equipped with a huge claw on the middle toe of each foot. This claw may have extended more than 35 centimeters (15 inches). Wielding that claw in a single, leaping strike, *Utahraptor* could have slashed another dinosaur to death. Packs of *Utahraptors* were fully capable of bringing down even a large sauropod. Paleontologist James Kirkland, who named the predator, considers *Utahraptor* the most vicious of all dinosaurs, as well as one of the most intelligent.

Utahraptor was discovered in eastern Utah in 1991, and was identified by its slender 25-centimeter-long (9 inch) claw core. Skull material, hind limb bones, and tail vertebrae were found among remains in a quarry near Moab, Utah, in 1975. It was officially described and named in 1993.

VALDORAPTOR

(VAL-duh-RAP-tor)

Type Species: *oweni* (OH-uh-nye)
Status: Doubtful
Classification:
  Order: Saurischia
  Suborder: Theropoda
  Family: ?Allosauridae
Name: Latin *valdo* = wealden + Latin *raptor* = robber
Size: Large
Period: Early Cretaceous, 125 million to 119 million years ago
Place: England
Diet: Meat

 Valdoraptor was a large meat-eating dinosaur. It may have been a member of the *Allosauridae*, a family of large-to-giant carnivores, that had big heads, short necks, short forelimbs, and three-fingered, large-clawed hands.

 Poorly known, *Valdoraptor* was named from a partial foot bone that was originally misidentified as a bone of the ankylosaur *Hylaeosaurus*.

Valdoraptor oweni
foot

VALDOSAURUS

(VAL-duh-SAW-rus)

Type Species: *canaliculatus* (KAN-uh-LICK-yuh-LAT-us)

Classification:

Order:	Ornithischia
Suborder:	Ornithopoda
Family:	Dryosauridae

Name: Latin *valdo* = wealden + Greek *sauros* = lizard

Size: ?

Period: Early Cretaceous, 144 million to 113 million years ago

Place: England, Romania

Diet: Plants

Valdosaurus was a dryosaurid, one of a family of medium-sized plant-eaters with sharp-ridged cheek teeth, five-fingered hands, and long, stiffened tails.

Valdosaurus nigeriensis (nye-JEE-ree-EN-sis): This species is known only from a leg bone.

VECTENSIA

(veck-TEN-see-uh)

Type Species: (No specific name given)
Status: Invalid — *See ?Hylaeosaurus*
Classification:
  Order: Ornithischia
  Suborder: Ankylosauria
  Family: Nodosauridae
Name: Latin *vector* = bearer + Latin *ensis* = sword
Size: ?
Period: Late Cretaceous, ?97 million to ?65 million years ago
Place: England
Diet: Plants

    Vectensia was an armored dinosaur of the family Nodosauridae, ankylosaurs with large side spikes and clubless tails. Known from only a single armor plate, *Vectensia* probably refers to *Hylaeosaurus armatus*. However, its validity is very much in doubt.

VELOCIPES

(ve-LOS-i-pes)

Type Species: *gurichi* (GOOR-i-chee)
Status: Doubtful
Classification:
   Order: Saurischia
   Suborder: ?Theropoda
   Family: ?
Name: Latin *velox* = swift + Latin *pes* = foot
Size: ?
Period: Late Triassic, 228 million to 223 million years ago
Place: Germany
Diet: Meat

Velocipes was established on only one part of what may be a left-leg bone.

VELOCIRAPTOR

(ve-LOS-i-RAP-tor)

Type Species: *mongoliensis* (mong-GOH-lee-EN-sis)

Classification:

Order: Saurischia

Suborder: Theropoda

Family: Dromaeosauridae

Name: Latin *velox* = swift + Latin *raptor* = robber

Size: 1.8 meters (6 feet) long

Period: Late Cretaceous, ?late Santonian or early Campanian, 85 million to 80 million years ago

Place: Mongolia, China, ?Russia

Diet: Meat

Velociraptor, was swift, smart, and equipped with sharp teeth, large eyes, and long clawed fingers and toes. But it was not as fast as a cheetah, nor as smart as a chimpanzee, as characterized in the film *Jurassic Park.* It was no larger than a wolf.

Its most distinguishing and frightening feature was a sickle-like claw on the second toe of its hind foot. The significance of this claw was not realized until the 1964 discovery of *Deinonychus*, a related predator. With that find, the claw was understood as a slashing weapon, used by dinosaurs like *Deinonychus* and *Velociraptor* for attack.

VELOCIRAPTOR *continued*

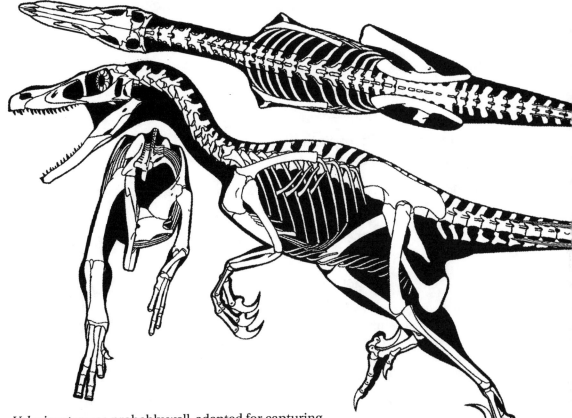

Velociraptor was probably well-adapted for capturing
and holding swift-moving, lightweight prey. Its long fingers could have held
on to victims, and the wide gape of its jaws indicate that it could handle relatively large prey.

One spectacular *Velociraptor* specimen was found in the Gobi Desert in
1971. The articulated skeleton was grasping a skeleton of *Protoceratops andrewsi*.
Protoceratops was probably struggling to defend itself or its eggs from the attacking *Velociraptor*, and both animals died simultaneously. This discovery revealed
that *Velociraptor* had a collar bone, a feature previously thought peculiar to birds.

This animal has been reported from Kazakhstan in Russia, and Shanxi in
China, but the material is indeterminate.

VELOCISAURUS

(ve-LOS-i-SAW-rus)

Type Species: *unicus* (YOO-ni-kus)
Classification:

Order:	Saurischia
Suborder:	Theropoda
Family:	Velocisauridae
Name:	Latin *velox* = swift + Greek *sauros* = lizard
Size:	Small
Period:	Late Cretaceous, 73 million to 65 million years ago
Place:	Argentina
Diet:	Meat

This small carnivore may be a later member of the ceratosaurs, a group of various-sized meat-eaters, some of which had a cranial crest or horns, or a dorsal fin. *Velocisaurus* is known only from limb and foot bones.

Velocisaurus unicus
foot

VOLKHEIMERIA

(VOL-kye-MEE-ree-uh)

Type Species: *chubutensis* (CHUB-oo-TEN-sis)

Classification:

Order:	Saurischia
Suborder:	Sauropoda
Family:	Brachiosauridae

Name: (Wolfgang) *Volkeimer*

Period: Middle Jurassic, 169 million to 163 million
years ago

Place: Argentina

Diet: Plants

    Volkheimeria was a brachiosaurid, a bulky sauropod with long front legs and an elevated neck. It was more primitive than its much larger South American relative, *Patagosaurus*. Its spinal bones were particularly primitive. The discovery of *Volkheimeria* and its relationship to brachiosaur-like dinosaurs found in North America and Africa supports the hypothesis that animals crossed between between South America and other continents during the Jurassic Period. Along with the discovery of *Patagosaurus* and the theropod *Piatnitzkysaurus*, *Volkheimeria* established that sauropods and carnosaurs lived in South America during the Jurassic Period.

VULCANODON

(vul-KAN-uh-don)

Type Species: *karibaensis* (kuh-REE-bay-EN-sis)

Classification:

Order:	Saurischia
Suborder:	Sauropoda
Family:	Vulcanodontidae
Name:	Latin *Vulcan* = Roman god of fire + Greek *odontos* = tooth
Size:	Large, 6.5 meters (20 feet) long
Period:	Early Jurassic, 208 million to 201 million years ago
Place:	Zimbabwe
Diet:	Plants

Though distinctive enough to merit its own family, this dinosaur could be either an advanced prosauropod or a primitive sauropod. *Vulcanodon* was a large animal, similar in many aspects to later sauropods. It had plump legs, a heavy body, a long neck, and an unusually high shoulder. Its primitive features included carnivore's teeth and prosauropod pelvic bones. Its sauropod features included solid, robust limb bones, a very long forearm, flattened nail-like claws, and a large, sharp big-toe claw.

Vulcanodon was first thought to be an advanced melanorosaurid, one of the large, more advanced prosauropods that tended to walk on all fours. More recently, it has been regarded as a primitive sauropod. Some scientists have argued that *Vulcanodon* should be recognized as the earliest known sauropod because of its large size, column-like legs and long forelimbs, pelvic structure, and four-legged gait.

Fossil footprints from several sites in Lesotho and attributed to sauropods could be those of *Vulcanodon*, which had a sauropod-like foot. These tracks include those named *Deuterosauropodopus*.

WAKINOSAURUS

(wa-KEE-noh-SAW-rus)

Type Species: *satoi* (SAT-oh-eye)
Status: Doubtful
Classification:
   Order: Saurischia
   Suborder: Theropoda
   Family: ?Megalosauridae
Name: *Wakino* (Subgroup) + Greek *sauros* = lizard
Size: ?
Period: Early Cretaceous, 144 million to 125 million years ago
Place: Japan
Diet: Meat

   Wakinosaurus is one of the few dinosaurs discovered in Japan. It was a ceratosaur, one of the various-sized meat-eaters, some of which had cranial crests or horns, and fins on their backs.

   Like other Japanese finds, *Wakinosaurus* is known only from fragmentary fossils, in this case a large incomplete tooth. This heavily serrated tooth most resembles the teeth of a carnivore, *Prodeinodon kwangshiensis*, found in China.

Wakinosaurus satoi tooth

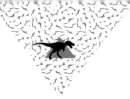

WALGETTOSUCHUS

(WAWL-get-uh-SOOK-us)

Type Species: *woodwardi* (WOOD-wur-dye)
Status: Doubtful — *See ?Rapator*
Classification:
   Order: Saurischia
   Suborder: Theropoda
   Family: ?
Name: Walgett (town in New South Wales) + Greek souchos = crocodile
Size: ?
Period: Early Cretaceous, 119 million to 113 million years ago
Place: Australia
Diet: Meat

   Walgettosuchus was a meat-eater belonging to the tetanurids, a widely diversified group of small-to-giant carnivorous dinosaurs with stiff tails.
Walgettosuchus's size and identity are mysteries, since it was named on an isolated, almost featureless, incomplete tip-of-the-tail vertebra discovered in Lightning Ridge, Australia.
   If more material were available, *Walgettosuchus* might prove to be identical to other small Australian theropods such as *Rapator*.

WALKERIA

(waw-KEE-ree-uh)

Type Species: *maleriensis* (muh-LAYR-ee-EN-sis)
Classification:
  Order: Saurischia
  Suborder: Theropoda
  Family: ?
Name: (Alick D.) *Walker*
Size: Small
Period: Late Triassic, 231 million to 225 million years ago
Place: India
Diet: Meat

Walkeria is the earliest and most primitive dinosaur yet found in Asia. A carnivorous dinosaur of unknown affinities, *Walkeria* was a small theropod, distinguished from other contemporary forms by the absence of a ridge below the openings in front of the eye, and by other features, such as unserrated teeth and a long, tapering snout.

The discovery of *Walkeria* in equally ancient rocks in Texas suggests a link between the dinosaurs of India and North America in what was then a single world continent.

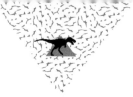

WANNANOSAURUS

(wah-NAN-uh-SAW-rus)

Type Species: *yansiensis* (YAN-see-EN-sis)
Classification:

Order:	Ornithischia
Suborder:	Pachycephalosauria
Family:	Homalocephalidae

Name: Wannan (locality) + Greek sauros = lizard
Size: Less than 1 meter (39 inches) long
Period: Late Cretaceous, 83 million to 73 million years ago
Place: China
Diet: ?Plants

Wannanosaurus may be the most primitive known flat-headed form of pachycephalosaur, or bone-headed dinosaur. *Wannanosaurus* had a completely flattened skull roof and large openings in its skull above its temples.

WUERHOSAURUS

(woo-AYR-huh-SAW-rus)

Type Species: *homheni* (HOM-he-nye)
Classification:
  Order: Ornithischia
  Suborder: Stegosauria
  Family: Stegosauridae
Name: Wuerho (town in Xinjiang, China) + Greek *sauros* = lizard
Size: 7 to 8 meters (approximately 23 to 27 feet) long
Period: Early Cretaceous, 138 million to 125 million years ago
Place: China
Diet: Plants

   Wuerhosaurus was a large plated dinosaur. It was similar to *Stegosaurus* in some anatomical features, though its plates and front limbs were smaller.
   Wuerhosaurus also had bones that were similar to corresponding bones in the stegosaurs *Lexovisaurus* and *Kentrosaurus*. *Wuerhosaurus* is the first stegosaur discovered from the Cretaceous Period, most others having lived in the preceding Late Jurassic Period.

WYLEYIA

(wye-LAY-uh)

Type Species: *valdensis* (val-DEN-sis)
Status: Doubtful
Classification:
  Order: ?Saurischia
  Suborder: ?Theropoda
  Family: ?
Name: (J.F.) Wyley
Size: Small
Period: Early Cretaceous, 125 million to 119 million years ago
Place: England
Diet: Meat

    This is a poorly preserved and understood animal which was first described as a bird. It had an upper arm bone similar to, but smaller than, that of the early avian, *Ichthyornis*. According to later scientific opinion, this bone was almost surely dinosaurian. *Wyleyia* was probably a small meat-eating dinosaur, but further identification cannot be made.

XENOTARSOSAURUS

(ZEE-noh-TAHR-suh-SAW-rus)

Type Species: *bonapartei* (BOH-nuh-PAHR-tye)
Classification:
    Order: Saurischia
    Suborder: Theropoda
    Family: ?Abelisauridae
Name: Greek *xenos* = stranger + Greek *tarsos* = flat of
                  the foot + Greek *sauros* = lizard
Size: Medium
Period: Late Cretaceous, ?83 million to
                  73 million years ago
Place: Argentina
Diet: Meat

    Xenotarsosaurus was a medium-sized, poorly-known theropod.
From the hind leg on which it was based, it appears to have been
slow. Although it was originally grouped with the South American
abelisaurs, it also shows some features resembling North
American carnivores.

*Xenotarsosaurus
bonapartei*
leg bone

XIAOSAURUS

(zhou-SAW-rus)

Type Species:	*dashanpensis* (DASH-un-PEN-sis)
Status:	Doubtful — *See ?Yandusaurus*
Classification:	
Order:	?Ornithischia
Suborder:	?
Family:	?
Name:	Chinese *xiao* = small + Greek *sauros* = lizard
Size:	About 1 meter (3.3 feet) long
Period:	Middle Jurassic, 169 million to 163 million years ago
Place:	China
Diet:	Plants

Xiaosaurus is based on fragmentary remains from a quarry in Dashanpu, central China, that has produced some of the best-preserved dinosaur remains yet known.

Not much is known of this dinosaur. It was originally described as a small, fast-running plant-eater with a high skull. Now it is grouped as an ornithischian, a member of that large and diverse group of bird-hipped herbivorous dinosaurs.

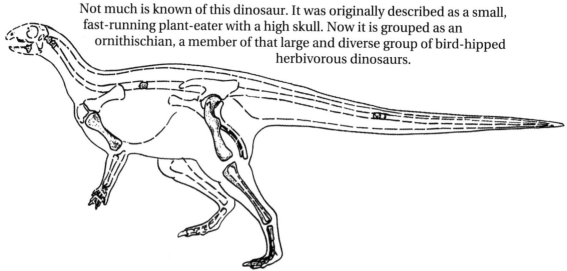

XUANHANOSAURUS

(ZHWAHN-han-uh-SAW-rus)

Type Species: *qilixianensis* (KWIL-ick-SEE-uh-NEN-sis)

Classification:

Order:	Saurischia
Suborder:	Theropoda
Family:	?Megalosauridae
Name:	Xuanhan (County in China) + Greek sauros = lizard
Size:	6 meters (over 20 feet) long
Period:	Middle Jurassic, 175 miillion to 163 million years ago
Place:	China
Diet:	Meat

   Xuanhanosaurus was a medium-sized, primitive form of meat-eater, distinguished by its long and massive forearms. When it was described in 1984, *Xuanhanosaurus* was thought to have walked on all fours because of the length of these forelimbs. This theory is not widely accepted today.

YALEOSAURUS
(YAY-luh-SAW-rus)

Type Species: *colurus* (KOL-uh-rus)
Status:　　　　Invalid — *See Anchisaurus*

YANDUSAURUS

(YAN-doo-SAW-rus)
(=?*Xiaosaurus*)

Type Species: *hongheensis* (HONG-hee-EN-sis)
Classification:

　　Order:　　　Ornithischia
　　Suborder:　Ornithopoda
　　Family:　　Hypsilophodontidae
Name:　　　　Yandum (town in China) + Greek *sauros* = lizard
Size:　　　　　1.5 meters (5 feet) long
Period:　　　　Middle Jurassic, 175 million to 163 million
　　　　　　　years ago
Place:　　　　China
Diet:　　　　　Plants

　　Yandusaurus was a slender, primitive, medium-sized hypsilophodontid— a primitive, bipedal, plant-eating dinosaur with a small head, cheek teeth, short forelimbs, and long hindlimbs.

YANGCHUANOSAURUS

(YANG-choo-AN-uh-SAW-rus)

Type Species: shangyouensis (SANG-yoo-EN-sis)
Classification:
   Order: Saurischia
   Suborder: Theropoda
   Family: ?Megalosauridae
Name: Yangchuan (District of Szechuan Province, China) + Greek sauros = lizard.
Size: 10 meters (33 feet) long
Period: Late Jurassic, 163 million to 145 million years ago
Place: China
Diet: Meat

   Yangchuanosaurus, a large carnivore with the general proportions of *Allosaurus*, may have belonged to the megalosaurid family. Its jaws were sizable, and equipped with large, sharply pointed teeth. Its body and tail were heavily built, and its arms relatively short. *Yangchuanosaurus* may have had a crest on its head and a fin down its back.

   Yanghuanosaurus magnus (MAG-nus): Based on an incomplete skull, *Y. magnus* was larger than the type species, having an estimated length of 10 meters (33 feet). Its heavily built skull measured 111 centimeters (about 43 inches) in length and 70 to 73 centimeters (about 27 inches) in height, making it one of the largest known megalosaurids. There was a double hornlike ridge on its nasal bones, suggesting that it may have had a crest.

YAVERLANDIA

(YAV-ur-LAN-dee-uh)

Type Species: *bitholus* (bye-THOL-us)
Classification:
  Order: Ornithischia
  Suborder: Pachycephalosauria
  Family: Pachycephalosauridae
Name: Yaverland (Battery)
Size: 90 centimeters (3 feet) long
Period: Early Cretaceous, 125 million to 119 million
               years ago
Place: England
Diet: Plants

A very small, primitive pachy-cephalosaur, one of the so-called bone-headed dinosaurs, *Yaverlandia* was named because of its thickened skull. Like all bone-heads, most of which were small, *Yaverlandia* was bipedal and ate plants.

This genus was founded on a skull cap small enough to hold in the palm of an adult hand. It is the oldest known pachy-cephalosaurid, and the only one with two domes, one attached to each frontal bone of the skull. The upper surface of the skull caps was pitted.

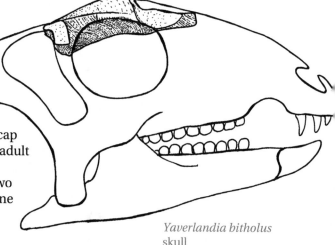

Yaverlandia bitholus skull

Yaverlandia seems to have been ancestral to the pachycephalosaurids *Stegoceras* and *Pachycephalosaurus*, but its skull more closely resembles that of other, contemporary, hypsilophodonts such as *Hypsilophodon*. This resemblance reflects the possible hypsilophodont ances-try of pachycephalosaurs.

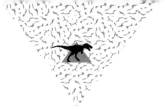
YUNNANOSAURUS

(yoo-NAN-uh-SAW-rus)

Type Species: *huangi* (HWANG-eye)

Classification:

    Order: Saurischia

    Suborder: Prosauropoda

    Family: Yunnanosauridae

Name: Yunnan (province of China) + Greek *sauros* = lizard

Size: ?

Period: Early Jurassic, 208 million to 194 million years ago

Place: China

Diet: Plants

    Yunnanosaurus was the first known member of a family of large prosauropods. Prosauropods were primitive plant-eaters with high, narrow heads and short snouts. Their teeth were similar to those of the larger, later plant-eaters, the sauropods.

    Yunnanosaurus's skeleton is similar to that of *Lufengosaurus hueni*. It is distinguished by the shape of the skull and teeth, and by different skeleton proportions, all of which suggest this animal was a juvenile.

ZAPSALIS

(zap-SAL-is)

Type Species: *abradens* (uh-BRAY-dunz)
Status: Doubtful — *See Paronychodon*

ZATOMUS

(zuh-TOH-mus)

Type Species: *sarcophagus* (sahr-KOF-uh-gus)
Status: Doubtful
Classification:
   Order: Saurischia
   Suborder: ?Theropoda
   Family: ?
Name: Greek *za* = very + Greek *tomos* = sharp
Size: Large
Period: Late Triassic, 225 million to 208 million years ago
Place: North Carolina
Diet: ?Meat

    This was a large and perhaps flesh-eating dinosaur. If it was, *Zatomus* is significant in establishing that such dinosaurs lived in the Late Triassic Period in eastern North America. *Zatomus* is known, however, only from a small tooth 23 millimeters (about .9 inches) in length. The tooth may well belong to something other than a dinosaur.

ZEPHYROSAURUS

(ZEF-i-ruh-SAW-rus)

Type Species: schaffi (SHAF-eye)
Classification:
  Order: Ornithischia
  Suborder: Ornithopoda
  Family: Hypsilophodontidae
Name: Greek zephuros = west wind + Greek sauros = lizard
Size: 1.8 meters (6 feet) long
Period: Early Cretaceous, 119 million to 113 million years ago
Place: Montana
Diet: Plants

Zephyrosaurus was a hypsilophodontid with a small head, cheek teeth, short front legs, and long hind legs. There is evidence that its skull was capable of flexing, a movement particularly useful in chewing.

Zephyrosaurus represents a previously unknown hypsilophodontid lineage which is distinct from that represented by *Hypsilophodon*. It differed from *Hypsilophodon* in several features, including cheek teeth that lacked sharp edges.

Zephyrosaurus schaffi skull

ZIGONGOSAURUS
(zee-GONG-uh-SAW-rus)

Type Species: fuxiensis (FOOK-see-EN-sis)
Status: Doubtful — *See Omeisaurus*

ZIZHONGOSAURUS

(zee-ZONG-uh-SAW-rus)

Type Species: chuanchiensis (CHOO-an-chee-EN-sis)
Classification:
  Order: Saurischia
  Suborder: Sauropoda
  Family: Vulcanodontidae
Name: Zizhong (county in China) + Greek *sauros* = lizard
Size: 9 meters (30 feet) long
Period: Early Jurassic, 208 million to 188 million
                years ago
Place: China
Diet: Plants

    Although little material has been found, *Zizhongosaurus* is known as a small, primitive sauropod. It bore a slight resemblance to the Indian sauropod, *Barapasaurus*. *Zizhongosaurus* established the presence of sauropods in China in the Early Jurassic Period, an early time in their worldwide evolution.

DINOSAURS BY PERIOD

Cretaceous Period

Abelisaurus
Acanthopholis
Acrocanthosaurus
Adasaurus
Aegyptosaurus
Aelosaurus
Aepisaurus
Alamosaurus
Albertosaurus
Alectrosaurus
Alioramus
Altispinax
Alvarezsaurus
Amargasaurus
Amtosaurus
Anatotitan
Anchiceratops
Andesaurus
Ankylosaurus
Anoplosaurus
Anserimimus
Antarctosaurus
Aragosaurus
Aralosaurus
Archaeornithoides
Archaeornithomimus
Argyrosaurus
Arrhinoceratops
Arstanosaurus
Asiaceratops
Asiatosaurus
Astrodon
Atlascopcosaurus
Aubylysodon
Austrosaurus
Avaceratops
Avimimus
Bactrosaurus
Bagaceratops
Bahariasaurus
Barsboldia
Baryonyx
Becklespinax
Betasuchus
Borogovia
Brachyceratops
Brachylophosaurus
Brachypodosaurus

Bradycneme
Caenagnathus
Calamosaurus
Calamospondylus
Campylodoniscus
Carcharodontosaurus
Carnotaurus
Ceratops
Chasmosaurus
Chiayusaurus
Chilantaisaurus
Chingkankousaurus
Chirostenotes
Chondrosteosaurus
Chubutisaurus
Cionodon
Claorhynchus
Clasmodosaurus
Clausaurus
Coeluroides
Compsosuchus
Conchoraptor
Corythosaurus
Craspedodon
Crataeomus
Craterosaurus
Daspletosaurus
Deinocheirus
Deinodon
Deinonychus
Diceratops
Diclonius
Dinosaurus
Diplotomodon
Dravidosaurus
Dromaeosaurus
Dromiceiomimus
Dryptosauroides
Dryptosaurus
Dysganus
Dyslocosaurus
Edmontonia
Edmontosaurus
Elmisaurus
Embasaurus
Enigmosaurus
Eoceratops
Epachthosaurus
Erectopus
Erlikosaurus
Eucentrosaurus
Euoplocephalus
Euronychodon

Gallimimus
Garudimimus
Genyodectes
Gilmoreosaurus
Goyocephale
Gravitholus
Gryposaurus
Hadrosaurus
Harpymimus
Heishansaurus
Heptasteornis
Hironosaurus
Hisanohamasaurus
Homalocephale
Hoplitosaurus
Hulsanpes
Hylaeosaurus
Hypacrosaurus
Hypselosaurus
Hypsibema
Hypsilophodon
Iguanodon
Indosaurus
Indosuchus
Ingenia
Inosaurus
Itemirus
Jaxartosaurus
Jubbulpuria
Kagasaurus
Kakuru
Kangnasaurus
Katsuyamasaurus
Kelmayisaurus
Kitadanisaurus
Koreanosaurus
Kritosaurus
Labocania
Laevisuchus
Lambeosaurus
Lametasaurus
Laplatasaurus
Leaellynasaurus
Leipsanosaurus
Leptoceratops
Lophorhothon
Loricosaurus
Macrurosaurus
Magyarosaurus
Maiasaura
Majungasaurus
Majungatholus
Maleevosaurus

Cretaceous Period *continued*

Maleevus
Mandschurosaurus
Megacervixosaurus
Microceratops
Microdontosaurus
Microhadrosaurus
Micropachycephalosaurus
Microsaurops
Microvenator
Minmi
Mongolosaurus
Monoclonius
Montanoceratops
Muttaburasaurus
Nanotyrannus
Nanshiungosaurus
Nemegtosaurus
Neuquensaurus
Nipponosaurus
Noasaurus
Nodosaurus
Notoceratops
Opisthocoelicaudia
Oplosaurus
Ornatotholus
Ornithodesmus
Ornithomimoides
Ornithomimus
Ornithotarsus
Orodromeus
Orthogoniosaurus
Orthomerus
Ouranosaurus
Oviraptor
Pachycephalosaurus
Pachyrhinosaurus
Palaeoscincus
Panoplosaurus
Paranthodon
Parasaurolophus
Parksosaurus
Paronychodon
Peishansaurus
Pelorosaurus
Pentaceratops
Phaedrolosaurus
Pinacosaurus
Pleurocoelus
Polyonax
Prenocephale
Priconodon
Probactrosaurus

Prodeinodon
Prosaurolophus
Protoceratops
Psittacosaurus
Quaesitosaurus
Rapator
Rebbachisaurus
Regnosaurus
Rhabdodon
Rhodanosaurus
Ricardoestesia
Saichania
Saltasaurus
Saurolophus
Sauropelta
Sauroplites
Saurornithoides
Saurornitholestes
Secernosaurus
Segnosaurus
Shamosaurus
Shanshanosaurus
Shantungosaurus
Silvisaurus
Spinosaurus
Stegoceras
Stegosaurides
Stenopelix
Struthiomimus
Struthiosaurus
Stygimoloch
Styracosaurus
Talarurus
Tanius
Tarascosaurus
Tarchia
Taveirosaurus
Telmatosaurus
Tenontosaurus
Thecocoelurus
Therizinosaurus
Thescelosaurus
Thespesius
Titanosaurus
Tochisaurus
Torosaurus
Trachodon
Triceratops
Troodon
Tugulusaurus
Turanoceratops
Tylocephale

Tyrannosaurus
Ugrosaurus
Ultrasaurus
Unquillosaurus
Utahraptor
Valdoraptor
Valdosaurus
Vectensia
Velociraptor
Velocisaurus
Wakinosaurus
Walgettosuchus
Wannanosaurus
Wuerhosaurus
Wyleyia
Xenotarsosaurus
Yaverlandia
Zephyrosaurus

Jurassic Period
Abrictosaurus
Agilisaurus
Algoasaurus
Allosaurus
Alocodon
Ammosaurus
Amphicoelias
Amygdalodon
Anchisaurus
Apatosaurus
Barapasaurus
Barosaurus
Bellusaurus
Bihariosaurus
Bothriospondylus
Brachiosaurus
Callovosaurus
Camarasaurus
Camptosaurus
Cardiodon
Cathetosaurus
Ceratosaurus
Cetiosauriscus
Cetiosaurus
Changdusaurus
Chaoyoungosaurus
Chialingosaurus
Chinsakiangosaurus
Chuandongosaurus
Chungkingosaurus
Coelurus
Compsognathus

Jurassic Period *continued*

Cryptodraco
Dacentrurus
Dachongosaurus
Damalasaurus
Dandakosaurus
Datousaurus
Dianchungosaurus
Dicraeosaurus
Dilophosaurus
Diplodocus
Dracopelta
Drinker
Dryosaurus
Dystrophaeus
Dystylosaurus
Echinodon
Elaphrosaurus
Emausaurus
Euhelopus
Eustreptospondylus
Fabrosaurus
Gasosaurus
Geranosaurus
Gigantosaurus
Gongbusaurus
Haplocanthosaurus
Heterodontosaurus
Huayangosaurus
Iliosuchus
Ischyrosaurus
Janenschia
Jiangjunmiaosaurus
Jurossosaurus
Kaijangosaurus
Kentrosaurus
Kotasaurus
Kunmingosaurus
Lanasaurus
Lancanjiangosaurus
Laosaurus
Lapparentosaurus
Lesothosaurus
Lexovisaurus
Lisboasaurus
Lufengosaurus
Lukousaurus
Lusitanosaurus
Lycorhinus
Macrodontophion
Magnosaurus
Mamenchisaurus
Marshosaurus

Massospondylus
Megalosaurus
Metriacanthosaurus
Monkonosaurus
Monolophosaurus
Morinosaurus
Nanosaurus
Neosodon
Ngexisaurus
Ohmdenosaurus
Omeisaurus
Ornitholestes
Oshanosaurus
Othnielia
Patagosaurus
Phyllodon
Piatnitzkysaurus
Piveteausaurus
Podokesaurus
Poekilopleuron
Priodontognathus
Proceratosaurus
Protognathosaurus
Rhoetosaurus
Sanpasaurus
Sarcolestes
Sarcosaurus
Scelidosaurus
Scutellosaurus
Segisaurus
Seismosaurus
Shunosaurus
Siamosaurus
Sinocoelurus
Sinosaurus
Stegosaurus
Stokesosaurus
Supersaurus
Syntarsus
Szechuanosaurus
Tatisaurus
Tawasaurus
Teinurosaurus
Tianchungosaurus
Tienshanosaurus
Torvosaurus
Trimucrodon
Tuojiangosaurus
Volkheimeria
Vulcanodon
Xiaosaurus
Xuanhanosaurus

Yandusaurus
Yangchuanosaurus
Yunnanosaurus
Zizhongosaurus

Triassic Period

Agrosaurus
Aliwalia
Arctosaurus
Azendohsaurus
Blikanasaurus
Camelotia
Coelophysis
Coloradisaurus
Dolichosuchus
Eoraptor
Euskelosaurus
Frenguellisaurus
Halticosaurus
Herrerasaurus
Ischisaurus
Likhoelesaurus
Liliensternus
Melanorosaurus
Mussaurus
Pachysauriscus
Palaeosauriscus
Picrodon
Pisanosaurus
Plateosaurus
Procompsognathus
Pterospondylus
Revueltosaurus
Rioarribasaurus
Riojasaurus
Roccosaurus
Saltopus
Sellosaurus
Staurikosaurus
Tanystrosuchus
Technosaurus
Thecodontosaurus
Thotobolosaurus
Velocipes
Walkeria
Zatomus

Unknown

Nurosaurus
Sangonghesaurus
Tichosteus

GEOGRAPHICAL INDEX

TRIASSIC

245 million to 208 million years ago. The first dinosaurs spread across the land, which was joined in one continent. Pterosaur, flying reptiles, first took to the air.

JURASSIC

208 million to 145 million years ago. The continent slowly split in two. The first bird appeared. So did giant plant-eating dinosaurs, and many kinds of meat-eating dinosaurs.

CRETACEOUS

145 million to 65 million years ago. The first flowers appeared. The land divided into several continents. Most of the dinosaurs we know come from the Cretaceous.

Billions of
Years Ago

**TIME
LINE**

4.6
Earth
Age

3.5
First Single
Cell Life